DEVELOPING LETTER-SOUND CONNECTIONS

A Strategy-Oriented
Alphabet Activities Program
for Beginning Readers & Writers

CYNTHIA CONWAY WARING

**THE CENTER FOR APPLIED
RESEARCH IN EDUCATION**
West Nyack, New York 10994

Library of Congress Cataloging-in-Publication Data

Waring, Cynthia Conway.
    Developing letter-sound connections : a strategy-oriented alphabet activities program for beginning readers & writers / Cynthia Conway Waring.
        p.   cm.
    ISBN 0-87628-137-4
    1. English language—Alphabet—Study and teaching (Primary)—Activity programs.   2. Reading—Phonetic method.   3. English language—Composition and exercises—Study and teaching (Primary)   4. Language arts (Primary)   5. Creative activities and seat work.
    I. Title.
LB1525.65.W37   1998
372.46′5—dc21   98-41346
                                                                                                                                  CIP

Artwork on pages 11, 22, 35 and 76
by Nathaniel G. Waring

THE ALASKA MOTHER GOOSE AND OTHER NORTH COUNTRY NURSERY RHYMES, by Shelley Gill, illustrations by Shannon Cartwright, copyright 1987 by Paws IV Publishing Company. Used by permission.

GRANDMOTHER'S NURSERY RHYMES: LULLABIES, TONGUE TWISTERS AND RIDDLES FROM SOUTH AMERICA, compiled by Nelly Palacio Jaramillo, © 1994 by Nelly Palacio Jaramillo. Reprinted by permission of Henry Holt and Company, Inc.

Printed in the United States of America

10   9   8   7   6   5   4   3   2   1

ISBN 0-87628-137-4

ATTENTION: CORPORATIONS AND SCHOOLS

The Center for Applied Research in Education books are available at quantity discounts with bulk purchase for educational, business, or sales promotional use. For information, please write to: Prentice Hall Special Sales, 240 Frisch Court, Paramus, New Jersey 07652. Please supply: title of book, ISBN number, quantity, how the book will be used, date needed.

THE CENTER FOR APPLIED RESEARCH IN EDUCATION
West Nyack, NY 10994
A Simon & Schuster Company

On the World Wide Web at http://www.phdirect.com

Prentice Hall International (UK) Limited, *London*
Prentice Hall of Australia Pty. Limited, *Sydney*
Prentice Hall Canada Inc., *Toronto*
Prentice Hall Hispanoamericana, S.A., *Mexico*
Prentice Hall of India Private Limited, *New Delhi*
Prentice Hall of Japan, Inc., *Tokyo*
Simon & Schuster Asia Pte. Ltd., *Singapore*
Editora Prentice Hall do Brasil, Ltda., *Rio de Janeiro*

DEDICATION

To Nathaniel, Molly, and Nat Waring

in celebration of our connections

ACKNOWLEDGMENTS

with thanks to

Susan Kolwicz, Bonnie Roy, and Cynthia Stowe
for believing in this book

and to

Nancy Braus of Everyone's Books in Brattleboro, Vermont,
for sharing a vision of multicultural literature

**Bonnie Adams, Jo Carino, Ted Hallstrom, Nancy H. Martin,
Dena Nelson, Linda Prybylo, and Alissa Sheinbach**
for helping me in their quiet ways

Kindergarten to third grade teachers:
**Sue Breines, Katie Bloomfield, Bernice Carew, Bob Dihlmann,
Sue Fletcher, Vivian Kucinski, Bonnie Roy,
Elinor Saltz, and Susie Secco**

for welcoming me into their classrooms, onto their teams, and into their lives

ABOUT THE AUTHOR

Cynthia Conway Waring has supported learners with special needs in the areas of reading, spelling, and written expression for more than twenty-five years. She has taught students from kindergarten age to adult in public and private settings in adult literacy, classroom, clinic, inclusion, resource room, and tutorial programs. Cynthia has made presentations at professional conferences and lectured in graduate-level courses. She has provided consultation, in-service workshops, and teacher training.

Cynthia's first book, *Developing Independent Readers: Strategy-Oriented Reading Activities for Learners with Special Needs,* was published by The Center for Applied Research in Education in 1995. Her article, "Keys and a Clue," was published in *Teaching Exceptional Children* in 1976.

Cynthia has an M.Ed. from the Reading Specialist Program at Lesley College, an M.A. in Special Education/Learning Disabilities from the University of Connecticut, and a B.A. in English-Honors and Psychology from the University of Massachusetts. She is certified as an elementary teacher (K–8), teacher of children with moderate special needs (N–12), reading specialist/consulting teacher of reading (K–12), and Orton-Gillingham therapist. Cynthia is a registered educational therapist and member of The Learning Disabilities Network (based in New England) and has completed the Lindamood Auditory Discrimination in Depth training.

Currently, Cynthia teaches students with special needs using *Developing Independent Readers* and *Developing Letter-Sound Connections* in Massachusetts as a reading specialist in the Amherst Public Schools, as a tutor at the Smith College Campus School in Northampton, and in private practice. She also conducts in-service workshops and teacher training and consults with teachers in elementary schools and adult literacy programs.

ABOUT THIS PROGRAM

Positive first experiences with print set the stage for a lifetime of reading and writing. Beginners who develop and apply productive strategies to seek meaning become independent readers and writers who *can* and *do* read and write both for enjoyment and for the fulfillment of their own personal goals. One of the important challenges for beginning readers and writers is to learn about the abstract symbols of the English language—letters and the sounds they represent. This program helps students develop the strategies they need to experience success from the beginning! *Developing Letter-Sound Connections* presents a variety of engaging, strategy-oriented activities, designed for large or small groups or individual students, that help beginning readers and writers to make meaningful connections between what they know and the letters and sounds they must learn and remember.

Theme-based key words and pictures for the twenty-six letters of the alphabet and consonant digraphs *ch*, *sh*, and *th* are central to the **Introductory Activities** and **Reinforcement Activities** in *Developing Letter-Sound Connections*. These key words and pictures provide consistency and continuity as reference tools for **Reference Activities** beginning in kindergarten and throughout the primary grades. Students refer to them as they read and write in their classrooms and at home.

Developing Letter-Sound Connections is a program for kindergarten teachers who are looking for letter-sound activities consistent with the rhythms and activities of their day. It is a resource for primary classroom, special education, reading, and Title I teachers whose students require direct group or individual instruction in letter-sound knowledge. It provides resources for students in kindergarten through grade 3 who continue to need letter-sound reference tools as they read and write. Teachers of older beginning readers and writers can adapt the suggested activities to meet their students' needs.

This book is organized into two sections—**Section I: How to Use This Program and Section II: Letter-Sound Units.**

Section I: How to Use This Program

Section I describes in detail the following activities that help beginning readers and writers develop productive strategies and make meaningful connections between what they know and letters and sounds. Students complete activities in large or small groups or individually.

1. Introductory Activities

The introductory lesson comprises several interrelated activities. The lesson requires approximately twenty minutes to complete.

- **Alphabet Sequence: Oral to Written Connections** Students connect the alphabet song to the written alphabet on charts that have the letters grouped in clusters as they are sung. Students practice strategies that help them locate letters and sounds on reference tools.
- **Literature, Theme, and Key Word/Picture Connections** The teacher reads aloud a featured picture book to establish the theme for the unit. Students and the teacher connect the book to the theme of the unit and to the corresponding key word and picture for the focus letter-sound. The key word and picture are part of the Letter-Sound-Key Word/Picture Card for each unit.
- **Connections with Familiar Objects in the Mystery Box** Students use initial sound and meaning clues provided by the teacher to predict, cross-check, and confirm or correct as they guess inedible and edible items in a Mystery Box whose names begin with the focus letter-sound. Later, students are offered opportunities to taste edible items or foods made from edible items.

2. Reference Activities

Combined with the Introductory Activities, the Reference Activities form the foundation of *Developing Letter-Sound Connections*. Reference Activities provide consistency and continuity for beginning readers and writers throughout the primary grades. Teachers provide the suggested reference tools for *all* students in their kindergarten through third-grade classrooms at school and at home. Students use them as they need them.

Letter-Sound Reference Tools for Beginning Readers and Writers

Students refer to the same letter-sound reference tools in their classrooms and at home beginning in kindergarten and throughout their primary years. Reference tools are enlarged as wall charts for group activities and reduced in size and arranged on 8 1/2" x 11" pages for individual student reference. They include (1) the upper- and lowercase **Alphabet in Song Clusters**, (2) the twenty-six **Letter-Sound-Key Word/Picture Cards in Alphabetical Order**,

(3) **Letter-Sound-Key Word/Picture Cards for Consonant Digraphs and Short Vowels**, and (4) the **Horizontal Wall Alphabet**.

3. Reinforcement Activities

Teachers select Reinforcement Activities to meet the needs of their students and as time allows. Students complete Reinforcement Activities during shared, partner, and independent reading time and during project or activity time in their classrooms and at home.

- **Theme-Related Books and Literature Extension Connections** Throughout each letter-sound unit, the teacher reads aloud theme-related books chosen from the annotated book list and makes them available to children. Each alphabetical list includes a variety of fiction and nonfiction books, such as alphabet, counting, easy-to-read, interactive, picture, rebus, short chapter, and wordless. Students engage in activities related to the books that introduce, reinforce, and extend the theme. Activities include art, composition, cooking, dance and movement, discussion, drama and puppetry, math, music, and science.

- **Mystery Box Connections** Students play with the items in the Mystery Box and dramatize and dictate a story about them. The teacher transcribes the dictated story and color-codes the focus letter. Students then listen to the story read to them, edit and illustrate it, and practice left-to-right reading sequence as they count the number of times the letter recurs. The story becomes part of students' Story Books. Students take roles as teacher/leader and student as they engage in the Mystery Box activity in small groups. Later, they sort items and pictures beginning with focus and review sounds into boxes labeled with key word pictures.

- **Rhyme, Song, Fingerplay, and Tongue Twister Connections** The teacher shares with students short pieces written on charts that are familiar to students from their oral language experiences and that feature the focus letter-sound. Together, during group shared reading, they highlight the theme, letter, and sound and interact with the pieces through a variety of multisensory activities. Later, individual students illustrate the piece and circle or highlight the focus letter with colored pencil.

- **Cloze Sentence Connections** During a group activity, students listen to sentences read aloud that feature the color-coded focus letter. They practice prediction, cross-checking, confirmation, and self-correction strategies to determine words that are written but not read aloud (in a cloze procedure). In independent follow-up activities appropriate to their learning styles, students locate and match, glue on, trace, or write focus letters in the context of the presented cloze sentences. To complete all activites, students practice left-to-right reading sequence as they count the times the letter recurs in the sentences.

- **Multisensory Prewriting Connections** Prewriting activities involve multisensory input and output, large and small muscles, two and three dimensions, and vertical and horizontal formats. For reinforcement at school and at home, students construct Activities Books that contain activities completed on paper.

- **Connecting with Published and Student-Made Alphabet Books and Dictionaries** Students practice alphabet sequence and letter-sound knowledge at school and at home as they locate focus and review letter pages, identify the pictures, and complete related activities in published alphabet books and dictionaries and in those they construct themselves.

- **Connecting with Environmental Print** With guidance in and out of school, students notice focus and review letters in the environment—in the classroom, throughout the school, in the neighborhood and community, and at home.

- **Home-School Connections** A sample letter to students' families describes activities that highlight and reinforce letter-sound connections out of school. Students refer to reference tools at home as well as at school, and they construct Story Books, Activities Books, and Student-Made Dictionaries that they take home to share with their families.

Section II: Letter-Sound Units

The twenty-nine units of *Developing Letter-Sound Connections* focus on each of the alphabet letters and on consonant digraphs *ch*, *sh*, and *th*. Each unit is in two sections: **Teacher Reference** and **Reproducible Masters for Photocopying**.

Teacher Reference

Resources for teacher reference for each unit include:

- **Annotated Book List**
- **Literature Extension Activities**
- **Items for the Mystery Box**
- **Rhymes, Songs, Fingerplays, and Tongue Twisters**
- **Cloze Sentences**

Reproducible Masters for Photocopying

Reproducible masters for photocopying for each unit include:

- **Rhyme, Song, Fingerplay, and Tongue Twister Independent Activity Sheets**
- **Cloze Sentence Independent Activity Sheets**
- **Activities Book Cover, Wall Alphabet Letter and Picture, Story Book Page,** and **Student-Made Dictionary Page**

  (This last page of each letter-sound unit can be reduced, as needed, and used for each purpose.)

CONTENTS

ABOUT THIS PROGRAM, ix

SECTION I: HOW TO USE THIS PROGRAM, 1

1. Introductory Activities, 3

Alphabet Sequence: Oral to Written Connections, 3
    Daily Alphabet Song Practice with Voice-Print Match, 3
    Stopping at a Specific Letter in the Alphabet, 4
    Saying or Singing the Alphabet up to the New Focus Letter, 5

Literature,Theme, and Key Word/Picture Connections, 6
    Review Letter-Sound-Key Word/Picture Cards, 6
    The Read-Aloud Book, 8
    Introduction of the Focus Letter-Sound-Key Word/Picture Card, 9

Connections with Familiar Objects in the Mystery Box, 11
    Mystery Box Whole-Group Activity, 11

2. Reference Activities, 14

Introducing the Reference Tools, 14
    Alphabet in Song Clusters, 14
    Letter-Sound-Key Word/Picture Cards in Alphabetical Order and for
        Consonant Digraphs and Short Vowels, 15
    Horizontal Wall Alphabet, 15

Using the Reference Tools Throughout the Primary Grades, 16

Constructing the Reference Tools, 16

Reproducible Masters for Photocopying:
    Alphabet in Song Clusters, 19
    Letter-Sound-Key Word/Picture Cards in Alphabetical Order, 20
    Letter-Sound-Key Word/Picture Cards for Consonant Digraphs and
        Short Vowels, 21

3. Reinforcement Activities, 22

Theme-Related Books and Literature Extension Connections, 22

Mystery Box Connections, 22
    Stories and Story Books, 23
    Small-Group Activity, 25
    Sorting Mystery Box Items and Pictures, 26

Rhyme, Song, Fingerplay, and Tongue Twister Connections, 27
    Group Shared-Reading Activity, 27
    Independent Activity, 29

Cloze Sentence Connections, 30
    Group Shared-Reading Activity, 30
    Independent Activity, 33

Multisensory Prewriting Connections, 35
    Forming Uppercase Letters with Grover, 35
    Letter-Tracing Activities, 36
    Play-Doh® or Clay Letters, 38
    Construction of the Wall-Size Outline Letters, 38
    Tactile or Kinesthetic/Motor Activities Without Visual Input, 39
    Activities with Upper- and Lowercase Magnetic Letters, 42
    Alphabet Letter-Stamp Activities, 45

*Connecting with Published and Student-Made Alphabet Books and
    Dictionaries, 46*
    Published Alphabet Books and Dictionaries, 46
    Student-Made Books: Story Books, Activities Books, and Dictionaries, 47

Connecting with Environmental Print, 50
    In the Classroom, 50
    Throughout the School, 50
    In the Neighborhood and Community, 51
    At Home, 51

Home-School Connections, 51
    Reference Tools, 52
    Wall Alphabet, 52
    Student-Made Alphabet Books and Dictionary, 52
    A Letter to Families, 53
    Reproducible Master for Photocopying: Activities That Encourage
        Awareness of Letters and Sounds, 54

SECTION II: LETTER-SOUND UNITS, 57

Aa   apple   59

Teacher Reference, 59
    Annotated Book List, 59
    Literature Extension Activities, 62
    Items for the Mystery Box, 63
    Rhymes, Songs, Fingerplays, and Tongue Twisters, 63
    Cloze Sentences, 64

Reproducible Masters for Photocopying, 65
Rhyme, Song, Fingerplay, and Tongue Twister Independent Activity
Sheets, 65
Cloze Sentence Independent Activity Sheets, 68
Activities Book Cover, Wall Alphabet Letter and Picture, Story Book
Page, and Student-Made Dictionary Page, 70

Bb   bed   71

Teacher Reference, 71
Annotated Book List, 71
Literature Extension Activities, 75
Items for the Mystery Box, 77
Rhymes, Songs, Fingerplays, and Tongue Twisters, 77
Cloze Sentences, 78

Reproducible Masters for Photocopying, 79
Rhyme, Song, Fingerplay, and Tongue Twister Independent Activity
Sheets, 79
Cloze Sentence Independent Activity Sheets, 82
Activities Book Cover and Wall Alphabet Letter and Picture, Story
Book Page, and Student-Made Dictionary Page, 84

Cc   cat   85

Teacher Reference, 85
Annotated Book List, 85
Literature Extension Activities, 89
Items for the Mystery Box, 90
Rhymes, Songs, Fingerplays, and Tongue Twisters, 90
Cloze Sentences, 90

Reproducible Masters for Photocopying, 92
Rhyme, Song, Fingerplay, and Tongue Twister Independent Activity
Sheets, 92
Cloze Sentence Independent Activity Sheets, 95
Activities Book Cover and Wall Alphabet Letter and Picture, Story
Book Page, and Student-Made Dictionary Page, 97

Dd   dog   98

Teacher Reference, 98
Annotated Book List, 98
Literature Extension Activities, 102

Items for the Mystery Box, 103
Rhymes, Songs, Fingerplays, and Tongue Twisters, 104
Cloze Sentences, 104

Reproducible Masters for Photocopying, 106
Rhyme, Song, Fingerplay, and Tongue Twister Independent Activity
    Sheets, 106
Cloze Sentence Independent Activity Sheets, 109
Activities Book Cover and Wall Alphabet Letter and Picture, Story
    Book Page, and Student-Made Dictionary Page, 111

Ee   elephant   112

Teacher Reference, 112
Annotated Book List, 112
Literature Extension Activities, 116
Items for the Mystery Box, 117
Rhymes, Songs, Fingerplays, and Tongue Twisters, 117
Cloze Sentences, 118

Reproducible Masters for Photocopying, 119
Rhyme, Song, Fingerplay, and Tongue Twister Independent Activity
    Sheets, 119
Cloze Sentence Independent Activity Sheets, 122
Activities Book Cover and Wall Alphabet Letter and Picture, Story
    Book Page, and Student-Made Dictionary Page, 124

Ff   fish   125

Teacher Reference, 125
Annotated Book List, 125
Literature Extension Activities, 129
Items for the Mystery Box, 130
Rhymes, Songs, Fingerplays, and Tongue Twisters, 130
Cloze Sentences, 131

Reproducible Masters for Photocopying, 132
Rhyme, Song, Fingerplay, and Tongue Twister Independent Activity
    Sheets, 132
Cloze Sentence Independent Activity Sheets, 135
Activities Book Cover and Wall Alphabet Letter and Picture, Story
    Book Page, and Student-Made Dictionary Page, 137

Gg   goat   138

Teacher Reference, 138

       Annotated Book List, 138

       Literature Extension Activities, 140

       Items for the Mystery Box, 141

       Rhymes, Songs, Fingerplays, and Tongue Twisters, 142

       Cloze Sentences, 142

Reproducible Masters for Photocopying, 144

       Rhyme, Song, Fingerplay, and Tongue Twister Independent Activity
          Sheets, 144

       Cloze Sentence Independent Activity Sheets, 147

       Activities Book Cover and Wall Alphabet Letter and Picture, Story
          Book Page, and Student-Made Dictionary Page, 149

Hh   hat   150

Teacher Reference, 150

       Annotated Book List, 150

       Literature Extension Activities, 153

       Items for the Mystery Box, 154

       Rhymes, Songs, Fingerplays, and Tongue Twisters, 155

       Cloze Sentences, 155

Reproducible Masters for Photocopying, 157

       Rhyme, Song, Fingerplay, and Tongue Twister Independent Activity
          Sheets, 157

       Cloze Sentence Independent Activity Sheets, 160

       Activities Book Cover and Wall Alphabet Letter and Picture, Story
          Book Page, and Student-Made Dictionary Page, 162

Ii   igloo   163

Teacher Reference, 163

       Annotated Book List, 163

       Literature Extension Activities, 167

       Items for the Mystery Box, 168

       Rhymes, Songs, Fingerplays, and Tongue Twisters, 168

       Cloze Sentences, 168

Reproducible Masters for Photocopying, 170

       Rhyme, Song, Fingerplay, and Tongue Twister Independent Activity
          Sheets, 170

Cloze Sentence Independent Activity Sheets, 173
Activities Book Cover and Wall Alphabet Letter and Picture, Story
    Book Page, and Student-Made Dictionary Page, 175

Jj   jump   176

Teacher Reference, 176
Annotated Book List, 176
Literature Extension Activities, 179
Items for the Mystery Box, 180
Rhymes, Songs, Fingerplays, and Tongue Twisters, 180
Cloze Sentences, 181

Reproducible Masters for Photocopying, 182
Rhyme, Song, Fingerplay, and Tongue Twister Independent Activity
    Sheets, 182
Cloze Sentence Independent Activity Sheets, 185
Activities Book Cover and Wall Alphabet Letter and Picture, Story
    Book Page, and Student-Made Dictionary Page, 187

Kk   kangaroo   188

Teacher Reference, 188
Annotated Book List, 188
Literature Extension Activities, 189
Items for the Mystery Box, 190
Rhymes, Songs, Fingerplays, and Tongue Twisters, 191
Cloze Sentences, 191

Reproducible Masters for Photocopying, 193
Rhyme, Song, Fingerplay, and Tongue Twister Independent Activity
    Sheets, 193
Cloze Sentence Independent Activity Sheets, 196
Activities Book Cover and Wall Alphabet Letter and Picture, Story
    Book Page, and Student-Made Dictionary Page, 198

Ll   lion   199

Teacher Reference, 199
Annotated Book List, 199
Literature Extension Activities, 202
Items for the Mystery Box, 203
Rhymes, Songs, Fingerplays, and Tongue Twisters, 203
Cloze Sentences, 204

Reproducible Masters for Photocopying, 205
Rhyme, Song, Fingerplay, and Tongue Twister Independent Activity
Sheets, 205
Cloze Sentence Independent Activity Sheets, 208
Activities Book Cover and Wall Alphabet Letter and Picture, Story
Book Page, and Student-Made Dictionary Page, 210

Mm   mountain   211

Teacher Reference, 211
Annotated Book List, 211
Literature Extension Activities, 214
Items for the Mystery Box, 215
Rhymes, Songs, Fingerplays, and Tongue Twisters, 216
Cloze Sentences, 216

Reproducible Masters for Photocopying, 218
Rhyme, Song, Fingerplay, and Tongue Twister Independent Activity
Sheets, 218
Cloze Sentence Independent Activity Sheets, 221
Activities Book Cover and Wall Alphabet Letter and Picture, Story
Book Page, and Student-Made Dictionary Page, 223

Nn   nest   224

Teacher Reference, 224
Annotated Book List, 224
Literature Extension Activities, 226
Items for the Mystery Box, 227
Rhymes, Songs, Fingerplays, and Tongue Twisters, 227
Cloze Sentences, 228

Reproducible Masters for Photocopying, 229
Rhyme, Song, Fingerplay, and Tongue Twister Independent Activity
Sheets, 229
Cloze Sentence Independent Activity Sheets, 232
Activities Book Cover and Wall Alphabet Letter and Picture, Story
Book Page, and Student-Made Dictionary Page, 234

Oo   octopus   235

Teacher Reference, 235
Annotated Book List, 235
Literature Extension Activities, 236

Items for the Mystery Box, 237
Rhymes, Songs, Fingerplays, and Tongue Twisters, 237
Cloze Sentences, 237

Reproducible Masters for Photocopying, 239
Rhyme, Song, Fingerplay, and Tongue Twister Independent Activity
    Sheets, 239
Cloze Sentence Independent Activity Sheets, 242
Activities Book Cover and Wall Alphabet Letter and Picture, Story
    Book Page, and Student-Made Dictionary Page, 244

Pp   pumpkin   245

Teacher Reference, 245
Annotated Book List, 245
Literature Extension Activities, 248
Items for the Mystery Box, 249
Rhymes, Songs, Fingerplays, and Tongue Twisters, 250
Cloze Sentences, 250

Reproducible Masters for Photocopying, 251
Rhyme, Song, Fingerplay, and Tongue Twister Independent Activity
    Sheets, 251
Cloze Sentence Independent Activity Sheets, 254
Activities Book Cover and Wall Alphabet Letter and Picture, Story
    Book Page, and Student-Made Dictionary Page, 256

QU qu   quilt   257

Teacher Reference, 257
Annotated Book List, 257
Literature Extension Activities, 260
Items for the Mystery Box, 261
Rhymes, Songs, Fingerplays, and Tongue Twisters, 262
Cloze Sentences, 262

Reproducible Masters for Photocopying, 264
Rhyme, Song, Fingerplay, and Tongue Twister Independent Activity
    Sheets, 264
Cloze Sentence Independent Activity Sheets, 267
Activities Book Cover and Wall Alphabet Letter and Picture, Story
    Book Page, and Student-Made Dictionary Page, 269

Rr   rabbit   270

Teacher Reference, 270
  Annotated Book List, 270
  Literature Extension Activities, 273
  Items for the Mystery Box, 274
  Rhymes, Songs, Fingerplays, and Tongue Twisters, 275
  Cloze Sentences, 275

Reproducible Masters for Photocopying, 277
  Rhyme, Song, Fingerplay, and Tongue Twister Independent Activity
    Sheets, 277
  Cloze Sentence Independent Activity Sheets, 280
  Activities Book Cover and Wall Alphabet Letter and Picture, Story
    Book Page, and Student-Made Dictionary Page, 282

Ss   snake   283

Teacher Reference, 283
  Annotated Book List, 283
  Literature Extension Activities, 286
  Items for the Mystery Box, 286
  Rhymes, Songs, Fingerplays, and Tongue Twisters, 287
  Cloze Sentences, 287

Reproducible Masters for Photocopying, 289
  Rhyme, Song, Fingerplay, and Tongue Twister Independent Activity
    Sheets, 289
  Cloze Sentence Independent Activity Sheets, 292
  Activities Book Cover and Wall Alphabet Letter and Picture, Story
    Book Page, and Student-Made Dictionary Page, 294

Tt   turtle   295

Teacher Reference, 295
  Annotated Book List, 295
  Literature Extension Activities, 299
  Items for the Mystery Box, 300
  Rhymes, Songs, Fingerplays, and Tongue Twisters, 300
  Cloze Sentences, 301

Reproducible Masters for Photocopying, 302
  Rhyme, Song, Fingerplay, and Tongue Twister Independent Activity
    Sheets, 302

Cloze Sentence Independent Activity Sheets, 305
Activities Book Cover and Wall Alphabet Letter and Picture, Story
      Book Page, and Student-Made Dictionary Page, 307

Uu   umbrella   308

Teacher Reference, 308
      Annotated Book List, 308
      Literature Extension Activities, 311
      Items for the Mystery Box, 312
      Rhymes, Songs, Fingerplays, and Tongue Twisters, 312
      Cloze Sentences, 312

Reproducible Masters for Photocopying, 314
      Rhyme, Song, Fingerplay, and Tongue Twister Independent Activity
            Sheets, 314
      Cloze Sentence Independent Activity Sheets, 317
      Activities Book Cover and Wall Alphabet Letter and Picture, Story
            Book Page, and Student-Made Dictionary Page, 319

Vv   valentine   320

Teacher Reference, 320
      Annotated Book List, 320
      Literature Extension Activities, 322
      Items for the Mystery Box, 323
      Rhymes, Songs, Fingerplays, and Tongue Twisters, 323
      Cloze Sentences, 323

Reproducible Masters for Photocopying, 325
      Rhyme, Song, Fingerplay, and Tongue Twister Independent Activity
            Sheets, 325
      Cloze Sentence Independent Activity Sheets, 328
      Activities Book Cover and Wall Alphabet Letter and Picture, Story
            Book Page, and Student-Made Dictionary Page, 330

Ww   water   331

Teacher Reference, 331
      Annotated Book List, 331
      Literature Extension Activities, 336
      Items for the Mystery Box, 337
      Rhymes, Songs, Fingerplays, and Tongue Twisters, 337
      Cloze Sentences, 338

Reproducible Masters for Photocopying, 339
Rhyme, Song, Fingerplay, and Tongue Twister Independent Activity
Sheets, 339
Cloze Sentence Independent Activity Sheets, 342
Activities Book Cover and Wall Alphabet Letter and Picture, Story
Book Page, and Student-Made Dictionary Page, 344

Xx   fox   345

Teacher Reference, 345
Annotated Book List, 345
Literature Extension Activities, 349
Items for the Mystery Box, 349
Rhymes, Songs, Fingerplays, and Tongue Twisters, 350
Cloze Sentences, 350

Reproducible Masters for Photocopying, 351
Rhyme, Song, Fingerplay, and Tongue Twister Independent Activity
Sheets, 351
Cloze Sentence Independent Activity Sheets, 354
Activities Book Cover and Wall Alphabet Letter and Picture, Story
Book Page, and Student-Made Dictionary Page, 356

Yy   yarn   357

Teacher Reference, 357
Annotated Book List, 357
Literature Extension Activities, 360
Items for the Mystery Box, 361
Rhymes, Songs, Fingerplays, and Tongue Twisters, 362
Cloze Sentences, 362

Reproducible Masters for Photocopying, 363
Rhyme, Song, Fingerplay, and Tongue Twister Independent Activity
Sheets, 363
Cloze Sentence Independent Activity Sheets, 366
Activities Book Cover and Wall Alphabet Letter and Picture, Story
Book Page, and Student-Made Dictionary Page, 368

Zz   zebra   369

Teacher Reference, 369
Annotated Book List, 369
Literature Extension Activities, 370

Items for the Mystery Box, 371
Rhymes, Songs, Fingerplays, and Tongue Twisters, 371
Cloze Sentences, 372

Reproducible Masters for Photocopying, 373
Rhyme, Song, Fingerplay, and Tongue Twister Independent Activity
    Sheets, 373
Cloze Sentence Independent Activity Sheets, 376
Activities Book Cover and Wall Alphabet Letter and Picture, Story
    Book Page, and Student-Made Dictionary Page, 378

CH ch   chair   379

Teacher Reference, 379
Annotated Book List, 379
Literature Extension Activities, 382
Items for the Mystery Box, 383
Rhymes, Songs, Fingerplays, and Tongue Twisters, 383
Cloze Sentences, 383

Reproducible Masters for Photocopying, 385
Rhyme, Song, Fingerplay, and Tongue Twister Independent Activity
    Sheets, 385
Cloze Sentence Independent Activity Sheets, 388
Activities Book Cover and Wall Alphabet Letter and Picture, Story
    Book Page, and Student-Made Dictionary Page, 390

SH sh   shark   391

Teacher Reference, 391
Annotated Book List, 391
Literature Extension Activities, 394
Items for the Mystery Box, 395
Rhymes, Songs, Fingerplays, and Tongue Twisters, 395
Cloze Sentences, 395

Reproducible Masters for Photocopying, 397
Rhyme, Song, Fingerplay, and Tongue Twister Independent Activity
    Sheets, 397
Cloze Sentence Independent Activity Sheets, 400
Activities Book Cover and Wall Alphabet Letter and Picture, Story
    Book Page, and Student-Made Dictionary Page, 402

TH th   thumb   403

Teacher Reference, 403
Annotated Book List, 403
Literature Extension Activities, 404
Items for the Mystery Box, 405
Rhymes, Songs, Fingerplays, and Tongue Twisters, 406
Cloze Sentences, 406

Reproducible Masters for Photocopying, 408
Rhyme, Song, Fingerplay, and Tongue Twister Independent Activity
      Sheets, 408
Cloze Sentence Independent Activity Sheets, 411
Activities Book Cover and Wall Alphabet Letter and Picture, Story
      Book Page, and Student-Made Dictionary Page, 413

**APPENDIX A: Reproducible Masters for Letter-
                 Sound-Key Word/Picture Cards and
                 Card Mask, 415**

**APPENDIX B: Books That Contain Rhymes,
                 Songs, Fingerplays, and Tongue
                 Twisters, 424**

Section I

HOW TO USE THIS PROGRAM

Developing Letter-Sound Connections contains twenty-nine units with Introductory, Reference, and Reinforcement Activities for each letter of the alphabet and for consonant digraphs *ch*, *sh*, and *th*. All activities are designed for use with large or small groups or with individual students.

The introductory lesson comprises several interrelated **Introductory Activities**. The lesson requires approximately twenty minutes to complete. It is described in this section as it might occur in a kindergarten classroom setting with the whole class.

Combined with the Introductory Activities, the **Reference Activities** form the foundation of *Developing Letter-Sound Connections*. Reference Activities provide consistency and continuity for beginning readers and writers throughout the primary grades. Teachers provide the suggested reference tools for all students in kindergarten through third-grade at school and at home. Students use them as they need them.

Teachers select **Reinforcement Activities** from those suggested to meet the needs of their students and as time allows. Students complete Reinforcement Activities during shared, partner, and independent reading time and during project or activity time in their classrooms and at home.

The descriptions of each activity in this section include a brief introduction, a list of materials, and teacher directions.

1. Introductory Activities

ALPHABET SEQUENCE:
Oral to Written Connections

Students connect the alphabet song to the written alphabet on charts that have the letters grouped in clusters as they are sung. Students practice strategies that help them locate letters and sounds on reference tools.

Daily Alphabet Song Practice with Voice-Print Match

Children frequently enter kindergarten able to sing the alphabet to the tune of "Twinkle Twinkle Little Star." Therefore, oral knowledge of the alphabet song is an ideal place to begin focus on letter-sound knowledge. Many students, however, are not yet able to connect the names of the letters they sing to the written letters of the alphabet. It is helpful for these students to have daily practice with voice-print match, along with their whole class during meeting or calendar time.

abcd efg
hijk
lmnop
qrs tuv
wxyz

Daily practice matching the letter name to its visual symbol serves several purposes. It helps all students to slow down and sing L, M, N, O as separate letters rather than as a single conglomerate (as many children tend to do). It enables those students who do not yet know the alphabet song, or who leave out letters when they sing it, to learn it in a supportive environment with their peers as models. Students practice left-to-right reading sequence and the return sweep of the eyes from the right at the end of one line to the left and down to the next line of print. Daily practice establishes the alphabet, and alphabetical order, as an important and valued reference tool.

Materials

- Pointer
- Enlarged reference tool with the upper- and lowercase Alphabet in Song Clusters (hung on the wall at a height where students can see and reach easily)
- Horizontal wall alphabet with upper- and lowercase letters

Reference Tool: A reproducible master for the reference tool with the upper- and lowercase Alphabet in Song Clusters is provided on p. 19 of the Reference Activities section. Written presentation of the letters in clusters, as they are sung in the alphabet song, provides a visual-spatial representation of the organization of letters as students have learned it in the song. This gives students additional cues that help them to locate the letters as they are learning them and, later, to locate them on their individual reference charts as they read and write. When duplicated as presented, this tool is an individual student reference tool. When enlarged, it becomes a wall chart for group activities.

Enlarge and copy the master onto an 11″ × 17″ piece of unlined paper. Cut around each group of letters and affix them to a 12″ × 18″ or 18″ × 24″ piece of colored oak tag, leaving space between each row of letters, so the letters appear in the format identical to the individual student reference tool. Presentation of the alphabet chart in the same format helps students transfer to the individual reference chart.

Horizontal Wall Alphabet: Construct a horizontal wall alphabet using the reproducible masters for a wall-size outlined upper- and lowercase letter pair from the Wall Alphabet Letter and Picture, at the end of each letter-sound unit, following the directions in Reference Activities, p. 17. You can also purchase a commercially made alphabet with or without key word/pictures. With students, color or fill in the outlined letters in one of the ways described in Multisensory Prewriting Connections (Reinforcement Activities, pp. 38-39).

Directions

1. At first, point to each letter on the Alphabet in Song Clusters chart as the group sings the song.
2. Later, with teacher guidance, individual students use the pointer to lead the group.
3. Finally, individual students point to each letter independently as the class sings.

Stopping at a Specific Letter in the Alphabet

The ability to stop at a specific letter in the alphabet is an important strategy. Students use it when they refer to their alphabet reference tools to locate a letter or sound as they write or read.

At the beginning of the program, introduce the strategy of stopping at a specific letter in the alphabet with a read-aloud of **The Gunniwolf** by A. Delaney. Students participate by singing the alphabet song in its entirety and to a given letter.

Materials

- Pointer
- Enlarged reference tool—upper- and lowercase Alphabet in Song Clusters (hung at an easy height)

- Horizontal wall alphabet with upper- and lowercase letters
- **The Gunniwolf**, retold and illustrated by A. Delaney (New York: Harper & Row, 1988)

In the beginning of **The Gunniwolf**, a little girl is afraid of the Gunniwolf, but when she wanders into the woods where he lives, she discovers that the alphabet song she sings while she picks flowers puts him to sleep. This discovery allows her to return to the woods whenever she likes; she can sing the song to keep herself safe.

Directions

1. Ask students to tell where in the classroom they might find a written alphabet.
2. As students identify the Alphabet in Song Clusters and the horizontal wall alphabet, point to each reference tool. Tell students that the Alphabet in Song Clusters will help them as they help you read that day's story.
3. Introduce **The Gunniwolf** as a piece of fiction (fantasy, make-believe, or other term familiar to students). Throughout the activity, remind students (as needed) that the story is not real. Together, preview the book; look at the illustrations of the Gunniwolf—at the beginning of the book, where just a bit of the rather silly-looking Gunniwolf is revealed in the background—and later, where more of his body is shown. Preview to the end of the book, where the last illustration shows the little girl safely and happily picking flowers while the Gunniwolf naps nearby.
4. Invite students to help read the book. Explain that their job is to sing the alphabet song as you point to the Alphabet in Song Clusters and to stop when the pointer stops at a letter. Challenge students to watch the pointer carefully so they will not be tricked!
5. Then, read **The Gunniwolf** aloud. Every time the girl sings the alphabet song, point to each letter on the Alphabet in Song Clusters as students sing. Several times in the book, the girl stops singing before the end of the alphabet, when the Gunniwolf falls asleep.

Saying or Singing the Alphabet up to the New Focus Letter

The following activity is the first activity of several that make up the introductory lesson for each letter-sound unit. Practice with this activity helps students develop the ability to stop singing the alphabet song at a specific point to locate a letter or sound.

Materials

- Pointer
- Enlarged reference tool—upper- and lowercase Alphabet in Song Clusters (hung at an easy height)

Directions

1. At the beginning of the introductory lesson for each letter-sound unit, sing or say the alphabet up to and including the previous focus letter with the students.
2. Use a pointer (or have a student use it) to point to the corresponding letter as it is sung by the group of students (or individual student in tutorial).

Literature, Theme, and Key Word/Picture Connections

Read aloud a featured book to establish the theme for the unit. With students, connect the featured book and theme to the corresponding Letter-Sound-Key Word/Picture Card.

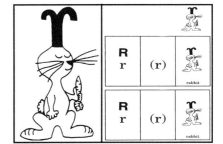

Review Letter-Sound-Key Word/Picture Cards

Before you introduce a new letter-sound and unit, students review the Letter-Sound-Key Word/Picture Cards from previous units.

Materials

- One envelope for review card storage
- One Letter-Sound-Key Word/Picture Card for each review letter-sound for each group of students (or individual student in tutorial)
- One Card Mask made from colored card stock or oak tag
- Enlarged reference tool—upper- and lowercase Alphabet in Song Clusters (hung at an easy height)

Letter-Sound-Key Word/Picture Cards are approximately 3" × 5" in size. Make the cards by photocopying onto card stock the reproducible masters in Appendix A. Each card is divided vertically by lines into three segments or frames, with the following information represented:

1. On the left is the letter or letters that represent a phoneme/sound.

2. In the middle is the sound represented by the letters, enclosed in parentheses.

3. On the right is the key word/picture. For all sounds, letters are embedded in the picture. This gives students a meaningful visual clue to aid memory.

A card is used as a mask to cover the last two frames (middle and right) of each Letter-Sound-Key Word/Picture Card during the one-frame-exposed activity described in item 4 of Directions. A template for making the Card Mask is also included in Appendix A.

Note: The representation for sounds used in *Developing Letter-Sound Connections* is simple and makes sense to students. At the beginning of the program, explain that the sounds the letters represent are written between marks called parentheses. (Some dictionaries use diagonal lines to represent respellings; as appropriate, you and your students can look at different dictionary respellings and discuss how they differ from those represented in this program.)

Directions

1. In group presentation, sit in front of students. In tutorial, you and the student sit facing each other at a table. Present the cards, one at a time, with the symbols toward the students. Hold the pack with your left hand (to students' right) and turn cards with your right hand (to students' left). This provides a movement that cues readers to return their eyes to the left of each card, as in the return sweep of the eyes from the right in the line above in reading text.

2. During beginning units, show students all three frames of each card. Students read each section of the card in order from left to right: (1) the *name* of the letter(s), (2) the *sound* the letter(s) represent, and (3) the *key word/picture*. Present the cards in alphabetical order. Encourage students to refer to the Alphabet in Song Clusters, which is displayed in clear view of all students, as they need to.

3. Later in the program, when appropriate, present the review cards in random order.

4. Finally, when most or all of the letters of the alphabet have been presented, show students the cards in random order, with only the first frame of each card exposed (the frame on the left). Cover the second and third frames of each card with the mask. Remove each card from the pack with your right hand and hold the mask in place with your left hand. In this more difficult task, students name the exposed letter(s) and give the sound and key word from memory. When useful, point to or guide students to point to the section under the mask that represents

each response. Memory and retrieval appear to be aided by this additional spatial and motor cue.

At the beginning of the program, teach students to check their response by showing them all three frames of each card successfully read, and then asking, "Are you right? Take a look and check to be sure." Cards of which students are unsure or which they read unsuccessfully are returned immediately to the pack for additional tries and practice during this activity. Students enjoy having their pile of cards read successfully to compare with the teacher's pile (which is usually nonexistent because students are provided with several opportunities for success with challenging cards).

5. At the end of this activity, students watch as you store the review cards in an envelope marked for this purpose.

The Read-Aloud Book

Read aloud a featured book to establish the theme for the unit. Choose a book from the Annotated Book List, found in the Teacher Reference section of each letter-sound unit.

Materials

* The featured picture book for the letter-sound unit
* One wall-size key word/picture (reproducible master at the end of each letter-sound unit)
* One small key word/picture
* One Letter-Sound-Key Word/Picture Card (Appendix A—reproduced from the master on card stock)
* One Letter-Sound Key Word/Picture Card (reproduced from the master on unlined paper)
* Removable label or correction tape
* Enlarged reference tool—upper- and lowercase Alphabet in Song Clusters (hung at an easy height)
* Horizontal wall alphabet with upper- and lowercase letters

Before you present this activity, prepare the read-aloud book. Use removable tape to attach the small key word/picture to the upper right-hand corner of the title page of the book. A piece of tape folded onto itself in a loop, with the sticky side exposed and attached to the back of the picture works well. Just below the key word/picture, tape the two Letter-Sound-Key Word/Picture Cards, with the third frame directly below the key word/picture so that the pictures line up. Tape the card copied onto card stock first and tape the card copied onto unlined paper directly below it. Tape the wall-size key word/picture to the left-hand page opposite the title page. Do not show these items to students until the appropriate time following the read-aloud.

Directions

1. After they have sung the alphabet song up to and including the previous focus letter, ask students to guess the letter about which you are thinking. A wide range of guesses occurs during the first units of the program while students are discovering the alphabetic sequence that organizes the units. Students often sing the alphabet song or scan an alphabet chart to choose a familiar or favorite letter, or they may offer the letter that begins their names. Ask a student who volunteers to remind her or his peers where in the classroom they could find letters of the alphabet. If necessary, guide students to observe and refer to the Alphabet in Song Clusters and the horizontal wall alphabet.

   Respond to guesses or predictions in a nonevaluative way, as in brainstorming. Ask students to share the reasoning behind their guesses: "Hmmm. Why do think it might be *c*?" for example. Many students detect the alphabetic sequence early on in the program. Others need more experiences before they notice that the units progress in order through the alphabet. Students articulate and reveal this information to their peers through their responses to the query.

2. After several students have made predictions and shared their reasoning, show students the cover of the featured read-aloud book. Say, "Here is some more information." Direct students' attention to the picture and letters (especially in the title) on the cover in their search for confirmations or corrections of their initial guesses.

   Here, and throughout the program, you consistently model a critical reading strategy. Do not tell students if they are correct; direct their attention or provide additional information or clues so that students can confirm or self-correct. This practice, and the habit it establishes, contributes significantly to the development of independent readers and writers who actively use their own resources and strategies to work out challenges.

3. When students have made and confirmed or corrected a number of predictions, leave them with the query concerning the identity of the focus letter as you begin reading the book: "Listen to this story and see if you still think it is *c* (or other predicted letters)."

Introduction of the Focus Letter-Sound-Key Word/Picture Card

With students, connect the featured book to the theme of the unit and to the corresponding key word/picture for the focus letter-sound.

Materials

- Same materials as for the Read-Aloud Book
- Hand-held mirrors for individuals or small groups of students

Directions

1. After students have listened to and interacted with the read-aloud book through discussion, ask students to identify the focus letter and sound and to provide or review reasons for that choice. Encourage students to use information from the story, book cover, and alphabet charts to support their responses.

2. Open to the title page of the book and the page opposite, revealing the small key word/picture, the two Letter-Sound-Key Word/Picture Cards, and the wall-size key word/picture.

3. A student places the small key word/picture below the appropriate letter on the Alphabet in Song Clusters.

4. Another student places the new card (copied onto unlined paper) next to the last review letter card on the meeting area bulletin board near the calendar and the Alphabet in Song Clusters. With teacher guidance, students group cards on the bulletin board in song clusters with one cluster per line:

a b c d

e f g

h i j k

l m n o p

q r s

t u v

w x y z

5. If the horizontal wall alphabet is hung so that students can reach it easily, a student puts the new wall-size key word/picture in place below the appropriate letter. If it is hung where students cannot reach it, students watch as you place the wall-size key word/picture below or next to the appropriate upper- and lowercase letter of the horizontal wall alphabet.

6. Show students the focus Letter-Sound-Key Word/Picture Card (copied onto card stock). In unison, students read aloud the card.

7. With students, say the focus sound several times. Distribute hand-held mirrors to individuals or small groups of students. Students look at their mouths as they form the sound. They talk about the position of the lips, tongue, teeth, and roof of the mouth (palate) during articulation.

8. In preparation for the next activity, place the focus Letter-Sound-Key Word/Picture Card (copied onto card stock) on an easel or chart stand (or in another location) where it can be seen easily by all students.

Connections with Familiar Objects in the Mystery Box

Immediately following the Introduction of the Focus Letter-Sound-Key Word/Picture Card activity, present a whole-group activity in which students use initial sound and meaning clues to predict, cross-check, and confirm or correct as they guess inedible and edible items in a Mystery Box whose names begin with the focus letter-sound. Later, offer students opportunities to taste the edible items and foods made from edible items.

Mystery Box Whole-Group Activity

Materials

- The focus Letter-Sound-Key Word/Picture Card for the unit (copied onto card stock)
- A round hatbox with a lid, with holes in the box for your hands that enable you to reach inside the box to take out items without lifting the lid
- Mystery Box items whose names begin with the focus letter-sound for the unit. These include inedible items (small toys, ornaments, objects, or photographs or pictures that represent common items or animals) and edible items (in plastic storage bags or containers, as appropriate)

Cut two round holes approximately 3 1/2" in diameter, placed approximately 12" from the center of one circle to the center of the second, and centered in the side of the box facing you (as in the drawing above). Cut two rectangular pieces of felt approximately 9" × 6". Tape the rectangles of felt inside the box to hang over each hole so that students are unable to see the items in the box before you take them out and reveal them.

An alphabetical list of suggested items for the Mystery Box is provided in the Teacher Reference section of each letter-sound unit. Inedible and edible items are listed separately. The key-word item, which relates to the theme of the unit, appears in bold print in the list. Select items from those suggested, typically ten to fifteen items. It is difficult for young children to sustain attention for more than this number of items.

A gallon-size plastic freezer or storage bag with a zip closure works well to store inedible items until they are introduced in alphabetical order in the letter-sound units. Add fresh edible items for each unit to the Mystery Box. Students help store in the classroom inedible items whose names begin with review focus letter-sounds. They sort items into boxes labeled with key word/pictures (described in the Mystery Box Connections section of Reinforcement Activities on p. 26).

Directions

1. Immediately after the Introduction of the Focus Letter-Sound-Key Word/Picture Card activity, display the new card in view of all students—on an easel or chart stand.

2. Sit down and place the Mystery Box on your lap.

3. Explain to students (at the beginning of the program) and remind students (later in the program) that the names of all of the items in the Mystery Box begin with the focus letter-sound.

4. Reach into the box with both hands and choose one item at a time at random.

5. Give meaning clues about its identity. Present clues that are general at first, then gradually give clues that are more specific. Students combine this information with the initial sound to make guesses or predictions. Begin clue giving by reminding students to prepare their mouths for their guesses by saying the focus sound. Offer additional reminders during the activity as appropriate. Students raise their hands when they have a prediction, and you call on one student following each clue.

   Clues include category (function/purpose/use), description (size, weight, shape, color, texture/feel, material, parts, noise, movements, smell, and temperature), contrast and comparison, and something related to the featured read-aloud book. For an elephant, for example, you might give the following clues: (1) This is a toy of an animal. (2) The real animal is very large (or huge). (3) It is a heavy animal. (4) This animal is often gray. (5) Its skin is often thick, wrinkled, and baggy. (6) This animal has large, floppy ears, (7) ivory tusks, and (8) a trunk. (9) It makes a trumpeting sound. (10) It walks in Africa or India where it lives. (11) It is much larger than a horse. (12) The main character in **Horton Hatches the Egg** is an _____ . You can occasionally offer a cloze sentence as a clue—a sentence in which the name of the item is omitted. An example of a cloze sentence for an elephant might be "At the zoo, I saw an _____ waving its trunk above its huge, gray head."

   If students have been unsuccessful in their attempts to identify or name the item after you have supplied the types of meaning clues described above, offer a sound clue in the form of a rhyming word. You might say "It begins with (e) and rhymes with telephant."

During this activity, as throughout *Developing Letter-Sound Connections*, respond to students' guesses or predictions in a nonevaluative way. Do not tell students if they are correct, but immediately give an additional clue. The new clue provides more information so that students can confirm or self-correct.

6. When students have responded to several clues with predictions and confirmations or corrections, take the item out of the box with one hand and show it to the students.

7. Then, place the item where students can see it easily.

8. When you have given clues for all of the items in the Mystery Box for the focus letter, show students that the box is empty.

9. Ask students to help complete the activity by naming each item you hold up for all to see. Before they begin this rapid naming task, remind students to prepare their mouths for naming the items by saying the focus sound. Then, pick up at random and show each item; the students name it as you put it back into the Mystery Box.

10. With the students, sort the items into inedible and edible. Students may later use the inedible items in the Mystery Box to complete reinforcement activities in the Mystery Box Connections section (see p. 22).

11. Later, provide edible items with color-coded labels. Write the name of each item with all letters except the focus letter in black marker and the focus letter in red marker. Offer students opporunities to taste the edible items.

Note: At the beginning of the year, determine any medical or religious factors that may affect students' abilities to eat edible items. Also, substitute or add edible items that reflect the experiences and cultures of your students or that correspond to themes or units of study in the classroom or school. Encourage students, families, and community members to bring to school, suggest, or prepare with the class foods from their cultures that begin with the focus letter-sound or that have edible items in the list as ingredients. Similarly, and as time permits, you can follow favorite recipes to prepare foods with your students.

12. Near the snack area, display Lois Ehlert's alphabet book, **Eating the Alphabet: Fruits and Vegetables from A to Z** (New York: Harcourt Brace Jovanovich, Inc., 1989). The book features full-page colored paintings of fruits and vegetables for each letter of the alphabet and a glossary that traces the origins, all over the world, of the foods presented.

2. Reference Activities

CONNECTIONS, CONSISTENCY, AND CONTINUITY THROUGHOUT THE PRIMARY GRADES: LETTER-SOUND REFERENCE TOOLS FOR BEGINNING READERS AND WRITERS

In the *Developing Letter-Sound Connections* program, students use the same reference tools in their classrooms and at home throughout the primary years. This helps establish and reinforce connections between the activities that focus specifically on letters and sounds and the activities that make up the rest of the day, both in and out of school. Further, this provides consistency and continuity for students from kindergarten through grade 3 (or longer, to meet individual needs). Teachers provide *all* students in primary classrooms with the reference tools, and students use them as they need them.

Introducing the Reference Tools

Typically, teachers begin to introduce the *Developing Letter-Sound Connections* program at the start of kindergarten. Together, teacher and students construct and use the following reference tools as they complete the Introductory Activities for each letter-sound unit.

1. Alphabet in Song Clusters
2. Letter-Sound-Key Word/Picture Cards in Alphabetical Order
3. Letter-Sound-Key Word/Picture Cards for Consonant Digraphs and Short Vowels
4. Horizontal Wall Alphabet

Alphabet in Song Clusters

A chart-size reference tool with the upper- and lowercase Alphabet in Song Clusters hangs on a bulletin board in the kindergarten meeting area near the calendar at a height where students can see and reach it easily. At the beginning of the year, the chart includes the upper- and lowercase letters in song clusters only. Throughout the year, students add key word/pictures as they progress alphabetically through the letter-sound units. Students hang key word/pictures for consonant digraphs *ch*, *sh*, and *th* below the alphabet during the final three units of the program.

During daily meeting, kindergarten students practice matching the alphabet letter names to the written letters when they sing the alphabet song as a teacher or student leader points to each letter on the Alphabet in Song Clusters chart. As well, they practice left-to-right reading sequence and the return sweep of the eyes from the right at the end of one line to the left and down to the next line of print.

Letter-Sound-Key Word/Picture Cards in Alphabetical Order and for Consonant Digraphs and Short Vowels

During the introduction of the focus Letter-Sound-Key Word/Picture Card for each letter-sound unit, kindergarten students place a copy of the new card next to the last review letter card on the meeting area bulletin board. They place it near the calendar and next to the enlarged reference tool with the upper- and lowercase Alphabet in Song Clusters. With teacher guidance, students group cards in song clusters with one cluster per line:

a b c d

e f g

h i j k

l m n o p

q r s

t u v

w x y z

Daily, during meeting, kindergarten students read the cards up to and including the focus card. They practice association of letter name, sound, and key word; left-to-right reading sequence; and the return sweep of the eyes from the right to the left and down to the next line.

Horizontal Wall Alphabet

At the beginning of the kindergarten year, hang on the wall horizontally the wall-size upper- and lowercase letter pairs for each letter in alphabetical order. Leave spaces for the corresponding key word/pictures that are added, one at a time, as letter-sound units are introduced.

During the introduction of the focus Letter-Sound-Key Word/Picture Card for each letter-sound unit (see p. 9), you or the students can place the wall-size key word/picture next to or below the appropriate letter of the horizontal wall alphabet. If the wall alphabet is hung where students can reach it, a student puts the new picture for each unit in place. If it is hung where students cannot reach it, students watch as you put it in place.

Using the Reference Tools Throughout the Primary Grades

Teachers in every primary classroom provide *all* students with the reference tools; therefore, there is no stigma associated with using them. All students feel free to use the tools as they need them.

Individual reference tools, reproduced onto 8 1/2″ × 11″ unlined paper, are the Alphabet in Song Clusters, Letter-Sound-Key Word/Picture Cards in Alphabetical Order, and Letter-Sound-Key Word/Picture Cards for Consonant Digraphs and Short Vowels. Students keep these reference tools in a pocket of a writing or reading folder or in a separate reference tools section in a three-ring binder. The teacher sends or mails home two copies of these reference tools for each student—one copy for use at home and the second to keep in a wallet or pocketbook or in the family vehicle for use outside school.

During the kindergarten year, when the *Developing Letter-Sound Connections* program is introduced, students refer to the horizontal wall alphabet as they progress through the alphabet and corresponding activities. They add key word/pictures to the upper- and lowercase letter pairs as letter-sound units are introduced. During the primary years following the introduction of the program, typically from first grade on, the teacher hangs the complete upper- and lowercase alphabet with corresponding key word/pictures beside or below them at the start of the year. Some students and their families benefit from having a wall alphabet at home. In this case, the teacher sends or mails home copies of the Wall Alphabet letters and pictures or full-size copies of the Letter-Sound-Key Word/Picture Cards for hanging in alphabetical order.

Constructing the Reference Tools

Alphabet in Song Clusters, Letter-Sound-Key Word/Picture Cards in Alphabetical Order, and Letter-Sound-Key Word/Picture Cards for Consonant Digraphs and Short Vowels

Materials

- Reproducible masters for photocopying (provided at the end of this section)

- Unlined 8 1/2″ × 11″ paper
- Oak tag (plain or in a variety of colors)
- Glue or rubber cement
- Three-hole punch
- Laminator and clear laminating material

Directions

1. Copy the master for each reference tool onto unlined paper.
2. Prepare each tool in one of three ways:
   a. Glue the copied page onto oak tag.
   b. Glue the copied page onto oak tag and laminate it.
   c. Make holes in the left side of the copied page with a three-hole punch to fit into students' loose-leaf binders.

Horizontal Wall Alphabet

Materials

- Reproducible masters for photocopying (provided in each letter-sound unit)
- Unlined 8 1/2″ × 11″ paper
- Oak tag (plain or in a variety of colors)
- Glue or rubber cement
- Laminator and clear laminating material

Directions

Kindergarten and primary teachers use the reproducible masters for the Wall Alphabet Letter and Picture in each letter-sound unit to construct their own horizontal wall alphabet.

1. Cut vertically to separate the upper- and lowercase letter pair (on the left) from the key word/picture (on the right).
2. With students, color the key word/pictures, if desired.
3. Another approach is to fill in the outlined letters in one of the ways described in the Multisensory Prewriting Connections section, Construction of the Wall-Size Outline Letters (p. 38).
4. Glue the copied pages onto oak tag and laminate it.

Note: You may purchase a commercially made alphabet with or without key word/pictures, or use other teacher-made alphabets. Then, hang the key word/picture, as it is introduced, below or next to the appropriate letter of the alphabet.

A B C D   E F G
a b c d   e f g

H I J K
h i j k

L M N O P
l m n o p

Q R S   T U V
q r s   t u v

W X Y Z
w x y z

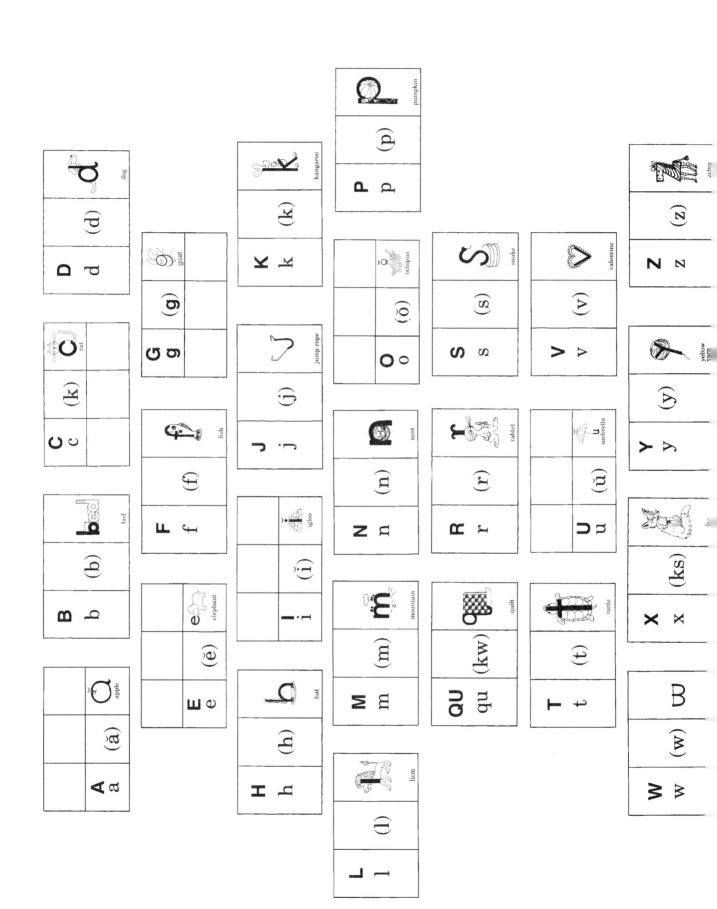

A a	(ă)	apple
B b	(b)	bed
C c	(k)	cat
D d	(d)	dog
E e	(ĕ)	elephant
F f	(f)	fish
G g	(g)	goat
H h	(h)	hat
I i	(ĭ)	igloo
J j	(j)	jump rope
K k	(k)	kangaroo
L l	(l)	lion
M m	(m)	mountain
N n	(n)	nest
O o	(ŏ)	octopus
P p	(p)	pumpkin
QU qu	(kw)	quilt
R r	(r)	rabbit
S s	(s)	snake
T t	(t)	turtle
U u	(ŭ)	umbrella
V v	(v)	valentine
W w	(w)	
X x	(ks)	
Y y	(y)	yellow yarn
Z z	(z)	zebra

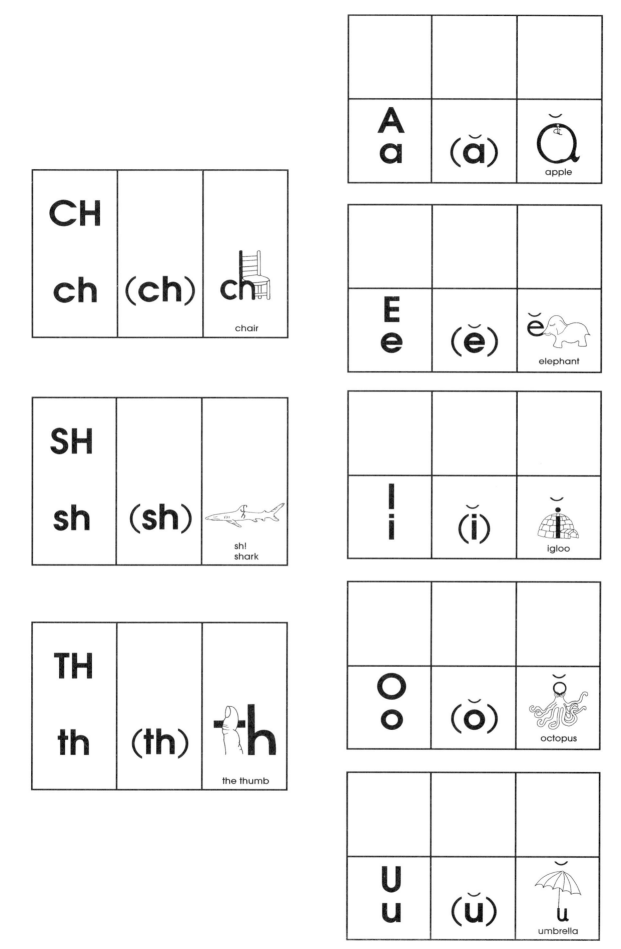

CH		
ch	(ch)	ch
		chair

SH		
sh	(sh)	
		sh! shark

TH		
th	(th)	th
		the thumb

A a	(ă)	ă apple

E e	(ĕ)	ĕ elephant

I i	(ĭ)	ĭ igloo

O o	(ŏ)	ŏ octopus

U u	(ŭ)	ŭ umbrella

3. Reinforcement Activities

Theme-Related Books
and
Literature Extension Connections

During each unit, students complete literature-based activities that introduce, extend, and reinforce the theme. As they respond to the books and engage in related activities, students make connections that help them learn and remember focus letters and sounds.

The Teacher Reference section of each letter-sound unit contains an alphabetical annotated list of books. The books are related to the theme and key word of each unit, and they depict the lives, challenges, and victories of people of diverse cultures, ages, and times in history. Each list includes a variety of fiction and nonfiction books: alphabet, counting, easy-to-read, interactive, picture, rebus, short chapter, and wordless.

discussion   art   oral composition   drama   dance   puppetry   math   movement   cooking   music   science

During the unit, the teacher makes available throughout the day the featured read-aloud book (described in the Introductory Activities section, p. 8) and additional theme-related books. The teacher (or another adult or a student) reads books aloud to students. He or she displays books in the theme or library area of the classroom. Students look at or read books independently or with a partner during daily independent reading time.

Literature Extension Activities that correspond to the theme books follow the annotated book list in the Teacher Reference section. Activities include art, composition, cooking, dance and movement, discussion, drama and puppetry, math, music, and science. Field-trip activities provide introductory and extension experiences and background information, and they are opportunities to focus on environmental print.

Mystery Box Connections

Students use the items from the Mystery Box to complete a variety of small-group and individual reinforcement activities suggested for each letter-sound unit.

Stories and Story Books

After they have completed the introductory Mystery Box Whole-Group Activity, described on p. 11, students interact with the items in the Mystery Box and dramatize and dictate stories about them. Through their stories, students connect their oral language to the written text. Color-coding helps students identify the focus letter in context. The illustrated stories become part of students' Story Books.

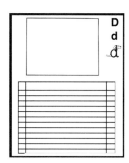

Materials

- Mystery Box items for the focus letter-sound
- Lined 8 1/2″ × 11″ composition paper (cut to 7 1/4″ × 6″ and 7 1/4″ × 10″)
- Unlined white drawing paper (5 1/2″ × 4 1/4″—half of a piece of 8 1/2″ × 11″ paper)
- Graphite and colored pencils
- Red and black thin markers
- Story Book Page reproduced on unlined white paper (8 1/2″ × 11″)

Reduce the Wall Alphabet Page at the end of each letter-sound unit to make your Story Book Page. Copy the master onto one side of the paper and leave the back side blank. There are two options when copying the master:

a. Copy the masters as they are, with the key word/picture to the right of each upper- and lowercase letter pair.

b. Cover the key word/picture with removable label tape or correction tape. Copy key word/pictures for students to glue onto the pages. Students can then glue on a key word/picture below the upper- and lowercase letter pair on each first page.

Directions

1. Individual students (or students in pairs or small groups) explore and play with the items from the Mystery Box.

2. Students then choose four to six items, in addition to the key-word item, which is always included, to use as they dramatize and dictate a story.

Note: Some students benefit, at first, from creating a round-robin story with the teacher, another adult, or another student before they dictate their own stories.

3. Write the dictated story in rough draft form on lined composition paper. As a student dictates, ask guiding questions, as appropriate, to encourage use of narrative elements and clear transitions.

4. Read the draft of the story to the student(s). Students make any necessary changes, and you revise accordingly.

5. Students refer to the selected items from the Mystery Box as they use a graphite pencil (first) and then colored pencils to illustrate the story on the 5 1/2″ × 4 1/4″ unlined paper provided. (It may be more appropriate for students to illustrate the story later, in item 10, below.)

6. Later, transcribe the draft of the story onto lined composition paper. Use black thin marker to write all letters except the focus letter, which you write with red thin marker.

Note: Occasionally, a student with partial or total color blindness is unable to distinguish one or more colors. In this case, write the focus letter with bolder, thicker lines in addition to color-coding with red thin marker.

7. Before you show and read aloud the transcribed story to students, glue the story onto the first and second pages of the Story Book. Glue on the student illustration, completed in item 5, above, or leave room for the illustration, which students glue on when they complete it in item 10, below. You or the students glue the illustration at the top of the first page (to the left of the upper- and lowercase focus letter(s) and key word/picture in the upper right-hand corner). Write the first page of the story on a partial piece of lined composition paper (approximately 7 1/4″ × 6″), which you cut to fit below the illustration. Glue the first and subsequent full pages (on 7 1/4″ × 10″ lined composition paper) onto the back of the Story Book Page. For these full pages, put glue on the top 1/2″ only of each lined composition paper page and glue the 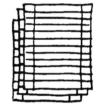 pages in steps down the back side of the page, as in the illustration. Thus, you prepare the Story Books so that there is only one page (two sides) for each focus letter. In this way, students can flip easily through the Story Books page by page (and letter by letter) to locate a specific letter page.

8. Hand the books to students to locate the focus letter page. Encourage students to flip through the book letter by letter (and page by page) in alphabetical order, from the front of the Story Book, to locate the appropriate page.

9. Read the transcribed story to students. Make any revisions and editing changes that students request as students watch; explain the process and editing symbols (the caret, for example).

10. Students illustrate the story at this point if they did not do so in item 5, above. Students refer to the selected items from the Mystery Box as they illustrate.

11. Finally, with teacher guidance as necessary, students use the pointer finger of the writing hand or a pointer to point to and count each focus

letter as they track from left to right in each line of the transcribed story. In addition to voice-print match and left-to-right reading sequence, students practice the return sweep of the eyes from the right at the end of one line to the left and down to begin the next line of print.

12. Throughout the *Developing Letter-Sound Connections* program, help students compile their dictated stories into a Story Book with a student-illustrated cover.

13. The Story Book is one of several student-made alphabet books and dictionaries that students construct during the *Developing Letter-Sound Connections* program. The Connecting with Published and Student-Made Alphabet Books and Dictionaries section (p. 46) describes ways in which students practice alphabet and letter-sound skills as they use these reference books.

Note: While this reinforcement activity is highly motivating and valuable, it is time- and labor-intensive. It is remarkable how much beginning writers can compose as they dramatize and dictate a story with props! You may want to consider ways to make completion of this activity more practical. Suggestions include the following:

a. Other adults (assistant teachers, parents, or community volunteers) take dictation and transcribe stories.

b. Individual students in a class take turns and dictate a story for one or two letter-sound(s) for the entire program (depending on class size). They compile one group Story Book for the classroom library.

c. Pairs of students or students in small groups compose a cooperative story. You or a volunteer can color-code the original transcription. Students take turns tracking and counting the focus letter in the original transcription, which is displayed in the classroom library. Each student in a pair or group receives a black-on-white copy.

d. Individual students with special needs complete the activity in tutorial.

Small-Group Activity

With teacher support or independently, students in pairs or small groups take roles as teacher/leader and student(s) and engage in the Mystery Box activity (as it has been modeled in the introductory Mystery Box Whole-Group Activity, p. 11).

Materials

- The focus Letter-Sound-Key Word/Picture Card for the unit
- The Mystery Box

- Items from the Mystery Box whose names begin with the focus letter-sound for the unit

Directions

As appropriate, help student leaders to formulate and present clues that include category (function/purpose/use), description, contrast or comparison, reference to the featured read-aloud book for the unit, cloze sentence, and/or rhyming (described in detail in the Mystery Box Whole-Group Activity in the Introductory Activities section).

Sorting Mystery Box Items and Pictures

At the end of each unit, students place the items for the focus letter-sound from the Mystery Box into the appropriate storage box (prepared with copies of the Letter-Sound-Key Word/Picture Card on the end and lid). Students store boxes where they are easily accessible in the classroom. Before they store the Mystery Box items for the unit, they complete the following optional activity.

Materials

- Inedible items from the Mystery Box whose names begin with the focus letter-sound for the current unit and items for the Mystery Box from review units (including photographs or pictures of items drawn by students or teacher)
- Mystery Box item storage boxes

Prepare a shoe box with a lid for each letter-sound unit. Cover each box and lid with plain paper and glue a copy of the Letter-Sound-Key Word/Picture Card onto one end of the box and onto the lid.

Directions

1. With students, combine the contents of storage boxes for focus and review letters in one place (on a rug or table, for example).
2. Individually or in pairs or small groups, students sort items into the appropriate Mystery Box item storage boxes. They refer to the key word/pictures on the end and on the lid of each box.
3. When students complete the twenty-nine units of *Developing Letter-Sound Connections,* transfer Mystery Box items from the storage boxes to individual gallon-size plastic freezer or storage bags with zip closures (one bag for each letter-sound unit) for storage until you present the program to a new group of students.

Rhyme, Song, Fingerplay, and Tongue Twister Connections

The teacher presents short pieces that are familiar to students from their oral language experiences or that become familiar from experiences provided in their classrooms. Students interact with the written pieces through a variety of multisensory activities during group shared reading. In an independent follow-up activity, individual students illustrate their own copies of the piece, and they circle or highlight with colored pencil, and then count, the focus letter.

> **Note:** As with all resource books, teachers adapt the suggested activities to match the experiences and meet the needs of their own students. They change materials and procedures to those that are familiar to their students and that reflect their local cultures. This is especially important for this activity. In addition to the suggested pieces—or in their place—you can use short pieces familiar to your students: rhymes (ball bouncing, hand, nursery, rope jumping, sleep, street, and other popular or traditional rhymes), songs, fingerplays, and tongue twisters, plus alliterative sentences, chants, poems, and other forms of oral language.

Group Shared-Reading Activity

Materials

- Published book(s) that contain the selected pieces
- Oak tag weight chart or easel paper for each piece
- Black and red thick permanent markers
- Plastic acetate cover sheet or lamination
- Thick water-base washable markers
- Chart stand or easel
- Pointer
- Reproducible master for photocopying for Rhyme, Song, Fingerplay, and Tongue-Twister Independent Activity sheets (provided in each letter-sound unit)

Each unit includes a list of Rhymes, Songs, Fingerplays, and Tongue Twisters that presents pieces alphabetically in two sections: (1) those that relate to the theme, and (2) those that feature the focus letter-sound but do not relate to the theme. Pieces for which reproducible masters are provided for use in the Independent Activity are marked with an asterisk (*).

Following the first line of each piece are numbers that correspond to books in which it may be found, listed alphabetically in Appendix B. Typically, the text for pieces is taken from early collections of the rhymes (many from the late 1800s to 1915), which are more faithful to the rhyme and rhythm of the original rhymes. If no number(s) follow a piece, the piece was located only in an early source that is out of print, or it was author-created, in which case the author's name follows in parentheses.

> *Note:* In a number of cases, pieces are listed for more than one letter-sound unit. It's beneficial to present pieces in subsequent units following their introduction. This provides excellent review and reinforcement for beginning readers and writers.

The two kinds of reproducible activity sheets either relate to the theme of the unit (presented first in each letter-sound unit) or feature the focus letter-sound but do not relate to the theme.

Refer to the reproducible master of the piece and write it by hand onto chart or easel paper with thick permanent markers. Add pictures to illustrate the piece as you choose. Prepare the chart for shared reading in one of the two following ways:

1. Use a thick black marker to write all letters except the focus letter, which you write with a thick red marker.

2. Use a thick black marker to write all letters including the focus letter. Cover the chart with a plastic acetate sheet during the activity or laminate the chart so that it can be washed off and reused.

Directions

1. Display the prepared piece on a chart stand or easel where all students can see it easily.

2. Read the piece aloud from one or more books that contain it (if available). If it is illustrated, compare and contrast with the students the different ways in which artists have interpreted the piece. Note different versions of the piece and discuss the ways in which literature from the oral tradition changes over time.

   If the piece is an excerpt from a longer piece, read aloud the full text. Sing the songs with students (along with an audiotape, or to live instrumental accompaniment, whenever possible). Listed books frequently suggest finger, hand, or body movements, or musical accompaniment for the piece.

3. Students listen and watch as you read the piece aloud (or sing, if it is a song) several times. Model voice-print match, left-to-right reading sequence, and return eye sweep as you use the pointer to point to each word.

4. Discuss the piece with students. Add finger, hand, or body movements to accompany the piece. Individual students or students in pairs or groups dramatize the piece. Together, they visualize an illustration for the piece and describe the picture they imagine would show its meaning.

5. Students join you in several subsequent choral readings (singing) of the piece, with accompanying movements as you point to the corresponding words.

6. If you have prepared the chart with red color-coded letters (as in option 1, described in the Materials section), individual students take turns using the pointer to point to and count focus letters.

   If you have prepared the chart with all black letters and use a plastic acetate cover sheet or laminated chart (as in option 2), individual students use a colored washable marker to circle each focus letter and then count them.

Guide and support students, as necessary, as they track from left to right in each line of text and from the right at the end of one line to the left and down to begin the next line of print.

Independent Activity

Materials

- Chart of the selected piece from the preceding Group Shared-Reading Activity (displayed where all students can see it easily)
- Graphite and colored pencils
- Individual copy of the piece for each student (prepared using the reproducible master for photocopying for Rhyme, Song, Fingerplay, and Tongue-Twister Independent Activity sheets in each letter-sound unit)

Directions

1. Immediately following the Group Shared-Reading Activity, individual students illustrate, below or next to the text, their copies of the selected piece. Teachers or peers reread the piece for students while they illustrate it, as needed.

2. Students use a graphite or colored pencil to circle or highlight the focus letter featured in the piece. They circle each focus letter or color over the letter in a circular motion sufficiently lightly so that it can be read easily.

3. Students point to and count the circled or highlighted letters. Guide students, as necessary, as they track from left to right in each line of text and from the right at the end of one line to the left and down to begin the next line of print.

Cloze Sentence Connections

Following a cloze procedure, groups of students listen to sentences read aloud that feature the focus letter-sound. Students use prediction, cross-checking, confirmation, and self-correction strategies to identify words beginning with the focus letter that are written but not read aloud. In an independent follow-up activity, individual students locate and match, glue on, trace, or write focus letters and words that contain focus letters in the context of the cloze sentences previously completed as a group activity. During both activities, students practice left-to-right reading sequence and return sweep of the eyes to the left of the following line as they locate and count the focus letter each time it recurs.

Group Shared-Reading Activity

Materials

- Reproducible master for photocopying for Cloze Sentence Independent Activity sheets (provided in each letter-sound unit)
- Oak tag weight chart or easel paper
- Black, red, and green thick permanent markers
- Plastic acetate cover sheet or lamination
- Thick water-base washable markers
- Chart stand or easel
- Pointer

Refer to the Cloze Sentences in the Teacher Reference section or to the reproducible Cloze Sentence Independent Activity sheets in each letter-sound unit and copy one or both of the two sets of four cloze sentences onto chart or easel paper with thick permanent marker. The Teacher Reference section presents the complete cloze sentences with the focus letter in bold print. Use green thick marker to underline the word that is underlined on the master.

Prepare the chart for the group shared-reading activity in one of the two following ways:

1. Use a thick black marker to write all letters except the focus letter; write it with thick red marker.
2. Use a thick black marker to write all letters including the focus letter. Cover the chart with a plastic acetate sheet during the activity or laminate the chart so that it can be washed off and reused.

Note: The cloze sentences presented first in the Teacher Reference section and on the Cloze Sentence Independent Activity sheets omit a word at or near the beginning of a sentence. This format provides students with opportunities to practice a reading-on strategy. When reading on, readers say "blank" when they encounter an unknown or challenging word; they read the text that follows the word to gather more information on which to base a response that fits in the blank. In this modified activity, students hear you say "blank" for the omitted written word and listen as you read the text that follows it.

Determining an unknown word at or near the beginning of a sentence is a more difficult task than identifying a word at or near the end of a sentence. In the latter task, the information on which the reader (or listener) bases a prediction precedes the omitted word and makes it an easier task. Some students need practice with the latter type of cloze activity before they are successful with the omission at or near the beginning of sentences. In this case (and for as long as your students need), present sentences in the latter format. These appear in parentheses following each cloze sentence in the Teacher Reference section of each unit. If you choose the second format, copy the cloze sentences in parentheses onto charts and make corresponding student activity pages.

Directions

1. When you first introduce this activity, guide students as they observe the nature of the modified cloze sentences. Support them as they notice that a single line or several lines of print make up a single idea or sentence (indicated by an uppercase letter at the beginning and an end mark—period, exclamation point, or question mark). Together, note that each sentence is indicated by a numeral and that the numerals progress in counting order from 1 onward. Students observe if you have written the focus letter in red every time it is written—and in initial, medial, and final positions in words. They note that one word in each *sentence* (not each line of text) is underlined and that the omitted word always begins with the focus letter-sound.

Note: In most, but not all, cases, the focus letter represents the sound represented on the Letter-Sound-Key Word/Picture Card. When it does not (including vowels in open, vowel-consonant *e*, vowel combination, and *r*-controlled syllables, and the soft sounds of *c* and *g* and consonants in consonant-digraph and silent-letter combinations), students may comment that they have noticed this. Welcome these observations, as they provide valuable opportunities to validate and celebrate students' careful attention to print. Further, these observations provide opportunities to introduce or review and discuss multiple sounds represented by letters. Explain as much as is appropriate for your students about the structure of the English language and syllable types, and the ways in which these affect the sound(s) represented by letters. The *Developing Letter-Sound Connections* program presents the closed (short) sounds of vowels so that young children may begin to attend to and learn this more difficult sound; students are easily able to add the open (long) sound of vowels later, as it is a much less difficult sound to hear and learn. The program presents only the hard sound of *c* and *g* because this facilitates young children's writing and rereading their beginning approximate spelling—with only one letter to represent the *s* sound and the *j* sound. You can use the Letter-Sound-Key Word/Picture Cards (provided in Appendix C of the companion program and book **Developing Independent Readers: Strategy-Oriented Reading Activities for Learners with Special Needs** by this author) to present the additional sounds represented by letters when appropriate for your students.

2. When students have finished sharing their observations about the modified cloze sentences, explain that you will read each sentence aloud but will not read the underlined word. Explain that students are to listen to the sentence and, as detectives, figure out the missing word.

3. Remind students to prepare their mouths for their predictions or guesses about the identity of the missing word by saying the focus sound.

4. Read each sentence aloud, one at a time; omit the underlined word and say "blank" in its place. Model voice-print match, left-to-right reading sequence, and return eye sweep as you use the pointer (or your finger in individual presentation) to point to each word.

5. By turns, students make predictions about the identity of the omitted word.

6. Reread the sentence with the predicted word.

7. With students, confirm or correct their predictions by cross-checking. Take information from one cueing system and check it against information from other cueing systems, and ask, "Could it be ____ ?" Use information from the letter-sound (grapho-phonic cueing system) and check whether the predicted word begins with the focus letter-sound. Use information from the sentence meaning (semantic cueing system) to check that the sentence makes sense with the predicted word inserted, and use information from language structure and order or grammar (syntactical cueing system) to check that the sentence sounds right (or sounds like talking). If the predicted word begins with the focus letter and makes sense and sounds right in the sentence, it is confirmed. If the prediction is not confirmed by cross-checking using the three cueing systems, help students revise or correct the prediction. Model and verbalize the strategies of prediction, cross-checking, and confirmation or correction more in the beginning of the program, and throughout as students need.

8. With students, proceed through the activity, sentence by sentence, until you complete it.

9. If you have prepared the chart with red color-coded letters (as in option 1 of the Materials section), students, by turns, use the pointer to point to and count focus letters. If you have prepared the chart with all black letters and are using a plastic acetate cover sheet or laminated chart (as in option 2), individual students use a colored washable marker to circle each focus letter and then count them. Guide and support students, as necessary, as they track from left to right in each line of text and from the right at the end of one line to the left and down to begin the next line of print.

Independent Activity

Materials

- Graphite and colored pencils
- Scissors
- Glue (or paste, glue sticks, or tape)
- Reproducible master for Cloze Sentence Independent Activity sheets (provided in each letter-sound unit)

Use removable label tape or correction tape to cover elements of the reproducible master when you photocopy the master to produce one or more of the following options. This variety of options allows you to provide individual students with independent activities appropriate to their learning styles, skills, and needs. While all students complete the same independent activity sheet, each individual completes it in her or his own way. Give individuals and small groups of students directions appropriate to the option selected for the activity sheet. Enlarge and copy the master to provide larger print for students when appropriate.

Note: In this activity, underlined words occur at the beginning of sentences (requiring an uppercase letter), in the context of sentences (requiring a lowercase letter), and in both contexts in a single word (requiring both upper- and lowercase letters). This provides students with opportunities to consider and practice the appropriate use of upper- and lowercase letters in different contexts. When you cover a focus letter for copying, cover the letter whenever it occurs in the underlined words.

1. Cover all letters except the focus letter in each word in the word list. Copy the sentences as they appear on the master, covering no letters or words.

2. Cover all letters except the focus letter in each word in the word list. Cover the focus letter each time it appears in the underlined word in each sentence.

3. Copy the words in the word list and in the sentences as they appear on the master, covering no letters or words.

4. Copy the words in the word list as they appear on the master. Cover the underlined words in the sentences.

Directions

Individual students complete the Cloze Sentence Independent Activity sheets in different ways corresponding to the option you have selected and the directions you have given them. The options are listed in progressive difficulty of task.

Regardless of which of the options they follow to complete the activity sheet, students finish the activity in the same way. They use a graphite or colored pencil to highlight the focus letter. They circle each focus letter or color over the letter in a circular motion sufficiently lightly so that it can be read easily. Students then point to and count the circled or highlighted letters. Guide students, as necessary, as they track from left to right in each line of text and from the right at the end of one line to the left and down to begin the next line of print.

1a. Students **locate** the focus letter for each word in the word list and the matching focus letter in the corresponding underlined word in the sentence with the same number. They **cut out** the focus letter in the word in the word list and **glue** it on top of the focus letter each time it appears in the underlined word.

1b. Students **locate** the focus letter for each word in the word list and the matching focus letter in the underlined word in the sentence with the same number. They **trace** the focus letter each time it appears in the underlined word.

2. Students **locate** the focus letter for each word in the word list and the blank space(s) in the corresponding underlined word in the sentence with the same number. They **write** the focus letter in the space(s) provided in the underlined word.

3a. Students **locate** each word in the word list and the matching underlined word in the sentence with the same number. They **cut out** each word in the word list and **glue** it on top of the corresponding underlined word.

3b. Students **locate** each word in the word list and the matching underlined word in the sentence with the same number. They **trace** all of the letters in the underlined word.

4. Students **locate** each word in the word list and the matching under-lined space in the sentence with the same number. They **write** all of the letters in the word in the underlined space.

Multisensory Prewriting Connections

Developing Letter-Sound Connections suggests a number of multisensory prewriting activities designed to engage learners with short attention spans. The activities use two and three dimensions and a variety of input and output modalities—visual, auditory, and  kinesthetic/motor/tactile—to aid learning and memory. Students complete activities in vertical and horizontal formats that provide opportunities to utilize feed-back from large and small muscles.

While letter formation, handwriting, and penmanship are beyond the scope of this book, teachers and students can use these prewriting activities to supplement a handwriting program when it is introduced in the classroom. Teachers have found that the principles that guide the prewriting activities described in this section have been highly effective in teaching letter formation, handwriting, and penmanship as well. Successful programs of this type frequently

1. introduce letters in groups by beginning stroke
2. are multisensory in nature and utilize tracing of models on surfaces with increased tactile feedback
3. use vertical as well as horizontal surfaces and large and small muscles
4. include oral descriptions of movements related to letter formation along with guided demonstrations
5. allow for practice out of the context of the writing process
6. assure the use of an efficient pencil grip

Note: As appropriate, record, in anecdotal notes about performance, whether students refer to reference tools as they complete the following activities.

Forming Uppercase Letters with Grover

Students explore letter shapes in three dimensions as they place the body of the plush Grover toy in the shape of uppercase letters. They refer to the illustrations in the book **Grover's Own Alphabet: a Jim Henson Sesame Street Muppet With Letters by Sal Murdocca.**

Materials

- One plush Grover toy (Jim Henson Productions, Inc., Sesame Street/Children's Television Workshop—available from Applause Inc., Woodland Hills, CA 91365)
- **Grover's Own Alphabet: A Jim Henson Sesame Street Muppet With Letters by Sal Murdocca** (A Sesame Street/Golden Book® published by Western Publishing Company, Inc., in cooperation with Children's Television Workshop, 1978).

     In the book, Grover interacts with an item that begins with a letter of the alphabet as he places his body in the shape of the uppercase letter.

Directions

1. For each focus letter of the alphabet, students locate the appropriate letter page in **Grover's Own Alphabet.**
2. Read aloud the text of the corresponding page of the book.
3. Students name the item on the page that begins with the focus letter.
4. Students refer to the illustration of Grover in the book as they place the body of the plush Grover toy in the shape of the uppercase focus letter. As needed, hold or support the body of the toy as students place the arms and legs appropriately.

Letter-Tracing Activities

Students use the pointer finger or the pointer and middle fingers of the writing hand to trace upper- and lowercase letter models written on *vertical and horizontal* surfaces that provide increased tactile feedback.

Materials

- Wide water-base, washable, nontoxic markers in a variety of colors
- Rough brown paper towels (institutional quality frequently found in schools and other public buildings)
- 8 1/2″ unlined paper
- Portable chalkboard
- Wall-mounted chalkboard
- Chalk in a variety of colors
- Chalkboard eraser
- Paintbrushes in a variety of sizes—1/2″ and upward
- A small container of water
- Wire mesh screening (typically used in window and door screens)

Prepare the wire mesh screening. Cut the mesh in a rectangle several inches larger than standard 8 1/2″ × 11″ paper. Bind it on four sides with strapping tape folded over to bond to itself and to the rough edge of the screen mesh.

Note: The following activities can also be completed with additional teacher-made and commercially available letters designed for tracing activities, such as sandpaper letters.

Directions

In the following activities, write the uppercase letter near the top of the page and the lowercase letter below it. Describe the movements you make as you write the letter. Schools, school systems, and commercially available penmanship programs frequently develop a set of verbal prompts for each letter that are used consistently. Use the verbalizations that are used locally.

Present each activity in a horizontal and a vertical format. Present the paper towel and paper activities on a horizontal surface (desk or tabletop) and on a vertical surface (taped or clipped to a chart stand or easel). If you are using a portable chalkboard for individual or small-group work, place it on a flat surface for the horizontal activity, or hold it vertically or prop it on a chart stand or easel. The wall-hung chalkboard provides a vertical surface.

Note: When tracing on a vertical surface, students extend a straight arm. This engages the upper arm muscles that have been observed to facilitate motor input and learning.

1. Students watch and listen as you describe your movements in forming upper- and lowercase focus letter pairs with wide colored markers on a rough brown paper towel.
2. Students name the letter and then use the pointer finger or the pointer and middle fingers of the writing hand to trace the uppercase letter, and then the lowercase letter, as they repeat the descriptions of the strokes. Support the verbalizations, as needed.
3. Verbalize the movements as you write focus upper- and lowercase letters on unlined paper while students watch and listen.
4. Students repeat the process described in item 2, above.
5. Place the wire screen mesh rectangle on top of the letters written on the unlined paper, and students follow the process in item 2 to trace the letters through the screen.
6. Write the upper- and lowercase focus letters on the chalkboard, following the procedures described in items 1 and 3.
7. Students trace the letters several times (as in item 2) until the letter is nearly erased.

8. Students dip a paintbrush in a small amount of water until just wet, and they trace the nearly erased chalk letters. Provide the support needed to assure that students begin tracing in the appropriate place and follow the verbal description of movements as it has been established in the preceding activities.

Play-Doh® or Clay Letters

Students construct three-dimensional upper- and lowercase letters with Play-Doh® or clay on top of a written model.

Materials

- Unlined paper (8 1/2″ × 11″) on which the upper- and lowercase forms of the focus letter have been written, with the uppercase letter near the top and the lowercase letter below it. (The letter written on unlined paper from the tracing activity described above works well for this activity.)
- Play-Doh® modeling compound or modeling clay in one color or a variety of colors

Directions

1. Students name the focus letter and then use the pointer finger or the pointer and middle fingers of the writing hand to trace the uppercase letter, and then the lowercase letter, as they repeat the descriptions of the strokes involved in its formation. Support the verbalizations, as needed.
2. Students roll small amounts of Play-Doh® or clay between the palms of their hands to form a ball. They continue to roll the ball between their palms to form a thin, cylindrical "snake."
3. They place as many of the "snakes" as needed onto the lines of the letter models on unlined paper to form the upper- and lowercase letters.
4. When they have completed their letters, students return the Play-Doh® or clay to the storage container to be reused.

Construction of the Wall-Size Outline Letters

Students explore letter shapes as they fill in wall-size outlined upper- and lowercase letter pairs.

Materials

- Wall-size outlined upper- and lowercase letter pairs (using the reproducible Wall Alphabet Letter and Picture at the end of each letter-sound unit)
- Some or all of the following materials:
  1. Small key word/pictures for the focus letter
  2. Upper- and lowercase letter pairs for the focus letter
  3. Pictures of items whose names begin with the focus letter, drawn by students
  4. Pictures or photographs of items whose names begin with the focus letter that students (or you) have cut from magazines, catalogs, newspapers, calendars, or other sources
  5. Small items whose names begin with the focus letter. For the letter *b*, for example: beans (dried), buttons, beads, banana chips (dried), balloons, birdseed, or dog biscuits or bones
     The following books provide suggestions for items that begin with each letter of the alphabet and that may be used with this activity:
     ALPHABETivities: 175 Ready-to-Use Activities From A to Z, Claudia Krause (West Nyack, NY: The Center for Applied Research in Education, 1986).
     The Complete Letter Book: Multisensory Activities for Teaching Sounds and Letters, Michele Borba and Dan Ungaro (Carthage, IL: Good Apple, Inc., 1980)

Directions

1. Individual students or students in groups fill in the wall-size outline letters for their own Activities Books, to accompany the classroom horizontal wall alphabet, or to display in the classroom or school. The classroom horizontal alphabet is described on p. 17 in the Reference Activities section of this book.
2. With students, cut around the key word/pictures or the upper- and lowercase letter pairs. Leave a small border of paper around each picture.
3. Students glue or paste key word/pictures, upper- and lowercase letter pairs, student-drawn pictures, photographs or pictures cut from magazines, or small items to fill in the upper- and lowercase outlined letters.

Tactile or Kinesthetic/Motor Activities Without Visual Input

Students focus on input from modalities other than the visual as they identify letters with tactile, kinesthetic, motor (and auditory) input.

Guided Tracing of Letters on Rough Surfaces:
Tactile, Kinesthetic, Motor (and Auditory) Input

Hold the pointer finger or the pointer and middle fingers of the student's writing hand and guide the tracing of a focus or review letter onto a surface that provides maximum tactile feedback

Materials

- Letter-Sound-Key Word/Picture Cards for focus and review letters
- Assorted materials that provide increased tactile feedback
  The upper- and lowercase letter pairs on rough brown paper towels and traced on paper through wire screening, described in Letter-Tracing Activities (p. 36), work well for this activity. Upper- and lowercase three-dimensional magnetic letters also work well for this activity. While the student traces the magnetic letter, you hold it in the standard spatial orientation (right side up).

Note: When you do these activities in a vertical format, gently hold the student's arm extended straight ahead. This engages the upper arm muscles, which have been observed to facilitate motor input and learning.

Directions

1. Arrange the Letter-Sound-Key Word/Picture Cards in random order. Refer to one card at a time and do not show it to the student until item 7, below.
2. The student averts or closes her or his eyes.
3. Hold the pointer finger or the pointer and middle fingers of the student's writing hand and guide the tracing of the focus or review letter, chosen at random, in a horizontal or vertical format.
4. The student names the letter he or she has traced.
5. Repeat the guided tracing of the letter if the student has not correctly identified the letter.
6. Only if necessary, add verbal prompts to the task. Describe the movements involved in writing the letter as they were introduced in the Letter-Tracing Activities.
7. When the student has correctly identified the letter, show her or him the corresponding card. At first, say, "Check to see if you are right." Later, after the student is familiar with the procedure, place the card in front of the student to check.

Guided Letter Formation
with Kinesthetic/Motor (and Auditory) Input

Hold the pointer finger or pointer and middle fingers of the student's writing hand and guide the formation of a focus or review letter in the air.

Materials

- Letter-Sound-Key Word/Picture Cards for focus and review letters

Directions

1. Arrange the Letter-Sound-Key Word/Picture Cards in random order. Refer to one card at a time and do not show it to the student until item 7, below.
2. The student averts or closes her or his eyes.
3. Hold the pointer finger or the pointer and middle fingers of the student's writing hand and guide the formation, in the air straight in front of the student, of a focus or review letter chosen at random.
4. The student names the letter he or she has formed.
5. Repeat the guided formation of the letter if the student has not correctly identified the letter.
6. Only if necessary, add verbal prompts to the task. Describe the movements involved in writing the letter as they were introduced in the Letter-Tracing Activities.
7. When the student has correctly identified the letter, show her or him the corresponding card. At first, say, "Check to see if you are right." Later, after the student is familiar with the procedure, place the card in front of the student to check.

Recognition and Naming of a Letter
Formed on the Student's Back or in the Student's Palm:
Tactile (and Auditory) Input

Form a focus or review letter with your finger on the student's back or in the palm of the student's hand; the student recognizes and names it.

Materials

- Letter-Sound-Key Word/Picture Cards for focus and review letters

Directions

1. Arrange the Letter-Sound-Key Word/Picture Cards in random order. Refer to one card at a time and do not show it to the student until item 6, below.

2. If a student is comfortable with this activity, use your finger to form a focus or review letter on the outside of the student's shirt on the student's back, or in the palm of the student's writing hand. Students can also do this activity in pairs.

3. The student names the letter he or she felt formed on her or his back or palm.

4. Repeat the guided formation of the letter if the student has not correctly identified the letter.

5. Only if necessary, add verbal prompts to the task. Describe the movements involved in writing the letter as they were introduced in the Letter Tracing Activities.

6. When the student has correctly identified the letter, show her or him the corresponding card. At first, say, "Check to see if you are right." Later, after the student is familiar with the procedure, place the card in front of the student to check.

Activities with Upper- and Lowercase Magnetic Letters

Students practice alphabet sequence and associate names and sounds with focus and review upper- and lowercase magnetic letters.

Materials

- Letter-Sound-Key Word/Picture Cards for focus and review letters
- Five or six sets of uppercase magnetic letters for complete alphabet
- Five or six sets of lowercase magnetic letters for complete alphabet
- Two or three sets of magnetic numerals 0 to 9
- Small (sandwich size) plastic storage bags (one bag for each letter of the alphabet)
- Large (quart size) plastic storage bag (for all of the numerals)
- Small box with a lid (for storage of focus and review letters)
- Magnetic letter board or metal cookie sheet

Use these materials for all of the Activities With Upper- and Lowercase Magnetic Letters. Use of magnetic letter sets manufactured by several different companies is optimal. Letters that appear in different colors and fonts provide students with opportunities to develop flexibility in letter recognition.

Before the program begins, place the upper- and lowercase magnetic letter for each of the twenty-six letters of the alphabet from each of the five or six sets in a separate plastic storage bag—one bag for each letter.

At the beginning of the program, place two or three of each magnetic numeral into the small box. Numerals serve as distractors while you introduce the first five focus letters. After students have completed the first five units, there are sufficient letters to serve as distractors, and you remove the numerals from the small box.

At the beginning of each unit, transfer the five or six upper- and lowercase focus letters from the small storage bag to the small box. Add the focus letter to the review letters in the box. Review letters introduced in previous units remain in the box throughout the program.

Directions

Naming Individual Upper- and Lowercase Letters

1. Take one upper- or lowercase magnetic letter at a time at random out of the small box and show it to students.
2. Students name the presented letter.
3. The activity continues until students have named all upper- and lowercase review letters and the focus letter.

Locating Individual Upper- and Lowercase Letters Named but Not Shown

1. At the beginning of the activity, you and the students remove all focus and review upper- and lowercase magnetic letters (and numerals for units 1–5) from the small box. Place them with the magnet down and the letter or numeral facing students on a table or desk (horizontal format) or on a magnetic letter board or metal cookie sheet (vertical format). Check with students that all letters and numerals are in standard orientation for reading.
2. Arrange the Letter-Sound-Key Word/Picture Cards in random order. Refer to one card at a time and do not show it to students until item 5, below.
3. Name (but do not show students) a focus or review letter one at a time at random.
4. Students repeat the name of the letter and locate or point to one upper-case and one lowercase letter named.
5. When students have correctly located or pointed to each letter, show them the corresponding card. At first, say, "Check to see if you are right." Later, after students are familiar with the procedure, place the card in front of students to check.
6. The activity continues until students have located upper- and lowercase forms of all review letters and the focus letter.

Locating Upper- and Lowercase Focus and Review Letters from Among Distractors

1. After students have completed the previous activity, shuffle the cards (but do not show students) and name a focus or review letter one at a time at random.

2. Students repeat the name of the letter and pick up all of the upper- and lowercase forms of the letter. As students locate each one, they place letters on the horizontal or vertical surface in a horizontal line from left to right (in reading sequence). They place uppercase letters in a top line and lowercase letters in a line directly below.

3. When students have correctly located each letter, show them the corresponding card. At first, say, "Check to see if you are right." Later, after students are familiar with the procedure, place the card in front of students to check.

4. The activity continues until students have located and placed in lines upper- and lowercase forms of all review letters and the focus letter. In units 1–5, the numerals that serve as distractors remain on the table or desk at the end of the activity.

Arranging Upper- and Lowercase Letters in Alphabetical Order

1. After students have completed the Locating Upper- and Lowercase Focus and Review Letters From Among Distractors activity, they remove one uppercase and one lowercase form of each letter and arrange them in alphabetical order. They place letters on the horizontal or vertical surface in a horizontal line from left to right (in reading sequence), placing uppercase letters in a top line and lowercase letters in a line directly below. They form multiple sets of double lines, as needed, to complete the alphabet up to the focus letter.

2. Students say or sing the alphabet up to and including the focus letter and voice-print match, letter pair by letter pair, to check the sequence for order and completeness.

Note: Students can also complete this activity using the Letter-Sound-Key Word/Picture Cards for focus and review letters. They make alphabet trains in lines from left to right on a horizontal surface— on the floor or on a table or desk.

Associating Upper- and Lowercase Letters with the Sounds They Represent

1. After students have completed the Arranging Upper- and Lowercase Letters in Alphabetical Order activity, shuffle the cards and refer to one card at a time; do not show it to students until item 4, below.

2. Say the sound represented by a review or focus letter(s) in random order, as shown on the cards.

3. Students name the letter(s) and locate or point to, or pick up and move the upper- and lowercase letter form of the appropriate letter(s).

4. When students have correctly identified each letter, show them the corresponding card. At first, say, "Check to see if you are right." Later, after students are familiar with the procedure, place the card in front of students to check.

5. This part of the activity continues until students have located or moved upper- and lowercase forms of all review letters and the focus letter.

6. After students complete items 3 and 4 of this activity, show them one upper- *or* lowercase letter at a time (not in pairs for this part of the activity).

7. Students say the sound(s) it represents.

8. This part of the activity continues until students have said the appropriate sound(s) associated with each upper- and lowercase review and focus letter presented separately.

Note: Students can also complete this activity using the Letter-Sound-Key Word/Picture Cards for focus and review letters.

Alphabet Letter-Stamp Activities

Students complete a variety of activities with upper- and lowercase letter stamps.

Materials

- 8 1/2″ unlined paper
- Stamp pads in a variety of colors: red, blue, green, black, purple
- Child-size gloves (The one-size-fits-all stretch knit gloves work well for small hands. Students wear them as they use the stamp pads.)
- Uppercase manuscript letters set
- Lowercase manuscript letters set

Prepare the letter sets for each unit. Present the letters up to and including the focus letter. Store the remainder of the letters until needed.

Some alphabet stamps have a thin, black baseline printed at or near the bottom of each stamp to aid in standard orientation of letters. If stamps do not have one printed on, add a baseline with black permanent marker.

Directions

1. Present the upper- and lowercase letter stamps, up to and including the focus letter, in random order.

2. Students match upper- and lowercase letter pairs.

3. Students place letters in alphabetical order.

a. Students place upper- and lowercase letters (separately) in alphabetical order from left to right on a flat surface (table, desk, floor), or

b. On a flat surface, students place upper- and lowercase letter pairs in alphabetical order, with the uppercase letter above the lowercase letter in each pair.

   They point to each letter stamp or letter-stamp pair and say or sing the alphabet song up to and including the focus letter to check for order and completeness.

4. Students make designs on their papers using the stamps, stamp pads, and paper. They use the focus letter stamps (upper- and lowercase) to make one or more designs. Students use focus and review stamps to make separate designs. As needed, remind students to orient the letters with the baseline at the bottom.

5. Students can also use alphabet letter stamps to do the activities described for magnetic letters (p. 42).

Connecting with Published and Student-Made Alphabet Books and Dictionaries

Students practice alphabet sequence and letter-sound knowledge at school and at home as they locate focus letter pages, identify pictures, and complete related activities in published alphabet books and dictionaries and in those they construct themselves.

Published Alphabet Books and Dictionaries

A large number of beautifully illustrated alphabet books and dictionaries are currently available. These include books on a wide range of topics and in a variety of formats. Some published alphabet books and dictionaries present pictures and photographs of items and words not within a young child's experience or vocabulary. These books provide rich opportunities for families and teachers to engage students and offer contexts for expanding children's experiences and vocabulary. Published alphabet books or dictionaries with representations of familiar items, suggested in the following Materials section, provide different kinds of learning opportunities. Students use them to connect the names of familiar items with the letters and sounds they are in the process of learning.

Materials

- One or several published alphabet books or dictionaries that present pictures or photographs of items familiar to students
- Removable label or correction tape

Note: Frequently, published alphabet books and dictionaries include on a page items whose names begin with the same letter but not with the same sound—for example, items whose names begin with hard and soft *c* or *g* ; items whose names begin with *c* and *ch, s* and *sh*, or *t* and *th*; or words with silent letters *wr* and *w* or *kn* and *k*. To avoid confusion, prepare the pages of the published books with removable tape. Cut small pieces of tape and place a piece next to only those items whose names begin with the focus sound.

Directions

1. Present one or several published alphabet books or dictionaries.
2. Students locate the focus letter page in each book. They say or sing the alphabet in sequence as they flip, page by page, through the book from the front, to locate the focus letter.
3. When they have located the appropriate page(s), students name the letter. Encourage students to prepare their mouths to say the name of all of the items on the page(s) by saying the focus sound.
4. They "read the pictures"; students say the name of each item pictured or marked with tape. Students practice saying and hearing the sound repeatedly as they complete the activity. They use the initial sound to confirm or correct their responses. If a student responds to an item with a name that does not begin with the focus sound, encourage her or him to cross-check and revise or correct using the initial sound cue.
5. Students repeat the process with several alphabet books or dictionaries.

Student-Made Books: Story Books, Activities Books, and Dictionaries

Students make three types of books organized by alphabet sequence during the *Developing Letter-Sound Connections* program: Story Books, Activities Books, and Dictionaries. Students use the books as reading material and as reference books in the classroom during independent and partner reading time; during project, activity, or writing time; and at home.

Story Books

Students compile their Mystery Box Stories—dramatized and dictated stories inspired by the items in the Mystery Box—into Story Books with student-illustrated covers. Materials and directions for making Story Books are on p. 23 of the Mystery Box Connections section.

Activities Books

Students include in their Activities Books the reinforcement activities that are completed on paper. These may include Literature Extension Activities; Rhyme, Song, Fingerplay, and Tongue-Twister Independent Activities; Cloze Sentence Independent Activity sheets; and Multisensory Prewriting Activities.

Students construct the Activities Books in one of two ways:

a. Students make one small book with activities for the focus letter-sound of the unit only. They add color and illustrations to the Activities Book Cover made by photocopying the reproducible master at the end of each letter-sound unit.

b. Students compile all of the activities from the program in one large book. Thus, there is one chapter of the book for activities for each letter-sound unit, included as students complete them in order throughout the program. The Activities Book Cover is the chapter/section marker for each letter-sound unit within the large book. Students make an original illustrated and labeled cover.

Student-Made Dictionary

Use the reproducible master for photocopying at the end of each letter-sound unit to prepare a blank student-made dictionary for individual students or for a group or class. Choose between two options when you copy the master:

a. Copy the master as it is, with the key word/picture to the right of each upper- and lowercase pair. (*Note:* Reduce it and position it in the upper right-hand corner of the page.) The dictionary is ready for the suggested activities once students have made a cover and it has been made into a book with staples or hole punches and rings.

b. Cover the key word/picture with removable label or correction tape before you copy the reduced and correctly positioned master. This provides a blank space below each upper- and lowercase letter pair where students glue on key word/pictures, copied for this purpose, during the corresponding letter-sound unit.

Students complete their student-made dictionaries in one or a combination of the following ways. As a letter-sound is introduced in the *Developing Letter-Sound Connections* program:

a. Students draw pictures of items whose names begin with a letter-sound on the corresponding page of the dictionary.

b. Students cut out pictures or photographs of items whose names begin with a letter-sound from magazines, catalogs, newspapers, calendars, and other sources and glue them onto the corresponding page of the dictionary.

c. After students locate the corresponding page in their dictionary, you or another adult (or students when they begin to write in their classrooms) can record words of interest or high frequency that begin with the letter-sound. Students use the dictionary as a reference tool when they write or read.

d. Students glue onto the corresponding dictionary page small items whose names begin with the focus letter. For *b,* for example, use beans (dried), buttons, beads, banana chips (dried), balloons, birdseed, or dog biscuits or bones. The two books **ALPHABETivities** and **The Complete Letter Book**, cited on p. 39, provide suggestions for items that begin with each letter of the alphabet.

Directions

1. Students share their completed books with their peers and with adults. They describe the content, demonstrate the activities they have completed, and explain how they constructed the books.

2. Teachers, family members, or other students read aloud selections and discuss the accompanying illustrations.

3. You and family members respond to students' observations about print and point out conventions of print: alphabetical sequence, left-to-right and top-to-bottom reading and writing sequence, return sweep of the eyes from the right at the end of one line and down to the next line of print, upper- and lowercase letters, indentations for paragraphs, quotation marks, end marks (periods, question marks, and exclamation points), boldface type, italics, and so on.

4. Students repeat selected activites in the books for reinforcement. They retrace a letter written on a paper towel, for example, or they construct it again on the written model with Play-Doh® or clay.

5. Students use the books to practice reading through the alphabet in sequence, locating a letter in alphabet sequence, reading (naming) pictures with names that begin with a letter-sound, and connecting letter(s)

with the sound (s) they represent. The Letter to Families, pp. 54-56, describes each of these activities.

Connecting with Environmental Print

Throughout the *Developing Letter-Sound Connections* program, look for opportunities to help students notice focus and review letters in environmental print in their classroom, school, neighborhood, and community. In the letter you send home, suggest ways in which family members can help students notice letters and sounds during their everyday activities outside school.

In the Classroom

The reference tools, books, and charts suggested as part of the *Developing Letter-Sound Connections* program provide students with opportunities to focus on print as they use them. In addition, you help students to notice focus and review letters on other kinds of print that are part of the daily life of the classroom: *j* on the job board, *s* on the schedule, *l* on the weekly lunch menu, and so on.

You can also bring into the classroom familiar items whose names begin with the focus letter-sound—Rice Krispies® and Special K® for *k*, for example. Take photographs of high-visibility print in the community and bring them into school for a letter-sound bulletin board or scrapbook—Burger King® and Bus Stop for *b*, Stop and Shop® for *s*, and McDonald's® for *m*, for example.

With students, play games of "I Spy" or "I See the Letter _____" in the classroom. The leader locates a focus or review letter in the print in the classroom. He or she tells other players the name of the letter; (1) the leader gives clues to help players locate it, or (2) players take turns asking questions of the leader. As a variation of these games, use the sound of the letter. The leader chooses an item in the classroom that begins with a focus or review sound. He or she identifies the sound, and (1) the leader gives clues to help players identify it, or (2) players take turns asking questions of the leader.

Small groups of students can go on scavenger hunts in the classroom. Prepare a list for each group of children that combines letters, numerals, color-coding, rebus/pictures, and a few high-frequency words.

Throughout the School

Help students to focus on print in other classrooms and throughout the school—inside the building and on the grounds. Students take frequent in-school field trips throughout the program. They predict and then count the number of

Exit signs in the school building during the x unit, for example. Students predict the letters they will see on the name of the school and then go outside to look at the sign on the school building to confirm or correct their guesses. At the appropriate time in the program, encourage students to notice the first letter of the principal's, secretary's, nurse's, or other staff's names on the signs near their rooms. They focus on the letters in signs inside and outside the school building—on the doors of the girls' and boys' bathrooms, the cafeteria or lunchroom, the staffroom, art and music rooms, and nurse's office. Students can play short games of "I Spy" or "I See Something . . . (Letter or Sound)" as they wait in line for lunch, for an assembly, and so on.

In the Neighborhood and Community

In addition to looking at photographs of high-visibility print that you bring into the classroom, students notice letters in their neighborhoods and communities on field trips. Students point out the focus and review letters they see as they walk or ride—on signs, license plates, vehicles, billboards, mailboxes, buildings, and so on. Take photographs during field trips to add to letter-sound bulletin boards or scrapbooks.

Near the end of the *Developing Letter-Sound Connections* program, when they have completed the z unit, play the Alphabet Game with students during field trips as they walk or ride and as they tour public buildings or stores. As a team, you and students try to find each letter of the alphabet in order on signs and license plates or on displays, boxes, and jars, and so on. Play games of "I Spy" and "I See Something" with letter names and sounds.

At Home

The Home-School Connections section describes resources from school that family members can use to help students focus on letters and sounds at home and outside school. Included in the section is a sample letter to students' families; it suggests activities that highlight and reinforce letter-sound connections.

Home-School Connections

In addition to the varied connections you make with the families of your students through conferences, phone calls, planned and unplanned visits to the classroom, and written communications, you send or mail home a number of resources that relate directly to the *Developing Letter-Sound Connections* program. When you send home each resource, suggest to families ways students might use it outside school.

Reference Tools

At appropriate times during the program, send or mail home two copies for each student of each of the 8 1/2″ × 11″ reference tools described in the Reference Activities section (p. 14). These are

1. Alphabet in Song Clusters
2. Letter-Sound-Key Word/Picture Cards in Alphabetical Order
3. Letter-Sound-Key Word/Picture Cards for Consonant Digraphs and Short Vowels.

Families may keep one copy at home and another copy in a wallet or pocketbook, or in the family vehicle for reference away from home.

Wall Alphabet

Some students and their families benefit from having a wall alphabet at home. In this case, copy onto unlined paper (1) the reproducible masters for the Letter-Sound-Key Word/Picture Cards, provided in Appendix A, or (2) the Wall Alphabet Letters and Pictures, provided in the letter-sound units. As the program is introduced in kindergarten, send or mail home a copy of the focus card or wall-size key word/picture when you have introduced it in a unit. Later in primary grades, send the complete alphabet. Students and their families hang the cards or alphabet in order in a bedroom, on the kitchen wall, on the refrigerator, or in another prominent place at home where they see them frequently.

As time allows, or for individual students, enclose a short, handwritten, color-coded note to accompany the copy of the card or key word/picture. Write each letter except the focus letter with black thin marker, and write the focus letter in red thin marker.

Student-Made Alphabet Books and Dictionary

During the *Developing Letter-Sound Connections* program, students take home their three books organized by alphabet sequence: Story Books, Activities Books, and Dictionary. When you send home each book, explain to students' families (through a conference, phone conversation, or written communication) the process involved in making the book. Suggest ways in which students and families might use the books outside school.

Each letter-sound unit contains a reproducible master for making the books. Connecting with Published and Student-Made Alphabet Books and Dictionaries (p. 46) describes materials and directions for their construction.

A Letter to Families

The following letter describes activities that highlight and reinforce letter-sound connections outside school. Revise or copy the master and attach a cover letter. If family members are unable to read this information, make arrangements to have it read aloud or provide an audiotape of the letter read aloud (and tape player, if needed).

Activities That Encourage Awareness of Letters and Sounds

A.   ENCOURAGING YOUR CHILD'S AWARENESS OF PRINT

As you go about your day, occasionally point out and name letters (just as you pointed out and named a plane in the sky when your child was younger). You may want either (a) to make a comment and model for your child or (b) to encourage your child to give a response.

1.   As you ride in a car, bus, train, or subway
   a.   "I see a yellow *M* up ahead." (McDonald's®)
   b.   "What are the letters on that sign?" (STOP)

2.   In the kitchen
   a.   "Look! The word 'eggs' has two *g*'s in it."
   b.   "Please hand me the cookbook with the *N* on it."

3.   In the supermarket
   a.   "I'm looking for the meat department. That's an 'm'. Here it is." (pointing out the *m*)
   b.   "Can you find the cereal on this shelf that has a big, red *K* on it?" (Special K®)

B.   ALPHABET GAMES AT HOME, WHILE TRAVELING, AT THE SUPERMARKET . . . ANYWHERE

In addition to the one at home, you may want to keep an alphabet chart handy for your child's reference in the car, or in your wallet or pocketbook for when you are traveling.

1.   ALPHABET GAME

While you ride in the car, travel by public transportation, or move through the supermarket, as a team try to find each letter of the alphabet in order on signs and license plates or on displays, boxes, or jars.

2.   I SPY or I SEE SOMETHING (Letter names or sounds)
   a.   The leader looks around the room, car/bus/train, or supermarket (or gathers a small collection of toys or objects) and chooses one item but does not tell the other players.
   b.   The leader gives the name (or sound) of the letter that begins the name of the item.
   c.   Players take turns asking questions about the item, or the leader gives clues (tells category or how it is used, describes it, or compares or contrasts it with other items).
   d.   The player who guesses the item is the next leader.

3.   ADDING ON ITEMS IN ALPHABETICAL ORDER: I WAS GOING ON A TRIP
   a.   The first player says, "I was going on a trip, and I took (for example) an apple." (names an item that begins with *a*)
   b.   The second player says, "I was going on a trip, and I took an apple and (for example) a book." (repeats the first item and adds an item that begins with *b*)
   c.   The third player (or the player who takes the third turn) says, "I was going on a trip, and I took an apple, a book, and (for example) a cat." (repeats all previous items in order and adds an item that begins with *c*)

      d.   Players continue throughout the alphabet in sequence.

  4.   OBJECT SORT

      a.   The leader gathers a number of toys, objects, or pictures—many of whose names begin with the same letter and sound and some that do not—and 29 separate pieces of paper with the 26 letters of the alphabet and *ch*, *sh*, and *th* written on them.

      b.   The leader says a sound, and a player tells the name of the letter(s) that spells the sound, or the leader names a letter(s) and a player tells the sound that the letter(s) spell.

      c.   A player chooses the piece of paper with the named letter(s) written on it and places it on a flat surface.

      d.   A player sorts the objects by placing all of the objects that begin with the letter(s)/sound in one pile next to that piece of paper, and all of the others in another pile.

      e.   The game may be made more difficult by having more than one letter(s)/sound. A player sorts objects into more than one pile.

C. READING TO YOUR CHILD

  1.   Talk about and label the parts of the book as you read (words, pictures/illustrations, title, author, illustrator, cover, front of the book, table of contents, and so on).

  2.   Talk about the story yourself and make predictions about possible events or endings. Then, use the following pictures and story to confirm ("Yes! I was right.") or revise your guesses ("Actually, _____ happened. What a surprise!"). After you have modeled for your child, often encourage her or him to make and confirm or correct predictions about the stories you share.

  3.   Often ask, and help your child to ask, open-ended questions about the story. For example:

      a.   "Why, do you suppose . . . ?"

      b.   "What makes you think . . . ?"

      c.   "I wonder why (or how or when) . . . !"

  4.   Ask, "What do you notice when you look at this page?"

      a.   Point out and discuss details in the pictures (expressions on faces, marks showing movement, and so on) and relate these details to the story meaning.

      b.   Point out and discuss interesting or unusual features of letters or words in the pictures or words (**boldface type,** *italics*, squiggly letters, repeated words, and so on), and relate these features to the story meaning.

      c.   Note how rhyming words often look, as well as sound, the same.

      d.   Point out words that begin with the same letter.

      e.   Note repeated words.

  5.   Ask "What do you notice when you hear me read that?"

      a.   Note rhyming words.

      b.   Point out words that begin with the same sound.

      c.   Discuss words or groups of words that mean the same, have opposite meanings, or have many, unusual, or unfamiliar meanings.

  6.   Occasionally, leave out a word for your child to fill in or say as you read and give the first sound of the word as a clue. For example:

The three little kittens
They lost their m_____ . (mittens)

D. READING ALPHABET BOOKS AND DICTIONARIES WITH YOUR CHILD

A large number of beautifully illustrated alphabet books on a wide range of topics are currently available. Some present items not within a young child's experience or vocabulary. These books are wonderful for sharing and for expanding your child's experiences and vocabulary. We have found, though, that alphabet books with pictures of familiar, everyday objects are most useful for activity 2c, below.

Your child has made alphabet story books, activities books, and a dictionary in school this year. You can share them with your child as you do the published books.

1. READING THROUGH ALPHABET BOOKS AND DICTIONARIES IN SEQUENCE
   a. Start at the beginning of the book and say "a" (pointing to *a* on the page).
   b. Show your child how to anticipate the next page by predicting the next letter: *b*.
   c. Ask the child to turn the page to confirm or correct that prediction.
   d. Continue throughout the alphabet in sequence, having the child predict the next letter each time and then confirm or correct (encouraging the child to sing or say the alphabet, or to use an alphabet chart as a reference, only as needed).

2. LOCATING A LETTER AND IDENTIFYING THE NAMES OF PICTURES THAT BEGIN WITH THE SOUND THE LETTER SPELLS
   a. Name a letter (or give the sound that a letter spells and have the child name the letter).
   b. Have the child locate the letter in the book (encouraging the child to sing or say the alphabet, or use an alphabet chart as a reference, only as needed).
   c. After the child locates the letter, have her or him locate and "read" (name) all of the pictures that begin with the letter and sound.

3. CONNECTING SOUNDS, LETTERS, AND KEY WORD/PICTURES

You and your child can do the following activity with any of the alphabet books he or she has made at school: Story Books, Activities Books, or Dictionary.

   a. Locate any letter on a page in one of the books. Do not show your child the letter or name the key word/picture.
   b. Say the sound that the letter spells.
   c. Have the child say the name of the letter and the key word/picture.
   d. Show the page—letter and picture—so that the child can confirm or correct her or his response.

4. USING THE STUDENT-MADE DICTIONARY

Your child may want to use the dictionary that he or she made at school in one or several of the following ways:

   a. Your child may want to glue small objects that begin with a letter or sound onto that page in the dictionary.
   b. He or she may want to draw pictures—or to cut out of magazines, catalogs, newspapers, or calendars—pictures that begin with a letter or sound, and glue them onto that page in the dictionary.
   c. You or your child (when he or she begins to write) may write words of special interest on the corresponding page in the dictionary.

Section II

LETTER-SOUND UNITS

Section II of *Developing Letter-Sound Connections* contains the twenty-nine letter-sound units—one thematic unit for each letter of the alphabet and for consonant digraphs *ch*, *sh*, and *th*. Each letter-sound unit is made up of two sections: **Teacher Reference** and **Reproducible Masters for Photocopying**.

The first part of each letter-sound unit, **Teacher Reference**, contains resources for teachers. The alphabetical *Annotated Book List* includes a variety of theme-related fiction and nonfiction books: alphabet, counting, interactive, picture, rebus, short chapter, and wordless. *Literature Extension Activities* introduce, reinforce, and extend the theme of books from the book list, and include art, composition, cooking, dance and movement, discussion, drama and puppetry, math, music, and science. *Items for the Mystery Box* includes separate alphabetical lists of inedible and edible items for Mystery Box activities. The list of *Rhymes, Songs, Fingerplays, and Tongue Twisters* presents alphabetically the first line of each piece in two lists: (1) those that relate to the theme, and (2) those that feature the focus letter but do not relate to the theme. Pieces for which reproducible masters are provided are marked with an asterisk. Following each entry are numbers that correspond to books in which it may be found, listed alphabetically in Appendix B. *Cloze Sentences* are completed cloze sentences, with the word that is deleted in the Independent Activity underlined and with the focus letter in bold print. The list includes sentences in two formats: The first omits a word at or near the beginning (as they appear on the Independent Activity); the second, in parentheses, omits the word at or near the end.

The second part of each letter-sound unit, **Reproducible Masters for Photocopying**, provides the following masters for photocopying for each letter-sound unit: three masters for Rhyme, Song, Fingerplay, and Tongue-Twister Independent Activity sheets, two masters for Cloze Sentence Independent Activity sheets, and one master for the Activities Book Cover, Wall Alphabet Letter and Picture, Story Book Page, and Student-Made Dictionary Page.

A a apple

TEACHER REFERENCE

Annotated Book List

The Apple Bird, Brian Wildsmith (Oxford: Oxford University Press, 1983). In this wordless book, a slight bird transforms as it eats an apple larger than itself, and, when it naps at the end of the book, it resembles the apple it has eaten—in shape as well as size!

Apple Picking Time, Michele Benoit Slawson, illustrated by Deborah Kogan Ray (New York: Crown Publishers, Inc., 1994). At the end of the day, after Anna, her mother, father, and grandparents finish harvesting apples at the orchard, Anna proudly cashes in her ticket with the half-moon punch that she receives for filling her bin for the first time in her life.

Apples, Nonny Hogrogian (New York: Macmillan Publishing Co., 1972). The colorful double-page illustrations in this wordless book show apple cores, discarded by the children and animals in a village, growing into an apple orchard.

Apples and Pumpkins, Anne Rockwell, pictures by Lizzy Rockwell (New York: Simon & Schuster Children's Publishing, 1989). Simple, supportive text and illustrations in this book depict a young girl's visit to a farm to prepare for Halloween, where she and her family pick apples to give as treats and a pumpkin that they carve into a jack-o'-lantern.

Apples of Your Eye: Rookie Read-About Science, Allan Fowler (Chicago: Childrens Press, 1994). Brief text and accompanying brightly colored photographs show children and adults interacting with apples, explain the meaning of the saying "apple of our eye," and show interesting facts about apples: uses, growing environment and seasons, storage, life cycle, grafting process, and varieties.

Apple Tree, Barrie Watts (Englewood Cliffs, New Jersey: Silver Burdett, 1986). Colored photographs and line drawings trace the development of apples throughout the year, with bold headings for readers just beginning and easy-to-read text for more developed beginning readers. Includes index.

Apple Tree! Apple Tree!: A Just One More Book Just for You, Mary Blocksma, illustrated by Sandra Cox Kalthoff (Chicago: Childrens Press, 1983). In this book that uses only 59 words, a personified apple tree gives gifts to its friends who visit but always leave. The tree discovers kindness repaid the following spring when an apple seed, planted by its friend Worm, grows into a friend that will not leave.

An Apple Tree Through the Year, Claudia Schnieper, translated from the German by Gerd Kirchner, photographs by Othmar Baumli (Minneapolis: Carolrhoda Books, Inc., 1987). Colored photographs, including a large number of close-ups, and diagrams combine with informative text to follow an apple tree through the four seasons and describe its growth cycle and relationship to other elements in the orchard. Key terms, which appear in bold print in the text, are defined in a glossary. Contains a separate section that explains the grafting process and an index.

Apple Valley Year, Ann Turner, illustrated by Sandi Wickersham Resnick (New York: Macmillan Publishing Company, 1993). Detailed text and illustrations follow the activities of the Clark family and the animals in an apple orchard through the four seasons of one year.

First Apple, Ching Yeung Russell, illustrated by Christopher Zhong-Yuan Zhang (New York: Penguin Books USA Inc., 1994). In this short chapter book, neither Ying nor her beloved grandmother has ever tasted an apple because they are so expensive in China in the 1940s that only the rich can buy them. Ying sets her resolve to earn the money to buy one for her grandmother's seventy-first birthday. Though a number of misadventures thwart Ying's plans, she is rewarded, in the end, for her honesty and courage.

How Do Apples Grow?: A Let's Read-and-Find-Out Science, Betsy Maestro, illustrated by Giulio Maestro (New York: HarperCollins Publishers, 1992). This informative book combines clearly written text, illustrations, and labeled diagrams to describe the life cycle of an apple from winter to fall, including the relationship of the parts of the apple to the process of fertilization.

How to Make an Apple Pie and See the World, Marjorie Priceman (New York: Alfred A. Knopf, 1994). When a young girl discovers that the market is closed, she travels around the globe to obtain the ingredients she needs to make an apple pie—wheat in Italy, a hen for eggs in France, cinnamon in Sri Lanka, a cow for milk in England, salt from the Atlantic Ocean, sugar in Jamaica, and apples in Vermont. Includes a world map with the girl's destinations and forms of transportation marked plus a recipe for apple pie.

Johnny Appleseed, Patricia Demouth, illustrated by Michael Montgomery (New York: Grosset & Dunlap, Inc., 1996). This easy-to-read book from the All Aboard Reading series, with a few lines of large print per page, presents the life of the gentle man, John Chapman, the legendary Johnny Appleseed, who befriended people—indigenous and pioneer—and animals as he traveled west to plant apple trees.

Johnny Appleseed: A Tall Tale Retold and Illustrated, Steven Kellogg (New York: William Morrow and Company, Inc., 1988). Kellogg combines factual incidents and exaggerated tales to celebrate, in text and characteristic action-filled illustrations, the life of John Chapman, who left Massachusetts to travel west to plant apple orchards, clear land, and supply seeds and saplings for pioneer families, and whose life took on mythic proportions as the legendary Johnny Appleseed. An author's note describes the literature on which Kellogg based his book.

Johnny Appleseed, Reeve Lindbergh, illustrated by Kathy Jakobsen (Boston: Little, Brown and Company, 1990). Lindbergh's introduction and author's note provide the historical context for her poem that traces the legendary journey of John Chapman, who planted and distributed apple seeds and seedlings and established nurseries for settlers of the midwestern frontier. The text is complemented by rich full-page and border paintings and a map.

Johnny Appleseed, Eva Moore, illustrated by Beatrice Darwin (New York: Scholastic Inc., 1964, 1970). In this book for beginning readers arranged in nine chapters, the author presents, in story form, the details (commonly known and as she imagines they may have happened) of the life of Johnny Appleseed, born John Chapman in Massachusetts, whose life of generosity and peace, as he traveled west by foot for over forty years, sharing apple seeds and planting orchards, became a legend.

Latkes and Applesauce: A Hanukkah Story, Fran Manushkin, illustrated by Robin Spowart (New York: Scholastic Inc.,1990). The text of this story captures the cadence of the speech of the Eastern European family, housebound because of a blizzard, for whom potatoes and apples for their Hanukkah latkes and applesauce are miraculously provided by a cat and dog with whom they share their meager provisions. An author's note provides a history of Hanukkah, a recipe for potato latkes, and information about the game of dreidel.

The Life and Times of the Apple, Charles Micucci (New York: Orchard Books, 1992). Each set of two pages in this informative book, illustrated with watercolor and pencil drawings, diagrams, maps, time line, graphs, and family tree, is devoted to an aspect of the apple including parts of the fruit and flower, plant relatives, reproduction and cross-fertilization, grafting, life cycle, pollination, harvesting, uses, production throughout the world, varieties, history, popular sayings, and the legend of Johnny Appleseed.

Much Bigger than Martin, Steven Kellogg (New York: The Dial Press, 1976). Tired of being bossed around and left out by his older brother Martin, Henry remembers that his grandfather told him that apples make people grow, and he eats a bagful. Though the apples fail to help Henry grow bigger than his brother, they help bring about some important changes in their relationship.

Picking Apples & Pumpkins, Amy and Richard Hutchings, photographs by Richard Hutchings (New York: Scholastic Inc., 1994). Colorful photographs show two young girls, their two friends, parents, and grandmother as they pick Macoun and Delicious apples in an orchard and pumpkins in a patch, then return home to make an apple pie and carve jack-o'-lanterns.

The Seasons of Arnold's Apple Tree, Gail Gibbons (San Diego: Harcourt Brace & Company, 1984). In this book with a line or two of text per page that accompany brightly colored simple drawings, the apple tree on the hill is Arnold's secret place and his friend, and he enjoys special activities with it appropriate to each season of the year—activities that reveal facts about apple trees. Includes information about a cider press and an apple pie recipe.

The Story of Johnny Appleseed, Aliki (New York: Aladdin Paperbacks, 1963). This easy-to-read version of the story of John Chapman's life emphasizes the relationships with people and the natural world enjoyed by the man who has come to be known as Johnny Appleseed.

Sweet Dried Apples: A Vietnamese Wartime Childhood, Rosemary Breckler, illustrated by Deborah Kogan Ray (Boston: Houghton Mifflin Company, 1996). A young girl, forced to flee her war-ravaged homeland of Vietnam, describes her treasured relationship with her grandfather, an herb doctor, including memories of the delicious dried apples that he used to flavor his bitter-tasting remedies.

Ten Apples Up on Top!, Theo. LeSieg, illustrated by Roy McKie (New York: Random House, 1961). A lion, dog, and tiger—once engaged in good-natured competition to determine who could balance the largest number of apples on his head while performing a variety of tricks—join forces to keep their piles from falling when challenged by a group of bears.

What's So Terrible About Swallowing an Apple Seed?, Harriet Lerner and Susan Goldhor (New York: HarperCollins Publishers, 1996). Until a friend helps her see the truth, Rosie imagines the problems that would result if, as her big sister told her, the apple seed she swallowed grew into an apple tree with branches coming out her ears. Later, regretting her lie, her sister helps her imagine the benefits.

Literature Extension Activities

1. After they look carefully at the illustrations in ***Apples***, students tell the story in their own words. You can scribe or record on audiotape the student stories, if desired, and students illustrate their versions.

2. With students, compare and contrast apples and pumpkins as or after you read ***Apples and Pumpkins*** and ***Picking Apples & Pumpkins***. Compile a list or data matrix showing similarities and differences, or create a Venn diagram. Considerations include size, shape, color, attributes of skin, seeds (edible/inedible, size, shape, color), when harvested, location of growth (trees/vines), how eaten, other products, and so on.

3. As or after you share ***First Apple*** with students, eat slices of fresh apple, a treat possible only for the wealthy in China in the 1940s.

4. Inspired by the recipes in ***How to Make an Apple Pie and See the World*** and ***The Seasons of Arnold's Apple Tree,*** or using a favorite

recipe from students, community members, or your own file, make and enjoy an apple pie with your students.

5. After students listen to **Johnny Appleseed** by Reeve Lindbergh (and other books about the legendary character by Aliki, Demuth, Kellogg, and Moore), help them mark on their classroom map of the United States John Chapman's journey from his birthplace in Leominster, Massachusetts, throughout the Midwest.

Items for the Mystery Box

Inedible Items: abacus, accordion, acrobat, actor, actress, alarm clock, albatross, album, alligator, alphabet, ambulance, anchor, animals (variety), anteater, antenna, ant hill, antlers, ants, arrow, athlete, ax, astronaut

Edible Items: alfalfa sprouts, almonds, almond butter, alphabet cereal, alphabet pasta, alphabet soup, anadama bread, anchovies, animal crackers, antipasto salad, **apple**, applesauce, apricots, asparagus, avocado

Rhymes, Songs, Fingerplays, and Tongue Twisters

Apple Theme

An apple a day: 5, 33
Apple on a stick: 4
An apple pie, when it looks nice: 28
Apples, peaches, creamery butter: 4
"As I went up the apple tree": 36, 46, 51
A was an apple pie: 3, 5, 28, 33, 34, 46, 76
Here is the tree with leaves so green: 34
Here's to thee, good apple tree: 46
*If all the world were apple pie: 3, 5, 28, 33, 50, 53, 58
Johnny gave me apples: 4
*Oh, dear! what can the matter be?: 28, 50, 73
Once I found an apple pip: 34
Strawberry, apple, my jam tart: 4

*There was an old woman lived under the hill: 5, 28, 34, 38, 40, 46, 50, 73, 76
Tongue Twisters: 74, 80
Up in the green orchard there is a green tree: 5, 46
Way up high in the apple tree: 12, 75
With apples by the fire: 5, 73

Letter-Sound a (a)

The ants go marching: 55
Dance to your daddy: 29, 32, 33, 34, 62, 73
There was a man lived in the moon: 5, 26, 41, 62
Tongue Twisters: 1, 13, 60, 74, 80

Cloze Sentences

1. An <u>alligator</u> is **an** animal that looks **a** lot like **a** crocodile.
   (An animal that looks **a** lot like **a** crocodile is an <u>alligator</u>.)

2. An <u>apple</u> is **a** fruit that can be red, yellow, or green **and** that grows on **an** apple tree.
   (**A** fruit that can be red, yellow, or green **and** that grows on **an** apple tree is an <u>apple</u>.)

3. An <u>ant</u> is an insect that lives in **an** anthill and likes picnics.
   (An insect that lives in **an** anthill and likes picnics is an <u>ant</u>.)

4. An <u>ambulance</u> is **a** fast vehicle that **a** sick person can ride in to the hospital.
   (**A** fast vehicle you can ride in to the hospital if you **are** sick is **an** <u>ambulance</u>.)

1. An <u>astronaut</u> is **a** person from the U.S.**A.** who travels in space in **a** spaceship.
   (**A** person from the U.S.**A.** who travels in space in **a** spaceship is **an** <u>astronaut</u>.)

2. <u>Antlers</u> are horns that grow on **a** deer.
   (Horns that grow on **a** deer are <u>antlers</u>.)

3. <u>Animals</u> that you might see **at a** zoo are lions, zebras, elephants, **and** monkeys.
   (Lions, zebras, elephants, **and** monkeys **are** <u>animals</u> you might see **at a** zoo.)

4. The <u>alphabet</u> is another name for the **ABC**'s.
   (**Another** name for the **ABC**'s is the <u>alphabet</u>.)

A a

If all the world were apple pie,

And all the seas were ink,

And all the trees were bread and cheese,

What should we have for drink?

Name _____   Date _____

A a

Oh, dear! what can the matter be?

Two old women got up an apple tree;

One came down,

And the other stayed till Saturday.

Name _____   Date _____

A a

There was an old woman lived under the hill,
And if she's not gone she lives there still.
Baked apples she sold, and cranberry pies,
And she's the old woman that never told lies.

Name _____   Date _____

A a

COMPLETE IT

alligator
1

apple
2

ant
3

ambulance
4

An <u>alligator</u> is an animal that looks a lot like
     1
a crocodile.

An <u>apple</u> is a fruit that can be red, yellow, or
    2
green and that grows on an apple tree.

An <u>ant</u> is an insect that lives in an anthill and
   3
likes picnics.

An <u>ambulance</u> is a fast vehicle that a sick
      4
person can ride in to the hospital.

Name _____   Date _____

A a

COMPLETE IT

astronaut
1

Antlers
2

Animals
3

alphabet
4

An <u>astronaut</u> is a person from the U.S.A. who
   1
travels in space in a spaceship.

<u>Antlers</u> are horns that grow on a deer.
  2

<u>Animals</u> that you might see at a zoo are lions,
  3
zebras, elephants, and monkeys.

The <u>alphabet</u> is another name for the
     4
ABC's.

Name _____   Date _____

B b   bed

TEACHER REFERENCE

Annotated Book List

Asleep, Asleep, Mirra Ginsburg, inspired by a verse of A. Vvedensky, illustrated by Nancy Tafuri (New York: Greenwillow Books, 1992). Couplets that accompany double-page illustrations affirm that everyone and everything is asleep in the woods and fields that surround a young child who, with the exception of the wind and his mother, is the only one awake.

The Bed Book, Sylvia Plath, illustrated by Emily Arnold McCully (New York: Harper & Row Publishers, 1976). In rhyme and illustration, the book invites readers to expand their ideas about beds, and the imagination, not the sky, is the limit for the number of inventive beds, including Jet-Propelled, Tank, Snack (complete with a free vending machine), Pocket-size (just add water and it grows to full size), Elephant, Acrobat, and Spottable (where spills don't matter).

Bedtime for Frances, Russell Hoban, illustrated by Garth Williams (New York: Harper & Row, 1960). In a series of episodes, little Frances the badger and her wise parents successfully deal with a common childhood fear—noises and sights at bedtime.

Can't You Sleep, Little Bear?, Martin Waddell, illustrated by Barbara Firth (New York: The Trumpet Club, 1988). Patient Big Bear helps Little Bear with fears of the dark— first with lanterns, and then with a walk out of their cave into the night, where the moon and stars and the safety of Big Bear's warm arms bring on the long-awaited sleep.

Dr. Seuss's Sleep Book, Dr. Seuss (New York: Random House, 1962). With his characteristic rhyming, tongue-twisting text and humorous illustrations, Seuss presents the unusual habits, routines, and beds of a number of imaginary creatures readying themselves for, engaged in, or awakening from sleep.

The Five-Dog Night, Eileen Christelow (New York: Clarion Books, 1993). Ezra worries his neighbor, Old Betty, when he refuses her advice for keeping warm at night, but she is no longer concerned when she discovers that Ezra describes the degree of cold by the number of dogs he invites into his bed for warmth.

Five Little Monkeys Jumping on the Bed, Eileen Christelow (New York: Clarion Books, 1989). Christelow's interpretation of this familiar counting rhyme—a cumulative

71

story in reverse—has a humorous surprise ending. When the monkeys finally fall asleep, their mother jumps on the bed!

A Giraffe on the Moon, Sandy Nightingale (San Diego: Harcourt Brace & Company, 1991). Humorous two-page colored illustrations, with a phrase of descriptive rhyming text, show a number of fanciful dreams that a young child might have, including dinosaurs on skis, a snowman at the beach, and an elephant in a sandwich!

Goodnight Moon, Margaret Wise Brown, illustrated by Clement Hurd (New York: Harper & Row, 1947). In rhyming verse, a young rabbit says goodnight to things in his bedroom (shown in black and white) as the room (pictured in color) darkens and night progresses.

Go to Bed!, Virginia Miller (Cambridge, Massachusetts: Candlewick Press, 1993). Getting little Bartholomew bear to bed is not an easy task until his own series of antics and protests tires him out, and he falls asleep—with a yawn and final sleepy protest "Nah."

Grandfather Twilight, Barbara Berger (New York: Philomel Books, 1984). Poetic in text and illustration, this simple tale follows Grandfather Twilight, who releases the moon into the sky every evening from an infinite strand of pearls.

Grandma Gets Grumpy, Anna Grossnickle Hines (New York: Clarion Books, 1988). During a sleepover at Grandma's house, five young cousins discover that the grandmother who loves and enjoys them also has limits to her patience.

Home: A Collaboration of Thirty Distinguished Authors and Illustrators of Children's Books to Aid the Homeless, edited by Michael J. Rosen (New York: HarperCollins Publishers, 1992). In "**My Bed**," written by Franz Brandenberg and illustrated by Aliki, captions and a series of colorful illustrations present a number of roles—animate and inanimate—a small boy can play while in his bed. In "**Under the Bed**," written by Jon Scieszka and illustrated by Lane Smith, a boy catalogues the rich variety of items that end up under his bed, where he's been told he needs to clean.

HUSH!: A Thai Lullaby, Minfong Ho, pictures by Holly Meade (New York: Orchard Books, 1996). Cut-paper and ink illustrations accompany this lullaby, set in the author's homeland of Thailand, in which, until she falls asleep herself, a mother quiets a series of animals—mosquito, lizard, cat, mouse, frog, pig, duck, monkey, water buffalo, and elephant—so that they do not awaken her baby who, at the book's end, is the only one awake!

I Hear a Noise, Diane Goode (New York: E. P. Dutton, 1988). One night, a child and his mother are whisked out his bedroom window by a monster who takes them home. The adventure is short-lived; the monster's mother scolds it and makes it take them back!

Ira Sleeps Over, Bernard Waber (New York: Scholastic Inc., 1972). Ira faces his own worries and the taunts of his older sister as he makes a monumental decision—whether to take his teddy bear along to his first sleepover.

Isabella's Bed, Alison Lester (Boston: Houghton Mifflin Co., 1991). A fantasy ride on the bed in their grandmother's attic enables Anna and Luis to begin to unlock the mystery of Isabella, its owner, and to get their grandmother to begin to tell them about her youth in South America.

I Want to Sleep in Your Bed!, Harriet Ziefert, illustrated by Mavis Smith (New York: The Trumpet Club, 1990). After their bedtime ritual, everyone in the house is asleep— parakeet, dog, baby brother, and Mommy and Daddy—everyone, that is, except Susan, who wants to sleep in her parents' bed.

Jesse Bear, What Will You Wear?, Nancy White Carlstrom (New York: Scholastic, 1986). Detailed illustrations provide clues to meaning in this predictable rhyming book that follows Jesse Bear and his family from morning to bedtime of a busy day.

K Is for Kiss Goodnight: A Bedtime Alphabet, Jill Sardegna, pictures by Michael Hays (New York: Bantam Doubleday Dell Publishing Group, Inc., 1994). Rich, full-page colored drawings illustrate descriptive phrases beginning with each letter of the alphabet and show three young children and their parents—African American, Asian American, and European American—as they prepare for bed and sleep.

Little Rabbit Goes to Sleep, Tony Johnston, illustrated by Harvey Stevenson (New York: HarperCollins Publishers, 1994). A little rabbit tries all the tricks he knows to help himself go to sleep, but the night feels too dark and large and scary until he watches the night sky with his grandfather, who answers his questions and quiets his fears.

Mouse Tales, Arnold Lobel (New York: HarperCollins Publishers, 1972). In this collection of short tales, Papa mouse sits by their bed and tells one bedtime story for each of the mouse boys until all seven of them are asleep.

The Napping House, Audrey Wood, illustrated by Don Wood (San Diego: Harcourt Brace Jovanovich, 1984). In this cumulative story, everyone except a flea is sleeping— "snoring granny, dreaming child, dozing dog, snoozing cat, slumbering mouse"—until the flea "bites the mouse, who scares the cat, who claws the dog. . . . "

No Jumping on the Bed!, Tedd Arnold (New York: Dial Books for Young Readers, 1987). Walter's father has warned him again and again not to jump on the bed or he might crash through the floor, but, unable to resist, Walter jumps. Then, Walter and his bed fall through floor after floor of his apartment building, taking the inhabitants of the apartments below and their possessions on a fantastic adventure.

Owl at Home, Arnold Lobel (New York: Scholastic Inc., 1975). In a collection of stories, Owl is alone at home, but he is entertained by the winter wind, bumps in his bed, sad thoughts, a challenge to himself, and his new friend—the moon. In **"Strange Bumps,"** in bed at night, Owl is frightened by two bumps under the blankets that mysteriously move every time his legs move!

Papa's Bedtime Story, Mary Lee Donovan, illustrated by Kimberly Bulcken Root (New York: The Trumpet Club, 1993). A young child asks for a bedtime story, and Papa responds with a collection of two-page stories in which a series of young animals that live near their home in the mountains ask their fathers for a bedtime story. The pattern continues until the child falls asleep.

Porcupine's Pajama Party, Terry Webb Harshman, illustrated by Doug Cushman (New York: Harper & Row, 1988). When he invites his friends Owl and Otter to sleep at his house, Porcupine discovers that being together makes everything more fun— making cookies, watching a scary movie on TV, and being scared in the dark.

The Princess and the Pea, adapted from Hans Christian Andersen and illustrated by Janet Stevens (New York: Scholastic Inc., 1982). Animals dressed in royal finery are the characters in this version of the tale, in which a princess proves herself a *real* princess and worthy of marrying the prince when she feels a tiny pea the queen has placed beneath twenty featherbeds and mattresses on her bed to test her.

Roll Over!, Mordicai Gerstein (New York: Crown Publishers, 1984). In Gerstein's version of the familiar fingerplay and counting rhyme, when a little boy says "roll over," one by one, the ten animals (with alliterative names) who are hiding in his bed fall out and are revealed as the reader opens a fold-out flap on each page, leaving the boy alone and asleep in the bed in the end.

Sleep Tight, B. G. Hennessy, illustrated by Anthony Carnabuci (New York: The Trumpet Club, 1992). Rhyming couplets enumerate the animals and familiar items in a young boy and girl's world that are sleeping as the children prepare for sleep in their beds.

Sun Is Falling Night Is Calling, Laura Leuck, illustrated by Ora Eitan (New York: The Trumpet Club, 1994). The gentle rhyming verses show a rabbit mother and child as they share the familiar and comforting routines of bedtime.

Tell Me a Story, Mama, Angela Johnson, illustrated by David Soman (New York: The Trumpet Club, 1989). At bedtime, a young girl asks her mother to retell stories of her mother's childhood, but the beloved stories are so familiar that it is the girl, instead, who recounts them.

There's an Alligator Under My Bed, Mercer Mayer (New York: Dial Books for Young Readers, 1987). Even though neither he nor his parents have ever seen it, a young boy is certain that there is an alligator under his bed, so he devises a clever plan to lead it out of the house and lock it in the garage.

Time for Bed, Mem Fox, illustrated by Jane Dyer (San Diego: Harcourt Brace & Company, 1993). Double full-page watercolor paintings illustrate rhyming lines in which the parents of a variety of young—mouse, gosling, kitten, calf, foal, fish, sheep, bird, bee, snake, puppy, deer, and child—prepare their little ones for bed.

Time for Bed, the Babysitter Said, Peggy Perry Anderson (Boston: Houghton Mifflin Company, 1987). An illustration and a few words of text on each page make this an easy-to-read story of Joe, the frog, who resists his babysitter's attempts to put him to bed until he offers the simple explanation: She didn't say please or thank you.

Tucking Mommy In, Morag Loh, illustrated by Donna Rawlins (New York: Orchard Books, 1987). In this gentle story illustrated with warm, vibrant colors, two young girls help their tired mother get ready for bed, tuck her in, and tell her a bedtime story before their father comes home from work and tucks the sleepy sisters into their own beds.

Tuck-Me-In Tales: Bedtime Stories from Around the World, Margaret Read MacDonald, illustrated by Yvonne Davis (Little Rock, Arkansas: August House LittleFolk, 1996). Written by a storyteller, folklorist, and children's librarian, this collection of five traditional tales for bedtime includes stories from Siberia, Japan, Liberia, Argentina, and the British Isles. Author's notes suggest ways to read or tell the stories (with music for two) and provide background information about each tale.

When Sheep Cannot Sleep: The Counting Book, Satoshi Kitamura (New York: Farrar, Straus & Giroux, 1986). When Wooly the sheep suffers from insomnia, he takes a walk and counts increasing numbers of objects until, finally, he counts his family and friends and falls asleep.

Literature Extension Activities

1. After they listen to ***The Bed Book*** read aloud, students invent and construct beds of their own design in three dimensions. They use boxes of varied sizes, paper towel tubes, paper, and a variety of art and recycled materials, or they use modeling clay to construct their beds. Students name their beds and tell or dramatize each bed's special features. They share reasons they would like to have a bed like the one they have invented.

2. Students provide interpretive movements, use puppets to perform, or dramatize ***Five Little Monkeys Jumping on the Bed***.

    a. Students interpret the book in dance, fingerplay, movement, or rhythm by clapping and stamping their feet to the pronounced beat of the counting rhyme. (Share with students the hand and finger motions suggested in three books of fingerplays listed in Appendix B: No. 12 for "Five Little Monkeys," No. 19 for "Two Little Monkeys," and No. 78 for "Three Little Monkeys.")

    b. Students make and use finger, stick, or sock puppets to dramatize the rhyme.

    c. Students, in roles as each of the five little monkeys, their mother, and the doctor present a play. They make and use simple costumes, props, and set.

3. After they hear "**My Bed**" in ***Home: A Collaboration of Thirty Distinguished Authors and Illustrators of Children's Books to Aid the Homeless*** read aloud, take turns with the students in acting out for others to guess the different roles they play in their own beds. Compile a

list of roles, and individuals illustrate them for a class book or wall display.

For "homework," students (you, too, of course) make a list, using pictures or words, of the treasures they find under their beds after they listen to **"Under the Bed."**

4. After students listen to ***Roll Over!*** read aloud, interpret the fingerplay dramatically with your students. (Share with students versions of the fingerplay in books listed in Appendix B: hand and finger motions suggested for "Ten in the Bed" in No.12 and the musical accompaniment and suggested dramatic activity for "Five in the Bed" in No. 29.)

   Students construct a small or big book version of ***Roll Over!*** modeled after the book, then listen to and share the completed class book during shared group, partner, or individual reading time. Provide the patterned text and illustrations of the large bed with the following changes: (1) Substitute the number of students in the class for the numeral 10 on the first page; (2) add pages to the book to correspond to the number of students in the class so that there is a page for each student; (3) draw yourself (or another character) in the illustration of the bed as the main character; and (4) leave blank space on the inside of the fold-out flaps so that each student can write her or his name and draw a picture of herself or himself falling out of the bed.

5. After they have listened to ***There's an Alligator Under My Bed*** read aloud, students create an extended ending or sequel to the book in one or several of the following ways:

   a. Students draw pictures to illustrate an ending or sequel.

   b. Individual or small groups of students tell an ending or sequel.

   c. Individual students, pairs, or small groups of students cooperatively compose orally and dictate an ending or sequel to you, and students illustrate it.

Students use their two hands to form a mouse-size bed with bedposts similar to the ones in the key word/picture for the unit and in ***There's an Alligator Under My Bed***. They hold their hands as in the diagram shown.

In pairs, students trace around their partner's hands in the bed position held flat onto a piece of unlined drawing paper. Students then complete the illustration of the bed by drawing a pillow, sheets, blanket, and a person or mouse sleeping in it. *Note*: Having them form a bed with their hands in this manner is a highly effective technique for helping students, who tend to confuse them, to distinguish between lowercase *b* and *d*.

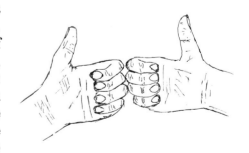

Items for the Mystery Box

Whenever possible, select items for this unit that are **b**lack, **b**lue, or **b**rown in color.

Inedible Items: baboon, baby, backhoe, backpack, badge, bag, ball, ballet slippers, balloon, bandage, bandana, bank, barn, barrette, basket, bat (animal), bat (baseball), bathing suit, bathtub, beanbag, bear, beaver, **bed**, bee, beetle, bell, belt, bib, bicycle, binoculars, bird, blanket, block, boat, bone, bonnet, book, bookcase, bookmark, boots, bottle, bow (arrow), bow (hair), bow tie, box, boy, bracelet, bridge, broom, brush, bubbles (in jar with wand), bucket, bug, bulldozer, bunny, bureau, bus, butterfly, button

Edible Items: bacon, bagel, baklava, banana, banana bread, banana chips (dried), barley, basil, bean salad, beans (baked), beans (green, yellow), beef, beets, berries (blackberries, blueberries, raspberries, strawberries), biscuits, blintzes, blueberry muffins, blueberry pie, bologna, borscht, bread (quick sweet), bread (yeast), breadsticks, breakfast foods (variety), broccoli, brownies, bubble gum, buns, burritos, brussels sprouts, butter

Rhymes, Songs, Fingerplays, and Tongue Twisters

Bed Theme

Come, let's to bed: 5, 34, 46, 50, 76
Diddle, diddle dumpling, my son John: 3, 5, 28, 33, 34, 38, 39, 40, 42, 46, 50, 53, 73, 76
Good night, sleep tight: 5
Go to bed late: 5, 34, 51
*It's raining, it's pouring: 5, 34, 36, 42, 51, 73, 76, 78
The Man in the Moon looked out of the moon: 28, 50, 73, 76
Tongue Twisters: 80

Letter-Sound b (b)

Anna Banana: 4
Baa, baa, black sheep: 3, 5, 9,19, 20, 26, 28, 29, 32, 33, 34, 38, 39, 40, 41, 42, 43, 46, 50, 52, 53, 58, 62, 67, 73, 76
Bye, baby bunting: 5, 20, 28, 32, 33, 34, 38, 39, 40, 50, 73, 76

Little Boy Blue, come blow your horn: 5, 25, 26, 28, 29, 33, 34, 38, 39, 40, 42, 43, 46, 50, 53, 58, 62, 73, 76
Oh, we can play on the big bass drum: 29
Old Mother Hubbard: 5, 20, 25, 28, 32, 33, 34, 37, 38, 39, 42, 43, 45, 46, 50, 58, 73, 76
*Pat a cake, pat a cake, baker's man: 3, 5, 20, 28, 29, 31, 33, 34, 37, 38, 39, 40, 41, 42, 43, 46, 53, 58, 62, 73, 76
*Rub-a-dub-dub: 5, 20, 28, 32, 33, 34, 37, 40, 42, 46, 73, 76
Rock-a-bye, baby, on the tree top: 5, 6, 20, 28, 29, 33, 34, 38, 39, 40, 41, 46, 50, 52, 53, 58, 62, 67, 73, 76
Teddy Bear, Teddy Bear: 3, 4, 48, 51, 64, 78, 79
Tongue Twisters: 1, 7, 13, 60, 74, 80

Cloze Sentences

1. <u>B</u>alloons are fun to **b**low up at a **b**irthday party.
   (At a **b**irthday party, it is fun to **b**low up <u>**b**alloons</u>.)
2. <u>B</u>arns are **b**uildings on a farm where cows and horses live.
   (On a farm, cows and horses live in a **b**uilding called a <u>**b**arn</u>.)
3. A small <u>b</u>ed called a cri**b** is where **b**abies sometimes sleep.
   (**B**abies sometimes sleep in a cri**b,** which is a small <u>**b**ed</u>.)
4. In a paper <u>b</u>ag, I take home the food I **b**uy at the grocery store.
   (I take home the food I **b**uy at the grocery store in a paper <u>**b**ag</u>.)

1. <u>B</u>i**b**s under **b**abies' chins can keep **b**abies' clothes clean when they eat.
   (To keep their clothes clean when they eat, **b**abies often wear <u>**b**i**b**s</u> under their chins.)
2. **B**y putting a <u>b</u>andage on a cut, you may keep it clean.
   (When you get a cut you may keep it clean **b**y putting on a <u>**b**andage</u>.)
3. A <u>b</u>oat is a small ship used for riding on water.
   (A small ship for riding on the water is a <u>**b**oat</u>.)
4. In a <u>b</u>ox is the way cereal usually comes when you **b**uy it at the store.
   (When you **b**uy cereal at the store, it usually comes in a <u>**b**ox</u>.)

B b

It's raining, it's pouring,

The old man is snoring.

He got into bed

And bumped his head

And couldn't get up in the morning.

Name _____ Date _____

B b

Pat a cake, pat a cake, baker's man,

Bake me a cake as fast as you can.

Pat it and prick it, and mark it with a B,

And put it in the oven for Baby and Me.

Name _____   Date _____

Rhymes . . . 2

B b

RUB-A-DUB-DUB

Rub-a-dub-dub,

Three men in a tub,

And who do you think they be?

The butcher, the baker,

The candlestick-maker;

Turn 'em out, knaves all three!

Name _____   Date _____

B b

COMPLETE IT

Balloons	Barns
1	2
bed	bag
3	4

<u>Balloons</u> are fun to blow up at a birthday party.
 1

<u>Barns</u> are buildings on a farm where cows and
 2
horses live.

A small <u>bed</u> called a crib is where babies
 3
sometimes sleep.

In a paper <u>bag</u>, I take home the food I buy at
 4
the grocery store.

Name _____   Date _____

Cloze Sentences . . . 1

B b

COMPLETE IT

Bibs 1	bandage 2
boat 3	box 4

<u>Bibs</u> under babies' chins can keep babies' clothes
1
clean when they eat.

By putting a <u>bandage</u> on a cut, you may keep it
2
clean.

A <u>boat</u> is a small ship used for riding on water.
3

In a <u>box</u> is the way cereal usually comes when
4
you buy it at the store.

Name _____   Date _____

B

b

bed

C c cat

TEACHER REFERENCE

Annotated Book List

Amazing Cats: Eyewitness Juniors, Alexandra Parsons, photographed by Jerry Young (New York: Alfred A. Knopf, 1990). Colored drawings and photographs complement short text passages that highlight the habits and traits of common and unusual members of the cat family—wild and domesticated—from all over the world. Includes table of contents and index.

Annie and the Wild Animals, Jan Brett (Boston: Houghton Mifflin Company, 1985). When her cat disappears one snowy day, Annie puts out corn cakes to attract a new pet, but the moose, wildcat, bear, and stag that crowd her yard are not what she had hoped for. In spring, the animals return to their homes, as does Annie's cat—with three kittens!

Back Soon, Diana Hendry, illustrated by Carol Thompson (Mahwah, New Jersey: BridgeWater Books/Troll Associates, Inc., 1993). Tired of being left with family members while his mother goes out, Herbert initiates some adventures of his own at home so that she will miss *him,* and he discovers that he enjoys having some time to himself, too.

Cat and Cat-face, Chyng Feng Sun, illustrated by Lesley Liu (Boston: Houghton Mifflin Company, 1996). A gentle pansy, called Cat-face in Chinese, and a lively cat discover that understanding their differences and giving each other time apart, as well as together, are part of becoming friends.

Cat: Eyewitness Books, Juliet Clutton-Brock (New York: Alfred A. Knopf, 1991). Collections of colored photographs, drawings, and objects along with fact-filled text and captions compose the pages of this informative book about domestic and wild cats. Contains table of contents and index.

Cat and Rat: The Legend of the Chinese Zodiac, Ed Young (New York: Henry Holt and Company, 1995). The pourquoi story, which traces the origin of the Chinese zodiac to a race of the animals invited by the Jade Emperor of Heaven to compete for a place among its twelve signs, reveals why there is no year of the cat and explains why cat and rat, once best friends, are now enemies.

Cats: A First Discovery Book, Gallimard Jeunesse and Pascale de Bourgoing, illustrated by Henri Galeron (New York: Scholastic Inc., 1989). In this spiral-bound informative book designed for young readers, see-through plastic pages allow readers to see the front and back of illustrations, and a plastic covering protects all pages. Information presented includes body parts, breeds, vision and hearing, body language, grooming, kittens, habits, wild feline relatives, and a history of domesticated cats.

The Cat Who Lost His Purr, Michele Coxon (New York: Penguin Books USA, Inc., 1991). Bootle, the cat, awakens to an empty house one morning to discover that he's lost his purr, and he sets off to find it, rejecting the sounds that he hears that are not his purr and entertaining himself with adventure after adventure, until his two-legged family returns home at the end of the day and, suddenly, his purr returns.

The Christmas Day Kitten, James Herriot, illustrations by Ruth Brown (New York: St. Martin's Press, 1976, 1986). A shy stray cat, who visits for a few minutes several times each week to warm herself in front of the fireplace at the home of Mrs. Pickering and her three basset hounds, disappears for several weeks and returns to die on Christmas Day, but not until she has presented her final gift—a spunky newborn kitten.

Cross-Country Cat, Mary Calhoun, illustrated by Erick Ingraham (New York: Mulberry Books, 1979). Because Henry the cat is able to walk on his hind legs, he is able to use the cross-country skis and poles fashioned for him by his boy, The Kid, to find his way to his human family after he is accidentally left behind in a cabin in the mountains.

Duckat, Gaelyn Gordon, illustrated by Chris Gaskin (New York: Scholastic Inc., 1992). The duck that Mabel finds at her door on Monday acts just like a cat when it meows, hates water, scratches, drinks milk from a bowl, catches mice, pounces on Mabel's toes, chases a ball of yarn, sleeps by the fire, climbs trees, and washes behind its ears. The fantasy appears to come to an end when the duck flies to escape a dog, goes for a swim in a pond, and quacks; but on the last page it is Tuesday, and Mable finds a cat at her door—a cat that quacks—and the duck, who now talks!

Have You Seen My Cat?, Eric Carle (New York: Scholastic, 1987). Two repeated lines and illustrations tell the story of a boy who travels around the world to look for his lost cat and is disappointed that the variety of cats (wild and domesticated) people show him are not his, until he finds his cat and the reason she has been missing—a litter of kittens.

Hi, Cat!, Ezra Jack Keats (New York: Macmillan Company, 1970). Peter (introduced as a younger child in ***A Snowy Day*** by the same author) isn't sure how he feels about the new cat on the block that follows him everywhere after he greets it, especially after it spoils every act of the show that he and Archie put on for the other kids.

The Kids' Cat Book, Tomie de Paola (New York: Holiday House, Inc., 1979). During a young boy's visit to Granny Twinkle's to pick out a free kitten, Granny provides information about a variety of breeds of cats including physical description, habits, care and feeding, place of origin, and history. Stories of cats in ancient Egypt and Rome, in the Middle Ages, in England during the time of Queen Victoria, and in literature are included in the history. Also contains a list of interesting facts about cats.

Millions of Cats, Wanda Gág (New York: Coward-McCann, 1928, 1956). Seventy years after its first publication, this story of the old man who sets out to get a cat for his wife, and returns with trillions of cats because he cannot choose just one, continues to be a classic. The text—especially the often-repeated rhythmic refrain—and the detailed black-and-white illustrations of countless cats distinguish this book.

Mister King, Raija Siekkinen, translated from the Finnish by Tim Steffa, illustrated by Hannu Taina (Minneapolis: Carolrhoda Books, Inc., 1986). In this modern fable, a lonely king who hasn't a single subject does not enjoy his beautiful house and kingdom until a huge cat arrives at his door.

Moses the Kitten, James Herriot, illustrated by Peter Barrett (New York: St. Martin's Press, 1974, 1984). Moses, a stray kitten rescued by a Yorkshire farmer and his wife, receives nourishment and nurture from an unlikely source—a mother pig suckling her litter of twelve piglets!

Mr. Putter and Tabby Bake the Cake, Cynthia Rylant, illustrated by Arthur Howard (San Diego: Harcourt Brace & Company, 1994). This easy-to-read chapter book is one in a series of books about Mr. Putter and his cat. During one Christmas season, Mr. Putter worries that his neighbor is eating too much fruitcake, so he and Tabby set out to make her a "light and airy" cake, which turns out not to be as easy as he thought, to involve a number of misadventures, and to take a *lot* of time!

Mrs. Katz and Tush, Patricia Polacco (New York: Bantam Doubleday Dell Publishing Group, Inc., 1992). Larnel offers Mrs. Katz a kitten for company after her husband dies, and so begins the close relationship of a lonely woman and a young boy. They discover important similarities in the experiences of their Jewish and African American peoples.

Mrs. Peachtree and the Eighth Avenue Cat, Erica Silverman, illustrations by Ellen Beier (New York: Simon & Schuster Children's Publishing Division, 1994). In this story, set in the 1890s in New York City, Mrs. Peachtree is *not* interested in having a cat— especially the scraggly stray that keeps coming to her tea shop. Soon, however, she finds herself feeding him, going out to look for him at night during a rainstorm, and, finally, naming him and calling him her own.

My Cat Jack, Patricia Casey (Cambridge, Massachusetts: Candlewick Press, 1994). One sentence in enlarged print for each double page describes a cat involved in a number of activities, shown in the full-page ink, crayon, and watercolor illustrations.

My Cats Nick & Nora, Isabelle Harper & Barry Mosher (New York: The Blue Sky Press, 1995). Mosher's watercolors and brief text capture the energy of a Sunday afternoon of adventures shared by two young cousins and two lively cats.

My New Kitten, Joanna Cole, photographs by Margaret Miller (New York: Morrow Junior Books, 1995). Close-up color photographs follow a young girl as she observes the development of a litter of kittens from birth until eight weeks of age when she takes home one of the kittens as a pet.

The Old Ladies Who Liked Cats, Carol Green, illustrated by Loretta Krupinski (New York: HarperCollins Publishers, 1991). Based on a story Charles Darwin told about clover and cats, this folk tale tells how the ecological balance of a small island is upset when the wise elder women are forbidden to let their cats outside at night.

Only the Cat Saw, Ashley Wolff (New York: Walker and Company, 1985). As they ready for bed and as they sleep, Amy's busy family misses the nocturnal world that only their cat sees, but in the morning the cat sleeps, and Amy notices their daytime world.

Oscar, Cat-About-Town, James Herriot, illustrated by Ruth Brown (New York: St. Martin's Press, 1977, 1990). The Herriots wonder why Oscar, the stray cat they have taken into their home, keeps disappearing, until they discover that his love of people, especially in groups, draws him to visit local social events.

Our Cat Flossie, Ruth Brown (New York: Dutton Children's Books, 1986). One line of text and a painting in muted colors on each page capture the activities and humor in the life of a city cat, Flossie.

Pretend You're a Cat, Jean Marzollo, pictures by Jerry Pinkney (New York: Penguin Books USA, Inc., 1990). Each double page includes a series of questions in a rhymed pattern, directed to the reader, and an illustration. The questions describe typical activities or actions of an animal and ask, "Can you ___?" and the illustration shows the featured animal and a young child or children engaging in the suggested activities, pretending to be the animal. Featured animals are a cat, dog, fish, bee, chick, bird, squirrel, pig, cow, horse, seal, snake, and bear.

Six-Dinner Sid, Inga Moore (New York: Simon & Schuster, Inc., 1991). No one on his street knows that Sid, the cat, lives at six different houses in order to eat six dinners a day. An observant veterinarian informs his owners, who limit his dinners to one a day—until Sid moves to six new homes on a new street!

Smoky Night, Eve Bunting, illustrated by David Diaz (San Diego: Harcourt Brace & Company, 1994). Stunning acrylic paintings on photographed collage and found-object backgrounds illustrate the story: Two families and their two cats are brought together when a fire during the Los Angeles riots forces them out of their apartment building and into an emergency shelter.

Storm in the Night, Mary Stolz, illustrated by Pat Cummings (New York: Harper & Row, Publishers, 1988). When the lights go out during a thunderstorm, Thomas and his cat listen as grandfather tells a story of how his love for his dog forced him to confront his fears during a similar storm when he was a boy.

The Third-Story Cat, Leslie Baker (Boston: Little, Brown and Company, 1987). A cat escapes her apartment home to have the city adventures she has long desired to experience and returns home satisfied—for the moment.

Tikvah Means Hope, Patricia Polacco (New York: A Doubleday Book for Young Readers, 1994). Tikvah, the cat, lives up to her name, which means hope, when she survives—

along with the Sukkah (stick and palm branch hut for the Sukkoth, or thanksgiving, celebration)—the firestorm that devastated Oakland, California. An author's note provides additional information about the effects of the firestorm on the people, animals, land, and vegetation of Oakland.

Whiskers & Rhymes, Arnold Lobel (New York: Greenwillow Books, 1985). Cats dressed in human clothing are the characters in the illustrations for this collection of humorous short rhymes that cover a variety of subjects with engaging rhythms reminiscent of nursery rhymes.

Who Says a Dog Goes Bow-wow?, Hand De Zutter, illustrated by Suse MacDonald (New York: Bantam Doubleday Dell Books for Young Readers, 1993). Each page, illustrated in cut-paper collage, presents the phonetic representation of the sound of an animal as it is said by people in a number of countries and cultures around the world.

Literature Extension Activities

1. An author's note accompanying ***Cat and Rat: The Legend of the Chinese Zodiac*** provides infromation about the Chinese zodiac and includes a chart that matches birth years 1900 to 2007 to the corresponding animal that rules each year. It also describes the characteristics of the animal—characteristics that are believed to be shared by persons born during that year. With students, find your sign and theirs in the Chinese zodiac and have them tell whether they do or do not think they share personality traits with the animal during whose year they were born. If not, they choose an animal they feel they *are* most like.

2. Create with students, My Cat books, inspired by ***My Cat Jack*** and following the "My cat is a ____ cat" and "He's a ____ cat" pattern that alternates throughout the book.

3. As a group project, you and your students illustrate a chart of the ecological chain of which they are part, similar to the one of the island described in ***The Old Ladies Who Liked Cats***. Discuss what might happen to the balance of nature if any one element were suddenly missing from the chain.

4. After you share ***Only the Cat Saw*** in read-aloud, compile with students a list of things that cats (or people) might see at night when they are usually sleeping.

5. Like the children pictured in ***Pretend You're a Cat***, with students, in groups or individually, dramatize the activities or actions prompted by the questions on each page—and those they generate themselves—to pretend to be cats, other animals in the book, or any other animals. In another activity, mime activities or actions for others to guess the identity of the animal (as in charades).

Note: The two books **Smoky Night** and **Tikvah Means Hope** may be difficult for students who have experienced fires in or near their homes. As with all sensitive topics, use care when presenting these books.

Items for the Mystery Box

Inedible Items: cab, cactus, calculator, calendar, camel, camera, can, candle, cane (for walking), canoe, cap, cape, car, card (greeting), card (playing), cardboard, carpet, carriage (baby), carriage (horse), castle, **cat**, catalog, caterpillar, cat food, clay, clock, clogs, cloth, clown, coat, cobra, coffee, coin, collar, comb, comics, cook, corduroy, cork, corn (decorative), cotton balls, couch, cow, cowboy, crab, crayon, cricket, crocodile, crow, crown, crutch, cup, curtain

Edible Items: cabbage, cake, calzone, candy bar, candy cane, cannoli, cantaloupe, caramels, carrot, carrot cake, cashew butter, cashews, cauliflower, clams, clementine, cocoa, coconut, cod, coffee ice cream, collard greens, cone (ice cream), cookies, corn, cornbread, Cornflakes™, cornmeal, cornmeal mush, couscous, crabmeat, crackers, cranberries, cranberry bread, cream, crepes, croissant, cucumber, cupcakes, currants, custard

Rhymes, Songs, Fingerplays, and Tongue Twisters

Cat Theme

As I was going to St. Ives: 5, 9, 28, 33, 34, 37, 39, 46, 50, 73, 76
*Great A, little a: 5, 28, 33, 40, 50, 73
*Hey, diddle, diddle: 3, 5, 9, 20, 25, 26, 28, 32, 33, 34, 37, 38, 39, 40, 41, 42, 43, 46, 49, 50, 52, 53, 58, 62, 67, 73, 76
I had a cat and the cat pleased me: 8, 17, 51, 73
Pussy cat, pussy cat: 5, 9, 25, 26, 28, 33, 34, 37, 38, 39, 40, 42, 46, 50, 52, 58, 62, 73, 76

There were once two cats of Kilkenny: 20, 25, 28, 33, 50, 51, 73, 76
Tongue Twisters: 13, 54, 80

Letter-Sound c (k)

Little Boy Blue, come blow your horn: 5, 25, 26, 28, 29, 33, 34, 38, 39, 40, 42, 43, 46, 50, 53, 58, 62, 73, 76
Come, butter, come: 20
*There was a crooked man: 5, 9, 26, 28, 32, 33, 34, 37, 39, 46, 50, 62, 73, 76
Tongue Twisters: 1, 7, 13, 60, 80

Cloze Sentences

1. <u>C</u>ars, buses, vans, and tru<u>c</u>ks are vehi<u>c</u>les you <u>c</u>an ride in to s<u>c</u>hool.
    (You <u>c</u>an ride to s<u>c</u>hool in a bus, a van, a truck, or a <u>car</u>.)

2. A <u>c</u>at can meow, and it can lick its fur to clean itself.

(An animal that meows and licks its fur to clean itself is a <u>c</u>at.)

3. <u>C</u>arrots are orange vegetables that rabbits love to eat.

(Orange vegetables that rabbits love to eat are <u>c</u>arrots.)

4. A <u>cup</u> is a container for drinking coffee, tea, or hot cocoa.

(Your mom or dad may drink coffee or tea, and you may drink hot cocoa in a <u>cup</u>.)

1. You can use a <u>comb</u> or a brush to fix your hair.

(You can fix your hair with a brush or a <u>comb</u>.)

2. <u>C</u>orn is a vegetable that you can eat on the cob.

(A vegetable that you can eat on the cob is <u>c</u>orn.)

3. A <u>c</u>ard that says "get well" is something you may send to someone when he or she is sick.

(When someone is sick, you may send her or him a get-well <u>c</u>ard.)

4. The <u>c</u>andles are something you blow out before you cut your birthday cake.

(Before you cut your birthday cake, you blow out the <u>c</u>andles.)

C c

Hey, diddle, diddle,

The cat and the fiddle,

The cow jumped over the moon;

The little dog laughed

To see such sport,

And the dish ran away with the spoon.

Name _____   Date _____

C c

Great A, little a,

Bouncing B;

The cat's in the cupboard,

And she can't see.

Name _____   Date _____

C c

There was a crooked man,
And he went a crooked mile,

He found a crooked sixpence
Against a crooked stile;

He bought a crooked cat,
Which caught a crooked mouse,

And they all lived together
In a crooked little house.

Name _____   Date _____

Rhymes . . . 3

C c

COMPLETE IT

Cars
1

cat
2

Carrots
3

cup
4

Cars, buses, vans, and trucks are vehicles you
1
can ride in to school.

A _cat_ can meow, and it can lick its fur to clean
2
itself.

Carrots are orange vegetables that rabbits love
3
to eat.

A _cup_ is a container for drinking coffee, tea, or
4
hot cocoa.

Name _____   Date _____

C c

COMPLETE IT

comb
1

Corn
2

card
3

candles
4

You can use a <u>comb</u> or a brush to fix your hair.
1

<u>Corn</u> is a vegetable that you can eat on the
2
cob.

A <u>card</u> that says "get well" is something you may
3
send to someone when he or she is sick.

The <u>candles</u> are something you blow out before
4
you cut your birthday cake.

Name _____   Date _____

D d   *dog*

TEACHER REFERENCE

Annotated Book List

Amazing Wolves, Dogs & Foxes: Eyewitness Juniors, Mary Ling, Photographed by Jerry Young (New York: Alfred A. Knopf, 1991). Colored photographs and drawings and accompanying text provide information about the traits and habits of the variety of wild animals that are relatives of the domesticated dog, including wolves (from whom pet dogs are descended) and foxes. Contains table of contents and index.

Amos: The Story of an Old Dog and His Couch, Susan Seligson and Howie Schneider (Boston: Little, Brown and Company, 1987). The kids have grown and moved away, and his owners never take him with them when they go out, so Amos, the dog, is bored and lonely until he discovers that his couch comes alive with a touch, and then he's off with a loud VAROOM as he enjoys hilarious adventures in town atop his magical vehicle, surprising and entertaining human and animal friends on his way.

Biscuit, Alyssa Satin Capucilli, pictures by Pat Schories (New York: HarperCollins Publishers, 1996). In this book—from the My First I Can Read Book® series, with a predictable, repetitive pattern and supportive illustrations that provide clues to text meaning—not unlike his human counterparts, Biscuit, the dog, wants the little girl who owns him to do a number of things before he goes to sleep at night.

Bonesy and Isabel, Michael J. Rosen, illustrated by James Ransome (San Diego: Harcourt Brace & Company, 1995). It is the twelve-year old Labrador retriever named Bonesy who provides the companionship that supports Isabel as she makes the transition from her birth country of El Salvador to her new life in her adopted home in the United States, who listens to her as she learns and practices pronouncing English, and who, by his death, helps Isabel and her new parents, by sharing their grief, become a family.

The Bookshop Dog, Cynthia Rylant (New York: The Blue Sky Press, 1996). Neighbors and customers of Martha Jane's Bookshop vie to care for the dog after whom the shop is named while the owner is briefly hospitalized, but it is Martha Jane, herself, who chooses her own sitter.

Boomer's Big Day, Constance W. McGeorge, illustrated by Mary Whyte (San Francisco: Chronicle Books, 1994). Nothing is as it usually is on moving day, and until he is able to eat from his familiar food dish, find his old tennis ball, sleep in his own bed and dig in the yard, sniff the new smells, chase a squirrel, and make new canine friends at the new house, Boomer, the golden retriever, is disoriented and confused.

Dog: Eyewitness Books, Juliet Clutton-Brock (New York: Alfred A. Knopf, 1991). Photographs of wild and domesticated dogs and related objects complement text that presents information about a variety of breeds, domestication, evolution of the dog family, young, and habits (including talents that equip dogs for specific functions and work). Includes a section about care for a pet dog, a table of contents, and an index.

A Dog's Tale, Seymour Reit, illustrated by Kate Flanagan (New York: Bantam Doubleday Dell Publishing Group, 1996). This humorous easy-to-read book from the Bank Street Ready-to-Read series with large print and short sentences is told from the point of view of a dog who trains his new owner and teaches her, step by step, how to care for him.

The Dog Who Had Kittens, Polly M. Robertus, illustrated by Janet Stevens (New York: Holiday House, 1988). At first, Baxter, the basset hound, is jealous of the attention given to Eloise and her new litter of kittens, but when the kittens are left alone with him he discovers that he *enjoys* caring for them. Baxter misses the kittens when they are old enough to leave their mother, but a new-found bond with Eloise and the prospect of more kittens someday console him.

The Dog Who Lost His Bob, Tom and Laura McNeal, illustrated by John Sandford (Morton Grove, Illinois: Albert Whitman & Company, 1996). One Sunday, Bob's dog, Phil, becomes lost while trying to escape his weekly bath, and, during the months he roams before he is returned to Bob, Phil discovers that the benefits of a loving home are well worth getting wet once a week.

Fido, Stephanie Calmenson, illustrated by Maxie Chambliss (New York: Scholastic Inc., 1987). Because his dog, Fido, bears a striking resemblance to Mr. Tinker, the head of a large company, he is able to dress the dog in his best suit and send Fido to work in his place when he is forced to take a sick day.

The First Dog, Jan Brett (San Diego: Harcourt Brace & Company, 1988). Illustrated with drawings of the animals and vegetation that lived alongside the human hunters and gatherers in Ice Age Europe and with borders based on artifacts and cave paintings of that time period, the story of Kip, the cave boy, and the Paleowolf who saves his life and whom he befriends suggests a way in which wild dogs may have become domesticated.

Floss, Kim Lewis (Cambridge, Massachusetts: Candlewick Press, 1992). Floss, the border collie, becomes a skilled working sheepdog, but she never forgets the joys of playing ball with children when she was a pup, and she and her master learn to appreciate the importance of a balance of work and play as he allows her to play soccer with the children when her work on the farm in northern England is done.

Give a Dog a Bone: Stories, Poems, Jokes, and Riddles About Dogs, compiled by Joanna Cole and Stephanie Calmenson (New York: Scholastic Inc., 1996). This richly illustrated anthology pays tribute to dogs in poem, story, rebus, joke, riddle, and factual form.

Go, Dog. Go!, P. D. Eastman (New York: Random House, Inc., 1961). In this classic book for beginners, readers use highly supportive clues from the illustrations as they learn to read the phrases and sentences that describe the activities of a variety of dogs, discover a long line of dogs in cars on their way to a festive dog party in a tree, and follow a subplot in which one dog tries to impress another with a number of increasingly elaborate hats.

Good Dog, Carl, Alexandra Day (New York: Simon & Schuster Books for Young Readers, 1985). In this wordless book, while his owner leaves him in charge of the baby when she goes out, Carl, the rottweiler, and his small companion enjoy a number of humorous (and messy) adventures, but Carl cleans up all of the evidence before she returns.

Harry the Dirty Dog, Gene Zion, pictures by Margaret Bloy Graham (New York: Harper & Row, Publishers, 1956). In this classic first book in the series about Harry, the little white dog with spots, Harry buries the scrub brush and runs away from home to avoid having a bath, and his adventures make him so dirty that, when he returns home hungry and tired, he is not recognized by his owners even when he performs some familiar tricks until he uncovers the scrub brush, jumps into the bathtub, and takes a soapy bath.

Henry and Mudge Get the Cold Shivers, Cynthia Rylant, pictures by Sucie Stevenson (New York: Macmillan Publishing Company, 1989). In this easy-to-read book in the Henry and Mudge series, Henry's dog, Mudge, always takes care of him when he is sick, so when Mudge becomes ill, concerned Henry enthusiastically takes care of his pet.

Hunky Dory Ate It, Katie Evans, pictures by Janet Morgan Stoeke (New York: Penguin Books USA Inc., 1992). The hero of ***Hunky Dory Found It*** by the same author stars in this book for beginning readers with enlarged print and rhyming verses in which Hunky Dory, the dog, eats everything in sight until he becomes ill and discovers *one* thing that he does not like to eat—the medicine the vet gives him.

Knoxville, Tennessee, Nikki Giovanni, illustrated by Larry Johnson (New York: Scholastic Inc., 1968, 1994). With her family's dogs, a young girl celebrates her favorite season, summer, while at home with her parents and with her grandmother in the mountains.

The Last Puppy, Frank Asch (New York: Simon & Schuster Children's Publishing Division, 1989). One puppy from a large litter is saddened to be last to do everything, especially be chosen as someone's pet, but it discovers that it is first in one important way when it is taken home by a little boy who tells it that it is *his* first puppy.

Martha Speaks, Susan Meddaugh (Boston: Houghton Mifflin Company, 1992). In this book about Martha, the dog, who first speaks after eating alphabet soup, her owners enjoy her unusual talent until they become aware of the problems her nonstop talking and frankness bring, and they ask her to stop talking. When Martha calls the police to report a burglar, they agree on the importance of knowing the appropriate times and ways to speak.

Monday Run-Day, Nick Sharratt (Cambridge, Massachusetts: Candlewick Press, 1992). A dog is shown on each double page enjoying a special activity that rhymes with the featured day of the week—from "Sunday bun-day" sharing a platter of raisin buns with canine friends to "Saturday splatter-day" splashing in mud puddles with a doggy pal.

My Dog Rosie, Isabelle Harper and Barry Moser (New York: The Blue Sky Press, 1994). While her grandfather works in his art studio, a preschooler cares for his ever-patient rottweiler, Rosie (short for Franklin Roosevelt) in this story with human and canine characters from Moser's own life.

My New Puppy, Harriet Hains, photographed by Steve Shott, illustrated by Conny Jude (London: Dorling Kindersley Limited, 1992). Colored photographs on painted backgrounds show a young boy as he enjoys and cares for his new puppy.

The Old Woman Who Named Things, Cynthia Rylant, illustrated by Kathryn Brown (San Diego: Harcourt Brace & Company, 1996). An old woman who has outlived all of her friends names only the things in her life that she is certain will outlive *her*—including her house, "Franklin," and her chair, "Fred"—but refuses to name a stray dog until the fear of losing him helps her take the risk, and she reaps the joy of a new friendship.

Our New Puppy, Isabelle Harper and Barry Moser (New York: The Blue Sky Press, 1996). In Moser's third collaboration with his granddaughter, not unlike his human counterparts who are siblings, Rosie, the dog, must adjust to the arrival of eight-week-old puppy, Floyd.

Pinkerton, Behave!, Steven Kellogg (New York: Dial Press, 1979). Pinkerton the dog's frustrating behavior causes him to be expelled from obedience school, but when his owners realize that they must give him commands opposite from what is needed, he saves them from a burglar and becomes a hero. One in a series of books about Pinkerton.

Spot A Dog: A Child's Book of Art, Lucy Micklethwait (London: Dorling Kindersley Limited, 1995). The author uses an adjective to describe a dog and invites the reader to locate it in each of thirteen paintings by famous artists reproduced in full-page format.

Tuan, Eva Bonholm-Olsson, illustrated by Pham van Dôn, translated by Dianne Jonasson (New York: Farrar, Straus & Giroux, 1986, 1988). Illustrated on silk by Phan van Don, one of Vietman's best-known artists, the book captures the daily life of a small boy, Tuan, and his family—a life interrupted by a bite from a dog with rabies and the challenge of locating medicine in time to save Tuan's life.

Walter's Tail, Lisa Campbell Ernst (New York: Macmillan Publishing Company, 1992). Walter's continually moving tail is considered cute when he is a puppy, but, as he grows, his larger tail accidentally causes trouble. Walter and his owner are unable to shop in town until Walter uses his tail to make a rescue, and he becomes the town's hero.

Where's Spot?, Eric Hill (New York: G. P. Putnam's Sons, 1980). In this first interactive book about Spot, one predictable question in enlarged print and a simple, supportive illustration that gives clues to text meaning appear on each double page. Readers open flaps to find an answer to each question and to look, with his mother, for puppy Spot, who has not eaten his supper.

Whistle for Willie, Ezra Jack Keats (New York: Penguin Books, 1964). Peter, of *A Snowy Day* by the same author, tries and tries to learn how to whistle so that he can call his dog, Willie. Finally, his efforts are rewarded and appreciated by Willie and his parents and, most of all, by Peter himself, who feels quite grown-up as he enjoys his new skill.

Who Says a Dog Goes Bow-wow?, Hand De Zutter, illustrated by Suse MacDonald (New York: Bantam Doubleday Dell Books for Young Readers, 1993). Each page, illustrated in cut-paper collage, offers the phonetic representation of the sound of an animal as it is said by people in a number of countries and cultures around the world.

Why Do Dogs Do That?, Nancy White, illustrated by Gioia Fiammenghi (New York: Scholastic Inc., 1995). In a question-and-answer format, the author answers the questions children in her neighborhood have asked her about a wide range of topics related to dogs. Includes a description of the work of a golden retriever, trained at Canine Companions for Independence in California, to assist and follow the commands of a boy who uses a wheelchair.

Literature Extension Activities

1. After they hear *My Dog Rosie* read aloud, students enjoy Rosie's favorite story, pictured in the book: *Carl Goes Shopping* by Alexandra Day (New York: Farrar Straus & Giroux, 1989), a wordless book sequel to *Good Dog, Carl* by the same author, in which Carl, the dog, and the baby enjoy a romp through a department store while the dog is again left in charge.

2. After you share *My New Puppy*, with students, collect at least one photograph of every member of the class. Individuals who are able to do so bring in photographs from home, or you can take photographs of each student in the class. They then paint a colored background for their photographs, similar to the backgrounds in the book, onto which they glue

the photograph(s), trimmed to show only the student or teacher in action.

3. After you find the identified dog on the accompanying page of **Spot a Dog: A Child's Book of Art** with your students, they use adjectives to describe their own dogs, dogs in photographs, dogs in books, and in other contexts. They write and illustrate a class book using adjectives to describe dogs with the following text, patterned after the book, on alternating pages: Can you see a _____ dog? I can see a _____ dog. Can you spot a _____ dog? I can spot a _____ dog.

4. *Tuan*, written by Eva Boholm-Olsson who lived in Vietnam with her family, depicts the daily life of a small child, including one of the difficulties that challenge those living in that culture—the scarcity of medicine. Discuss with your students the similarities and differences between the Vietnamese culture, as presented in the book, and their own. Include in your discussion rabies in animals in your locale, precautions as well as medical treatments.

NOTE: Although *Tuan* ends happily, with the doctor able to locate the rabies vaccine needed to save Tuan's life in time for him to celebrate the Children's Festival with his mother, the subject matter of this book may not be appropriate for all young children.

5. As they enjoy **Who Says a Dog Goes Bow-wow?**, with your students, pronounce the sounds a dog makes in the following languages after you model them: Finnish, Turkish, Russian, Polish, Hebrew, Farsi, Danish, Lithuanian, Japanese, French, Dutch, Italian, Serbo-Croatian, Thai, Korean, Chinese, and English. Each of them chooses the sound he or she thinks best represents the sound of a dog or makes up her or his own sounds as the author suggests. They enjoy this process with the other animals presented in the book.

Items for the Mystery Box

Inedible Items: daffodil, daisy, dandelion, deer, dentist, desk, diamond, diaper, dice, dictionary, dime, dinosaur, dirt, dish, disk, doctor, **dog**, doghouse, doll, dollar, dolphin, dominoes, donkey, door, doorknob, dove, dragon, dragonfly, dreidel, dress, drill, drum, drumstick (musical), duck, dumptruck, dust (sawdust), dustpan

Edible Items: dal, Danish pastry, dates, desserts (variety), dill, dill pickles, dips (with vegetables), doughnuts, dressing (salad, on vegetables), dried fruits, drumstick (chicken, turkey), dumplings

Rhymes, Songs, Fingerplays, and Tongue Twisters

Dog Theme

Bow-wow-wow: 3, 20, 27, 28, 33, 46, 50, 73

Have a little dog and his name is Don: 27

Hey, diddle, diddle: 3, 5, 9, 20, 25, 26, 28, 32, 33, 34, 37, 38, 39, 40, 41, 42, 43, 46, 49, 50, 52, 53, 58, 62, 67, 73, 76

I had a cat and the cat pleased me: 8, 17, 51, 73

I had a dog and his name was Blue: 27

Old Dog Tray: 27

*Old Mother Hubbard: 5, 20, 25, 28, 32, 33, 34, 37, 38, 39, 42, 43, 45, 46, 50, 58, 73, 76

Where, oh where, has my little dog gone?: 5, 27, 34, 39, 62, 76

Letter Sound d (d)

*Dickery, dickery, dock: 5, 20, 25, 28, 29, 31, 32, 33, 34, 37, 38, 39, 40, 41, 42, 46, 49, 50, 53, 58, 62, 73, 76, 78

*Diddle, diddle dumpling, my son John: 3, 5, 28, 33, 34, 38, 39, 40, 42, 46, 50, 53, 73, 76

Down by the bay: 10, 51, 55

The farmer in the dell: 26, 47, 79

Humpty Dumpty sat on a wall: 3, 5, 20, 25, 26, 28, 29, 32, 33, 34, 37, 38, 39, 40, 41, 42, 43, 46, 50, 52, 53, 58, 62, 67, 73, 76

Lavender's blue, diddle diddle: 26, 28, 29, 33, 34, 38, 41, 46, 51, 53, 62, 67, 73, 76

London Bridge is falling down: 5, 26, 28, 33, 34, 38, 46, 47, 50, 62, 79

Tongue Twisters: 1, 7, 13, 60, 74, 80

Cloze Sentences

1. A <u>d</u>entist is a **d**octor who helps take care of your teeth.

   (A **d**octor who helps take care of your teeth is a <u>d</u>entist.)

2. A <u>d</u>oor is something that you sometimes have to open to get in an**d** out of a room.

   (Sometimes, to get in an**d** out of a room, you have to open a <u>d</u>oor.)

3. A <u>d</u>og is an animal that wags its tail an**d** barks.

   (An animal that barks an**d** wags its tail is a <u>d</u>og.)

4. A <u>d</u>uck is an animal that loves to swim in water an**d** that quacks.
   (An animal that loves to swim in water an**d** that quacks is a <u>d</u>uck.)

1. A <u>d</u>oll is a toy that looks like a person.

   (A toy that looks like a person is a <u>d</u>oll.)

2. A <u>d</u>esk is a place where a teacher may sit to **d**o his or her paperwork.

   (A teacher may **d**o his or her paperwork sitting at a <u>d</u>esk.)

3. A **d**oughnut is a sweet foo**d** in the shape of a ring—roun**d** with a hole in the mi**dd**le.

    (A sweet foo**d** that is in the shape of a ring—roun**d** with a hole in the mi**dd**le — is a **d**oughnut.)

4. A **d**rum is a musical instrument in a ban**d**, orchestra, or a para**d**e that you beat with special sticks.

    (A musical instrument in a ban**d**, orchestra, or a para**d**e that you beat with special sticks is a **d**rum.)

D d

Old Mother Hubbard
Went to the cupboard
To get her poor dog a bone.

But when she got there
The cupboard was bare,
And so the poor dog had none.

Name _____ Date _____

D d

Dickery, dickery, dock,

The mouse ran up the clock;

The clock struck one,

The mouse ran down.

Dickery, dickery, dock.

Name _____   Date _____

D d

Diddle, diddle, dumpling, my son John,

Went to bed with his stockings on.

One stocking off and one stocking on,

Diddle, diddle, dumpling, my son John.

Name _____   Date _____

D d

COMPLETE IT

dentist	door
1	2
dog	duck
3	4

A <u>dentist</u> is a doctor who helps take care of
  1
your teeth.

A <u>door</u> is something that you sometimes have to
  2
open to get in and out of a room.

A <u>dog</u> is an animal that wags its tail and barks.
  3

A <u>duck</u> is an animal that loves to swim in water
  4
and that quacks.

Name _____ Date _____

D d

COMPLETE IT

doll   desk
1   2
doughnut   drum
3   4

A <u>doll</u> is a toy that looks like a person.
   1

A <u>desk</u> is a place where a teacher may sit to
   2
do his or her paperwork.

A <u>doughnut</u> is a sweet food in the shape of a
     3
ring—round with a hole in the middle.

A <u>drum</u> is a musical instrument in a band,
   1
orchestra, or a parade that you beat with special
sticks.

Name _____   Date _____

© 1999 by Cynthia Conway Waring

Cloze Sentences . . . 2

D d

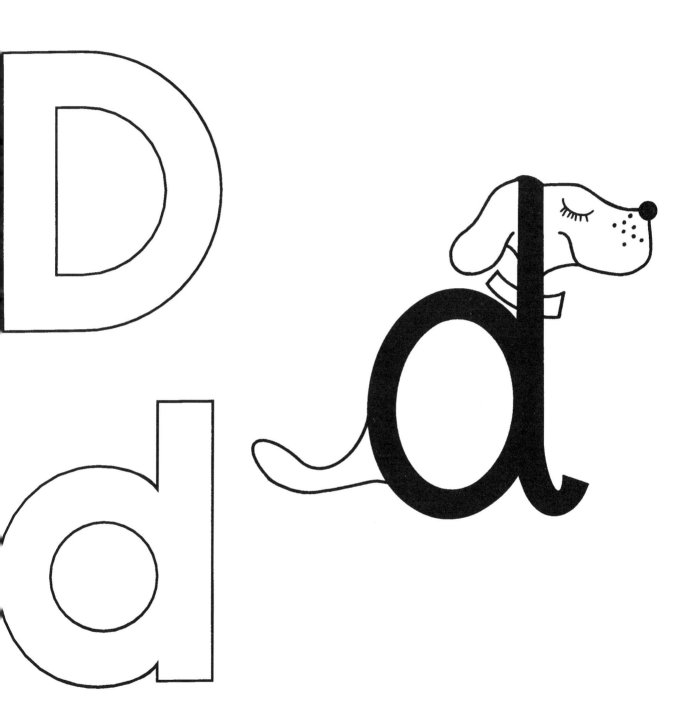

E e elephant

Teacher Reference

Annotated Book List

The Ant and the Elephant, Bill Peet (Boston: Houghton Mifflin Company, 1972). A series of grouchy and self-centered animals—ant, mud turtle, hornbill bird, giraffe, lion, and rhinoceros—refuse to help one another. When a kind elephant saves each of them from his or her predicament, not one thanks the elephant nor helps him when he is in trouble except the ant (and 95 thousand of his friends)!

The Blind Men and the Elephant, retold by Karen Backstein, illustrated by Annie Mitra (New York: Scholastic Inc., 1992). In this easy-to-read retelling of the Indian fable, six blind men who touch a different part of the animal cannot agree about what an elephant is like until they benefit from the prince's wisdom and come to understand that to know something one must know all of its parts.

Don't Leave an Elephant to Go and Chase a Bird, retold by James Berry, illustrated by Ann Grifalconi (New York: Simon & Schuster Children's Publishing Division, 1996). In this retelling of a tale from Ghana, West Africa, illustrated with colored illustrations suggested by traditional wood carvings and sculptures, after trading items with a series of people he meets, the trickster, Anancy the Spiderman, is distracted by a bird and misses out on his final trade, for an elephant, and must go home empty-handed.

Elephant, Judy Allen, illustrated by Tudor Humphries (Cambridge, Massachusetts: Candlewick Press, 1993). Her great-grandmother's ivory necklace with the elephants gives young Hannah a dream that helps her understand the experience of the African elephants whose lives were taken by her great-grandfather, a hunter who sold their tusks to ivory dealers. She is then compelled to ask forgiveness of an elephant at a game reserve by returning the necklace to her. Includes a fact sheet about African and Asian elelphants, information about dangers to elephants and efforts to protect them, and an address for sending questions to The Elephant Research Foundation.

Elephant: Eyewitness Books, Ian Redmond, photographed by Dave King (New York: Alfred A. Knopf, 1993). This informative book with colored photographs of elephants interacting with their environment and people presents the characteristics, family tree and living relatives, anatomy, habits, historical roles, and threats to survival of the huge mammal.

The Elephant Alphabet Book, Gene Yates (Chicago: Kidsbooks, Inc., 1995). Amusements and activities enjoyed by elephants, one for each letter of the alphabet, are celebrated in alliterative text and humorous illustrations in which an elephant's body forms the featured uppercase letter.

Elephant Families: Let's-Read-And-Find-Out Science, Arthur Dorros (New York: HarperCollins Publishers, 1994). Colored illustrations and simple text reveal physical characteristics, habits, types, and habitat of elephants in the context of the activities of a multigenerational family.

Elephants Aloft, Kathi Appelt, illustrated by Keith Baker (San Diego: Harcourt Brace & Company, 1993). One preposition in enlarged print on each illustrated double page describes a part of the journey in a hot air balloon of young elephants Rama and Raja who leave their home in Asia to visit their Aunt Rwanda in Africa.

The Elephant's Child, Rudyard Kipling, illustrated by Lorinda Bryan Cauley (San Diego: Harcourt Brace Jovanovich, 1983). This illustrated single tale selected from Kipling's *Just So Stories* is the story of the result of the elephant child's " 'satiable curiousity" about what the crocodile eats for dinner and explains why, as the result, elephants now have long trunks.

The Elephant's Child, Rudyard Kipling, illustrated by Jan Mogensen (New York: Crocodile Books, USA, 1988). Luminous watercolor paintings illustrate the details of this humorous pourquoi story, from Kipling's *Just So Stories*, of why, because of the elephant child's " 'satiable curiosity," all elephants now have long, useful trunks.

Ella, Bill Peet (Boston: Houghton Mifflin Company, 1964). Conceited Ella elephant runs away from the circus and returns, after months of being forced to do hard farm work, no longer spoiled and bad tempered.

Englebert the Elephant, Tom Paxton, illustrated by Steven Kellogg (New York: William Morrow & Company, Inc., 1990). By accident, Englebert the Elephant receives an invitation to the queen's ball, and there he dazzles everyone with his skill at dancing and his dainty appetite and manners at dinner. He is then honored as the queen's dancing partner and with a gift from her majesty herself, in this book introducing Englebert in rhyming verse.

Horton Hatches the Egg, Dr. Seuss (New York: Random House, 1940, 1968). Gentle and kind Horton the Elephant is the embodiment of faithfulness as he sits (and sits and sits . . . for fifty-one weeks), despite taunting and dangers, on the egg in the nest of a lazy bird who abandons it. His sterling qualities are rewarded, in the end, with the emergence of an elephant-bird that looks remarkably like him!

Horton Hears a Who!, Dr. Seuss (New York: Random House, 1954, 1982). Loyal and persistent Horton the Elephant (from *Horton Hatches the Egg* by the same author) defies the ridicule and threats from other animals to assert the integrity of all persons, even those too small to be seen, as he saves the inhabitants of the entire town of Whoville that live on a speck of dust.

How to Weigh an Elephant, Bob Barner (New York: Bantam Doubleday Dell, 1995). In this book designed for young children, readers observe a problem-solving approach of hypothesis formulation and testing to explore measurement (weight) and estimation, as an elephant uses a balance scale to determine which animals may ride together and which must ride singly in an elevator that can carry only his weight. Includes stickers and instructions for related activities extending the investigation of the concepts using common objects.

Just a Little Bit, Ann Tompert, illustrated by Lynn Munsinger (Boston: Houghton Mifflin Company, 1993). In hopes of enjoying a seesaw together, friends Elephant and Mouse ask a series of animals who happen by to sit on Mouse's end, but not until a small beetle adds its weight does the seesaw go up and down.

Little Elephant, Miela Ford, photographs by Tana Hoban (New York: Greenwillow Books, 1994). Single lines of text caption full-page photographs that capture the movements of a young elephant in a zoo that leaves its mother to enjoy playing in the water of a nearby pool and then returns to the safety of its mother's side.

My Friend Harry, Kim Lewis (Cambridge, Massachusetts: Candlewick Press, 1995). Harry, the stuffed elephant, begins to show wear after being constant companion to James through days and nights on his family's farm, on vacation, and even on the second day of school (because it was *Harry* who wasn't yet accustomed to being on his own).

Never Mail an Elephant, Mike Thaler, illustrated by Jerry Smath (Mahwah, New Jersey: Troll Communications L.L.C., 1994). It's a good thing that a young boy's cousin lives next door so he can make a last-minute delivery, because even after all his hard work—wrapping it in paper and securing it with string, marking the address, affixing *lots* of stamps, and stuffing it into the corner mailbox—he doesn't have any luck when he tries to mail her birthday present, a full-size elephant!

Never ***Ride Your Elephant to School***, Doug Johnson, illustrated by Abby Carter (New York: Henry Holt and Company, 1995). This humorous picture book warns the reader about some of the possible perils of taking an elephant to elementary school.

Ollie the Elephant, Burny Bos, illustrated by Hans de Beer (New York: North-South Books, 1989). Disappointed that he did not receive a baby brother for his birthday, Ollie the elephant sets out to find one. In the process, he experiences the way of life of several animals he meets on his way, becomes homesick and lost, and discovers to his delight, when he returns home, that his mother and father plan to have more children in the future.

Peanut Butter and Jelly: A Play Rhyme, illustrated by Nadine Bernard Westcott (New York: Penguin Books USA Inc., 1987). In this variation of a traditional play rhyme, five elephants help a brother, sister, and chef, who construct and eat a giant peanut butter and jelly sandwich made from scratch—from kneading the bread dough to squashing the peanuts and grapes. An author's note suggests hand and body actions to accompany the verses and refrain of the rhyme.

*A **Quiet Night In***, Jill Murphy (Cambridge, Massachusetts: Candlewick Press, 1993). In this fourth story about the Large family, Mrs. Large, the elephant, plans to put the four elephant children to bed early, so that she and their father can have a quiet night in to celebrate his birthday, but it turns out to be much quieter than she expected when the tired parents fall asleep on the couch before the children, who put themselves to bed.

The Rajah's Rice: A Mathematical Folktale from India, adapted by David Barry, illustrated by Donna Perrone (New York: W. H. Freeman and Company, 1994). A young girl from India, Chandra, the bather of the Rajah's elephants, uses her love for and knowledge of mathematics to collect from the greedy Rajah a reward of rice large enough to feed the starving villagers, plus ownership of the land they farm, for helping the elephants recover from grave illness. A note to parents and teachers explains the process of repeated doubling (exponential mathematics) on which this folktale is based.

The Right Number of Elephants, Jeff Sheppard, illustrated by Felicia Bond (New York: HarperCollins Publishers, 1990). A little girl determines the number of elephants appropriate for ten humorous situations in this counting book that counts down from 10 to 1.

17 Kings and 42 Elephants, Margaret Mahy, illustrated by Patricia MacCarthy (New York: Dial Books for Young Readers, 1972, 1987). Humorous rhyming verse, illustrated with batik paintings on silk, describes a procession of seventeen kings as they journey with forty-two elephants through the jungle.

SATO and the Elephants, Juanita Havill, illustrated by Jean and Mou-Sien Tseng (New York: Lothrop, Lee & Shepard Books, 1993). In a story based on the experiences of a modern Japanese ivory carver, when Sato, a master carver, discovers a bullet in the ivory he is carving, the painful reality of the slaughter of elephants for their tusks makes it impossible for him to do the work he loves using ivory, and he becomes a stone carver. A note from the author provides background information about her creation of the story and the killing of elephants for the sale of ivory.

The Story of Babar the Little Elephant, Jean De Brunhoff, translated from the French by Merle S. Haas (New York: Random House, 1933, 1960). The sophisticated ways of humans he learns in a nearby city, where Babar flees after his mother's death, cause the elephants in the forest to choose him as king upon his return, in the first book in a series of books about Babar.

The Trouble with Elephants, Chris Riddell (New York: HarperCollins Publishers, 1988). Despite the imagined troubles they bring, described in large print text with humorous fanciful illustrations, a little girl who treasures her stuffed elephant toy shows readers that elephants are extremely lovable.

Uncle Elephant, Arnold Lobel (New York: Harper & Row, Publishers, 1981). In an easy-to-read book with nine short chapters, a young elephant's loving and playful uncle takes care of him until his parents, lost at sea, return home.

The Way Home, Judith Benet Richardson, pictures by Salley Mavor (New York: Macmillan Publishing Company, 1994). The pictures, made in fabric relief (which combines soft sculpture, dyeing, wrapping, embroidery, and appliqué) distinguish this story of a wise elephant mother who teaches her young daughter, Savi, a gentle lesson about obedience. When Savi refuses to leave the beach at the end of the day, she leaves Savi a trail of bananas to lead the tired and hungry elephant to the safety of home! An author's note explains the process involved in creating the artwork for this book.

We'll Ride Elephants Through Brooklyn, Susan L. Roth (New York: Farrar Straus & Giroux, 1989). With the aid of brightly colored collage illustrations, a little girl describes in detail the events surrounding riding elephants in a parade through Brooklyn that celebrates her grandfather's return to health, a parade that Grandpa, fully recovered, is able to enjoy at the book's end.

Literature Extension Activities

1. Students dramatize—as a play with simple props, costumes, and setting—the story of *The Ant and the Elephant* after they have heard it read aloud.

2. After you share *Elephant,* by Judy Allen, with students, compose a group letter, or students can dictate or write individual letters and mail them to The Elephant Research Foundation, with questions they generate during the unit to which they are unable to discover answers themselves. *Note:* The Foundation replies to letters accompanied by a stamped, self-addressed envelope.

3. As you read aloud *The Elephant's Child*, students join in chorally as the repeated phrase "the great grey-green, greasy Limpopo River, all set about with fever-trees" recurs.

   With students, try your hand at painting, with watercolors, a scene on the banks of the Limpopo River or their favorite animals or scene from the book.

4. After you read **Never *Ride Your Elephant to School***, with your students, compare and contrast this book about an elephant with two books written by Laura Joffe Numeroff and illustrated by Felicia Bond that follow a similar pattern about a mouse and a moose: *If You Give a Mouse a Cookie* (New York: Scholastic Inc., 1985) in which, in this ultimate "if . . . then" book, a boy sets off a circular chain of events, which exhausts him and may continue indefinitely, when he gives a cookie to a mouse, and *If You Give a Moose a Muffin* (New York: Scholastic Inc., 1991) in which a boy starts a similar chain of events that may never stop when he gives a muffin to a hungry and artistic moose, who turns the house upside down with his enthusiasm.

5. After students enjoy several rereadings of the play rhyme **Peanut Butter and Jelly** with accompanying hand and body actions, make and eat peanut butter and jelly sandwiches with your students.

6. With students, create a class counting book in which they describe—in words and pictures—appropriate situations for 10 to 1 elephants patterned after **The Right Number of Elephants.**

Items for the Mystery Box

Inedible Items: echo *(Note:* Say words, phrases, and sentences into the Mystery Box and make your voice sound like an echo coming out of the box.), egg (decorated or plastic), elastic band, elastic (hair), elbow, **elephant**, elevator, eleven, elf, elk, embroidery, empty *(Note:* Show the Mystery Box at the end of the activity!), engine (fire), engine (train), engine (vehicle), entrance or enter sign, envelope, eraser (chalkboard), eraser (pencil), escalator, exit sign

Edible Items: egg drop soup, egg foo yong, eggplant, eggnog, egg rolls, eggs (fried, green with ham!, hard boiled, poached, scrambled), egg salad, enchiladas, endive, English muffins, escarole

Rhymes, Songs, Fingerplays, and Tongue Twisters

Elephant Theme

A grasshopper stepped on an elephant's toe: 51

Daddy's taking us to the zoo tomorrow: 17

The elephant carries a great big trunk: 51

The elephant goes like this, like that: 12, 29

Elephant/Right foot, left foot, see me go: 48

Elephants walking: 51

Eletelephony/Once there was an elephant: 51

*Eleven elephants elegantly equipped (Tongue Twister)

Here we go to the zoo in the park: 3

*Miss Mary Mack, Mack, Mack, She asked her mother, mother, mother: 36, 51, 53, 55, 79

Old Noah did build himself an ark: 3, 77

One little elephant went out one day: 29

Tongue Twisters: 1, 13, 60, 74, 80

Letter-Sound e (e)

*Jenny Wren last week was wed
Tongue Twisters: 60, 80

Cloze Sentences

1. An <u>entrance</u> sign tells you a way you can go into a building.

   (A sign that tells you a way you can go into a building is an <u>entrance</u> sign.)

2. An <u>egg</u> has a shell, and it is laid by a hen or a bird.

   (A thing with a shell that a hen or a bird lays is an <u>egg</u>.)

3. An <u>exit</u> sign tells you a way you can go out of a building.

   (A sign that tells you a way you can go out of a building is an <u>exit</u> sign.)

4. An <u>elephant</u> is a big, gray animal with a trunk.

   (A big, gray animal with a trunk is an <u>elephant</u>.)

1. A box is <u>empty</u> when it has nothing in it.

   (When it has nothing in it, a box is <u>empty</u>.)

2. An <u>envelope</u> is what you put a letter in when you mail it.

   (When you mail a letter, you put it in an <u>envelope</u>.)

3. An <u>engine</u> is under the hood of a car, and it is the part of the car that makes it go.

   (The part of a car that is under the hood and that makes the car go is an <u>engine</u>.)

4. Your <u>elbow</u> is the part of your arm that you can bend.

   (The part of your arm that you can bend is your <u>elbow</u>.)

E e

She asked her mother, mother, mother,

For fifteen cents, cents, cents,

To see the elephant, elephant, elephant,

Jump over the fence, fence, fence.

Name _____   Date _____

E e

Eleven elephants elegantly equipped

Eleven elephants elegantly equipped

Eleven elephants elegantly equipped

Name _____   Date _____

Rhymes . . . 2

E e

JENNY WREN

Jenny Wren last week was wed,
And built her nest in grandpa's shed;
Look in next week and you shall see
Two little eggs, and maybe three.

Name _____   Date _____

E e

COMPLETE IT

entrance   egg
1   2
exit   elephant
3   4

An <u>entrance</u> sign tells you a way you can go
1
into a building.

An <u>egg</u> has a shell, and it is laid by a hen or a
2
bird.

An <u>exit</u> sign tells you a way you can go out of a
3
building.

An <u>elephant</u> is a big, gray animal with a trunk.
4

Name _____ Date _____

Cloze Sentences . . . 1

E e

COMPLETE IT

empty
1

envelope
2

engine
3

elbow
4

A box is <u>empty</u> when it has nothing in it.
        1

An <u>envelope</u> is what you put a letter in when
       2
you mail it.

An <u>engine</u> is under the hood of a car, and it is
      3
the part of the car that makes it go.

Your <u>elbow</u> is the part of your arm that you can
      4
bend.

Name _____   Date _____

F f fish

TEACHER REFERENCE

Annotated Book List

Amazing Fish: Eyewitness Juniors, Mary Ling, photographed by Jerry Young (New York: Alfred A. Knopf, 1991). Collections of colored photographs and drawings amplify text that provides information about the physical characteristics of fish (including color, shape, and body parts) and their habits (in particular, feeding and hunting) with special focus sections on sharks, rays, eels, sea horses, and salmon.

Anna's Athabaskan Summer, Arnold Griese, illustrated by Charles Ragins (Honesdale, Pennsylvania: Boyds Mills Press, 1995). Anna learns about the traditions and beliefs of her Athabaskan people while she and her mother and grandmother spend the summer at the fish camp, and she looks forward to sharing her knowledge and understanding with her sister or brother soon to be born.

Big Al, Andrew Clements, illustrated by Yoshi (New York: Simon & Schuster Books for Young Readers, 1988). Because he is scary-looking, none of the other fish will befriend kindhearted and lonely Al, who makes a number of failed attempts to change his appearance. Just as he is about to lose hope, Al bravely saves some fish caught in a net who come to know and appreciate their new friend's true nature.

Blue Sea, Robert Kalan, illustrated by Donald Crews (New York: William Morrow & Company, Inc., 1979). In this book with a small number of words and a repetitive, predictable pattern, a little fish escapes and leaves behind the big, bigger, and biggest fish, who pursue and attempt to eat him, by swimming through progressively smaller holes.

Brian Wildsmith's Fishes, Brian Wildsmith (New York: Franklin Watts, Inc., 1968). "A battery of barracuda," "a fleet of bass," and a variety of other fish labeled with the specific name that applies to their group swim across the full-page colored paintings that illustrate this book. An author's note explains the origin of several terms for groups of fish.

The Carp in the Bathtub, Barbara Cohen, illustrated by Joan Halpern (New York: Lothrop, Lee and Shepard, 1972). Every year, Leah and Harry's mother buys the carp for her famous gefilte fish live a week before Passover and keeps it fresh in the bathtub. The year Leah is nine, the carp is different somehow, so he becomes the children's friend

125

named Joe, and they join forces to save him until their wise father, who recognizes their desire for a pet, brings home a cat.

Fish Eyes: A Book You Can Count On, Lois Ehlert (San Diego: Harcourt Brace Jovanovich, Inc., 1990). The "I" of the story turns itself into a small fish that invites the reader to follow as it sees an ascending number (from one to ten) of brightly colored fish (labeled with a numeral and descriptive phrase, with cut-out eyes that reveal colors on the preceding and following pages) and adds the number of fish on each page to one fish, itself.

Fish for Supper, M. B. Goffstein (New York: E. P. Dutton, 1976). With an economy of text and strokes of the pen in the uncluttered line drawings, the author presents the story of grandmother's day fishing on a lake and her subsequent fish dinner, her daily custom.

Fish Is Fish, Leo Lionni (New York: Alfred A. Knopf, 1970). When a tadpole becomes a frog, he is no longer content to remain in the pond with his friend minnow, so he ventures on land. When he returns, the minnow imagines the things the frog describes as unusual fish (with bird wings, cow horns and udder, and people clothing). After he is rescued by the frog when he leaps out of the pond to see them himself, the minnow admits the differences between fish and amphibians and is content with his life in the water.

Freaky Fish Facts: An Amazing Nature Pop-Up Book, illustrations by Paul Mirocha (New York: HarperCollins Publishers). A short passage describes a fascinating habit of each of five fish with movable parts that pop out of this informative book: males that carry gaff-topsail catfish eggs and young in their mouths, flashlight fish with glowing bacteria in pouches under their eyes, archer fish that shoot insects with water, catfish that use breathing pouches as they "walk" on land, and goosefish that use spines on their backs like fishing rods to catch fish to eat.

The Girl Who Swam with the Fish: An Athabascan Legend, Michelle Renner, illustrated by Christine Cox (Anchorage: Alaska Northwest Books, 1995). Waiting for the salmon to return to the Alaskan river where her family have made their seasonal fishing camp, a girl falls into the water and, changed into a salmon, learns about the fish and how they desire to be treated. An author's note traces the sources of this legend.

Go Fish, Mary Stolz, illustrated by Pat Cummings (New York: HarperCollins Publishers, 1991). Thomas and Grandfather (introduced in ***Storm in the Night*** by the same author) enjoy sharing a day fishing together in the Gulf of Mexico, fish dinner, a game of "Go Fish," and an evening on the porch with a story handed down through the generations by their ancestors from Benin, Africa—the Yorubas—and embellished by Grandfather.

Louis the Fish, Arthur Yorinks, pictures by Richard Egielski (New York: Farrar, Straus & Giroux, 1980). Obsessed with fish, Louis, son and grandson of butchers, is happy to get away from two things that he hates—meat and his job as a butcher—when, finally, he becomes a fish, free at last to swim around in a tank at a pet store.

The Magic Fish, Freya Littledale, illustrated by Winslow Pinney Pels (New York: Scholastic, 1966, 1985). When a poor fisherman puts back a fish he caught who is really a prince who can grant wishes, his wife greedily demands more and more wishes for wealth and power until the fish sends her and the fisherman back to their original life in an old hut.

McElligot's Pool, Dr. Seuss (New York: Random House, 1947, 1974). Patient young Marco contemplates the possibility of an underground connection between McElligot's Pool, where he is fishing, and the sea and imagines the fantastic fish that he might catch if he waits long enough.

The Memory Box, Mary Bahr, illustrated by David Cunningham (Norton Grove, Illinois: Albert Whitman & Company, 1992). During Zach's vacation fishing at the lake with his grandparents, after Gramps learns that he has Alzheimer's disease, he and Gramps start to fill a Memory Box with paper scraps, with old and new memories, and stories written on them, photographs, and souvenirs to help them all remember.

A Million Fish ... More or Less, Patricia C. McKissack, illustrated by Dena Schutzer (New York: Alfred A. Knopf, Inc., 1992). Inspired by the tall tales Papa-Daddy and Elder Abbajon tell about the strange events that occur while fishing on the bayou, young Hugh Thomas begins to tell them a tale about his day during which strange events caused him to lose all but three of the million (more or less) fish he'd caught.

My Visit to the Aquarium, Aliki Brandenberg (New York: HarperCollins Publishers, 1993). The detailed illustrations in this book that presents three young children's visit to an aquarium are a celebration of diversity—not only in the fish and other aquatic life from around the world but also in the people who explore the aquarium.

The Ocean Alphabet Book, Jerry Pallotta, illustrated by Frank Mazzola, Jr. (Boston: Quinlan Press, 1986). Interesting facts and full-page illustrations fill the pages of this informational alphabet book about fish and other creatures from the sea.

Ocean Parade: A Counting Book, Patricia MacCarthy (New York: Dial Books for Young Readers, 1990). Batik paintings on silk picture a variety of fish and the adjectives that describe their number, colors, size, patterns, and shapes.

On the Riverbank, Charles Temple, illustrated by Melanie Hall (Boston: Houghton Mifflin Company, 1992). In rollicking rhyming verse perfect for read-aloud, it's June, school has just let out, and a young boy and his parents enjoy a moonlit evening cat-fishing.

Picture Science Fish, Joy Richardson (New York: Franklin Watts, Inc., 1993). Full-paged color photographs illustrate this informational book about a variety of fish, and easy-to-read text in bold type describes their habits and characteristics. Contains a simple index.

The Rainbow Fish, Marcus Pfister (New York: North-South Books, 1992). Shiny silver highlights with designs that form the fish scales distinguish the illustrations in the story of Rainbow Fish whose vanity about his unique sparkling scales alienates everyone until he gives all but one of his scales to the other fish, and he learns the joy of friendship.

A River Dream, Allen Say (Boston: Houghton Mifflin Company, 1988). In a gentle story illustrated with Say's remarkable watercolors, the fly box that his uncle sends him while Mark is sick with a high fever reminds Mark of their shared fishing adventures the previous summer and creates a fantasy fishing adventure that includes his uncle and begins, magically, in a river where the street had been outside Mark's bedroom window.

Rosie's Fishing Trip, Amy Hest, illustrated by Paul Howard (Cambridge, Massachusetts: Candlewick Press, 1994). Young Rosie happily returns the small fish that she catches to its home in the pond where she and Grandpa share the more important aspects of a fishing trip—a picnic breakfast, his poems, her drawings, and, most important of all, each other's company.

A Salmon for Simon, Betty Waterton, illustrated by Ann Blades (New York: Atheneum, 1980). As the salmon swim past the island near the west coast of Canada where he lives, Simon makes a difficult decision when, rather than keep his catch, he digs a channel to the sea to save the life of a fish dropped at his feet by an eagle.

Swimmy, Leo Lionni (New York: Random House, 1963). In a classic story about the power of cooperation, a small fish named Swimmy helps a school of small fish save themselves from a big fish by swimming together to look like a giant fish, with Swimmy as the eye.

Today I'm Going Fishing with My Dad, N. L. Sharp, pictures by Chris L. Demarest (Honesdale, Pennsylvania: Boyds Mills Press, Inc., 1993). A young boy doesn't really enjoy fishing; in fact, there are many things he remembers that he *hates* about it, but he enjoys the predictability of the traditions they share and, most of all, the treasure of time alone with his dad.

Tommy's Mommy's Fish, Nancy Dingman Watson, illustrated by Thomas Aldren Dingman Watson (New York: Viking, 1971, 1996). Tommy learns about his mother's love from a gift he does *not* give her for her birthday when the striped bass he tries to catch for her until after dark gets away, and he discovers that he is relieved.

The Underwater Alphabet Book, Jerry Pallotta, illustrated by Edgar Stewart (Watertown, Massachusetts: Charlesbridge Publishing, 1991). This alphabet book provides information about the fish and other animals that live among the corals in a coral reef.

What About My Goldfish?, Pamela D. Greenwood, illustrated by Jennifer Plecas (New York: Clarion Books, 1993). In this book with short chapters, when Jamie's family moves to a new city, his concern for and the company of his pet dog and goldfish help him make the adjustment and new friends.

What's It Like to Be a Fish?: Let's-Read-and-Find-Out Science, Wendy Pfeffer, illustrated by Holly Keller (New York: HarperCollins Publishers, 1996). The informational book describes ways in which a fish is designed for life underwater—including a close look at the design and functions of body parts and feeding habits—and provides instructions for preparing a goldfish bowl.

When I Was Little, Toyomi Igus, illustrated by Higgins Bond (Orange, New Jersey: Just Us Books, 1992). Leaving his city home to go fishing every summer with Grandpa Will is Noel's favorite activity, and it is during these times that his grandfather shares stories about his childhood.

Where's That Fish?, Barbara Brenner and Bernice Chardiet, illustrated by Carol Schwartz (New York: Scholastic Inc., 1994). In this Hide & Seek Science book, each double-page underwater illustration includes an invitation to the reader to find a number of the featured fish described in a short text passage and an "It's a Fact" section that provides additional information.

Literature Extension Activities

1. Inspired by ***Brian Wildsmith's Fishes,*** and with your support, students think of the terms for groups of animals other than fish—a herd of cows or horses; a flock of birds, ducks, or geese; and a litter of kittens or puppies, for example—and make an illustrated book of their discoveries in addition to a variety of groups of fish.

2. As Thomas and Grandfather do in ***Go Fish***, enjoy a game of "Go Fish" with your students. Simple directions for this classic card game, plus strategy hints and variations, can be found in ***The Book of Cards for Kids*** by Gail MacColl, illustrations by Simms Taback (New York: Workman Publishing, 1992).

3. After you read and discuss ***The Memory Box*** with students, begin a Memory Box for the school year. Place in a special box written or dictated and illustrated old and new class memories and stories, photographs, and souvenir objects to help students celebrate and remember their times together.

4. If possible, enjoy a field trip to an aquarium with your students, then compare and contrast your visit with that of the three children in ***My Visit to the Aquarium.***

5. After they enjoy ***Ocean Parade: A Counting Book***, students, in pairs, each draw a number of the same type of fish on a piece of paper without showing their picture to their partners. They then take turns describing their fish picture for the partner to draw, including the following information: number, colors, sizes, patterns, and shapes. The partners reverse roles. When the second directed picture is completed, the partners compare original and directed pictures. After all pairs of students com-

plete the activity, come together with your students in a group and discuss their experiences during the activity and the importance of describing words (adjectives) in conveying in detail how something looks.

6. As you read **On the Riverbank** aloud, you and the students move your bodies, clap your hands, or tap your feet to the irresistible rhythm of the rhyming verses.

7. After you share **When I Was Little** in read-aloud, have students create their own books contrasting the present with when they were younger, alternating illustrations— black and white for the past and colored for the present—as in the book by Toyomi Igus.

Items for the Mystery Box

Inedible Items: fairy, fan, farmer, feather, feet (animal, human), feet (measuring—on measuring tape), felt, fence, fern, fiddle, file (fingernail), file (tool), fingerpaint, fin, finger, fire engine, fire extinguisher, fire fighter, fireplace, first (prize ribbon, medal, trophy), **fish**, fishing pole, five, flag, flamingo, flashlight, flower, flute, fly, foot (animal, human), foot (measuring—on a ruler or measuring tape), football, fork, fossil, four, fox, frame, frog, fruit (assorted), frying pan, funnel, fur

Edible Items: farfel, felafel, feta cheese, Fig Newtons®, figs, fish (tuna), flan, flapjacks, fortune cookies, frajitas, frankfurters, French fries, French toast, fried rice, fritters, frosting (on cupcakes or graham crackers), fruit (variety), fruitcake, fudge, fudgicles

Rhymes, Songs, Fingerplays, and Tongue Twisters

Fish Theme

Dance to your daddy: 29, 32, 33, 34, 62, 73
Down by the river: 4
Fishes swim in clear water: 5
Fishy, fishy in the brook: 5, 34, 46, 51
*Five Frenchmen foolishly fishing for flies (Tongue Twister)
Five little fishies swimming in a pool: 78
*Little Tommy Tittlemouse: 5, 25, 28, 33, 34, 40, 46, 50, 73, 76

Oh, a-hunting we will go: 44, 47, 79
*One, two, three, four, five: 3, 14, 25, 28, 32, 34, 39, 41, 46, 50, 51, 73, 76, 79
Terence McDiddler: 5
There was once a fish: 5
Three jolly fishermen: 55
Tongue Twisters: 13, 60, 80

Letter-Sound f (f)

Tongue Twisters: 1, 7, 13, 60, 74, 80

Cloze Sentences

1. Five <u>fingers</u> are something you have on your hand.
   (On your hand you have five <u>fingers</u>.)
2. A <u>frog</u> is an animal that lives near water, jumps, and looks like a toad.
   (An animal that lives near water, jumps, and looks like a toad is a <u>frog</u>.)
3. A <u>fish</u> is an animal that has **fins** and that swims in water.
   (An animal that has **fins** and that swims in water is a <u>fish</u>.)
4. On your <u>face</u> is where you wear a smile when something is **funny**.
   (When something is **funny**, you wear a smile on your <u>face</u>.).

1. <u>Fur</u> that is soft is something that cats have on their bodies.
   (On the bodies of cats is something soft called <u>fur</u>.)
2. <u>Feathers</u> are something that birds have on their bodies. They do not have **fur**.
   (Birds do not have **fur** on their bodies. They have <u>feathers</u>.)
3. A <u>fork</u>, a knife, and a spoon are things you may use when you eat **food** at a meal.
   (When you eat **food** at a meal, you may use a knife, a spoon, and a <u>fork</u>.)
4. On a <u>farm</u>, you may find cows, sheep, chickens, and pigs living together.
   (You may **find** cows, sheep, chickens, and pigs living together on a <u>farm</u>.)

F f

One, two, three, four, five,

Once I caught a fish alive;

Six, seven, eight, nine, ten,

I have let it go again.

Why did you let it go?

Because it bit my finger so.

Which finger did it bite?

The little finger on the right.

Name _____   Date _____

F f

Little Tommy Tittlemouse
Lived in a little house;
He caught fishes
In other men's ditches.

Name _____   Date _____

F f

Five Frenchmen foolishly fishing for flies

Five Frenchmen foolishly fishing for flies

Five Frenchmen foolishly fishing for flies

Name _____   Date _____

Rhymes . . . 3

F f

COMPLETE IT

fingers	frog
1	2
fish	face
3	4

Five <u>fingers</u> are something you have on your
      1
hand.

A <u>frog</u> is an animal that lives near water, jumps,
    2
and looks like a toad.

A <u>fish</u> is an animal that has fins and that swims
    3
in water.

On your <u>face</u> is where you wear a smile when
        4
something is funny.

Name _____ Date _____

F f

COMPLETE IT

Fur	Feathers
1	2
fork	farm
3	4

<u>Fur</u> that is soft is something that cats have on
  1
their bodies.

<u>Feathers</u> are something that birds have on their
    2
bodies. They do not have fur.

A <u>fork</u>, a knife, and a spoon are things you may
   3
use when you eat food at a meal.

On a <u>farm</u>, you may find cows, sheep, chickens,
    4
and pigs living together.

Name _____ Date _____

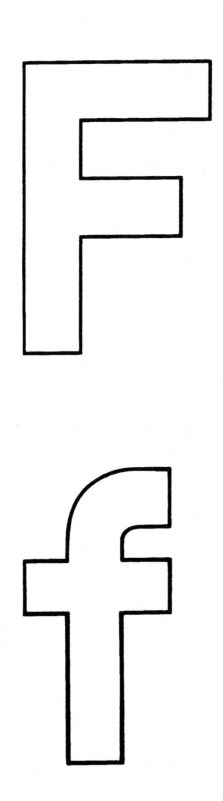

G g *goat*

TEACHER REFERENCE

Annotated Book List

Animal Fact/Animal Fable, Seymour Simon, illustrated by Diane de Groat (New York: Crown Publishers, Inc., 1979). This colorfully and accurately illustrated book presents scientific observations and factual information about the behavior of a variety of animals in an unusual and engaging format. For each animal, a true or false statement is presented on a right-hand page; the reader guesses whether it is a fact or a fable (fiction) and turns the page to find out. In "**Goats Will Eat Almost Anything**," the myth that goats eat tin cans is traced to their tendency to eat the glue on the can labels, and information is provided about the factual food preferences of goats.

The Goat in the Rug, as told to Charles L. Blood and Martin Link by Geraldine, illustrated by Nancy Winslow Parker (New York: Macmillan Publishing Company, 1976). Geraldine the goat describes each step in the process of making her mohair into a Navaho rug—clipping, washing and drying, carding, spinning, dyeing, and weaving. Contains a glossary of vocabulary with diagrams.

Goat's Trail, Brian Wildsmith (New York: Alfred A. Knopf, 1986). Cut-out windows and doors allow readers to look ahead and back at the illustrations accompanying the story of a wild goat, lonely in his mountain home, who causes a noisy uproar in the town in the valley he visits when he frees and takes with him all of the animals he meets on his way.

Gregory, the Terrible Eater, Mitchell Sharmat, illustrated by Jose Aruego and Ariane Dewey (New York: Scholastic Inc., 1980). Gregory the goat worries his parents when he refuses to eat the cans, boxes, and bottle caps they offer him and prefers to eat fruits and vegetables, but—with the help of Dr. Ram and a plan of their own—mother and father goat help their family reach a mealtime compromise.

The Magic Tablecloth, the Magic Goat, and the Hitting Stick, Freya Littledale, illustrated by Alfred Olschewski (New York: Scholastic, 1971, 1972). Olschewski's illustrations interpret Littledale's text for the "Peter and the North Wind" story of the North Wind's provision for the basic needs of a poor boy and his mother through three magic objects—a cloth, a goat, and a stick.

Over the Green Hills, Rachel Isadora (New York: Greenwillow Books, 1992). Zolani ties a gift of a wet sack of mussels onto the back of one of their strong young goats and, with his mother and baby Noma, sets out across the Transkei, on the east coast of South Africa, to visit his Grandma Zindzi, enjoying the company of friends and the beauty of the countryside as they go.

Peter and the North Wind:* Retold from the Norse Tale *The Lad Who Went to the North Wind, Freya Littledale, illustrated by Troy Howell (New York: Scholastic, 1971, 1988). After it blows their flour away, Peter goes to the North Wind to get the flour back and receives a magic cloth that gives food, a magic goat that makes gold, and a magic stick that hits on command and protects Peter from an innkeeper who tries to steal his magic objects.

The Rough, Gruff Goat Brothers Rap, Bernice and Jon Chardiet, illustrated by J. C. Suares (New York: Scholastic, 1993). This contemporary interpretation of the traditional "Three Billy Goats Gruff" story, with the troll as the keeper of a toll bridge, is told in rhyme and set to rap rhythm with background music and chorus on a companion audiotape.

The Summer of Stanley, Natalie Kinsey-Warnock, illustrated by Donald Gates (New York: Cobblehill Books/Dutton, 1997). As if things weren't difficult enough in 1945, with her father fighting in the war, Molly's grandfather gives her a *goat* for her ninth birthday! Molly's disappointment and the troubles Stanley, the goat, causes around the farm are soon forgotten, however, when he saves Molly's younger brother from drowning.

The Three Billy Goats Gruff, P. C. Asbjornsen and J. E. Moe, taken from the translation of G. W. Dasent, illustrated by Marcia Brown (San Diego: Harcourt Brace Jovanovich, 1957, 1985). On their way to the hillside to eat, three billy goats outwit a hungry troll who lives under the bridge they must cross. They persuade him to let the smaller two pass by, and the third and largest goat tosses the troll into the river.

The Three Billy Goats Gruff, Paul Galdone (New York: Clarion Books, 1973). The details and perspective of Galdone's illustrations capture the drama of the story of three billy goat brothers who outsmart the ugly troll by persuading him to wait to eat the third goat, who is the largest—and strong enough to toss the troll into the river.

The Three Billy Goats GRUFF, retold by Ellen Rudin, illustrated by Lilian Obligado (Racine, Washington: Western Publishing Company, Inc., 1982). In a small book designed for young readers to hold, when the littlest Billy Goat Gruff cannot wait any longer to cross the bridge to reach the field of grass on the other side of the stream, his two bigger brothers accompany him—a good thing, since the biggest goat is able to protect them all from the mean troll who lives under the bridge.

The Three Billy Goats Gruff, retold and illustrated by Janet Stevens (San Diego: Harcourt Brace & Company, 1987). In this large picture book version of the traditional tale illustrated in watercolor, colored pencil, and pastel, the goats don clothing appropriate to their age and size (with the littlest in diapers and with a pacifier) to help them convince the troll that he should wait for the bigger and fatter third billy goat Gruff (who wears a black leather jacket and dark sunglasses)!

The Three Bill Goats Gruff: A Norwegian Folktale, illustrated by Ellen Appleby (New York: Scholastic,1984). In turn, the three billy goats—from youngest to oldest— cross a bridge under which a mean troll lives, and the first two are able to persuade him to wait for the last and largest goat, who puts an end to him.

The Three Bill Goats Gruff: A Norwegian Folk Tale with Woodcuts, Susan Blair (New York: Scholastic, 1963). Blair's detailed woodcut illustrations interpret the well- known story of three billy goats who use their wits and their largest brother's strength to outsmart and overcome the troll so that they can pass over his bridge on their way to the hillside to eat.

Woolly Sheep and Hungry Goats: Rookie Read-About Science, Allan Fowler (Danbury, Connecticut: Children's Press, 1993). Simple, brief, easy-to-read text in enlarged type and accompanying brightly colored photographs provide information about wild goats and sheep in the Rocky Mountains, including physical description, habits, food, and products. Includes a word-and-photograph glossary of important words and an index.

Literature Extension Activities

1. While and after you read ***Gregory, the Terrible Eater***, discuss with students healthy food (people food) and junk food (goat food) as they are presented in the book. Students then sort items you present in a picnic basket into the following two categories: *Healthy or People Food* (such as carrots, apples, and grapes) and *Junk or Goat Food* (such as soap, tin can, and string). Students then eat some of the healthy food, if they choose.

   Discuss with students the food of real goats, and challenge the accuracy of the premise that goats eat trash on which ***Gregory, the Terrible Eater*** is based. Use such resource books and materials as "**Goats Will Eat Almost Anything**" in ***Animal Fact/Animal Fable*** and ***Woolly Sheep and Hungry Goats***, suggested for this unit. Students discover that goats prefer (as does Gregory goat) to eat fruit, vegetables, grass, plant leaves, and tree bark and that goats chew tin can labels to reach the glue but do not eat the metal cans.

2. An author's note accompanying ***Over the Green Hills*** provides information about the Transkei, designated by the government of South Africa as one of the black rural homelands considered an independent state, and about some of the vocabulary specific to that area. With students, locate on a map or globe the Transkei on the east coast of South Africa, on the Indian Ocean.

   After students enjoy ***Over the Green Hills*** in read-aloud, have them share stories—in discussion and in illustration—of trips they have made to visit their grandmothers (or other special family members or friends).

LETTER-SOUND UNITS   **141**

As Rachel Isadora describes in her book, the stories include information about their form of transportation, gifts they have taken with them, people they have seen during their trip, the appearance of the countryside as they traveled, and details of their arrival.

3. With students, listen and move to the audiotape of ***The Rough, Gruff Goat Brothers Rap*** (available through Scholastic Inc.) as they read along with the book.

4. As you share some or all of the seven versions of the "Three Billy Goats Gruff" story suggested for this unit, discuss, compare, and contrast the illustrations with students. Students choose their favorite illustrations for the tale, and they make puppets in the style of that version and present a shadow play of the story. They make a puppet for each character and for the narrator (that looks like the student narrating) and glue it onto chopsticks, craft or popsicle sticks, or pencils. The theater can be made by draping a single thickness of cloth over two chairs of equal height and placing a light source—a flashlight or lamp (a high-intensity lamp that is movable works well)—4" to 6" behind the cloth screen. Puppeteers sit behind the chairs and hold the puppets so that the bottoms of the characters' feet, when walking, are at the level of the chairs.

5. As you read ***Woolly Sheep and Hungry Goats,*** record with students, in list, data matrix, or Venn diagram form, what they know or discover about the similarities and differences between goats and sheep. Include information about where they live, physical description, habits, food, products, and names given males, females, and babies or young.

Items for the Mystery Box

Whenever possible, select items for this unit that are **g**old, **g**ray, or **g**reen in color.

Inedible Items: galoshes, game, garbage can, gas tank, gate, ghost, gift (wrapped box), girl, glass (drinking), glasses (eye), glider, glitter, globe, glove, glue, **goat**, goblet, goggles, gold, goldfish, goose, gopher, gorilla, gourd, graph, grass, grasshopper, guitar, gull (sea), gum, gumball

Edible Items: garbanzo beans (chick peas), garlic, garlic bread, gazpacho, gefilte fish, goat's cheese, goat's milk, gooseberries, gorp, goulash, graham crackers, granola, grapefruit, grape leaves (stuffed), grapes, grinders, guacamole, guava, gumdrops

Rhymes, Songs, Fingerplays, and Tongue Twisters

Goat Theme

Bill Grogan's goat: 27
Counting the Goats/Where is the goat? It's time for milking: 27
*Hush, little baby, don't say a word: 5, 6, 17, 21, 22, 29, 34, 51, 53, 61, 73, 76, 78
I went up the high hill: 46, 73
Mary had a William goat: 27
Oh, a hunting we will go: 44, 47, 79
Old Hogan's goat was feeling fine: 51
Phoebe rode a nanny goat: 28
Poor old Robinson Crusoe!: 5, 28, 33, 34, 50

Tongue Twisters: 13

Letter-Sound g (g)

Bubble gum, bubble gum, chew and blow: 4
Here are Grandma's glasses: 12, 14, 78
*Old Mother Goose/Old Mother Goose, when: 5, 28, 33, 34, 39, 40, 50, 73, 76
Three gray geese in a green field grazing: 5
*To market, to market, to buy a fat pig: 3, 5, 25, 28, 33, 34, 42, 46, 49, 50, 58, 76
Tongue Twisters: 1, 7, 13, 60, 74, 80

Cloze Sentences

1. Cars **go** on a **green** signal and stop at a red si**g**nal.
   (At a red signal, cars stop. At a **green** signal, cars **go**.)
2. Some of you are **girls**, and some of you are boys.
   (Some of you are boys, and some of you are **girls**.)
3. **Gas** in the tank makes a car **go**.
   (For a car to be able to **go**, it must have **gas** in the tank.)
4. I use a **glass** when I drink water, milk, juice, or soda.
   (When I drink water, milk, juice, or soda, I use a **glass**.)

1. **Gum** is something sticky and **g**ooey that I chew, and I can blow bubbles with it.
   (Something sticky and **g**ooey that I can chew and blow into bubbles is **g**um.)
2. I can use **glue** or tape to stick two thin**g**s to**g**ether.
   (I can stick two thin**g**s to**g**ether with tape or **g**lue.)
3. **Goats** are animals that some people think like to eat tin cans. Actually, **g**oats only chew the cans to reach the **g**lue on the labels!

(Animals that some people think like to eat tin cans are **g**oats. Actually, **g**oats only chew the cans to reach the **g**lue on the labels!)

4. In a **g**arden you can plant seeds and **g**row plants.

    (You can plant seeds and **g**row plants in a **g**arden.)

G g

Hush, little baby, don't say a word,

Papa's going to buy you a mocking bird.

If the mocking bird won't sing,

Papa's going to buy you a diamond ring.

If the diamond ring turns to brass,

Papa's going to buy you a looking-glass.

If the looking-glass gets broke,

Papa's going to buy you a billy-goat.

If that billy-goat runs away,

Papa's going to buy you another today.

Name _____   Date _____

G g

OLD MOTHER GOOSE

Old Mother Goose, when
She wanted to wander.
Would ride through the air
On a very fine gander.

Name _____   Date _____

G g

To market, to market, to buy a fat pig,
　　Home again, home again, jiggety-jig.

To market, to market, to buy a fat hog,
　　Home again, home again, jiggety-jog.

Name _____   Date _____

G g

COMPLETE IT

go
1

girls
2

Gas
3

glass
4

Cars <u>go</u> on a green signal and stop at a red
     1
signal.

Some of you are <u>girls</u>, and some of you are
          2
boys.

<u>Gas</u> in the tank makes a car go.
 3

I use a <u>glass</u> when I drink water, milk, juice, or
     4
soda.

Name _____   Date _____

G g

COMPLETE IT

Gum	glue
1	2
Goats	garden
3	4

<u>Gum</u> is something sticky and gooey that I chew,
1
and I can blow bubbles with it.

I can use <u>glue</u> or tape to stick two things
2
together.

<u>Goats</u> are animals that some people think like
3
to eat tin cans. Actually, goats only chew the cans
to reach the glue on the labels!

In a <u>garden</u> you can plant seeds and grow
4
plants.

Name _____   Date _____

H h   hat

TEACHER REFERENCE

Annotated Book List

Abe Lincoln's Hat, Martha Brenner, illustrated by Donald Cook (New York: Random House, Inc., 1994). This easy-to-read book describes a number of true humorous and serious incidents in the life of Abraham Lincoln while he was a lawyer, ran for senator, and became President, including stories about his tall, black hat, in which he kept important papers. Includes photographs of some of the people featured in the stories.

Aunt Flossie's Hats (and Crab Cakes Later), Elizabeth Fitzgerald Howard, illustrated by James Ransome (New York: Clarion Books, 1991). When Susan and her sister Sarah visit their great-great-aunt Flossie on a Sunday afternoon, they enjoy the stories she tells (inspired by the hats in her collection) and a special meal of crab cakes.

Caps for Sale, Esphyr Slobodkina (Reading, Massachusetts: Addison-Wesley Publishing Company, Inc., 1940, 1947, 1968). In this classic story with repeated lines, while a peddler naps under a tree, monkeys take all of the caps he carried on his head. The monkeys finally return his caps when he throws down his own cap in anger and they, in imitation, throw down the rest.

Casey's New Hat, Tricia Gardella, illustrated by Margot Apple (Boston: Houghton Mifflin Co., 1997). When Casey outgrows her old hat, none of the new ones in stores or those offered by family and friends on the ranch capture her fancy, except the old one, discarded by her grandfather, whose worn appearance and memory-evoking smells chronicle the years since her birth.

The Cat in the Hat, Dr. Seuss (New York: Random House, Inc., 1957, 1985). Rhyming text introduces the Cat in the Hat, who arrives one rainy day to entertain two bored children with his tricks of balancing and, finally, dropping an increasing number of items (including a protesting fish in its bowl). He introduces Things One and Two, whose play adds to the mess in the house, and cleans it all up with an ingenious invention before their mother returns home.

The Cat in the Hat Comes Back, Dr. Seuss (New York: Random House, Inc., 1958, 1986). When the fun-loving Cat in the Hat (from ***The Cat in the Hat*** by the same author) returns, he causes new troubles as his attempts to clean up the pink cat ring he

150

leaves in the bathtub create escalating messes until Little Cats Z to A from under his hat come to his aid.

Chicken Sunday, Patricia Polacco (New York: The Putnam & Grosset Book Group, 1992). A girl remembers Sundays with her friends and their mother, Miss Eula, and a special Easter when they made pysanky eggs to earn money to buy Miss Eula a hat she had admired.

Days with Frog and Toad, Arnold Lobel (New York: Harper & Row Publishers, Inc., 1979). This collection of stories celebrates the friendship of Frog and Toad as their relationship grows and deepens. In **"The Hat,"** when Frog gives Toad a hat for his birthday that is too big, Frog tells Toad to think big thoughts to make his head grow, and then, without Toad's knowledge, he shrinks the hat to the right size.

The Extraordinary Adventures of an Ordinary Hat, Wofram Hänel, illustrated by Christa Unzner-Fischer, translated by J. Alison James (New York: North-South Books, 1994). When a bowler hat, who daydreams in a hat-shop about adventures in faraway places and about a lovely straw hat, does not find the excitement he desires when he is finally purchased, he courageously escapes on the wind to South America, where his dreams come true.

Felix's Hat, Catherine Bancroft and Hanna Coale Gruenberg, pictures by Hanna Coale Gruenberg (New York: Macmillan Publishing Company, 1993). When Felix the frog loses the special hat that he always wears, members of his family, a dream, and a hand-me-down hat from his older brother help him deal with his loss.

The 500 Hats of Bartholomew Cubbins, Dr. Seuss (New York: Vanguard Press, Inc., 1938, 1965). When Bartholomew tries to remove his hat as the king passes (and every time after), a new hat appears in its place, and no one in the palace can make him take off his hat until 500 have left his head!

Happy Birthday, Moon, Frank Asch (New York: Simon & Schuster Books for Young Readers, 1982). Soft, luminous illustrations complement the story of a bear who, in his attempt to befriend the moon, talks with his own echo and devises a clever plan to give the moon a birthday gift—a hat that fits just right.

The Hat, Jan Brett (New York: G.P. Putnam's Sons, 1997). After Lisa hangs all of her woolens on the clothesline, a hedgehog investigates a stocking blown off by the wind, and it sticks on his head like a hat. This inspires the other animals to laugh, at first, and then to create their own hats from Lisa's woolens.

The Hat, Tomi Ungerer (New York: Parents' Magazine Press, 1970). A tall, black top hat blows onto the head of a poor man, causing him (with its brave and bold antics) to become a rich and decorated hero who marries the lovely Contessa, and then blows away to unknown places and future adventures.

A ***Hat for Minerva Louise***, Janet Morgan Stoeke (New York: Puffin Books, 1994). When Minerva, the hen, leaves her friends behind in the henhouse and goes outside to explore on a winter day, she searches for a hat to protect her from the cold and finds *two* hats—one for her head and one for her tail—in a pair of mittens!

Hats Hats Hats, Ann Morris, photographs by Ken Heyman (New York: William Morrow & Company, Inc., 1989). Colored photographs show a variety of hats (that are labeled with a few words on each page) worn by people of diverse ages from different cultures and places—Britain, Denmark, Egypt, El Salvador, France, India, Indonesia, Israel, Japan, Nigeria, Peru, and the United States. An index locates and describes each photograph.

Hello, Cat You Need a Hat, Rita Golden Gelman, pictures by Eric Gurney (New York: Scholastic Inc., 1979). A cat finally is successful in getting a mouse to stop making its persistent offers of a wide variety of hats to wear, but the mouse begins anew with shoes, in this humorous easy-to-read book.

Hilda Crumm's Hats, Linda Hendry (Toronto: HarperCollins Publishers Ltd., 1994). Hilda Crumm's habit of collecting junk begins to irritate the neighbors when it overflows her apartment, but, by chance as she cleans up, she discovers a new use for her treasures and begins a thriving custom-made hat business.

The Many Hats of Mr. Minches, Paulette Bourgeois, illustrated by Kathryn Naylor (Toronto, Canada: Stoddart Publishing Co. Ltd., 1994). Shy Dotty's wish to be "brave and wild and bold" comes true when the hats she wears, from among the hundreds that belong to Mr. and Mrs. Minches, who move into a fishing shack down the beach from her home, magically transform her.

Martin's Hats, Joan W. Blos, illustrated by Marc Simont (New York: William Morrow and Company, 1984). Throughout the adventure-packed day depicted in this colorful picture book, Martin dons a special hat for each role as explorer, partygoer, engineer, chef, police officer, postal carrier, fire fighter, construction worker, farmer, and, finally, sleeping boy in his nightcap!

Mattie's Hats Won't Wear That!, Elaine Greenstein (New York: Alfred A. Knopf, 1997). Tired of the unusual ornaments that Mattie uses to decorate them, the hats in her shop (that no one buys) long to be worn, and they finally find owners when they pick out their own decorations to express their individuality.

Old Hat New Hat, Stan and Jan Berenstain (New York: Random House, Inc., 1970). A few words in bold print on each page describe the adventure of a bear who decides to buy a new hat and the variety of hats that he rejects at a fancy hat store before he decides that his old hat is just right, after all.

Olive and the Magic Hat, Eileen Christelow (New York: Clarion Books, 1987). Thinking that the dress hat they are giving their father for his birthday is magic, Olive and Otis Opossum say some magic words, and the hat lands on the head of Mr. Foxley, who is increasingly convinced of its magic through their tricks to get it back.

The Purple Hat, Tracey Campbell Pearson (New York: Farrar, Straus & Giroux, 1997). Her purple hat, ordered from a catalogue, is just the thing to match Annie's purple coat and shoes (and bedroom!) until she loses it at school, inspiring a community search for the lost treasure.

She's Wearing a Dead Bird on Her Head!, Kathryn Lasky, illustrated by David Catrow (New York: Hyperion Books for Children, 1995). Feathers (and even entire birds) decorate the hats of fashionable women in Boston in 1896 until, in protest, two women organize a club of powerful women and men to protect the birds—the founders of the Massachusetts Audubon Society, Minna Hall and Marriet Hemenway. An author's note provides background information about the period of history and the writing of the book.

This Is the Hat: A Story in Rhyme, Nancy Van Laan, pictures by Holly Meade (New York: Hyperion Books for Children, 1992). Rhyming text and torn-paper collage illustrations contain colorful enlarged onomatopoetic words that contribute to the story of a hat, blown from a man's head, that is used by a series of animals and people for a variety of purposes before the man reclaims it.

A Three Hat Day, Laura Geringer, pictures by Arnold Lobel (New York: HarperCollins Publishers, 1985). In hat lover R. R. Pottle the Third's dreams about the woman he will marry, she is wearing the perfect hat; and so she is, when he meets her in a hat store while wearing three hats to cheer himself up.

Uncle Foster's Hat Tree, Doug Cushman (New York: Penguin Books USA Inc., 1988). In this easy-to-read book in chapters, Merle the mouse is bored at Uncle Foster's house until his uncle tells him an action-filled story about each hat on his hat tree—a jungle hat, garden hat, straw hat, and top hat—and they try them all on.

Uncle Nacho's Hat: El Sombrero Del Tío Nacho, adapted by Harriet Rohmer, illustrations by Mira Reisberg, Spanish version by Rosalma Zubizarreta (San Francisco: Children's Book Press, 1989). In this book with parallel English and Spanish text on each page, an adapted Nicaraguan folktale, Uncle Nacho resists change after his young niece gives him a new hat until she helps him realize that he's expending more energy letting go of his beloved old hat than looking to the future with his new one.

Who Took the Farmer's Hat?, Joan L. Nòdset, pictures by Fritz Siebel (New York: Harper & Row, Publishers, Inc., 1963). After his hat is blown off his head, a farmer finds that each in a series of animals thought it was an object that made sense in terms of its own experience, including a bird that uses the hat as a nest. The kind farmer sees the bird's perspective, leaves her the old hat, and buys a new one.

Literature Extension Activities

1. With a simple set and caps, students dramatize the tale of ***Caps for Sale*** as you reread it aloud.

2. In ***The Hat***, a companion book to Brett's ***The Mitten: A Ukrainian Folktale*** (Chapter 25), there are three dramas occurring in the border

on each page. Lisa leaves the story to the animals after the first pages, enters the border, and continues the activities of her day. The frame on the left of the border shows the character or event about to appear on the next page. The frame in the border on the top of the page shows Lisa's clothesline—filled with her airing woolens at the beginning of the book and becoming emptied as, one by one, the animals, who are inspired by hedgehog's accidental hat, take pieces of clothing to make their own improvised hats. After you share the book with students, complete the following activities:

a. Compare the creative use of clothing to make hats in *The Hat* and in *A Hat for Minerva Louise.*

b. Students design their own improvised hats from other pieces of clothing from the dress-up corner or area, or from home, and show them off in a parade like the parade of animals wearing Lisa's missing woolens in *The Hat*.

c. Compare and contrast Brett's use of borders in *The Hat* with her use of borders in other of her books including: *Annie and the Wild Animals* (Chapter 3), *The First Dog* (Chapter 4), and *The Mitten: A Ukrainian Folktale* (Chapter 25).

3. Throughout the unit, help students compile (and optionally illustrate) a list (or book) of different kinds of hats. Students may use, as resources, their own knowledge and experiences, plus such nonfiction books as *Hats Hats Hats* and the fictional books suggested for this unit.

4. After students enjoy the imaginary occupations and corresponding hats of Martin in *Martin's Hats*, they (and you) wear hats (from home or supplied by you) that show what they want to do as adults, or occupations of family, community members, or friends that they find interesting. Members of the group identify the occupations represented by the hats. Individuals add pantomimed gestures related to the occupations, as needed, to aid in identification.

5. After *Mattie's Hats Won't Wear That!* is read aloud, make hats with the students; and they can choose ornaments to decorate them, from a variety of items provided, to express their individuality!

Items for the Mystery Box

Inedible Items: hair, hammer, hammock, hand, handkerchief, hanger, harmonica, harp, **hat** *(Note:* Arrive at the meeting area for the Mystery Box Whole-Group Activity wearing several hats on top of one another. Silently remove one hat at a time, revealing those beneath.), hatchet, hawk, hay, head, heart, hedgehog, heel (shoe), heel (human), helicopter, helmet, hen, hinge, hippopotamus, hive, hobbyhorse, hog, holes (from a hole punch), holly, honeycomb, horn, hornet, horse, horseshoe, hose, house, hummingbird, hydrant

Edible Items: ham, hamburger, hamentashen, hazelnut cake, hazelnuts, hoisin sauce, hominy grits, honey, honeydew melon, horseradish sauce, hotdog, hot and sour soup, huckleberries, humus

Rhymes, Songs, Fingerplays, and Tongue Twisters

Hat Theme
*Bat, bat, come under my hat: 5, 28, 33, 50, 76

Christmas is coming, the geese are getting fat: 5, 73, 76, 78

Here are Grandma's glasses: 12, 14, 78

Hoddley, poddley, puddles and fogs: 5, 34, 73, 76

Jerry Hall: 5, 34, 50, 51, 73, 76

My hat has three corners: 12, 55

Riddle me, riddle me, what is that?: 5

Three young rats with black felt hats: 5, 25, 33, 34, 37, 73, 76

Tongue Twisters: 63

Letter-Sound h (h)
*Hot-cross buns! Hot-cross buns!: 3, 5, 28, 32, 34, 38, 39, 40, 41, 50, 62, 73, 76

*Humpty Dumpty sat on a wall: 3, 5, 20, 25, 26, 28, 29, 32, 33, 34, 37, 38, 39, 40, 41, 42, 43, 46, 50, 52, 53, 58, 62, 67, 73, 76

If I had a hammer: 17

If you're happy: 12, 55, 78

Jenny works with one hammer: 12

There was a little green house: 5, 28

Tongue Twisters: 1, 7, 13, 74, 80

Where is Thumbkin?: 12, 14, 31, 78

Cloze Sentences

1. My **hand** **h**as four fingers and a thumb.
   (I **have** four fingers and a thumb on my **hand**.)

2. **Happy** is **h**ow **h**e feels when **h**e is not sad.
   (When **h**e is not sad, **h**e feels **happy**.)

3. **Hangers** are something I use to **h**ang my clothes in a closet.
   (In a closet, I **h**ang my clothes on **hangers**.)

4. A **hook** is a thing for **h**anging my coat at school.
   (At school, I **h**ang my coat on a **hook**.)

1. The **horn** on my car makes a beep when I **h**onk it.
   (Beep is the sound when I **h**onk my car's **horn**.)

2. A **h**at is something I wear on top of my **h**air on my **h**ead.

   (On top of my **h**air on my **h**ead, I wear a **h**at.)

3. My **h**eart beats very fast when I run up a **h**ill.

   (When I run fast up a **h**ill, I can feel the beating of my **h**eart.)

4. A **h**ive is a place where bees make **h**oney.

   (Bees make **h**oney in a **h**ive.)

H h

Bat, bat,

Come under my hat,

And I'll give you a slice of bacon;

And when I bake

I'll give you a cake,

If I am not mistaken.

Name _____ Date _____

H h

Humpty Dumpty sat on a wall,

Humpty Dumpty had a great fall;

All the king's horses and all the king's men

Couldn't put Humpty Dumpty together again.

Name _____   Date _____

H h

HOT-CROSS BUNS!

Hot-cross buns!

Hot-cross buns!

One a penny, two a penny,

Hot-cross buns!

If you have no daughters,

Give them to your sons.

One a penny, two a penny,

Hot-cross buns!

Name _____ Date _____

H h

COMPLETE IT

hand	Happy
1	2
Hangers	hook
3	4

My <u>hand</u> has four fingers and a thumb.
   1

<u>Happy</u> is how he feels when he is not sad.
 2

<u>Hangers</u> are something I use to hang my
  3
clothes in a closet.

A <u>hook</u> is a thing for hanging my coat at
   4
school.

Name _____ Date _____

Cloze Sentences . . . 1

H h

COMPLETE IT

horn	hat
1	2
heart	hive
3	4

The <u>horn</u> on my car makes a beep when I honk
     1

it.

A <u>hat</u> is something I wear on top of my hair on
   2

my head.

My <u>heart</u> beats very fast when I run up a hill.
    3

A <u>hive</u> is a place where bees make honey.
   4

Name _____ Date _____

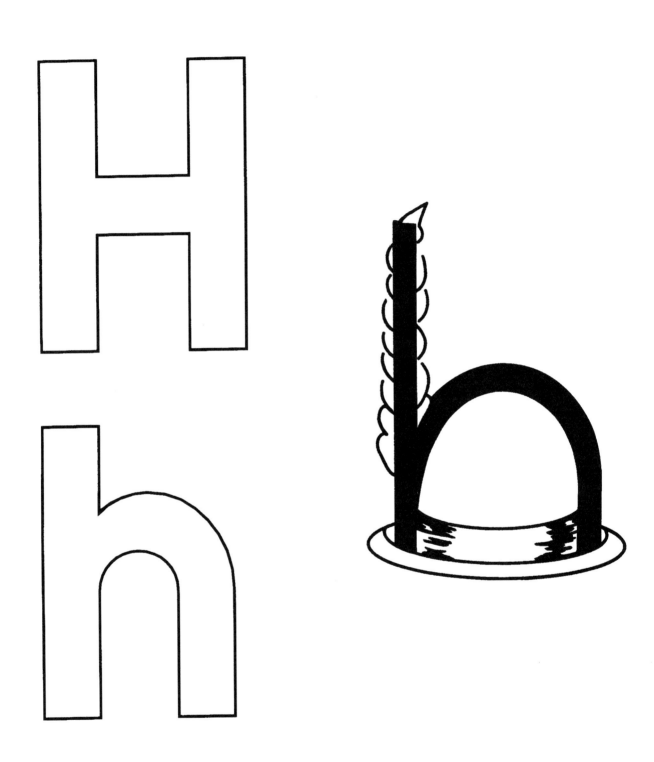

I i   igloo

TEACHER REFERENCE

Annotated Book List

Alaskan Eskimos and Aleuts, Mira Bartók and Christine Ronan (New York: HarperCollins Publishers, 1996). Colored photographs complement a sentence in large type on a page to present information about the lives of the Eskimo and Aleut peoples of Alaska and nearby islands. Contains a map and a glossary of key words.

Arctic & Antarctic: Eyewitness Books, Barbara Taylor, photographed by Geoff Brightling (New York: Alfred A. Knopf, 1995). Collections of colored photographs, drawings, and related objects and fact-filled text and captions present information about life in the polar regions, with detailed sections about people, animals, and vegetation. Includes contents and index.

Arctic Hunter, Diane Hoyt-Goldsmith, photographs by Lawrence Migdale (New York: Holiday House, 1992). Told from the point of view of a ten-year-old boy who lives far north of the Arctic Circle in Alaska, the book describes, in text and colored photographs, his multigenerational Inupiat family's spring fishing and hunting trip at their camp and provides information about contemporary and traditional life and ways. Provides a phonetic representation of each Inupiat word that appears in the text and contains a glossary.

Arctic Memories, Normee Ekoomiak (New York: Henry Holt and Company, 1988). In parallel text in Inuktitut and English languages illustrated with the author's paintings, drawings, and wall hangings, the author, an Inuk, shares memories of Inuit life and beliefs. An author's note is autobiographical, and editor's notes include information about Inuit people, language, and art.

Arctic Son, Jean Craighead George, paintings by Wendell Minor (New York: Hyperion Books for Children, 1997). In keeping with tradition, Luke is given an Eskimo name to go with his English name, and he learns, through his early childhood, about the natural wonders of the Arctic and the ways and language of his Inupiat friends.

Baseball Bats for Christmas, Michael Arvaarluk Kusugak, art by Vladyana Krykorka (New York: Annick Press (U.S.) Ltd., 1990). The Christmas of 1955, when Arvaarluk was seven, six trees were delivered by airplaine to Repulse Bay (at the north end of Hudson

Bay, on the Arctic Circle), where there are no "standing-ups" (trees), and Arvaarluk and his friends fashioned baseball bats from their branches.

Eskimo Boy: Life in an Inupiaq Eskimo Village, Russ Kendall (New York: Scholastic Inc., 1992). The book, illustrated with colored photographs and a map, shows the contemporary daily life of a seven-year-old Inupiaq boy, his family, and his village, who live on an island off the northwest coast of Alaska. Includes a glossary and an afterword that summarizes the history of Native Alaskans from their Asian origins to modern-day.

Frozen Land: Vanishing Cultures, Jan Reynolds (San Diego: Harcourt Brace & Company, 1993). Members of her multigenerational family teach a young girl the traditional and contemporary ways of her Inuit people, who hunt caribou and fish on the shores of an inlet of Hudson Bay, including how to build an igloo, in this book illustrated with a map and colored photographs. Contains an introduction and author's note.

Hide and Sneak, Michael Arvaarluk Kusugak (New York: Annick Press [U.S.] Ltd., 1992). As she plays hide and seek, a little girl ignores her mother's warning and is hidden by an Ijiraq, a tiny creature that hides someone forever, but she uses quick thinking and an inuksugaq (a pile of rocks made to look like a man, traditionally used in caribou hunting) to find her way home.

Houses and Homes, Ann Morris, photographs by Ken Heyman (New York: William Morrow & Company, 1992). Colored photographs present some of the similarities and differences in houses from different cultures and places—Bali, Britain, Canada, Colombia, France, Guatemala, Hong Kong, India, Italy, Kenya, the Netherlands, Nigeria, Papua New Guinea, Peru, Puerto Rico, Portugal, Russia, Thailand, United States—and emphasizes the similarity that makes each a home: love and family. Includes an index that describes each photograph and a map that locates each place.

Houses of Snow, Skin and Bones—Native Dwellings: The Far North, Bonnie Shemie (Plattsburgh, New York: Tundra Books of Northern New York: 1989). Author's notes introduce the challenge and ingenious solutions, using available materials, by northern people of providing shelter in the earth's coldest climate, followed by detailed drawings and discussions of traditional shelters: snow house or igloo (called igluvigak by the Inuit), quarmang or quarmak (dug-out of stone, skin, and whalebone), sod-house, and summer tents and tupiq.

How Snowshoe Hare Rescued the Sun: A Tale from the Arctic, retold by Emery Bernhard, illustrated by Durga Bernhard (New York: Holiday House,1993). When their foibles cause Bear and Wolf to fail to rescue the Sun from the demons under the earth, quiet but brave and strong Snowshoe Hare restores light to the cold and darkened sky, in the forms of Sun, Moon, and stars of the Milky Way in this pourquoi story from the Yuit people of northeast Siberia.

The Igloo, Charlotte and David Yue (Boston: Houghton Mifflin Company, 1988). This informational book of 117 pages, illustrated with black-and-white drawings, focuses upon the role of the igloo in the traditional and contemporary lives of the Eskimo people and includes details about the people, environment, and culture, including construction of and life in an igloo, clothing, food, family life, games and recreation, snow villages, transportation, and additional types of shelters.

Inunguak the Little Greenlander, Palle Peterson, illustrated by Jens Rosing (New York: Lothrop, Lee & Shepard Books, 1987). A map and notes from the author and illustrator that provide background about Greenland and the Inuit people precede the story of a boy who is ridiculed for his preference to listen to his grandfather tell the old stories and legends of the People rather than learn to be a hunter, until bad times befall his village. Then, he reminds others of the stories they have forgotten, which save them.

Ka-ha-si and the Loon: An Eskimo Legend, Terri Cohlene, illustrated by Charles Reasoner (Mahwah, New Jersey: Watermill Press, 1990). Given powers from his grandfather through a loon messenger, a boy helps his People when he finds food, defeats a giant, and protects the land from attacking mountains in this legend of the Eskimo people.

Long Claws: An Arctic Adventure, James Houston (New York: Penguin Books USA Inc., 1981). In a suspenseful and dramatic adventure story, a young fatherless Inuit brother and sister brave a blizzard and have an encounter with a hungry grizzly bear, called Long Claws by hunters, to bring a caribou home to their starving family.

Mama, Do You Love Me?, Barbara M. Joosse, illustrated by Barbara Lavallee (New York: Scholastic, 1991). A young child's mother responds to her series of questions with assurances of her unfailing love. The text and detailed illustrations, and a section with a glossary following, contain information about the native Arctic people—the Inuit.

My Arctic 1, 2, 3, Michael Arvaarluk Kusugak, art by Vladyana Krykorka (New York: Annick Press (U. S.) Ltd., 1996). The author's notes provide background information about his experiences growing up in Repulse Bay on the Arctic Circle and about the animals, people, and land and vegetation illustrated and described in this counting book. Includes a glossary.

Northern Lights the Soccer Trails, Michael Arvaarluk Kusugak, art by Vladyana Krykorka (New York: Annick Press (U. S.) Ltd., 1993). Kataujaq, sad and lonely as she misses her beloved mother who died from an illness, is consoled after she hears her grandmother's story about the soccer games played in the northern lights by the souls of those who have died.

Northern Lullaby, Nancy White Carlstrom, illustrated by Leo and Diane Dillon (New York: The Putnam & Grosset Group, 1992). Double-page luminous paintings illustrate the text of this gentle lullaby that bids goodnight, as a small child sleeps, to personified elements of Alaska: stars and moon, mountain and river, animals, vegetation, and northern lights.

On Mother's Lap, Ann Herbert Scott, illustrated by Glo Coalson (Boston: Houghton Mifflin Company, 1992). Young Michael is sure that there's enough room on Mother's lap under his reindeer blanket for his boat and doll and puppy as they rock in the rocking chair, but he needs his mother's assurance that there's enough room there for his baby sister when she awakens from her nap.

The Polar Bear Son: An Inuit Tale, retold and illustrated by Lydia Dabcovich (Boston: Houghton Mifflin Company, 1997). An old woman without family must fend for herself until she adopts a polar bear cub as her son. He provides well for her until she sends him away to protect him from jealous hunters, and she meets him only far out on the ice, where he continues for years to fulfill her needs. An author's note provides information about the Inuit, including their hunting and fishing, various dwellings, and storytelling.

A Promise Is a Promise, Robert Munsch & Michael Kusugak, art by Vladyana Krykorka (New York: Annick Press [U.S.] Ltd., 1988). A little girl defies her mother's warning about the ocean's troll-like Qallupilluit (who grab children without their parents), breaks her promise not to fish in the sea, and makes a second promise that endangers her brothers and sisters; however, her parents' clever plan saves the childrens' lives. An author's note provides information about a Qallupilluq, created to keep small children away from cracks in sea ice, and the background of this story.

A Ride on Mother's Back: A Day of Baby Carrying Around the World, Emery and Durga Bernhard (San Diego: Harcourt Brace & Company, 1996). Text, pictures, and authors' notes provide information about the ways people from different cultures carry their babies and about the experiences of carried babies in places around the world: Africa central/Mbuti, northern, Sahara Desert/Tuareg, and West/Mandingo; Amazon rain forest/Yanomama; Andes Mountains/Quechua; Bali/Balinese; Canada/Inuit; Guatemala/Maya; Nepal/Nepali; Papua New Guinea/ Papuans; Thailand/Hmong.

The Seal Oil Lamp: An Adaptation of an Eskimo Folktale, story and wood engravings by Dale De Armond (San Francisco: Sierra Club Books for Children, 1988). The kindness of a little boy is repaid by a mouse who saves his life when, by tradition, he is left to die because he is blind and is not expected to be able to hunt to support himself. The mouse people teach the boy a magic song that makes him a great whale hunter among his people. Contains a glossary.

The Secret of the Seal, Deborah Davis, illustrated by Judy LaBrasca (New York: Random House, Inc., 1989). A young Inuit boy discovers that, not only can he not kill the beautiful seal that emerges from an opening in the ice and whom he befriends and names, he must also protect her from his visiting uncle, who plans to capture a seal to sell to a zoo in the city where he lives.

A Sled Dog for Moshi, Jeanne Bushey, illustrated by Germaine Arnaktauyok (New York: Hyperion Books for Children, 1994). Moshi wishes she had a pet dog like the one her new friend from New York City owns, but her father refuses to give her one of his lead sled dog's pups until a sudden springtime blizzard and Moshi's good thinking change his mind. Includes a glossary and map.

This Place Is Cold: Imagine Living Here, Vicki Cobb, illustrated by Barbara Lavallee (New York: Walker and Company, 1989). The animals, climate, land, natural resources, people, transportation, vegetation, and waterways of Alaska are the areas of focus of this colorfully illustrated informational book.

Literature Extension Activities

1. After they listen to Kusugak's stories ***Baseball Bats for Christmas***, ***Hide and Sneak***, and ***Northern Lights the Soccer Trails,*** and to some or all of the nonfiction and fiction books suggested, students play familiar games enjoyed by Inuit and Inupiaq children including baseball, hide-and-seek, juggling, soccer, cat's cradle and other string games, and making angels in the snow.

2. Throughout the unit, you and students use, as resources, your own knowledge and experiences, plus ***Houses and Homes*** and other nonfiction and fiction books suggested, as you compile a list or book of different kinds of shelters (houses or homes) used by people in different places and cultures around the world. Include contemporary wooden arctic houses as well as the traditional shelters of arctic people: the snow house or igloo (iglu or igluvigak); dug-out of stone, skin, and whalebone (quarmang or quarmak); sod-house; and summer tents and tupiq presented in ***Houses of Snow, Skin and Bones—Native Dwellings: the Far North***. Optionally, children can illustrate the list or book.

3. As you investigate the role of the igloo (iglu or igluvigak) in the traditional and contemporary lives of the Eskimo people, using ***The Igloo*** and other informational and fictional books as resources, you and students create an igloo in the drama area in the classroom. As builders of an igloo do in the snow, mark a circle for the exterior wall of the igloo and parallel lines for the entrance passage; mark with tape on the floor or rug, or with markers on inexpensive paper available on rolls. Then, arrange the living quarters with the necessities students discover as they research the igloo. Necessities include a seal oil lamp, a frame for the cooking pot or tea kettle, a clothing drying rack, and a platform with bedding for sitting and sleeping, plus extra clothing, utensils, and tools assembled around the inside walls.

   Optionally, students can outline and outfit a storage room in front of the central living area, a room for dogs in severe weather in front of the storage room, and/or a cache next to the igloo to store food, harnesses, and outer clothing.

4. After they listen to ***Mama, Do You Love Me?*** read aloud, students (individually, in pairs, or in a group) create an illustrated "What If" book, pat-

terned after the published book. They supply incidents and items from their own culture.

Items for the Mystery Box

Inedible Items: **igloo**, iguana, inch (on a ruler or measuring tape), inchworm, infant, initials (yours, written), ink (in clear pen), ink bottle, inner tube, insect, instruments (musical, variety)

Edible Items: Indian corn (dried, not fresh; kernels or ground as grain; ears of the Native American cereal grass), Indian pudding, instant pudding

Rhymes, Songs, Fingerplays, and Tongue Twisters

Igloo Theme

*Twinkle, twinkle Northern Lights: 2

Letter-Sound i (i)

*A was an Apple pie: 3, 5, 28, 33, 34, 46, 76
Go in and out the window: 47
Here we go round the Mulberry bush: 5, 25, 26, 29, 33, 34, 38, 41, 47, 50, 62, 67, 73, 76, 78

Hush, little baby, don't say a word: 5, 6, 17, 21, 22, 29, 34, 51, 53, 61, 73, 76, 78
*This little piggy went to market: 3, 5, 14, 20, 25, 26, 28, 29, 31, 32, 33, 34, 37, 38, 39, 42, 43, 46, 50, 52, 73, 76
Tongue Twisters: 1, 13, 60, 74, 80

Cloze Sentences

1. The <u>ink</u> in a pen is the colored liquid that makes marks on the paper.
   (The colored liquid in a pen that makes marks on the paper is the <u>ink</u>.)
2. Musical <u>instruments</u> can be guitars, drums, or horns.
   (Guitars, drums, and horns are musical <u>instruments</u>.)
3. An <u>igloo</u> is a shelter made of blocks of hard snow by the Inuit people.
   (A shelter made of blocks of hard snow by the Inuit people is the <u>igloo</u>.)
4. An <u>infant</u> is another name for a human baby.
   (Another name for a human baby is an <u>infant</u>.)

1. An <u>insect</u>, another name for a bug, can be a bee, an ant, or a fly.
   (Another name for a bug that can be a bee, an ant, or a fly is an <u>insect</u>.)
2. If you say your <u>initials</u>, you say the letters that begin your first and last names.
   (The letters that begin your first and last names are your <u>initials</u>.)
3. <u>Inches</u> are the long marks on a ruler that you can use to measure objects.
   (The long marks on a ruler that you can use to measure objects are <u>inches</u>.)
4. An <u>inchworm</u> is a worm that is about an inch long.
   (A worm that is about an inch long is an <u>inchworm</u>.)

I i

Twinkle, twinkle
Northern Lights,
sparkle in the
arctic night.
Up above the clouds so high,
blue-green ribbons
in the sky.

Twinkle, twinkle
Northern Lights,
shimmer in my
dreams tonight.

Name _____   Date _____

I i

This little piggy went to market,

This little piggy stayed home.

This little piggy had roast beef,

This little piggy had none.

And this little piggy cried,
"Wee, wee, wee, wee!"
All the way home.

Name _____ Date _____

I i

A was an Apple pie;
    B bit it;
        C cut it;
            D dealt it;
                E ate it;
                    F fought for it;
G got it;
    H had it;
        J joined it;
            K kept it;
                L longed for it;
                    M mourned for it;
N nodded at it;
    O opened it;
        P peeped in it;
            Q quartered it;
                R ran for it;
                    S stole it;
T took it;
    V viewed it;
        W wanted it;
            X, Y, Z, and ampers-and,
                All wished for a piece in hand.

Name _____   Date _____

I i

COMPLETE IT

ink	instruments
1	2
igloo	infant
3	4

The <u>ink</u> in a pen is the colored liquid that makes
  1
marks on the paper.

Musical <u>instruments</u> can be guitars, drums, or
            2
horns.

An <u>igloo</u> is a shelter made of blocks of hard
     3
snow by the Inuit people.

An <u>infant</u> is another name for a human baby.
     4

Name _____   Date _____

I i

COMPLETE IT

insect   initials
1   2
Inches   inchworm
3   4

An <u>insect</u>, another name for a bug, can be a
       1
bee, an ant, or a fly.

If you say your <u>initials</u>, you say the letters that
                        2
begin your first and last names.

<u>Inches</u> are the long marks on a ruler that you
    3
can use to measure objects.

An <u>inchworm</u> is a worm that is about an inch
          4
long.

© 1999 by Cynthia Conway Waring

Name _____   Date _____

J j   jump

TEACHER REFERENCE

Annotated Book List

A Boy, a Dog and a Frog, Mercer Mayer (New York: The Dial Press, 1967). In this wordless book, a boy and his dog set out to capture a frog who avoids their net only to find that he misses them so much when they leave that he follows them home.

Amazing Frogs & Toads: Eyewitness Juniors, Barry Clarke, photographed by Jerry Young (New York: Alfred A. Knopf, 1990). Short passages of text and collections of photographs, drawings, and diagrams present information about the life cycle, habits, behaviors, and physical characteristics and adaptations that enable frogs and toads to live and survive in a variety of habitats including water, underground, and treetop.

Anna Banana: 101 Jump-Rope Rhymes, Joanna Cole, illustrated by Alan Tiegreen (New York: Beech Tree Books, 1989). This humorously illustrated collection lists more than one hundred traditional rope-jumping rhymes according to the type of jumping: straight, counting, fast, actions, missing, question and answer, fortune-telling, and running in and out. Includes instructions for related games when not evident from the rhymes, a brief history of rope jumping, a list of additional sources, and an index.

Fenton's Leap, Libba Moore Gray, illustrated by Jo-Ellen Bosson (New York: Simon & Schuster Books for Young Readers, 1994). Near-sighted Fenton, the frog, cannot see where he is jumping, so he survives a series of dangerous misadventures and suffers the insults of his peers until he saves a catfish, who gives him a pair of eyeglasses she retrieves from the swamp bottom.

Frog: Life Story, Michael Chinery, photography by Barrie Watts, illustrated by Martin Camm (Mahwah New Jersey: Troll Associates, 1991). Photographs and drawings illustrate the text, which describes the life cycle and predators of the frog, plus the body parts that make it such a successful jumper (up to two feet when frightened). Contains an engaging introductory summary, a section containing fascinating facts, and an index.

The Frog Alphabet Book, Jerry Pallotta, illustrated by Ralph Masiello (Watertown, Massachusetts: Charlesbridge Publishers, 1990). Information about a variety of frogs and other amphibians (including the narrow-mouthed frog who waddles rather than jumps) is presented through brief text and colorful drawings in this fascinating alphabet book.

Frog and Toad Are Friends, Arnold Lobel (New York: Harper & Row, Publishers, 1970). This easy-to-read collection of stories introduces a series of books about Frog and Toad and their all-too-human (and frequently humorous and touching) friendship, continued in ***Frog and Toad Together***, ***Frog and Toad All Year***, and ***Days with Frog and Toad*** by the same author. Frog and Toad Book Buddies, soft plastic dolls, are available from HarperCollins Publishers (1995).

Frog in Love, Max Velthuijs, translated by Anthea Bell (New York: Farrar, Straus & Giroux, 1989). Too shy to tell Duck that he is in love with her, Frog trains to break the world high jump record to impress her and is injured; but all is not lost, for Duck shows her fondness for him as she cares for him, which allows him to express his feelings.

The Frog Prince, adapted from the retelling by the Brothers Grimm by Paul Galdone (New York: McGraw-Hill, 1975). A princess unwittingly releases a prince from the spell that turned him into a frog when she allows him to become her companion after he recovers her golden ball from his well.

The Frog Prince, Edith H. Tarcov, illustrated by James Marshall (New York: Scholastic, 1974). A princess agrees to allow a frog to become her companion if he retrieves her golden ball from his well, but she is surprised when he comes to the castle to claim his reward and even more surprised when he turns into a prince.

Frogs, Gail Gibbons (New York: Holiday House, 1993). Clear, detailed drawings, diagrams, and text present information about frogs including stages of development, enemies, body parts and functions, hibernation, and role in the balance of nature. Special sections describe differences between frogs and toads, and provide interesting facts about these tremendous jumpers.

Frogs, Michael Tyler (Greenvale, New York: MONDO Publishing, 1996). Photographs, diagrams, drawings, and accompanying text present information about frogs—types, physical features, life cycle, food, and calls. Contains index.

Frogs: A First Discovery Book, Gallimard Jeunesse and Daniel Moignot, illustrated by Daniel Moignot (New York: Scholastic Inc., 1994). See-through plastic pages, colored illustrations, and simple text invite readers to discover facts about frogs—physical characteristics, life cycle, enemies, food, and amphibian relatives, including the toad.

Frog's Lunch, Dee Lillegard, illustrated by Jerry Zimmerman (New York: Scholastic Inc., 1994). In this supportive book with one to three lines of enlarged print on each page, accompanied by illustrations that provide clues to meaning, a fly comes along just in time for Frog's lunch.

Frogs, Toads, Lizards, and Salamanders, Nancy Winslow Parker and Joan Richards Wright, illustrated by Nancy Winslow Parker (New York: Greenwillow Books, 1990). A humorous illustrated rhyming couplet introduces each of sixteen amphibians or reptiles presented on the facing page with a simple, labeled scientific drawing and brief text. Contains picture glossaries, glossary, range maps, scientific classification, bibliography, and index.

Frogs and Toads and Tadpoles, Too: Rookie Read-About Science, Allan Fowler (Chicago: Childrens Press, 1992). Simple text and accompanying colored photographs provide information about the similarities and differences between frogs and toads.

From Tadpole to Frog: Let's-Read-and-Find-Out Science, Wendy Pfeffer, illustrated by Holly Keller (New York: HarperCollins Publishers, 1994). This informational book chronicles the stages of transformation of a bullfrog from fertilized egg to tadpole to full-grown frog, shows the process of hibernation, presents a frog's life through the seasons, describes several additional frogs, and provides a map indicating where bullfrogs live in the United States.

The Green Frogs: A Korean Folktale Retold, Yumi Heo (Boston: Houghton Mifflin Company, 1996). This pourquoi tale, which explains why green frogs cry out when it rains and why children in Korea who don't listen to their mother are called chung-gaeguri (green frogs), is the humorous story of a wise mother frog and her children who disobey by doing the opposite of everything she asks—even croaking backwards!

Green Wilma, Tedd Arnold (New York: Penguin Books USA Inc., 1993). In this humorous rhyming book, a little girl wakes up colored green and spends her day before, during, and after school acting just like a frog.

Hop Jump, Ellen Stoll Walsh (San Diego: Harcourt Brace & Co., Inc., 1993). Betsy, the frog, tires of the same hop jump of her peers, and, inspired by the motion of falling leaves, she dances. Soon, despite their initial reluctance, all of the frogs are hopping *and* dancing.

It's Mine!: A Fable by Leo Lionni, Leo Lionni (New York: Alfred A. Knopf, inc., 1985, 1986). The wise words and selfless action of a toad and survival of a disaster together help three frogs, who are always quarreling about ownership of the resources on the island where they live, to understand the meaning of community and sharing.

Jack Kent's Hop, Skip and Jump Book: A First Book of Action Words, Jack Kent (New York: Random House, 1974). Each double page presents a number of action verbs related to a single theme or activity illustrated with Kent's humorous colored drawings.

Jump, Frog, Jump, Robert Kalan, pictures by Byron Barton (New York: William Morrow & Co., Inc., 1981). In this rhythmic cumulative story that repeats the title, a frog narrowly escapes a series of animals and obstacles and three children when it attempts to catch and eat a fly and, in the end, is aided by one child who lifts a basket to let it go.

The Magic Moonberry Jump Ropes, Dakari Hru, pictures by E. B. Lewis (New York: Penguin Books USA Inc., 1996). Two young sisters are unable to interest their friends in their favorite activity, Double Dutch rope jumping, until their Uncle Zambezi gives them wish-granting jump ropes hand-dyed with moonberries from Tanzania, East Africa. Magically, as they try them out, they discover two new friends moving in next door. Includes a glossary/pronunciation guide for words in Swahili and an author's note that describes sisal and natural dyes grown in Africa and the background of the traditional jump-rope rhymes that appear in the story.

Ma'ii and Cousin Horned Toad: A Traditional Navajo Story, Shonto Begay (New York: Scholastic Inc., 1992). In this combination trickster and pourquoi story that explains why coyotes leave horned toads alone, lazy and greedy Coyote Ma'ii tries to take Horned Toad's farm from him by tricking him and swallowing him whole; but kind, hard-working and *smart* Toad outwits Ma'ii—from inside the coyote's stomach! Includes a glossary of Navajo words.

Peach & Blue, Sarah S. Kilborne, illustrated by Steve Johnson with Lou Fancher (New York: Alfred A. Knopf, 1994). When Blue, a toad, helps a peach see what is beyond the branch of her tree, she gives him two gifts—a new way of seeing his pond world and the love of a friend.

Splash!, Ann Jonas (New York: Mulberry Books, 1995). In this counting book, a series of animals that jump into and crawl out of a pond illustrate the processes of addition and subtraction as the reader responds to the repeated question "How many are in my pond?"

Tuesday, David Wiesner (New York: Clarion Books, 1991). In this Caldecott Medal–winning wordless book, one Tuesday evening, frogs rise out of the water and float on their lilypads through adventure after adventure in and around homes in a nearby town, then jump back to their pond at daybreak. They leave the townspeople and police to wonder about the lilypads they left behind and readers to imagine what will happen the next Tuesday when the pigs . . .

Literature Extension Activities

1. Students, individually or in a group, provide words for the story depicted in the illustrations of the wordless book, ***A Boy, a Dog and a Frog***. They record their story on an audiotape, dictate it to a teacher (another adult or child), or write it.
2. With students, play games of Leap Frog as Fenton and his cousins do in ***Fenton's Leap***.
3. With your students, compile what they know and what they discover about the differences and similarities between frogs and toads as you read ***Frogs and Toads and Tadpoles, Too*** and additional nonfiction and fiction books. Compare and contrast the two amphibian jumpers in a list, data matrix, or Venn diagram.
4. As you share ***It's Mine!: A Fable by Leo Lionni*** in read-aloud, have students identify different words for "jumped," including "leaped" and "hopped," that recur in the text. During a subsequent reading, students identify the "jump" words as you read. They raise their hands or jump (leap or hop) when they hear a "jump" word read aloud.
5. Inspired by the experiences with rope jumping of the children and adults in ***The Magic Moonberry Jump Ropes***, jump rope with the students at recess, in physical education, and whenever practical. Experiment with the rhymes in the book and those suggested in ***Anna Banana: 101***

Jump-Rope Rhymes to add to their repetoire of rope-jumping rhymes and activities.

6. After they have heard it read aloud, students dramatize the processes of addition and subtraction (and practice jumping) as they act out *Splash!* while you read it aloud. They use simple costumes or head pieces attached to oaktag headbands to establish their identities and blue paper or cloth for the pond. Actors and members of the audience join you as you repeat the question "How many are in my pond?" and they provide the answer.

Items for the Mystery Box

Inedible Items: jack (playing card), Jack-in-the-Box, Jack-o'-lantern, jacket, jacks (ball bouncing game), jaguar, jar, jay (blue jay), jeans, jeep, JELL-O® box, jellyfish, jet, jewelry (variety), jockey, jogging suit, joker (playing card), jumper (clothing), **jump rope** *(Note:* Arrive at the meeting area for the Mystery Box Whole-Group Activity silently jumping rope.), jug, juice box, junk

Edible Items: jam, JELL-O®, jelly, jelly beans, Jerusalem artichokes, Johnny-cake, juice (variety), junket, plus Hot Frogs made from pastry dough in *Roald Dahl's Revolting Recipes*, compiled by Josie Fison and Felicity Dahl, illustrated by Quentin Blake, photographs by Jan Baldwin (New York: Penguin Books USA Inc., 1994)

Rhymes, Songs, Fingerplays, and Tongue Twisters

Jump Theme

Anna Elise, she jumped with surprise: 5
*Jack be nimble: 5, 28, 32, 33, 34, 37, 38, 39, 40, 42, 43, 49, 50, 52, 58, 73, 76
*Here am I, Little jumping Joan: 5, 28, 33, 34, 38, 40, 50, 73, 76, 79
Miss Mary Mack, Mack, Mack,/she asked her mother for fifty cents: 36, 53, 79
Jack-in-the-Box: 29
Jack, Jack, jump the water: 79
Jump rope, jump rope: 4
Little Frog/A little frog in a pond am I: 75
Oliver jump: 4
There was a little grasshopper: 12

There was a man, he went mad: 5
Tongue Twisters: 1, 13

Letter-Sound j (j)

Jack and Jill went up the hill: 5, 20, 26, 28, 31, 32, 33, 34, 38, 39, 40, 46, 49, 50, 52
Jelly in the dish: 4
John Jacob Jingleheimer Schmidt: 55, 78
Johnny, Johnny, Johnny: 12, 14
Johnny over the ocean: 4
To market, to market, to buy a fat pig: 3, 5, 25, 28, 33, 34, 42, 46, 49, 50, 58, 76
Tongue Twisters: 13, 80
*There were two little blackbirds sitting on a hill: 12, 14, 28, 33, 78

Cloze Sentences

1. A <u>j</u>acket is a light coat **j**ust right for cool weather.

   (A light coat **j**ust right for cool weather is a <u>j</u>acket.)

2. <u>J</u>am or **j**elly is something I like to spread on my toast.

   (On my toast, I like to spread **j**elly or <u>j</u>am.)

3. <u>J</u>uice is something I like to drink at breakfast and at snack, and orange and apple are my favorites.

   (At breakfast and snack, I like to drink orange or apple <u>j</u>uice.)

4. When you <u>j</u>ump over something, you hop like a frog or a toad.

   (You hop like a frog or a toad when you <u>j</u>ump.)

1. A <u>j</u>ug is a container with a handle and a top that holds maple syrup, milk, **j**uice, and water.

   (A container with a handle and a top that holds maple syrup, milk, **j**uice, and water is a <u>j</u>ug.)

2. A <u>j</u>ack o'-lantern is a pumpkin that you carve into a face at Halloween.

   (A pumpkin that you carve into a face at Halloween is a <u>j</u>ack-o'-lantern.)

3. A <u>j</u>ar made out of glass or plastic is a container that can have **j**am, **j**elly, or peanut butter inside.

   (A glass or plastic container that can have **j**am, **j**elly, or peanut butter inside is a <u>j</u>ar.)

4. <u>J</u>ack and **J**ill went up the hill to fetch a pail of water.

   (In the rhyme, the girl and the boy who went up the hill to fetch a pail of water were **J**ill and <u>J</u>ack.)

J j

Jack, be nimble;

Jack, be quick;

Jack, jump over

The candlestick.

Name _____ Date _____

Rhymes . . . 1

J j

Here am I,
Little jumping Joan.
When nobody's with me,
I'm always alone.

Name _____   Date _____

J j

There were two little blackbirds sitting on a hill,

One named Jack and the other named Jill.

Fly away, Jack! Fly away, Jill!

Come again, Jack! Come again, Jill!

Name _____   Date _____

J j

COMPLETE IT

jacket   Jam
1   2
Juice   jump
3   4

A <u>jacket</u> is a light coat just right for cool
1
weather.

<u>Jam</u> or jelly is something I like to spread on my
2
toast.

<u>Juice</u> is something I like to drink at breakfast
3
and at snack, and orange and apple are my
favorites.

When you <u>jump</u> over something, you hop like a
4
frog or a toad.

Name _____   Date _____

J j

COMPLETE IT

jug	jack-o'-lantern
1	2
jar	Jack
3	4

A <u>jug</u> is a container with a handle and a top
    1
that holds maple syrup, milk, juice, and water.

A <u>jack-o'-lantern</u> is a pumpkin that you carve
      2
into a face at Halloween.

A <u>jar</u> made out of glass or plastic is a container
    3
that can have jam, jelly, or peanut butter inside.

<u>Jack</u> and Jill went up the hill to fetch a pail of
    4
water.

Name _____ Date _____

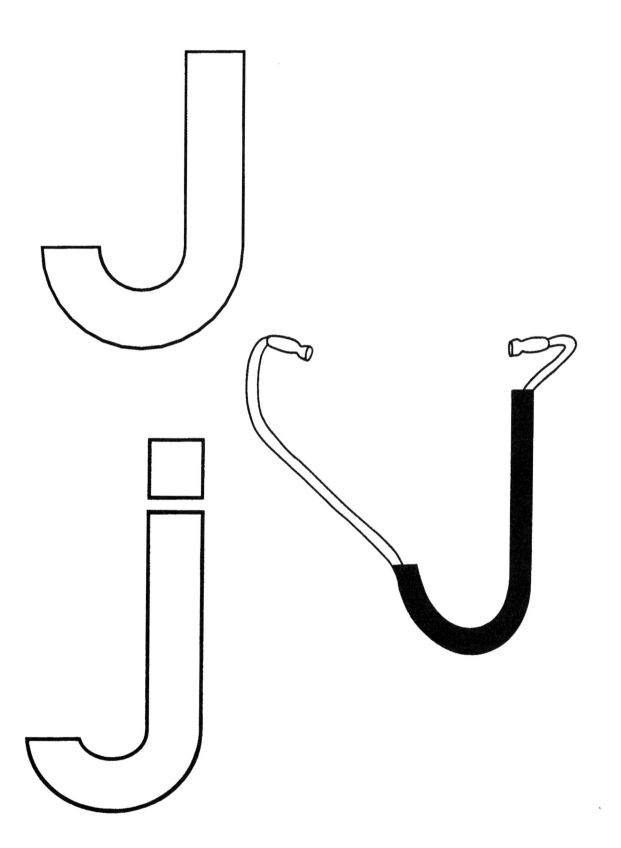

K k  kangaroo

TEACHER REFERENCE

Annotated Book List

Counting Kangaroos: **A Book About Numbers**, Marcia Leonard, pictures by Diane Palmisciano (Mahwah, New Jersey: Troll Associates, 1990). In this counting book, when grandma kangaroo asks her two grandchildren if they brought any toys to play with, she is surprised at the number of items, from one to ten of each, that they take out of their pouches and, with her help, have to clean up before lunch.

Joey, Jack Kent (Englewood Cliffs, New Jersey: Prentice-Hall, Inc., 1984). Worried that he might get lost, Joey's mother keeps him in her pouch until she can no longer stand the noise and weight of his three invited friends and their TV (and antenna), stereo, and musical instruments (including a grand piano). Then she orders everyone and everything out of her pouch and, finally, lets Joey go play.

Joey Runs Away, Jack Kent (New York: Simon & Schuster Books for Young Readers, 1985). Joey, introduced in ***Joey*** by the same author, runs away to avoid cleaning his room in his mother's pocket and tries out a number of pouchlike places to live, only to discover that none is right, until he is delivered from the postman's mailbag to his mother's pouch that fits exactly (even with a room inside to clean).

Kangaroo: Animals in the Wild, Vincent Serventy (Milwaukee: Raintree Publishers, 1983). This informational book, with three lines of bold-print text and a colored photograph on each page, provides facts about different members of the kangaroo family and the kangaroo's habitat, physical characteristics, habits, young, and enemies.

The Kangaroo from Woolloomooloo, Joy Cowley, illustrated by Rodney McRae (North Sydney, Australia: Murdoch Magazines Pty Ltd, 1991). In this supportive book with a predictable, repetitive pattern, a young child recounts the Australian animals he saw at the Sydney Zoo that interact with items and other animals that rhyme with their names.

Kangaroos: A New True Book, Emilie U. Lepthien (Chicago: Childrens Press, 1995). Text and captioned photographs provide information about the kangaroo, including characteristics and habits, care of young, predators and other threats to survival, and types of kangaroos and other marsupials. Contains a glossary with pronunciation guide for important terms, a table of contents, and an index.

Katy No-Pocket, Emmy Payne, Pictures by H. A. Rey (Boston: Houghton Mifflin Company, 1944, 1972). Mother animals of other species are not able to help Katy Kangaroo, who has no pocket, figure out how to carry her son, but a wise owl sends her to the city, where she is given a tool apron to wear that has enough pockets for her own and thirteen additional baby animals.

The Life Cycle of the Kangaroo, Paula Z. Hogan, illustrations by Gretchen Mayo (Austin, Texas: Steck-Vaughn Company, 1991). A colored drawing and two or three lines of text on each double page provide information about the habits, food and drink, enemies, and young of the kangaroo, and about other marsupials: opossum, koala, and wombat. Includes a glossary.

Norma Jean, Jumping Bean, Joanna Cole, illustrated by Lynn Munsinger (New York: Random House, 1987). In this easy-to-read book, Norma Jean, the kangaroo, alienates her classmates with her incessant jumping that interrupts their activities until she learns that there are appropriate times and places to jump.

The One in the Middle Is the Green Kangaroo, Judy Blume, illustrated by Amy Aitken (Scarsdale, New York: Bradbury Press, 1981). After he experiences success as the green kangaroo in the fifth- and sixth-grade play, second-grader Freddy is happier with his identity and no longer sees himself only as the middle sibling in his family.

Too Many Kangaroo Things To Do!, Stuart J. Murphy, illustrated by Kevin O'Malley. Kangaroo is disappointed when he finds that each of his friends has too many things to do to play with him on his birthday until he discovers, in the end, that each of them was preparing for his surprise birthday party. An author's note to adults and children suggests activities to extend the concepts of addition and multiplication introduced in the story.

What Do You Do with a Kangaroo?, Mercer Mayer (New York: Scholastic Inc., 1973). One by one, the animals with extravagant demands that intrude upon her activities find themselves no match for a feisty little girl who throws them out; but, when they return en masse, she finally gives in and lets them stay.

Literature Extension Activities

1. Individually, in pairs, or in groups, students make their own kangaroo counting books patterned after ***Counting Kangaroos: A Book About Numbers***. Students draw pictures of their favorite toys, in sets of from one to ten items, that come from the pouches of the kangaroo children.

2. With students, play a game modeled after ***The Kangaroo From Woolloomooloo***. First, substitute the name of a zoo for the Sydney Zoo. Then, by turns, students say aloud the name of an animal from their culture and an item or other animal with which it could interact, in realistic and fanciful contexts as in the book, that rhymes. After they make

their contribution, participants repeat the phrase that is repeated after each new animal in the book: "and the kangaroo from Woolloomooloo."

3. With students, explore the reference tools included in *Kangaroos*—table of contents, index, glossary, and pronunciation guide—and compare and contrast these different ways to locate information in a book.

4. In *Norma Jean, Jumping Bean*, Norma Jean, the kangaroo, learns that there are appropriate times and places to jump. With students, compile an illustrated list or class book of times that people (or kangaroos, like Norma Jean, who act like people) jump; for example, when they are surprised, when pole vaulting, over a puddle, on skis, and so on.

5. With students, compare and contrast the short chapter book *The One in the Middle Is the Green Kangaroo* with a picture book also about being the middle child in a family with three siblings: *Noisy Nora* by Rosemary Wells (New York: Dial Books for Young Readers, 1973), a humorous rhyming story in which Nora the mouse represents the plight of all middle siblings. She has to wait while Mother and Father are busy with baby Jack and big sister Kate—that is, until she gets their attention with some *Noise*!

   Students and teachers who occupy a position in their families similar to that of Freddy and Nora share their experiences and feelings (positive and negative), if they choose.

6. *Too Many Kangaroo Things To Do!*, from the Math Start series, provides a number of opportunities (with diagrams and equations provided in the text) for students to add or multiply the things each animal friend of Kangaroo must do to prepare for his birthday celebration. Students, who are interested and ready, explore these opportunities. They also engage in the suggested activities that extend the concepts introduced from the note to adults and children at the back of the book.

Items for the Mystery Box

Inedible Items: kaleidoscope, **kangaroo**, kayak, kazoo, kerchief, kernels (corn), ketchup bottle, kettle, keyboard, keyhole, keys, kid (child), kid (goat), kindergarten (photograph of the class), king (person), king (playing card), kite, kitten, kiwi (bird), koala bear

Edible Items: kale, kanahena (hominy or cornmeal mush of the Cherokee people), kebabs (made with a variety of fruits or vegetables), ketchup, Key lime pie, Hershey KISSES® chocolate candy, Kit-Kat® candy bar, Kellogg™ cereal (particularly Special K® and Rice Krispies®) kidney beans, kiwi (fruit), kohlrabi, kuchen, kugel, kumquat

Rhymes, Songs, Fingerplays, and Tongue Twisters

Kangaroo Theme

*Old Noah did build himself an ark: 3, 77

Tongue Twisters: 1, 13

The Zoo in the Park/This is the way the kangaroo hops: 3

Letter-Sound k (k)

*As I was going to St. Ives: 5, 9, 28, 33, 34, 37, 39, 46, 50, 73, 76

The Hokey-Pokey: 29, 79

Keep the kettle boiling: 4

Kookaburra sits in the old gum tree: 77

*Miss Mary Mack, Mack, Mack: 36, 51, 53, 55, 79

My little sister dressed in pink: 4

Pat a cake, pat a cake, baker's man: 3, 5, 20, 28, 29, 31, 33, 34, 37, 38, 39, 40, 41, 42, 43, 46, 53, 58, 62, 73, 76

Polly put the kettle on: 3, 5, 20, 26, 28, 29, 32, 33, 34, 40, 41, 46, 50, 62, 73, 76

This is the key of the kingdom: 5, 33, 34, 76

Tongue Twisters: 13, 60, 80

Twinkle, twinkle, little star: 6, 26, 28, 32, 34, 40, 42, 43, 49, 51, 53, 58, 62, 73, 76, 78

Cloze Sentences

1. A <u>kitten</u> is a baby cat.

   (A baby cat is a <u>kitten</u>.)

2. You can use a <u>key</u> to unloc**k** a door.

   (To unloc**k** a door, you can use a <u>key</u>.)

3. The <u>king</u> is the ruler of a **kingdom**, and he may be the husband of the queen.

   (The ruler of a **kingdom**, who may be the husband of the queen, is the <u>king</u>.)

4. In the <u>kitchen</u> is where many people **keep** their stove and refrigerator.

   (Many people **keep** their stove and refrigerator in the room called the <u>kitchen</u>.)

1. If you have a <u>kite</u>, you need a ball of strong string or yarn to fly it on a windy day.

   (You need a ball of strong string or yarn to fly a <u>kite</u> on a windy day.)

2. <u>Ketchup</u>, mustard, and relish are things you can put on a hot dog.

   (Things you can put on a hot dog are mustard, relish, and <u>ketchup</u>.)

3. When you <u>kick</u> a football, you hit it with your foot.

   (When you hit a football with your foot, you <u>kick</u> it.)

4. A <u>k</u>angaroo is an animal that hops and carries its baby in its pocket or pouch.

   (An animal that hops and carries its baby in its pocket or pouch is a <u>k</u>angaroo.)

K k

Old Noah did build himself an ark;

He built one out of hickory bark:

There's one wide river to cross.

The animals went in two by two,

The elephant and the kangaroo;

There's one wide river to cross.

Name _____   Date _____

K k

Miss Mary Mack, Mack, Mack,

All dressed in black, black, black,

With silver buttons, buttons, buttons,

All down her back, back, back.

Name _____   Date _____

K k

As I was going to St. Ives,

I met a man with seven wives.

Every wife had seven sacks,

Every sack had seven cats,

Every cat had seven kits;

Kits, cats, sacks, and wives,

How many were going to St. Ives?

Name _____   Date _____

K k

COMPLETE IT

kitten   key
1   2
king   kitchen
3   4

A <u>kitten</u> is a baby cat.
    1

You can use a <u>key</u> to unlock a door.
             2

The <u>king</u> is the ruler of a kingdom, and he may
      3
be the husband of the queen.

In the <u>kitchen</u> is where many people keep their
        4
stove and refrigerator.

Name _____   Date _____

Cloze Sentences . . . 1

K k

COMPLETE IT

kite	Ketchup
1	2
kick	kangaroo
3	4

If you have a <u>kite</u>, you need a ball of strong
            1

string or yarn to fly it on a windy day.

<u>Ketchup</u>, mustard, and relish are things you can
     2

put on a hot dog.

When you <u>kick</u> a football, you hit it with your
              3

foot.

A <u>kangaroo</u> is an animal that hops and carries
       4

its baby in its pocket or pouch.

Name _____   Date _____

L l   lion

TEACHER REFERENCE

Annotated Book List

Amazing Cats: Eyewitness Juniors, Alexandra Parsons, photographed by Jerry Young (New York: Alfred A. Knopf, 1990). Colored drawings and photographs complement short text passages that highlight the habits and traits of common and unusual members of the cat family—wild and domesticated—from all over the world. Includes table of contents and index.

Anansi and the Moss-Covered Rock, Eric A. Kimmel, illustrated by Janet Stevens (New York: Holiday House, 1988). In this trickster tale, with the help of a magic, moss-covered rock, lazy but cunning Anansi the Spider first tricks Lion and, then, all of the animals in the forest out of their food until Little Bush Deer, who's been watching all the time, turns the tables and teaches Anansi a lesson.

Andrew's Bath, David McPhail (Boston: Little, Brown and Company, 1984). The first time Andrew takes a bath by himself, he can't help the noise and splashing that keeps him from washing because a frog, hippo, alligator, and elephant join him, and he can't let out the water when his dad tells him because there's a thirsty lion in his way!

Androcles and the Lion, retold and illustrated by Dennis Nolan (San Diego: Harcourt Brace & Company, 1997). Glowing drawings in gold and brown illustrate this retelling of the fable of a wounded lion that saves the life of a runaway slave, Androcles, who had removed a thorn from its paw. An author's note traces the history of the original story of Androcles and the Lion.

Andy and the Lion: A Tale of Kindness Remembered or the Power of Gratitude, James Daugherty (New York: Puffin Books, 1938, 1966). A lion recognizes Andy (who had earlier pulled a thorn from its paw) during an attempted escape from the circus, and Andy is seen as a hero and given a medal for bravery.

The Big Boasting Battle, Hans Wilhelm (New York: Scholastic Inc., 1995). Horace, the lion, and Sylvester, the snake, engage in an escalating boasting contest during which they land, together, in a deep hole and learn to appreciate the value of each other's differences and strengths after they cooperate to get out.

Brave Lion, Scared Lion, Joan Stimson, illustrated by Meg Rutherford (New York: Scholastic Inc., 1997). When the timid brother of twins saves his boastful brother, who places himself in danger when he shows off, the two lion cubs learn that being brave means more than showing off, and that to overcome fear with an act of courage is true bravery.

Cat: Eyewitness Books, Juliet Clutton-Brock (New York: Alfred A. Knopf, 1991). Collections of colored photographs, drawings, and objects along with fact-filled text and captions compose the pages of this informative book about domestic and wild cats. Contains table of contents and index.

Eli, Bill Peet (Boston: Houghton Mifflin Company, 1978). Too old and feeble to keep company with young lions, Eli joins a flock of vultures for the food scraps they leave, but he vows he'll never befriend them until he saves one of the birds and becomes their hero, and they, in turn, save him from hunters.

The Green Lion of Zion Street, Julia Fields, illustrated by Jerry Pinkney (New York: Macmillan Publishing Company, 1988). The rhythm and rhyme of this poem and accompanying watercolor illustrations capture the drama as a group of children in the city discover that the scary lion they see, crouched above them as they wait for the bus on a foggy day, is only an immovable stone statue.

Hilary & the Lions, Frank Desaix, pictures by Debbi Durland Desaix (New York: Farrar, Straus & Giroux, 1990). When Hilary becomes separated from her parents on a crowded street during her first visit to New York City, the two marble lions that guard the library magically come alive, give Hilary an insider's tour of the city, and reunite her with her parents.

Hubert's Hair-Raising Adventure, Bill Peet (Boston: Houghton Mifflin Company, 1959). A kind elephant braves the dreaded swamp to bring back crocodile tears to restore the mane of Hubert, the vain lion, reduced to stubble in an accident that set it on fire.

I Spy a Lion: Animals in Art, devised and selected by Lucy Micklethwait (New York: Greenwillow Books, 1994). The author challenges the reader to find an animal in each of a number of works, presented in full-page reproductions, by distinguished painters from a variety of cultures and times in history.

Lazy Lion, Mwenye Hadithi and Adrienne Kennaway (Boston: Little, Brown and Company (Inc.), 1990). In this pourquoi tale, lazy Lion orders a variety of animals to make him a house, but he is dissatisfied with their efforts and even in heavy rain—when the animals take shelter in the homes they made—Lion does not find a house and wanders the African plain.

Lion: Animals in the Wild, Mary Hoffman (Milwaukee: Raintree Publishers, 1985). Stunning close-up and panoramic colored photographs and two to four lines of bold print text on a page provide information about aspects of the life of lions: physical characteristics; habits; habitat; young; family and community life; and hunting, food, and drink.

The Lion and the Little Red Bird, Elisa Kleven (New York: Penguin Books USA Inc., 1992). In this book, illustrated with collages of mixed-media, though they cannot understand each other's language, a gentle lion and a bird become companions and, as their friendship deepens, the bird comes to understand that the lion's tail keeps changing colors because he is an artist who uses his tail as a paintbrush!

A Lion at Bedtime, Debi Gliori (Hauppauge, New York: Barron's Educational Series, Inc., 1993). An otherwise brave boy, Ben, is afraid of the lion who comes into his bedroom every night until the lion climbs into bed with him one cold evening and Ben gets to know the lion close-up and conquers his fears.

Lion Dancer: Ernie Wan's Chinese New Year, Kate Waters and Madeline Slovenz-Low, photographs by Martha Cooper (New York: Scholastic Inc., 1990). Told from the point of view of a young boy who lives with his family in Chinatown, the text and colored photographs of this book show the preparation for and performance of his first Lion Dance for the Chinese New Year celebration in the streets of New York City. Includes a Chinese lunar calendar and Chinese horoscope.

A Lion for Lewis, Rosemary Wells (New York: Dial Books for Young Readers, 1982). Lewis's older brother and sister always assign him the least desirable role in their play until Lewis discovers a lion suit in the attic and the balance of power suddenly shifts to the youngest sibling—the master of the lion!

Lions, adapted by Cynthia Overbeck from *Lions/Raion* by Tokumitsu Iwagō, photographs by Tokumitsu Iwagō translated by Setsuko Takeuchi (Minneapolis, Minnesota: Lerner Publications Company, 1981). Informative text and colored photographs capture the daily challenges of lions and their families as they struggle to survive in the savannas on reserves in southern and eastern Africa.

The Lion's Whiskers: An Ethiopian Folktale, Nancy Raines Day, illustrated by Ann Grifalconi (New York: Scholastic Inc., 1995). A medicine man's wisdom provides the quest from which a woman learns how to become close to her reluctant stepson—by patiently awaiting the boy as she did a wild lion whose three whiskers were the goal of her first quest, in this book illustrated with collages made from textured materials and colored paper. An author's note traces this story to oral tradition in Ethiopia.

The Lonely Lioness and the Ostrich Chicks, retold by Verna Aardema, illustrated by Yumi Heo (New York: Alfred A. Knopf, 1996). In this retelling of a Masai folktale, Mother Ostrich asks a number of animals to help her recover her four chicks taken by a lonely motherless lioness—but it is only a clever mongoose who is able to outsmart the lioness.

Rabbit Makes a Monkey of Lion: A Swahili Tale, retold by Verna Aardema, illustrated by Jerry Pinkney (New York: Puffin Pied Piper/Dial Books for Young Readers, 1989). Try as he may, Lion can never catch the clever and fast trickster, Rabbit, who, Lion realizes, is behind the tricks the animals play on him to steal the honey from his calabash tree and to make a monkey (or fool) of him.

The Sabbath Lion: A Jewish Folktale from Algeria, retold by Howard Schwartz and Barbara Rush, illustrated by Stephen Fieser (New York: HarperCollins Publishers, 1992). The faith of ten-year-old Yosef is rewarded when a kind and gentle lion is sent to protect him as he travels alone through the desert. An author's note provides information about the Jewish Sabbath and about the origin of the folktale.

Sarah's Lion, Margaret Greaves, illustrated by Honey de Lacey (Hauppauge, New York: Barron's Educational Series, Inc., 1992). A lion that magically appears as the manifestation of her dreams helps a young princess escape the expectations, idleness, and confines of her position (with which her older sisters are content) to adventure into the world beyond her castle home.

Snow Lion, David McPhail (New York: Parents Magazine Press, 1982). Lion escapes the heat of the jungle in the mountains where he discovers snow, and, after failed attempts to bring snow to show his doubting friends, he leads his friends to its source. In gratitude, they make him a giant lion snow sculpture.

The Stone Lion, Alan Schroeder, pictures by Todd L. W. Doney (New York: Charles Scribner's Sons, 1994). Banished by her greedy elder son, a widow and her younger son make a humble home in the mountains of Tibet, where the boy discovers the Guardian of the Mountain, a lion carved in stone. The lion rewards the boy's kindness, honesty, and respect for the traditions and beliefs his mother has taught him, and punishes his brother for his selfishness which, in time, causes him to change his ways, ask for forgiveness, and give thanks.

The Very Hungry Lion, Gita Wolf, art by Indrapramit Roy (New York: Annick Press [U.S.] Ltd., 1996). After he is tricked by several clever animals, Singham, a hungry and *lazy* lion, who tries to find an easier way to get his food than chasing animals in the wild, discovers that hunting is the best way after all. For this story, from an ancient East Indian folktale, the hand silk-screened illustrations on paper made from rice husks and recycled fibers are based on an Indian folk painting style (Warli).

Literature Extension Activities

1. Students compare and contrast two very different treatments of the fable of Androcles and the Lion in the two books: ***Androcles and the Lion*** and ***Andy and the Lion: A Tale of Kindness Remembered or the Power of Gratitude***.

2. ***The Big Boasting Battle Book***, though fictional, reveals a number of the characteristics of lions about which Horace boasts. With students, take turns in the role of Horace, the lion, and present a series of mock boasting battles. Class members take the parts of other animals, one at a time, and counter the lion's boasts with strengths and characteristics of their species.

3. With students, respond to the author's challenge in ***I Spy a Lion: Animals in Art*** and locate the lion in the appropriate painting. Students point out and name other things they notice in the painting. They look, also, for animals from other letter-sound units: cat, dog, elephant, goat, rabbit, snake, and tortoise.

Students create and illustrate their own I Spy animal books patterned *after I Spy a Lion* and the author's invitation: "I Spy with my little eye a _____ . What do you spy?"

4. Compare and contrast with students the stepmother heroine in ***The Lion's Whiskers: An Ethiopian Folktale*** with the villainous stepmothers in other traditional tales.

5. After they have heard ***The Lonely Lioness and the Ostrich Chicks*** read aloud, students act out the movements and actions and imitate or echo the sounds (onamatopoetic) of the animal characters in subsequent readings.

Items for the Mystery Box

Inedible Items: lace, laces (boot or shoe), ladder, ladle, ladybug, lamb, lamp, lampshade, lantern, lasso, leaf, Lego® building blocks, leopard, leotard, leprechaun, letter (mail), letters (alphabetical), lid, lily, limb, link (chain), **lion**, lightbulb, lighthouse, lips (wax), lipstick, lizard, llama, lobster, lock, locket, log, loon

Edible Items: lamb, lasagna, latkes, leeks, lemon, lemonade, lemon pie, lentils, lentil soup, lettuce, licorice, lima beans, lime, limeade, linguine, lobster, lobster salad, lollipop, lo mein, lox

Rhymes, Songs, Fingerplays, and Tongue Twisters

Lion Theme

*The lion and the unicorn: 20, 32, 33, 34, 46, 50, 73, 76
Tongue Twisters: 1, 13

Letter-Sound l (l)

Here we go Looby Loo: 51, 67, 78
Hey, Lolly, Lolly: 77
*Jack and Jill went up the hill: 5, 20, 26, 28, 31, 32, 33, 34, 38, 39, 40, 46, 49, 50, 52, 53, 58, 62, 67, 73, 76, 78
Jack Sprat could eat no fat: 5, 25, 28, 33, 34, 37, 38, 39, 40, 41, 42, 46, 49, 50, 73, 76
Lazy Lucy: 29

*Mary had a little lamb: 5, 26, 28, 32, 33, 34, 39, 40, 41, 42, 43, 46, 49, 58, 62, 76
Rock-a-bye, baby, on the tree top: 5, 6, 20, 28, 29, 33, 34, 38, 39, 40, 41, 46, 50, 52, 53, 58, 62, 67, 73, 76
There's a hole in the bucket, dear Liza, dear Liza: 17, 55, 65
There was an old woman lived under the hill: 5, 28, 34, 38, 40, 46, 50, 73, 76
This little piggy went to market: 3, 5, 14, 20, 25, 26, 28, 29, 31, 32, 33, 34, 37, 38, 39, 42, 43, 46, 50, 52, 73, 76
Tongue Twisters: 7, 13, 60, 74, 80

Cloze Sentences

1. You can turn on a <u>light</u> if it is dark in a room.
   (If it is dark in a room, you can turn on a <u>light</u>.)
2. A <u>lollipop</u> is a kind of hard candy on a stick that you lick.
   (A kind of hard candy on a stick that you lick is a <u>lollipop</u>.)
3. I found three <u>letters</u> when I looked in the mailbox.
   (When I looked in the mailbox, I found three <u>letters</u>.)
4. You can <u>lock</u> the door with your key if you do not want anyone to come in.
   (If you do not want anyone to come in, you can use your key and <u>lock</u> the door.)

1. The <u>leaves</u> fall off the trees in the fall.
   (In the fall, the trees lose their <u>leaves</u>.)
2. A <u>lion</u> is a large, strong animal in the wild cat family that has a mane and roars.
   (A large, strong animal in the wild cat family that has a mane and roars is a <u>lion</u>.)
3. <u>Lemonade</u> is made from the sour yellow fruit called the lemon.
   (From the sour yellow fruit called the lemon, we make <u>lemonade</u>.)
4. <u>Lamb</u> is the name of a little baby sheep.
   (A little baby sheep is a <u>lamb</u>.)

L l

The lion and the unicorn

Were fighting for the crown;

The lion beat the unicorn

All round about the town.

Some gave them white bread,

And some gave them brown;

Some gave them plum-cake,

And sent them out of town.

Name _____   Date _____

L l

Mary had a little lamb, little lamb, little lamb.

Mary had a little lamb, its fleece was white as snow.

And everywhere that Mary went, Mary went, Mary went,

And everywhere that Mary went the lamb was sure to go.

It followed her to school one day, school one day, school one day.

It followed her to school one day that was against the rule.

It made the children laugh and play, laugh and play, laugh and play.

It made the children laugh and play to see a lamb at school.

© 1999 by Cynthia Conway Waring

Name _____   Date _____

L l

Jack and Jill went up the hill

To fetch a pail of water.

Jack fell down and broke his crown

And Jill came tumbling after.

Name _____   Date _____

L l

COMPLETE IT

light	lollipop
1	2
letters	lock
3	4

You can turn on a <u>light</u> if it is dark in a room.
    1

A <u>lollipop</u> is a kind of hard candy on a stick
   2
that you lick.

I found <u>three</u> letters when I looked in the
        3
mailbox.

You can <u>lock</u> the door with your key if you do
      4
not want anyone to come in.

Name _____   Date _____

L l

leaves
1

lion
2

Lemonade
3

Lamb
4

The <u>leaves</u> fall off the trees in the fall.
　　　1

A <u>lion</u> is a large, strong animal in the wild cat
　　2
family that has a mane and roars.

<u>Lemonade</u> is made from the sour yellow fruit
　　3
called the lemon.

<u>Lamb</u> is the name of a little baby sheep.
　4

Name _____   Date _____

M m mountain

TEACHER REFERENCE

Annotated Book List

Amber on the Mountain, Tony Johnston, illustrated by Robert Duncan (New York: Dial Books for Young Readers, 1994). When Anna's father comes to build a road, Amber teaches her about her mountain home and Anna teaches Amber to read. Then, when Anna returns home, Amber teaches herself to write so that they can continue their friendship.

Appalachia: The Voices of Sleeping Birds, Cynthia Rylant, illustrated by Barry Moser (San Diego: Harcourt Brace Jovanovich, 1991). Rylant's text and Moser's paintings create a quiet portrait of the people of the Appalachian Region—through the days and seasons of their lives in the mountains.

Climbing Kansas Mountains, George Shannon, illustrated by Thomas B. Allen (New York: Simon & Schuster Children's Publishing Division, 1993). A young boy and his father share a special adventure, just the two of them with no brothers along, as they climb to the top of a Kansas mountain—the grain elevator where his dad works—and celebrate the beauty of the surrounding expanses of flat farmland.

Clouds on the Mountain, Emilie Smith-Ayala, illustrated by Alice Priestly (New York: Annick Press [U.S.] Ltd, 1996). Colored-pencil drawings and text capture the drama of a mother, her three young sons, and a puppy caught in a sudden thunderstorm during their hike in the mountains.

Fire on the Mountain, Jane Kurtz, illustrated by E. B. Lewis (New York: Simon & Schuster Books for Young Readers, 1994). A courageous young shepherd boy wins a wager with a cruel and vain rich man by spending the night alone in the mountains. Then, with his sister, he outwits the man, who attempts to deny him what he had promised. An author's note explains the origin of this story from the oral tradition of Ethiopia.

Good Times on Grandfather Mountain, Jacqueline Briggs Martin, illustrated by Susan Gaber (New York: Orchard Books, 1992). Not only does the optimistic Washburn, who lives on Grandfather Mountain, look on the positive side of what, to others, would appear to be bad news; he whittles useful items out of what is left after the calamity!

High in the Mountains, Ruth Yaffe Radin, illustrated by Ed Young (New York: Macmillan Publishing Company, 1989). Young's rich illustrations in pastels complement Radin's description, from a child's point of view, of a day in the Colorado Rocky Mountains near her or his grandfather's home.

Hill of Fire, Thomas P. Lewis, pictures by Joan Sandin (New York: Harper & Row, Publishers, 1971). The easy-to-read story, based on the unexpected eruption of the Parícutin volcano in the cornfield of a farmer in Mexico in 1943, presents the effects the event may have had upon the farmer and his family and village.

How Mountains Are Made: Let's-Read-and-Find-Out Science, Kathleen Weidner Zoehfeld, illustrated by James Graham Hale (New York: HarperCollins Publishers, 1995). During a mountain-climbing trip, four children provide information about different types of mountains and explain how mountains are worn away and built up over the years. Illustrations, drawings, diagrams, maps, and conversational bubbles complement the text.

Let's Discover the Mountains, María Rius and J. M. Parramón, translated from Spanish by Jean Grasso Fitzpatrick (Woodbury, New York: Barron's Educational Series, Inc., 1986). One or two lines of large-print text for each detailed full-page illustration introduce a mountain environment. Includes a guide for parents and teachers.

The Lost Lake, Allen Say (Boston: Houghton Mifflin Company, 1989). During the first summer he lives with him, Luke finds that his father works all of the time and rarely talks to or interacts with him until their hiking and camping trip in the mountains helps Luke discover a deeper relationship with the dad he'd never truly known.

Ming Lo Moves the Mountain, Arnold Lobel (New York: William Morrow & Company, Inc., 1982). Several of a wise man's suggestions fail, but the last enables Ming Lo and his wife to enjoy their house out of the dark shadow of a nearby mountain. By doing the dance of the moving mountain with their eyes closed, piece by piece and step by step, they move, not the mountain, but their house and all of their possessions.

Mist Over the Mountains, Raymond Bial (Boston: Houghton Mifflin Company, 1997). Color and black-and-white photographs and informative text recall the people and region of Appalachia of the past and capture current life in the mountainous area.

A Mountain Alphabet, Margriet Ruurs, illustrated by Andrew Kiss (Toronto, Ontario: Tundra Books, 1996). Accompanied by an alliterative sentence, each painting of an aspect of a mountain habitat includes a number of items beginning with the featured letter and a hidden letter. Author's notes introduce the mountainous environment, add detailed information about each painting, and provide a key to the items to be discovered in each illustration.

Mountain Homes, Althea, illustrated by Barbara McGirr (Cambridge, England: Cambridge University Press, 1985). The informative book describes the animals and plants that survive extreme mountain conditions in places around the world. Includes an index and map of mountain ranges of the world.

Mountains, Neil Morris (New York: Crabtree Publishing Company, 1996). Photographs, diagrams, drawings, maps, and text present information about mountains: physical characteristics, weather, peoples, and plant and animal life. Contains a glossary and index.

Mountains, Seymour Simon (New York: Mulberry Books, 1994). Informative text and colored photographs introduce a number of mountain ranges throughout the world, describe ways in which mountains form and change, and explore the interrelationship among animals, humans, and vegetation in mountainous areas.

Mountains (Geography Detective), Philip Sauvain, illustrated by David Hogg (Minneapolis: Carolrhoda Books, Inc., 1996). Colored photographs, diagrams, maps, and a glossary with text provide information about mountains and "Geography Detective" and map-related questions invite interaction.

Mountains: Usborne First Travellers, Angela Wilkes, illustrated by Peter Dennis (London: Usborne Publishing Ltd, 1980). Text, illustrations, diagrams, and a map provide factual information about mountains of the world: physical characteristics, people, animals, vegetation, transportation, shelter, climbing, and recreation, with sections about avalanches, volcanoes, and glaciers and about Mount Everest and the Ruwenzori Mountains (Mountains of the Moon) in Africa.

Mountains and Volcanoes, Eileen Curran, illustrated by James Watling (Mahwah, New Jersey: Troll Associates, 1985). Repetitive-pattern, easy-to-read text, with a few words on a page, describes how mountains, including volcanoes, form and change.

The Mountains of Tibet, Mordicai Gerstein (New York: HarperCollins Publishers, 1987). A woodcutter from Tibet, who never fulfills his wishes to travel during his lifetime, dies as an old man and is given a chance to live again as anyone or anything anywhere in the galaxies. He discovers that he chooses his former life, but with one important difference—as a girl.

The Mountain That Loved a Bird, Alice McLerran, pictures by Eric Carle (Saxonville, Massachusetts: Picture Book Studio USA, 1985). After many years, the friendship and yearly visits of a bird and generations of her daughters help a barren mountain transform into a lush, green environment where, at last, a bird is able to stay and build her nest.

On Call Back Mountain, Eve Bunting, illustrated by Barry Moser (New York: The Blue Sky Press, 1997). Two young boys, who live at the base of Call Back Mountain, learn about loss and renewal as the forest, destroyed by a fire set by arson, grows back, and when their dear friend, who watches over the forest from the fire tower, dies.

Rocks in My Pockets, Marc Harshman and Bonnie Collins, illustrated by Toni Goffe (New York: Penguin Books USA Inc., 1991). The rocks from the soil that they keep in their pockets help the Woods family, who live on a farm on the top of a tall mountain, in many ways, including keeping them from blowing away, and they provide unexpected income when city people buy them as decorations.

The Stonecutter, Demi (New York: Crown Publishers, Inc., 1995). In this Chinese tale, an angel grants a discontented stonecutter's increasing wishes to become more powerful until, finally changed back into a stonecutter, he finds happiness in his original life and talent.

The Stone-Cutter: A Japanese Folk Tale, Gerald McDermott (New York: Penguin Books, 1975). A humble stonecutter's contentment as he cuts rock from a mountain pleases a magic spirit, who grants him wish after wish for increasing power. He becomes prince, sun, cloud, and mountain—a mountain being cut by a humble stonecutter—and there he remains, no longer watched over by the spirit.

They Could Still Be Mountains: Rookie Read-About Science, Allan Fowler (Chicago: Children's Press, 1997). This easy-to-read informational book with colored photographs focuses on different types of formations that are considered mountains and the animals, vegetation, waterways, and forms of recreation one might find there. Includes an index.

To Climb a Waterfall, Jean Craighead George, illustrated by Thomas Locker (New York: Philomel Books, 1995). George's text, which speaks directly to the reader, and Locker's richly detailed paintings complement each other effectively in this stunning picture book invitation to climb alongside a mountain waterfall.

Tonight Is Carnaval, Arthur Dorros, illustrated by the Club de Madres Virgen del Carmen of Lima, Peru (New York: Penguin Books USA, 1991). In this book illustrated with hand-quilted *arpilleras* (wall hangings used in storytelling), a boy who plays in the band, along with friends and members of his extended family, at the pre-Lenten Carnaval celebration in the high Andes Mountains, describes his everyday and Carnaval experiences. Contains a section, with colored photographs, that describes the process involved in making *arpilleras* and a glossary. Available also in a Spanish edition, ***Por fin es Carnaval***.

A Walk Up the Mountain, Caroline Arnold, illustrated by Freya Tanz (Englewood Cliffs, New Jersey: Silver Burdett Press, Inc., 1990). Easy-to-read text invites readers to take a nature walk in the mountains to discover information about vegetation and animals, geological forms, formation and metamorphosis of mountains, weather, waterways, glaciers, and mountain climbing. A map locates mountains of the world.

When I Was Young in the Mountains, Cynthia Rylant, illustrated by Diane Goode (New York: Penguin Books, 1982). A woman shares childhood memories of daily life with her extended family in a coal mining community in the Appalachian Mountains.

Literature Extension Activities

1. If there is opportunity, take a hiking field trip in the mountains with your students, or discover a special place where they can climb to appreciate a panoramic view near their homes, like the grain elevator the boy and his father climb in ***Climbing Kansas Mountains***. During or after

their adventure, students use pastels, as does the illustrator of the book, to draw what they see from their "mountain" vantage point.

2. ***Good Times on Grandfather Mountain*** follows a traditional good news/bad news pattern. Read other books that follow a good news/bad news pattern with your students, and they can create their own adventure stories.

   Read, for example, (1) ***Fortunately*** by Remy Charlip (New York: Four Winds Press, 1964), in which there is a good news/bad news pattern to the series of adventures a boy must brave between his home in New York City and a birthday party in Florida, and good events (fortunately) pictured with colored illustrations alternate with bad news (unfortunately) shown in black and white; or (2) ***That's Good! That's Bad!*** written by Margery Cuyler and illustrated by David Catrow (New York: Scholastic Inc., 1991) in which a round-trip jungle adventure of a boy who leaves the zoo on the end of the string of a helium balloon is told with a good news (That's good!)/bad news (That's bad!) pattern.

   Individuals or groups of students (round-robin, with each person adding the next event) tell or write and illustrate their own "Good News! Bad News!" adventure story. Authors and illustrators decide whether there will be a pattern to the drawings as well as to the text.

3. As you read aloud the words of the wise man, in ***Ming Lo Moves the Mountain***, students move their left and right feet as directed and experience, firsthand, the dance of the moving mountain.

4. With students, discuss and illustrate who or what and where they might like to be if they were given the choice given the woodcutter in ***The Mountains of Tibet***.

5. After they enjoy, in read-aloud, the two versions of the tale, compare and contrast ***The Stonecutter*** by Demi and ***The Stone-Cutter: A Japanese Folk Tale*** by Gerald McDermott with your students. Have students note, especially, the difference in the endings. Optionally, they compare and contrast the two "Stonecutter" stories and ***The Magic Fish*** (Chapter 6), tales that explore consequences of insatiable desires.

Items for the Mystery Box

Inedible Items: magazine, magic wand, magnet, magnifying glass, mail, mailbox, mammoth, map, marble, marionette, marker, mask, match(es) (burned out), medal, mermaid, meter (parking), microphone, microscope, milk carton, mirror, mitt (baseball), mitt (cooking), mitten, mobile, moccasins, mole, money (variety of bills and coins), monkey, moon, moose, mop, moth, motorcycle, **mountain**, mouse, mug, mule, mushroom, music (recorded on audiotape and played inside the Mystery Box as a clue), music (sheet), music box (Play it inside the Mystery Box as a clue.), mustache, mustard bottle

Edible Items: macadamia nuts, macaroni, macaroons, malted milk balls, malts, mango, manicotti, maple sugar candy, maple syrup, marmalade, marshmallows, matzo, matzo balls (in soup), mayonnaise, meatballs, meatloaf, melon (variety), milk, mincemeat pie, minestrone soup, mints, mint sauce, miso soup, M & M's® chocolate candy, mocha ice cream, molasses, moo shu, moussaka, mousse, mozzarella cheese, muffins (variety), mushrooms, mustard (condiment), mustard (spice)

Rhymes, Songs, Fingerplays, and Tongue Twisters

Mountain Theme

The bear went over the mountain: 51, 53, 55
Flying-man, Flying-man: 5
I love the mountains: 77
*She'll be comin' 'round the mountain: 17, 47, 55, 56, 57, 77, 78

Letter-Sound m (m)

Here we go round the mulberry bush: 5, 25, 26, 29, 33, 34, 38, 41, 47, 50, 62, 67, 73, 76, 78
Little Miss Muffet: 5, 20, 28, 32, 33, 34, 38, 39, 40, 43, 46, 50, 53, 58, 62, 73, 76

Mary had a little lamb: 5, 26, 28, 32, 33, 34, 39, 40, 41, 42, 43, 46, 49, 58, 62, 76
*Mistress, Mary, quite contrary: 5, 20, 28, 32, 33, 34, 38, 39, 40, 41, 46, 50, 52, 53, 62, 73, 76
Miss, miss, little miss, miss: 4
Oh, do you know the muffin man: 26, 33, 42, 47, 53, 79
Row, row, row your boat: 26, 29, 34, 77
*Three little kittens lost their mittens: 5, 9, 26, 27, 28, 33, 34, 37, 51, 62, 71, 72, 73, 76
To market, to market, to buy a fat pig: 3, 5, 25, 28, 33, 34, 42, 46, 49, 50, 58, 76
Tongue Twisters: 1, 13, 60, 74, 80

Cloze Sentences

1. <u>Mi</u>ce are small animals that some cats like to chase.
   (Some cats like to chase small animals called <u>mi</u>ce.)
2. <u>Mi</u>ttens keep your hands war<u>m</u>.
   (You can keep your hands war<u>m</u> if you wear <u>mi</u>ttens.)
3. A <u>m</u>ountain is a very big hill that you can cli<u>m</u>b.
   (A very big hill that you can cli<u>m</u>b is a <u>m</u>ountain.)
4. <u>Mi</u>lk is the drink that we get fro<u>m</u> cows.
   (The drink we get fro<u>m</u> cows is <u>mi</u>lk.)

1. <u>M</u>ustard is something that some people like on their hot dogs, and some people like ketchup or relish.

   (**So**me people like ketchup or relish on their hot dogs, and some people like **m**ustard.)

2. I **m**ight wear a <u>**m**ask</u> to cover **m**y face at Halloween.

   (At Halloween, I **m**ight cover **m**y face by wearing a <u>**m**ask</u>.)

3. <u>**M**arkers</u>, crayons, colored pencils, and chalk are things I **m**ight use when I draw.

   (When I draw, I **m**ight use crayons, colored pencils, chalk, or <u>**m**arkers</u>).

4. A <u>**m**ailbox</u> is a place I **m**ight look to see if I have gotten any letters, packages, or other **m**ail.

   (To see if I have gotten any letters, packages, or other **m**ail, I **m**ight look in a <u>**m**ailbox</u>.)

M m

She'll be comin' 'round the mountain when she comes.

She'll be comin' 'round the mountain when she comes.

She'll be comin' round the mountain,

She'll be comin' 'round the mountain,

She'll be comin' 'round the mountain when she comes.

Name _____   Date _____

M m

Three little kittens lost their mittens,

And they began to cry,

"Oh, Mother dear, we very much fear

That we have lost our mittens."

"What! Lost your mittens! You naughty kittens!

Then you shall have no pie."

"Mee-ow, mee-ow, mee-ow."

"No, you shall have no pie."

"Mee-ow, mee-ow, mee-ow."

Name _____   Date _____

M m

Mistress Mary, quite contrary,

How does your garden grow?

With silver bells and cockle shells

And pretty maids all in a row.

Name _____   Date _____

M m

COMPLETE IT

Mice
1

Mittens
2

mountain
3

Milk
4

<u>Mice</u> are small animals that some cats like to
1
chase.

<u>Mittens</u> keep your hands warm.
2

A <u>mountain</u> is a very big hill that you can
3
climb.

<u>Milk</u> is the drink that we get from cows.
4

Name _____   Date _____

M m

COMPLETE IT

Mustard   mask
1   2
Markers   mailbox
3   4

<u>Mustard</u> is something that some people like on
   1
their hot dogs, and some people like ketchup or relish.

I might wear a <u>mask</u> to cover my face at
                  2
Halloween.

<u>Markers</u>, crayons, colored pencils, and chalk are
   3
things I might use when I draw.

A <u>mailbox</u> is a place I might look to see if I have
      4
gotten any letters, packages, or other mail.

Name _____   Date _____

N n   nest

TEACHER REFERENCE

Annotated Book List

And So They Build, Bert Kitchen (Cambridge, Massachusetts: Candlewick Press, 1993). Detailed full-page illustrations and informative text describe twelve birds and other animals that build nests and other complex structures uniquely designed for survival.

Are You My Mother?, P. D. Eastman (New York: Random House, Inc., 1960). When a bird's mother leaves the nest to look for food for him just before he hatches, he sets out to find her and asks a series of animals, a car, a boat, and a plane if they are his mother. Finally, a steam shovel delivers him home just in time to meet his mother, whom he recognizes immediately.

The Best Nest, P. D. Eastman (New York: Random House, Inc., 1964). Mr. Bird loves their nest, but Mrs. Bird tires of it, so they reject a number of possible new locations and construct a nest atop a steeple bell, a highly unsuitable spot when it is rung. Mr. Bird searches frantically when Mrs. Bird disappears and finds her, a now content mother, in their old nest.

Birds' Nests, Eileen Curran, illustrated by Pamela Johnson (Mahwah, New Jersey: Troll Associates, 1985). Labeled illustrations and a line or two of text on each page identify different types of birds and describe various locations of nests, the processes involved in making different kinds of nests, and the reasons birds build nests.

Condor's Egg, Jonathan London, illustrated by James Chaffee (San Francisco: Chronicle Books, 1994). The last two surviving free-flying California condors in the wild secure a nest for their egg and protect it until the chick hatches. A note written by the Condor Recovery Program Coordinator describes the endangered condor, threats to its survival, and efforts to protect it. Includes addresses of sources of additional information.

Falcons Nest on Skyscrapers: Let's-Read-and-Find-Out Science, Priscilla Belz Jenkins, illustrated by Megan Lloyd (New York: HarperCollins Publishers, 1996). Illustrated text provides information about falcons and about a peregrine falcon that made a nest and successfully hatched and raised four young in a nest box on a ledge on the thirty-third story of a skyscraper in Baltimore. Contains information in an afterword about watching falcons, including locations of sanctuaries, observatories, and refuges, and an address to send for more information.

Flap Your Wings, P. D. Eastman (New York: Random House, Inc., 1969, 1977). A boy places an alligator egg that he finds by a pond in an empty nest, and Mr. and Mrs. Bird hatch it and raise the baby. When he is too big for the nest, they show him how to fly, and he jumps, flapping everything he has—right into the pond below, where he is immediately at home.

Grandmother's Pigeon, Louise Erdrich, illustrated by Jim LaMarche (New York: Hyperion Books for Children, 1996). Mysteries have always surrounded grandmother's life, but none as intriguing as the nest, among the collection in her room, from which three extinct passenger pigeons hatch!

Have You Seen Birds?, Joanne Oppenheim, illustrated by Barbara Reid (New York: Scholastic, 1986). Clay collage illustrations, combined with poetic text, show birds in action in a variety of habitats through the seasons.

Horton Hatches the Egg, Dr. Seuss (New York: Random House, 1940, 1968). Gentle and kind Horton the Elephant is the embodiment of faithfulness as he sits (and sits and sits . . . for fifty-one weeks), despite taunting and dangers, on the egg in the nest of a lazy bird who abandons it. His sterling qualities are rewarded, in the end, with the emergence of an elephant-bird that looks remarkably like him!

The Magic Finger, Roald Dahl, illustrated by Tony Ross (New York: Penguin Books USA Inc., 1966, 1989). In this short fiction book, an eight-year-old girl's neighbors vow never to hunt again after she uses her magic finger to turn them temporarily into birds who must fashion themselves a nest for refuge when four human-sized ducks take over their house and threaten to shoot *their* children.

The Nest, Brian Wildsmith (Oxford, England: Oxford University Press, 1983). In this wordless book, a pair of colorful birds mate, build a nest, and tend three eggs until their young hatch and leave the nest in what appears to be a leafless tree until, on the last page, their perch is revealed to be a deer's antlers!

The Nest: An Ecology Story Book, Chris Baines, illustrated by Penny Ives (New York: Crocodile Books, USA, 1990). Close-up, detailed illustrations and engaging text follow a black cock bird and his mate as they locate and build their nest and care for their eggs and, later, their fledgling babies.

A Nest Full of Eggs: Let's-Read-and-Find-Out Science, Priscilla Belz Jenkins, illustrated by Lizzy Rockwell (New York: HarperCollins Publishers, 1995). The informative book follows a pair of robins as they build their nest, lay their eggs, and nurture their young; describes the development of the robin within the egg; highlights the nature of feathers; presents a variety of different kinds of nests; and suggests ways in which children can help birds with their nest building.

No Roses for HARRY!, Gene Zion, pictures by Margaret Bloy Graham (New York: Harper & Row, Publishers, 1958). Harry, introduced in ***Harry the Dirty Dog*** by the same author, hates the wool sweater with the roses that the children's grandmother knit for him. Finally, after a number of unsuccessful tries, he is able to get rid of the sweater when a bird unravels it and uses the yarn to make a nest.

The Pinkish, Purplish, Bluish Egg, Bill Peet (Boston: Houghton Mifflin Company, 1963). After her children are grown, Myrtle the dove fills her empty nest with a large egg she finds in a cave, out of which hatches a griffin, who is an outcast until a heroic deed brings him acceptance.

Sarah, Plain and Tall, Patricia MacLachlan (New York: Harper & Row, 1985). In this short chapter book, Sarah answers an advertisement and leaves her seaside home in Maine to adjust to her new life as wife and mother of a man and his two young children on the western prairie of the United States. In Chapter 4, Sarah scatters the hair she cuts from Caleb's head for the birds to use for their nests, and, later, Caleb and Anna's father scatters his own.

Scrambled Eggs Super!, Dr. Seuss (New York: Random House, 1953). Anyone can make an egg dish with common hen eggs, but Peter T. Hooper goes to great lengths and performs daring feats to locate the nests of fanciful birds in imaginary places to procure the eggs he needs for his unique recipe, in this book with rhythmic rhyming text.

Swallows in the Birdhouse, Stephen R. Swinburne, illustrated by Robin Brickman (Brookfield, Connecticut: The Millbrook Press,1996). Photographs of three-dimensional watercolor sculptures illustrate this informative book in which two children construct a birdhouse as a nesting box for a pair of swallows, who build their nest and raise their babies before the fall migration. Includes facts about tree swallows and birdhouses and a glossary.

Urban Roosts: Where Birds Nest in the City, Barbara Bash (Boston: Little, Brown and Company Inc./Sierra Club Books, 1990). Watercolor illustrations and text introduce birds that make their nests in the midst of busy cities—a testimony to their remarkable ability to adapt to urban settings.

Literature Extension Activities

1. Whenever possible, you and your students—as well as family, school, and community members—lend abandoned nests to the classroom for a display during this unit. Using their own knowledge and experiences, and as they read the suggested fiction and nonfiction books, students compile a list of materials used in the construction of nests. Volunteers bring in samples of materials considered useful for nest building.

2. Students research and make clay models of a favorite bird, its nest, and its habitat in a specific season after they listen to ***Have You Seen Birds?*** and look closely at the clay collage illustrations.

3. After you have shared ***Swallows in the Birdhouse*** with students, experiment with three-dimensional watercolor to create scenes of birds.

Students paint the scenes first, using watercolors. They then cut out separate elements and fold and sculpt them before they glue them onto a plain-colored background, producing finished works similar to the illustrations in the book.

4. With support, students construct birdhouses appropriate for local species of birds and to their area and weather, inspired by the one the two children construct as a nesting box for a pair of swallows in ***Swallow in the Birdhouse***.

5. After you share ***Urban Roosts: Where Birds Nest in the City*** in read-aloud, you and students list the ingenious places presented in the book where birds have been found to build their nests in urban environments. Then, talk about the locations of birds' nests they have seen in cities. If they have not yet seen nests in urban settings, they consider keeping their eyes open for their next trip to the city! With students, compile a list of places you and they have seen nests built in rural settings. Discuss the positive and negative aspects of each location.

Items for the Mystery Box

Inedible Items: nail (used with hammer), nail (finger, glue-on), nail polish, napkin, necklace, necktie, needle, **nest**, net, newspaper, newt, nickel, nightgown, nine, nose, notebook, numbers (variety), nurse, nutcracker, nuts (variety or mixed, in a can), note (musical), note (written, short letter), nothing (Show students what is in the Mystery Box at the end of the activity.)

Edible Items: nachos, napoleons, navy beans, nectarines, noodle soup, noodles, nougat candy, nuggets (chicken), nut bread (quick, sweet), nutmeg, nuts (variety or mixed, in a can)

Rhymes, Songs, Fingerplays, and Tongue Twisters

Nest Theme

*Elizabeth, Elspeth, Betsy and Bess: 28, 33, 46, 50
Jenny Wren last week was wed
Kittens/Four little kittens: 19

Letter-Sound n (n)

Fireflies/Winking, blinking, winking, blinking: 75

*Hickety, pickety, my black hen: 5, 20, 28, 32, 33, 34, 38, 39, 46, 50, 53, 62, 73, 76
*Little Blue Ben, who lives in the glen: 34, 73
Nose, nose, jolly red nose: 5, 28
Tongue Twisters: 1, 7, 13, 60, 74, 80

Cloze Sentences

1. **Nine** is the **n**umber that comes after eight whe**n** we are cou**n**ting.
   (The **n**umber that comes after eight whe**n** we are cou**n**ting is **nine**.)

2. One **n**ickel is the coi**n** that is the same amou**n**t of mo**n**ey as five pe**nn**ies.
   (The coi**n** that is the same amou**n**t of mo**n**ey as five pe**nn**ies is o**n**e **n**ickel.)

3. Through my **n**ose a**n**d my mouth I ca**n** breathe.
   (I ca**n** breathe through my mouth a**n**d my **n**ose.)

4. A **n**est is something a bird builds whe**n** it **n**eeds a **n**ew home.
   (Whe**n** a bird **n**eeds a **n**ew home, it builds a **n**est.)

1. A **n**ewspaper is a good thing to read if you are i**n**terested i**n** the **n**ews.
   (If you are i**n**terested i**n** the **n**ews, a good thing to read is the **n**ewspaper.)

2. **N**uts are something that squirrels a**n**d chipmunks hide i**n** the fall.
   (I**n** the fall, squirrels a**n**d chipmunks hide **n**uts.)

3. A **n**ail is something that you ca**n** pound i**n**to wood with a hammer.
   (With a hammer, you ca**n** pound a **n**ail i**n**to wood.)

4. A **n**apkin is something you may use to wipe your face a**n**d hands at di**nn**er.
   (At di**nn**er, you may wipe your face a**n**d hands with a **n**apkin.)

N n

Elizabeth, Elspeth, Betsy and Bess,

They all went together to seek a bird's nest;

They found a bird's nest with five eggs in it,

They all took one and left four in it.

Name _____   Date _____

N n

Hickety, pickety, my black hen,
She lays eggs for gentlemen;
Gentlemen come every day
To see what my black hen does lay;
Sometimes nine and sometimes ten,
Hickety, pickety, my black hen.

Name _____   Date _____

N n

LITTLE BLUE BEN

Little blue Ben, that lives in the glen,

Keeps a blue cat and one blue hen.

Which laid of blue eggs a score and ten.

Where shall I find the little blue Ben?

Name _____   Date _____

N n

COMPLETE IT

Nine	nickel
1	2
nose	nest
3	4

<u>Nine</u> is the number that comes after eight when
1
we are counting.

One <u>nickel</u> is the coin that is the same amount
2
of money as five pennies.

Through my <u>nose</u> and my mouth I can breathe.
3

A <u>nest</u> is something a bird builds when it needs
4
a new home.

Name _____   Date _____

Cloze Sentences . . . 1

N n

COMPLETE IT

newspaper	Nuts
1	2
nail	napkin
3	4

A <u>newspaper</u> is a good thing to read if you are
1
interested in the news.

<u>Nuts</u> are something that squirrels and chipmunks
2
hide in the fall.

A <u>nail</u> is something that you can pound into
3
wood with a hammer.

A <u>napkin</u> is something you may use to wipe
4
your face and hands at dinner.

Name _____   Date _____

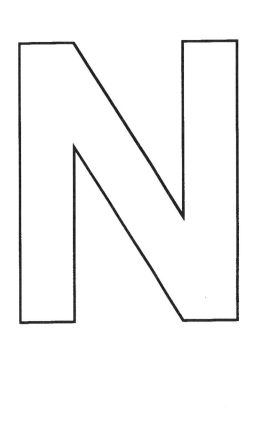

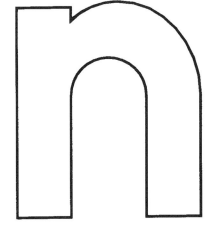

O o   octopus

TEACHER REFERENCE

Annotated Book List

Amazing Animal Disguises: Eyewitness Juniors, Sandie Sowler (New York: Alfred A. Knopf, Inc., 1992). Colored photographs and drawings complement text and captions that provide information about a variety of land and sea animals that use disguise, such as camouflage and mimicry, for protection, including the octopus that changes both the color and texture of its skin to match a rock on which it hides from enemies.

Dolphins at Daybreak, Mary Pope Osborne, illustrated by Sal Murdocca (New York: Random House, 1997). In order to become Master Librarians to help Morgan LeFay, Annie and Jack pilot a disabled minisubmarine, encounter an octopus and a hammerhead shark, are rescued by a pair of dolphins, and solve the first of four riddles in the ninth book in the "Magic Tree House" series.

The Greedy Gray Octopus, based on a story by Christel Buckley and her class, illustrations by David Pearson (Crystal Lake, Illinois: Rigby, 1988). In this book with a repetitive, predictable pattern, a hungry octopus invites a series of sea creatures to play with him, but each anticipates his intentions and is wise enough to refuse and flee. Finally, a shark accepts the octopus's invitation and eats *him*.

How to Hide an Octopus & Other Sea Creatures, Ruth Heller (New York: Grosset & Dunlap, Inc., 1985, 1992). Rhyming text provides information about a number of sea creatures that use camouflage as protection from their predators, and readers are invited to locate each animal, introduced in one illustration, using its camouflage in the next.

My Very Own Octopus, Bernard Most (San Diego: Harcourt Brace & Company, 1980, 1991). A boy wishes he had a pet, but family members are allergic to traditional pets, so he imagines a number of the benefits of having a pet that would make no one sneeze, a pet with eight arms—an octopus!

Nate the Great and the Stolen Base, Marjorie Weinman Sharmat, illustrations by Marc Simont (New York: Coward McCann Inc., 1992). Nate the Great, introduced in ***Nate the Great*** by the same author, and his dog Sludge solve a mystery to locate their friend Oliver's plastic toy octopus that their baseball team uses as second base.

Octopus Hug, Laurence Pringle, illustrated by Kate Salley Palmer (Honesdale, Pennsylvania: Boyds Mills Press, Inc., 1993). While their mother is out one evening, a young brother and sister learn about an octopus hug and other silly and wonderful games from their loving and playful father, and when their mom returns *she* finds out about an octopus hug when dad gives her one.

An Octopus Is Amazing: Let's-Read-and-Find-Out Science, Patricia Lauber, illustrated by Holly Keller (New York: HarperCollins Publishers, 1990). Simple drawings, diagrams, and text present fascinating information about the intelligent sea creature, the octopus: types, physical characteristics, habitat, protection, habits, food, locomotion, young, and problem-solving abilities.

Otto Is Different, Franz Brandenbery, illustrated by James Stevenson (New York: Greenwillow Books, 1985). When he wishes he didn't have to be different, Otto the octopus's parents help him appreciate the advantages of having eight arms—from getting work done four times faster, to being able to play hockey by himself and being a much-sought-after goalie, to receiving and giving hugs with eight arms instead of two!

Tickleoctopus, Audrey Wood, illustrated by Bill Morrison (Boston: Houghton Mifflin Company, 1980). Inspired by a tickling game she played with her son, the author creates a fantasy about a boy who catches an octopus while puddle-fishing and, with his Tickleoctopus, makes the rounds tickling and making laugh the once skeptical adults in his life.

Literature Extension Activities

1. The sea creatures in ***The Greedy Gray Octopus*** are described with a number of adjectives, many of which are color words. After they hear the book read aloud once, students identify the adjectives as they prepare simple costumes to accompany a dramatization of the story. They wear clothing that matches the principal color of a character, for example, and fashion a headpiece or body parts from art materials to identify the sea creature. Actors and actresses then provide the actions and speak chorally along with you (or memorize and say the dialogue themselves, if appropriate) as you read the text as narrator.

2. After they read about the benefits of having an octopus as a pet that the boy in ***My Very Own Octopus*** imagines and that his parents help him appreciate, generate and illustrate with your students more positive things an octopus could do as a pet in their own lives.

3. With students, draw or paint pictures of their favorite silly and loving games or activities, like those in ***Octopus Hug***, that they share or have shared with their dads, moms, other family members, or special people in their lives. In a group, they take turns describing the game or activity

they have illustrated. The completed drawings or paintings become a classroom or hall display or a class book.

4. After you share *An Octopus Is Amazing* and *Otto Is Different* in read-aloud, compile with students two lists of the advantages of being an octopus. On one chart, list strengths and benefits associated with the attributes of an octopus that they know, and that they learn from the informational book *An Octopus Is Amazing* and from other nonfiction sources. On a second chart, list the advantages of being an octopus that Otto comes to appreciate in the fictional book *Otto Is Different*. Compare and contrast the two lists in discussion with students.

Items for the Mystery Box

Inedible Items: **octopus**, off switch, officer (police), olive jar, on switch, operator (telephone), ostrich, otter, ox(en)

Edible Items: **octopus**, olive oil, olives, omelets, onions, oranges, oregano

Rhymes, Songs, Fingerplays, and Tongue Twisters

Octopus Theme

*Octopus offering olive omelets: (Tongue Twister: Cynthia Conway Waring)
Tongue Twisters: 1, 13

Letter-Sound o (o)

*Polly put the kettle on: 3, 5, 20, 26, 28, 29, 32, 33, 34, 40, 41, 46, 50, 62, 73, 76
*Once I saw a little bird: 33, 34, 42, 50, 51, 53, 73
Tongue Twisters: 13, 60, 74, 80

Cloze Sentences

1. The **on** switch makes a lamp light up and a computer start up.
   (The switch that makes a lamp light up and a computer start up is the **on** switch.)
2. An **operator** can give a person help when he **or** she presses "**o**" **on** the telephone.
   (When a person presses "**o**" **on** the telephone, he **or** she can get help from the **operator**.)

3. An <u>o</u>x is a large, strong animal that can pull heavy things, **often on** a farm.

   (A large, str**o**ng animal that can pull heavy things, **often on** a farm, is an <u>o</u>x.)

4. A p**o**lice <u>o</u>fficer will help a pers**o**n if he or she calls 911 **on** the teleph**o**ne.

   (If a person calls 911 **on** the teleph**o**ne, he or she will get help from a p**o**lice <u>o</u>fficer.)

1. The <u>o</u>ff switch makes a lamp and a c**o**mputer st**o**p being **on**.

   (The switch that makes a lamp and a c**o**mputer st**o**p being **on** is the <u>o</u>ff switch.)

2. An <u>o</u>live is s**o**mething that we can eat that is small and green and that c**o**mes in a jar, like a pickle.

   (**S**omething that we can eat that is small and green and that c**o**mes in a jar, like a pickle, is an <u>o</u>live.)

3. An <u>o</u>ct**o**pus is a sea animal that has a s**o**ft b**o**dy and eight arms with suckers **on** them.

   (A sea animal that has a s**o**ft b**o**dy and eight arms with suckers on them is an <u>o</u>ct**o**pus.)

4. An <u>o</u>strich is a big bird with a l**o**ng neck and l**o**ng legs that can run fast but cannot fly.

   (A big bird with a l**o**ng neck and l**o**ng legs that can run fast but cann**o**t fly is an <u>o</u>strich.)

Octopus offering olive omelets

Octopus offering olive omelets

Octopus offering olive omelets

Name _____   Date _____

O o

Polly, put the kettle on,
Polly, put the kettle on,
Polly, put the kettle on,
We'll all have tea.

Sukey, take if off again,
Sukey, take it off again,
Sukey, take it off again,
They've all gone away.

Name _____   Date _____

Rhymes . . . 2

Once I saw a little bird
Come hop, hop, hop,
And I said, "Little bird,
Won't you stop, stop, stop?"

I was going to the window
To say, "How do you do?"
But he shook his little tail,
And far away he flew.

Name _____   Date _____

O o

COMPLETE IT

on	operator
1	2
ox	officer
3	4

The <u>on</u> switch makes a lamp light up and a
    1
computer start up.

An <u>operator</u> can give a person help when he or
        2
she presses "o" on the telephone.

An <u>ox</u> is a large, strong animal that can pull
      3
heavy things, often on a farm.

A police <u>officer</u> will help a person if he or she
            4
calls 911 on the telephone.

Name _____   Date _____

COMPLETE IT

off	olive
1	2
octopus	ostrich
3	4

The <u>off</u> switch makes a lamp and a computer
    1
stop being on.

An <u>olive</u> is something that we can eat that is small
    2
and green and that comes in a jar, like a pickle.

An <u>octopus</u> is a sea animal that has a soft body
     3
and eight arms with suckers on them.

An <u>ostrich</u> is a big bird with a long neck and
    4
long legs that can run fast but cannot fly.

Name _____ Date _____

P p pumpkin

TEACHER REFERENCE

Annotated Book List

Apples and Pumpkins, Anne Rockwell, pictures by Lizzy Rockwell (New York: Simon & Schuster Children's Publishing, 1989). Simple, supportive text and illustrations in this book depict a young girl's visit to a farm to prepare for Halloween, where she and her family pick apples to give as treats and a pumpkin that they carve into a jack-o'-lantern.

Bear's Bargain, Frank Asch (New York: Simon & Schuster Books for Young Readers, 1985). Two friends, introduced in ***Happy Birthday, Moon*** by the same author, benefit from a bargain when Bear teaches Little Bird to be big with a pumpkin they grow from seed and Little Bird shows Bear how to fly with a kite they make.

The Big, BIG Pumpkin, Joan M. Lexau, pictures by Sue Lundgren (Middletown, Connecticut: Weekly Reader Books, 1985). Bear leaves home and, with his mother's advice and help from his new friend Crow and Crow's friends, he discovers that the enormous pumpkin he grows from a seed makes a wonderful home, with cut-out windows and a door.

The Biggest Pumpkin Ever, Steven Kroll, illustrated by Jeni Bassett (New York: Holiday House, Inc., 1984). Without each other's knowledge, two mice cultivate a pumpkin, one by day and one by night. When it grows to giant proportions and they discover each other's existence, they amiably figure out a way to share the product of their intense labor.

The Golden Flower: A Taino Myth from Puerto Rico, Nina Jaffe, illustrated by Enrique O. Sánchez (New York: Simon & Schuster Books for Young Readers, 1996). In this pourquoi story, a child plants seeds he finds in his barren world, from which a vine with a golden flower and then a yellow shining globe grow. From this shining pumpkin (calabaza) pour waters that cover the earth, leaving the island of Boriquén, or Puerto Rico. An afterword provides information about the traditional tale and the Taino people.

Grandma's Smile, Elaine Moore, pictures by Dan Andreasen (New York: William Morrow & Company, Inc., 1995). After they enjoy the varied events at an autumn festival, at first, Kim cannot choose the kind of face to be carved on her jack-o'-lantern for a contest. She soon realizes that her grandmother's smile is a fitting tribute to the loving relationship they share.

The Great Pumpkin Switch, Megan McDonald, Ted Lewin (New York: Orchard Books, 1992). Grandpa tells his grandchildren a story from his childhood, when he and his friend have to buy a large pumpkin to take the place of his sister's pumpkin that they accidentally smash.

The Halloween Performance, Felicia Bond (New York: Harper & Row, Publishers Inc., 1983). Readers are left to guess Roger the mouse's small but memorable role in the Halloween play until the preparations are completed, the performance is nearly over, and Roger appears—as the Halloween pumpkin.

How Spider Saved Halloween, Robert Kraus (New York: Scholastic Inc., 1973). Even with the help of friends, Spider finds that it is not easy to think of a costume that disguises his identity, until pal Ladybug's pumpkin, smashed by bullies, gives him an idea that saves the day. Colored orange, with a green construction paper stem and blacked-out front tooth, he makes the perfect Halloween pumpkin.

I'm a Seed, Jean Marzollo, illustrated by Judith Moffatt (New York: Scholastic Inc., 1996). In this book with large print, few words on a page, and striking collage illustrations, two seeds converse as they grow into mature plants, noting their differences during the process. In the end, they celebrate the marigold flowers and the pumpkins that they become.

In a Pumpkin Shell: Over 20 Pumpkin Projects for Kids, Jennifer Storey Gillis, illustrated by Patti Delmonté (Pownal, Vermont: Storey Communications, Inc., 1992). This activity book designed for children presents pumpkin facts, history, and legends, plus projects with pumpkins that include planting and growing, harvesting and storing, saving seeds, creating crafts, cooking from recipes, and completing a crossword puzzle.

It's Pumpkin Time!, Zoe Hall, illustrated by Shari Halpern (New York: Scholastic Inc., 1994). A young brother and sister share their preparations, starting in the summer, for their favorite holiday, Halloween, from planting seeds and tending the plants to harvesting and carving the pumpkins in time for trick-or-treating. Includes a page with words and pictures that describes how pumpkins grow underground.

Jack-o'-Lantern, Miriam Frost, illustrated by Steven Hauge (Bothell, Washington: The Wright Group, 1990). In a book of eight pages, children carve six pumpkins that express different emotions and, in the end, make them into a pumpkin pie.

The Little Old Lady Who Was Not Afraid of Anything, Linda Williams, illustrated by Megan Lloyd (New York: Harper & Row, Publishers, 1986). In this cumulative story, a plucky old woman encounters—as she walks home at night—shoes clomping, pants wiggling, a shirt shaking, gloves clapping, a hat nodding, and a pumpkin saying "Boo." She demonstrates not only her courage but also her inventiveness as she consoles them, after they fail to scare her, with a new purpose: They become the scarecrow in her garden.

Mother Pumpkin and Her Remarkable Gourd Family, Nadezhda Nadezhdina, translated by Tracy Kuehn (Moscow: Raduga Publishers/Chicago: Imported Publications, Inc., 1989). This illustrated collection includes riddles, information, history, stories, and poems from around the world about pumpkins and other members of the gourd family.

Picking Apples & Pumpkins, Amy and Richard Hutchings, photographs by Richard Hutchings (New York: Scholastic Inc., 1994). Colorful photographs show two young girls, their two friends, parents, and grandmother as they pick Macoun and Delicious apples in an orchard and pumpkins in a patch, then return home to make an apple pie and carve jack-o'-lanterns.

The Pumpkin, Joy Cowley, illustrations by Robyn Kahukiwa (Bothell, Washington: The Wright Group, 1982, 1990). In this eight-page book with repetitive pattern and text, a little girl and her sister, brother, father, and mother complete different tasks as they plant, hoe, water, pick, cut, and cook a pumpkin for their family to enjoy.

The Pumpkin Blanket, Deborah Turney Zawwÿn (Berkeley, California: Tricycle Press, 1990, 1995). Kindergarten-aged Clee gives up her beloved pumpkin quilt, mysteriously given to her by the Northern Lights, square by square, to cover and protect from the frost the pumpkins growing in their garden. When the pumpkins are harvested and the blanket is no longer needed (by child or pumpkins), the sky reclaims it.

The Pumpkin Fair, Eve Bunting, illustrated by Eileen Christelow (New York: Clarion Books, 1997). In this rhyming, rhythmic picture book, for a young girl, the highlight of the Pumpkin Fair—a celebration of pumpkin games, music, activities, and food—is winning a prize ribbon for the best-loved pumpkin for her small, undistinguished, and bumpy pumpkin.

The Pumpkin Man and the Crafty Creeper, Margaret Mahy, illustrated by Helen Craig (New York: Lothrop, Lee & Shepard Books, 1990). A bossy flowering vine tricks Mr. Parkin into taking her home and runs him ragged with her demands for personalized care, poetry, and entertainment (including a hired orchestra) until the vine's owner takes her back, and Mr. Parkin is freed to return to his first love—growing pumpkins (and *only* pumpkins).

Pumpkin Moonshine, Tasha Tudor (New York: Henry Z. Walck, Incorporated, 1938). In this small book, the pumpkin that Sylvie Ann and her dog pick from the cornfield on the hill rolls away from them and disturbs everyone in the barnyard. Later, with her grandfather's help, it becomes a wonderful pumpkin moonshine (jack-o'-lantern) and source of seeds for the next year's crop.

The Pumpkin Patch, Elizabeth King (New York: Penguin Books USA Inc., 1990). Colored photographs and text present the stages of growth of pumpkin plants and the varied activities of farm laborers who, from plowing the earth and planting the seeds to harvesting and selling, cultivate a large crop.

Pumpkin Pumpkin, Jeanne Titherington (New York: William Morrow & Company, Inc., 1986). This short book with large type, brief text, and detailed illustrations follows a pumpkin seed through stages of growth from the time Jaime plants it until he carves a jack-o'-lantern and harvests seeds for the following year.

Pumpkins: A Story for a Field, Mary Lyn Ray, illustrated by Barry Root (San Diego: Harcourt Brace & Company, 1992). A man sells everything except his bed, stove, and bathtub and, with the help of the field he loves (and a little magic), plants pumpkins that he sells to people around the world to save the field from being developed.

Literature Extension Activities

1. If you have not already done so during the first unit, compare and contrast apples and pumpkins as or after you read ***Apples and Pumpkins*** and ***Picking Apples & Pumpkins*** with your students. Compile a list or data matrix showing similarities and differences, or create a Venn diagram. Considerations include size, shape, color, attributes of skin, seeds (edible/inedible, size, shape, color), when harvested, location of growth (trees/vines), how eaten, other products, and so on.

2. In anticipation of this unit (while pumpkins are growing) or during this unit (if pumpkins grow while it is presented), visit a pumpkin patch with your students. Have them observe firsthand, over time, how marks scratched or carved into the skin of a pumpkin grow as the pumpkin grows. With students, draw a picture, as Bear draws a picture of Little Bird in ***Bear's Bargain***, or students can write their names or initials in the skin of individual pumpkins or contribute to a class pumpkin. Display the harvested pumpkins in the classroom or school.

3. After they hear ***I'm a Seed*** read aloud, students (individually or as a group) plant pumpkin seeds and flower or vegetable seeds. They record in a log book, in drawings with dictated or written labels, the growth process of each of the two kinds of seeds. They refer to their logs as they create individual or group books. They use their log illustrations and the repeated pattern of ***I'm a Seed*** to show the differences between the two seeds as they grow.

4. Share with students the fascinating facts, history, and legends about pumpkins from ***In a Pumpkin Shell: Over 20 Pumpkin Projects for***

Kids, and together you grow, create, cook, and complete pumpkin projects from the book.

5. ***It's Pumpkin Time!*** includes the address of the International Pumpkin Association, from which individuals can order information sheets about growing and cooking pumpkins. With students, compose an illustrated group letter to request these materials.

6. Students act out or draw their own jack-o'-lanterns, to accompany each page of ***Jack-o'-Lantern***, that show the emotions on the faces described by the adjectives in the text: happy, sad, scared, mad, silly, and sleepy. They compile and dramatize for others to guess a list of words that describe (adjectives) other emotions a jack-o'-lantern could show and draw jack-o'-lantern faces that show them. They dictate or write text, following the pattern of the book, and compile the text and illustrations into an individual or group collaborative book.

7. After they enjoy the not-very-scary ***The Little Old Lady Who Was Not Afraid of Anything*** in read-aloud, students who carry shoes, pants, shirt, gloves, hat, and jack-o'-lantern—and one student as the old woman—dramatize the story as you, the narrator, reread it.

Items for the Mystery Box

Whenever possible, select items for this unit that are **p**ink or **p**urple in color.

Inedible Items: paddle, pail, paint, paintbrush, pajamas, palm tree, pan, panda, pansy, panther, pants, paper, paper clip, parachute, parrot, paste, peacock, pearls, pebbles, peeler (vegetable), pelican, pen, pencil, penguin, pennant, penny, perfume, piano, picnic basket, pig, pigeon, piggy bank, pillow, pin (jewelry), pin (safety), piñata, pine cone, ping pong ball, pipe, pirate, pitcher, plane, plant, pocket, policeman, policewoman, polka dots, pony, porcupine, porpoise, pot, present (wrapped box), princess, **pumpkin**, puffin, puppet, puppy, purse, pussy willow, puzzle

Edible Items: paella, pancakes, papaya, parfait, parmesan cheese, parsley, parsnips, pasta (variety), peaches, peanut butter, peanuts, pears, pea soup, peas, pecans, pepper (black and red, seasoning), peppers (vegetable, in variety of colors), peppermint candy, pepperoncini peppers, pepperoni, persimmon, pesto, pickles, pilaf, pineapple, pine nuts, pirogi, pita bread, pizza, plums, pomegranates, popcorn, popovers, popsicles, potatoes (baked, boiled, fries, mashed), pretzels, prunes, pudding, punch, **pumpkin** bread, **pumpkin** pie, **pumpkin** seeds

Rhymes, Songs, Fingerplays, and Tongue Twisters

Pumpkin Theme

Five little pumpkins: 15
Jack-o'-Lantern/I am a pumpkin, big and round: 19
*Peter, Peter, pumpkin eater: 5, 20, 25, 28, 33, 39, 50, 52, 73, 76

Letter-Sound p (p)

Hush, little baby, don't say a word: 5, 6, 17, 21, 22, 29, 34, 51, 53, 61, 73, 76, 78
Pat a cake, pat a cake, baker's man: 3, 5, 20, 28, 29, 31, 33, 34, 37, 38, 39, 40, 41, 42, 43, 46, 53, 58, 62, 73, 76

Pawpaw Patch/Where oh where is pretty little Sally?: 47
*Pease-porridge hot: 3, 5, 25, 26, 28, 33, 34, 38, 39, 46, 50, 58, 62, 76, 79
*Peter Piper picked a peck of pickled peppers: 3, 5, 28, 33, 34, 39, 46, 50
Polly put the kettle on: 3, 5, 20, 26, 28, 29, 32, 33, 34, 40, 41, 46, 50, 62, 73, 76
Ten fat peas in a peapod pressed: 12
This little piggy went to market: 3, 5, 14, 20, 25, 26, 28, 29, 31, 32, 33, 34, 37, 38, 39, 42, 43, 46, 50, 52, 73, 76
Tongue Twisters: 1, 7, 13, 60, 74, 80

Cloze Sentences

1. My **p**illow is the thing I **p**ut my head on when I go to slee**p**.
   (When I go to slee**p**, I **p**ut my head on my **p**illow.)

2. A **p**encil is what I use when I want to be able to erase when I write.
   (When I want to be able to erase when I write, I use a **p**encil.)

3. A **p**upp**y** is the name of a baby dog.
   (A baby dog is called a **p**upp**y**.)

4. When I **p**aint, I like to **p**ut on a smock or an a**p**ron, stand at the easel, and use a clean brush.
   (I like to **p**ut on a smock or an a**p**ron, stand at the easel, and use a clean brush when I **p**aint.)

1. A **p**um**p**kin is the thing I carve into a jack-o'-lantern at Halloween.
   (At Halloween, I carve a jack-o'-lantern out of a **p**um**p**kin.)

2. A **p**an is something I **p**ut sou**p** in to cook it on the stove.
   (When I cook sou**p** on the stove, I **p**ut it in a **p**an.)

3. A **p**enn**y** is the coin that is the same as one cent.
   (The coin that is the same as one cent is a **p**enn**y**.)

4. My **p**late is where I **p**ut my food at dinner.
   (At dinner, I **p**ut my food on my **p**late.)

P p

Peter, Peter, pumpkin eater,

Had a wife and couldn't keep her;

He put her in a pumpkin shell,

And there he kept her very well.

Name _____   Date _____

P p

Peter Piper picked a peck of pickled peppers;

A peck of pickled peppers Peter Piper picked.

If Peter Piper picked a peck of pickled peppers,

Where's the peck of pickled peppers

Peter Piper picked?

Name _____   Date _____

P p

Pease-porridge hot,
Pease-porridge cold,
Pease-porridge in the pot
Nine days old.

Some like it hot,
Some like it cold,
Some like it in the pot
Nine days old.

Name _____   Date _____

P p

COMPLETE IT

pillow	pencil
1	2
puppy	paint
3	4

My <u>pillow</u> is the thing I put my head on when I
    1
go to sleep.

A <u>pencil</u> is what I use when I want to be able to
  2
erase when I write.

A <u>puppy</u> is the name of a baby dog.
  3

When I <u>paint</u>, I like to put on a smock or an
    4
apron, stand at the easel, and use a clean brush.

Name _____ Date _____

P p

COMPLETE IT

pumpkin	pan
1	2
penny	plate
3	4

A <u>pumpkin</u> is the thing I carve into a jack-o'-
    1
lantern at Halloween.

A <u>pan</u> is something I put soup in to cook it on
   2
the stove.

A <u>penny</u> is the coin that is the same as one
    3
cent.

My <u>plate</u> is where I put my food at dinner.
   4

Name _____   Date _____

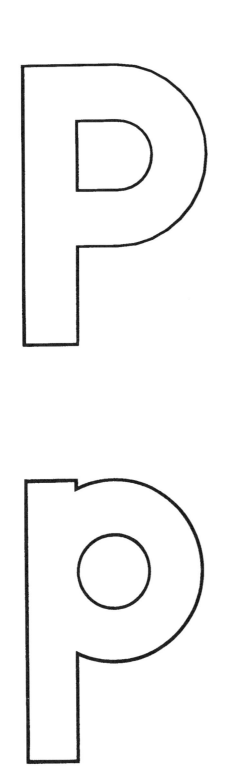

QU qu quilt

TEACHER REFERENCE

Annotated Book List

Aunt Harriet's Underground Railroad in the Sky, Faith Ringgold (New York: Crown Publishers, Inc., 1992). Cassie and her brother Be Be (from ***Tar Beach*** by the same author) learn about slavery—and freedom—while flying aboard a fantasy train on the Underground Railroad, whose conductor is Harriet Tubman. Contains background information about Harriet Tubman and the Underground Railroad, including a short bibliography of further readings and a map of routes.

The Canada Geese Quilt, Natalie Kinsey-Warnock, illustrated by Leslie W. Bowman (New York: Penguin Books USA Inc., 1989). In this short chapter book, ten-year-old Ariel's grandmother encourages Ariel's dream to be an artist and assures her of the constancy of her love that transcends the changes their family experiences—Grandma's stroke and the birth of Ariel's first sibling—when she makes a quilt based on one of Ariel's sketches of Canada geese.

The Crazy Quilt, Kristin Avery, illustrated by David McPhail (Glenview, Illinois: GoodYearBooks/Scott Foresman and Company, 1994). Young Tanya bear, inspired by the crazy quilt her mother made from favorite clothing of members of her extended family, surprises her immediate family with her own patchwork quilt, pieced from their favorite clothes taken without their knowledge!

Eight Hands Round: A Patchwork Alphabet, Ann Whitford Paul, illustrated by Jeanette Winter (New York: HarperCollins Publishers, 1991). This alphabet book presents twenty-six patchwork quilt patterns from the early United States and relates their possible origins to the activities and experiences of the people of the time that may have inspired them. An author's note provides background information about quilting when the United States was young.

The Josefina Story Quilt, Eleanor Coerr, illustrated by Bruce Degen (New York: Harper & Row, 1986). Pa is reluctant to let Faith take her old pet hen, Josefina, in their covered wagon as they travel west in 1850, and her misadventures nearly cause Josefina's demise, but she proves her worth along the way. Faith records their journey in a patchwork quilt.

Julius, Angela Johnson, pictures by Dav Pilkey (New York: Orchard Books, 1993). In this picture book illustrated with patchwork quilt borders, Julius, the fun-loving, enthusiastic (and messy) pig that Maya's grandfather brings her as a gift from Alaska—meant to teach her about fun and sharing—lives up to his expectations, and beyond.

The Keeping Quilt, Patricia Polacco (New York: Simon & Schuster, 1988). The author tells and illustrates the story of a quilt made from clothing of family members who immigrated with her great-grandmother to New York City from Russia—a quilt that has been a central part of her family's daily life and celebrations and has been passed from mother to daughter for four generations.

Luka's Quilt, Georgia Guback (New York: Greenwillow Books, 1994). When Luka's Tutu (grandmother) makes her a quilt that is not to her liking, Luka learns about the quilting traditions of their Hawaiian people, and they both learn about the benefits of compromise.

The Mountains of Quilt, Nancy Willard, illustrated by Tomie dePaola (San Diego: Harcourt Brace Jovanovich, Publishers, 1987). Grandmother makes crazy quilts from her bag of scraps, but none is as beautiful—or as magical—as the one whose center block is a magician's magic carpet that takes her on an adventure that changes her life.

The Patchwork Lady, Mary K. Whittington, illustrated by Jane Dyer (San Diego: Harcourt Brace & Company, 1991). The Patchwork Lady prepares refreshments and decorations for her birthday party, at which her friends surprise her with a patchwork quilt made of blocks that capture the patterns, colors, and elements of her home and life.

The Patchwork Quilt, Valerie Flournoy, illustrated by Jerry Pinkney (New York: Dial Books for Young Readers, 1985). Every day, Tanya's beloved Grandma sits in her favorite chair sewing pieces of fabric and the stories of the lives of her family into a patchwork quilt, until she becomes ill. Then, Tanya works on it until Grandma recovers and can finish it.

Patchwork Tales, Susan L. Roth and Ruth Phang (New York: Atheneum, 1984). In this book, illustrated with colorful wood block prints, a little girl's grandmother tells her the stories represented by each block in her mother's patchwork sampler quilt, and she asks her grandmother to sew her stories into a quilt for her. Includes directions for a simple, doll-size cloth patchwork quilt.

The Pumpkin Blanket, Deborah Turney Zawwÿn (Berkeley, California: Tricycle Press, 1990, 1995). Kindergarten-aged Clee gives up her beloved pumpkin quilt, mysteriously given to her by the Northern Lights, square by square, to cover and protect from the frost the pumpkins growing in their garden. When the pumpkins are harvested and the blanket is no longer needed (by child or pumpkins), the sky reclaims it.

The Quilt, Ann Jonas (New York: Penguin Books USA Inc., 1984). The fabric pieces in a quilt, made for a young girl to mark her rite of passage into a new grown-up bed, remind her of reassuring past events and inspire a dream adventure, in which she conquers her fears during her first night sleeping under it, as she searches for and finds her special stuffed dog.

The Quilt Story, Tony Johnston, illustrated by Tomie dePaola (New York: G. P. Putnam's Sons, 1985). When her family travels west in a covered wagon, the quilt Abigail's mother made provides a warm and comforting familiarity. Many years later, one of Abigail's young relatives discovers the quilt in the attic, and it accompanies her, too, to a new home.

The Rag Coat, Lauren Mills (Boston: Little, Brown and Company, 1991). Children in a small Appalachian coal mining town learn the meaning of community when the Quilting Mothers make Minna a coat from their cloth rags so that she can attend school.

Sam Johnson and the Blue Ribbon Quilt, Lisa Campbell Ernst (New York: Mulberry Paperback Books, 1983). When Sam Johnson is not allowed to join his wife's quilting club, he organizes an all-men's club to make a quilt for the county fair contest, but an accident on the way to the judging shows the men and women the advantages of cooperation over competition.

Sewing Quilts, Ann Turner, illustrated by Thomas B. Allen (New York: Macmillan Publishing Company, 1994). The patchwork quilt that a young girl and her mother and sister sew provides their family with reminders of their shared experiences and a sense of safety from the challenges of their pioneer life.

The Spinner's Gift, Gail Radley, illustrated by Paige Miglio (New York: North-South Books, 1994). The cloth for the queen's gown, woven from the thread spun by a poor spinner, is passed on and reused in a variety of forms until it returns, by chance, to the spinner, who makes it into a quilt for the queen's grandchild.

Sweet Clara and the Freedom Quilt, Deborah Hopkinson, illustrated by James Ransome (New York: Alfred A. Knopf, 1993). Aided by the quilt onto which she sews a map pattern of the Underground Railroad, Clara is reunited with her mother and sister and, with them and a friend, escapes to freedom.

Tar Beach, Faith Ringgold (New York: Random House, Inc., 1991). Ringgold's "Tar Beach" story quilt was adapted and combined with text and paintings in this book about Cassie's fantasy flight of the spirit, from the rooftop of her apartment building (Tar Beach) amid the stars above New York City.

Tonight Is Carnaval, Arthur Dorros, illustrated by the Club de Madres Virgen del Carmen of Lima, Peru (New York: Penguin Books USA, 1991). In this book, illustrated with hand-quilted *arpilleras* (wall hangings used in storytelling), a boy who plays in the band, along with friends and members of his extended family, at the pre-Lenten Carnaval celebration in the high Andes Mountains, describes his everyday and Carnaval experiences. Contains a section, with colored photographs, that describes the process involved in making *arpilleras,* and a glossary. Available also in a Spanish edition, ***Por fin es Carnaval***.

Literature Extension Activities

1. People from cultures around the world create quilts and other pieces of fabric art that are beautiful and functional, and that preserve, for generations, family and community history and stories. With students, explore this art form.

   * Share quilts that students, you, family or community members, or friends own or have made, and tell about the history, stories, and lives they represent.
   * Attend quilt exhibits at museums, historical societies, continuing education courses, and quilt supply stores.
   * Learn more about quilts and quilting from guest presenters and resource books and materials.

2. Extend students' exploration of quilts by making class quilts from fabric or paper.

Note: At the end of the unit, disassemble the class quilt(s) and return blocks to individual students, or give each student a photograph of herself or himself with the completed quilt(s) and place a photograph in a classroom album.

Quilts on Fabric Backgrounds

   * Draw pictures or designs in predrawn blocks with fabric crayons, pens, or markers.
   * Fasten (glue, paste) precut pieces of fabric into simple patchwork designs or crazy quilts. If possible, each person contributes a scrap of cloth that represents an important story or event in her or his life while part of the class community. (It is often helpful to plan the designs with movable geometric shapes and/or graph paper.)
   * Iron on or fasten (glue, paste) precut appliqué fabric designs.

Quilts on Paper Backgrounds

   * Assemble precut geometric shapes or appliqué designs from colored

paper or from light-colored paper (on which you and your students have drawn colored designs or pictures of memorable events from your time together) or from fabric into patchwork pattern, crazy quilt, or appliqué quilt designs.

* Construct a patchwork sampler quilt with paper blocks of class favorites in categories such as books, foods, animals, forms of transportation. Each class member draws a picture, on a block, of her or his favorite in a category for each quilt.

* Fasten (glue, paste) teacher-supplied photographs of each classroom community member onto paper blocks larger than the photographs, leaving borders that individuals illustrate with pictures that represent important things about themselves.

* Compile paper blocks on which individuals write their initials that they illuminate (decorate with designs as in the initial letters of words in old manuscripts and books) or surround with drawings of things important to them.

* Combine, with paper strips for borders, individuals' quilt blocks that show classroom experiences, drawn with pastels on colored paper, inspired by the illustrations in *Sewing Quilts*.

3. The illustrations for *Luka's Quilt* are done in cut-paper collage. After you share the book with students, experiment with this technique. Make two-dimensional leis, like the one Luka make during their Lei Day celebration, or a flower garden like Luka's family's.

4. In *The Rag Coat*, Minna's story quilt is not a bed covering. It is a coat. With students, make a list of quilted products and uses for quilts, including aprons, baby bibs and clothing, bed covers, bookmarks, change purses, coats, eyeglass cases, hats, hot pads, jackets, jewelry, ornaments, pants, pillow tops, pocketbooks, pot holders and mitts, shirts, tea cozies, vests, wall hangings, and so on.

Items for the Mystery Box

Inedible Items: quail, quart, quarter, quarterback, queen (person), queen (playing card), question mark, Quik® chocolate drink mix tin, quill pen, quills, **quilt**, quiver (of arrows)

Edible Items: Quaker® Oats cereal, quart (of juice, milk), quick breads (variety of sweet breads), Quik® chocolate drink mix, quince, quince juice, quinoa

Rhymes, Songs, Fingerplays, And Tongue Twisters

Quilt Theme

*Quiet queens quickly quilting: (Tongue Twister: Cynthia Conway Waring)
Tongue Twisters: 13

Letter-Sound qu (kw)

Hector Protector was dressed all in green: 5, 28, 33, 34, 40, 50, 73, 76
*I saw a ship a-sailing: 5, 28, 33, 34, 38, 39, 40, 50, 73, 76
Lavender's blue, diddle, diddle: 26, 28, 29, 33, 34, 38, 41, 46, 51, 53, 62, 67, 73, 76

Mother, Mother, I am sick: 4
Pussy cat, pussy cat: 5, 9, 25, 26, 28, 33, 34, 37, 38, 39, 40, 42, 46, 50, 52, 58, 62, 73, 76
Quack! Quack! Quack!/Five little ducks that I once knew: 12, 19
The Queen of Hearts: 3, 5, 28, 32, 33, 34, 35, 38, 39, 46, 50, 52, 73, 76
*Sing a song of sixpence: 3, 5, 26, 28, 29, 32, 33, 34, 37, 38, 39, 41, 46, 50, 52, 53, 58, 59, 62, 67, 73, 76
Tongue Twisters: 1, 63, 80

Cloze Sentences

1. A **qu**een can be a woman who rules a country, or she can be married to a king.

   (A woman who rules a country or who is married to a king is a **qu**een.)

2. A **qu**arter is a large, silver coin that is the same as twenty-five cents.

   (A large, silver coin that is the same as twenty-five cents is a **qu**arter.)

3. **Qu**ills are the stiff, sharp spines or hairs on a porcupine.

   (The stiff, sharp spines or hairs on a porcupine are **qu**ills.)

4. A **qu**estion mark is the mark that we put at the end of a sentence when we ask something that needs an answer.

   (The mark that we put at the end of a sentence when we ask something that needs an answer is a **qu**estion mark.)

1. A **qu**art is a way to measure the amount of li**qu**id, like milk, in a bottle or carton.

   (A way to measure the amount of li**qu**id, like milk, in a bottle or carton is a **qu**art.)

2. The **qu**arterback is one of the four players behind the line in the game of football.

   (One of the four players behind the line in football is the **qu**arterback.)

3. A **qu**ilt is a covering for a bed that is usually made from pieces of cloth sewn together.

(A covering for a bed that is usually made from pieces of cloth sewn together is a **qu**ilt.)

4. A **qu**iver is a case for holding arrows.

(A case for holding arrows is a **qu**iver.)

QU qu

Quiet queens quickly quilting

Quiet queens quickly quilting

Quiet queens quickly quilting

Name _____   Date _____

Rhymes . . . 1

QU qu

I SAW A SHIP A-SAILING

The captain was a duck,

With a packet on his back;

And when the ship began to move,

The captain said, "Quack! Quack!"

Name _____   Date _____

QU qu

SING A SONG OF SIXPENCE

The king was in his counting house
Counting out his money;

The Queen was in the parlor
Eating bread and honey.

Name _____   Date _____

QU qu

COMPLETE IT

queen	quarter
1	2
Quills	question
3	4

A <u>queen</u> can be a woman who rules a country,
   1
or she can be married to a king.

A <u>quarter</u> is a large, silver coin that is the same
    2
as twenty-five cents.

<u>Quills</u> are the stiff, sharp spines or hairs on a
   3
porcupine.

A <u>question</u> mark is the mark that we put at the
    4
end of a sentence when we ask something that
needs an answer.

Name _____   Date _____

QU qu

COMPLETE IT

quart	quarterback
1	2
quilt	quiver
3	4

A <u>quart</u> is a way to measure the amount of
    1
liquid, like milk, in a bottle or carton.

The <u>quarterback</u> is one of the four players
    2
behind the line in the game of football.

A <u>quilt</u> is a covering for a bed that is usually
    3
made from pieces of cloth sewn together.

A <u>quiver</u> is a case for holding arrows.
    4

Name _____   Date _____

Qu qu

R r   rabbit

TEACHER REFERENCE

Annotated Book List

Animal Lore & Legend—Rabbit: American Indian Legends, retold by D. L. Birchfield, additional text and book design by Vic Warren, illustrations by Diana Magnuson (New York: Scholastic Inc., 1996). In this easy-to-read book, nonfiction sections, with colored photographs that provide information about North American rabbits and hares, alternate with illustrated legends and trickster and pourquoi tales from the Cherokee and Taos nations about these animals. Includes a glossary.

"The Big Brag" in *Yertle the Turtle and Other Stories*, Dr. Seuss (New York: Random House, 1950, 1951, 1977, 1979, 1986). It's difficult to tell, in this story of competitive bragging in rhyme, whether the rabbit, with his exaggerated sense of hearing, or the bear, with his overblown sense of smell, will win the argument—until a worm, with eyesight good enough to recognize their foolishness, puts an end to their bravado.

Brother Rabbit: A Cambodian Tale, Minfong Ho & Saphan Ros, illustrated by Jennifer Hewitson (New York: Lothrop, Lee & Shepard Books, 1997). Ever cheerful, calm, and inventive, Brother Rabbit tricks crocodile, a woman, and two elephants with flattery and guile in this trickster tale, illustrated with striking watercolor-and-ink drawings with borders. An author's note relates Cambodian history and folktale tradition to this tale.

Ella and the Rabbit, Helen Cooper (New York: Crocodile Books, USA, 1990). When Ella awakens before her father and opens the door to his champion rabbit's hutch, it escapes, taking her on an exciting chase across the yard, and returns to its hutch *just* before Ella's dad arrives.

Foolish Rabbit's Big Mistake, Rafe Martin, illustrated by Ed Young (New York: G. P. Putnam's Sons, 1985). In possibly the oldest known Henny Penny story, animal after animal heeds rabbit's hysterical cries that "the earth's breaking up!" and follows him as he runs for his life, until a wise lion reassures them and teaches them a lesson.

Goodnight Moon, Margaret Wise Brown, illustrated by Clement Hurd (New York: Harper & Row, 1947). In rhyming verse, a young rabbit says goodnight to things in his

270

bedroom (shown in black and white) as the room (pictured in color) darkens with the coming night.

How Rabbit Tricked Otter and Other Cherokee Trickster Stories, told by Gayle Ross, illustrated by Murv Jacob (New York: HarperCollins Publishers, 1994). Storyteller Ross records a collection of fifteen trickster-hero and pourquoi tales from the oral tradition of the Cherokee culture that feature the most important character in the animal stories, the clever and mischievous Rabbit. Contains a foreword by Chief Wilma Mankiller, Principal Chief of the Cherokee Nation.

I Love You, Bunny Rabbit, Shulamith Levey Oppenheim, illustrated by Cyd Moore (New York: Bantam Doubleday Dell Books for Young Readers, 1995). When stains do not come out of Micah's beloved stuffed rabbit after he washes it at his mother's insistence, she thinks it is time for them to buy him a new rabbit, but after a trip to the toy store, during which Micah chooses his old rabbit, Micah reminds his mom that lovable little boys frequently also wear food stains!

Judge Rabbit and the Tree Spirit: A Folktale from Cambodia, told by Lina Mao Wall, adapted by Cathy Spagnoli, illustrated by Nancy Hom (San Francisco: Children's Book Press, 1991). Wise Judge Rabbit uses his problem-solving strengths to help a woman distinguish between her husband, who has returned from war, and a tree spirit that has taken on her husband's physical likeness and voice while he has been away, in this folktale with parallel text in English and Khmer. An author's note provides information about the many Judge Rabbit stories in Cambodian folktale tradition.

Let's Make Rabbits: A Fable, Leo Lionni (New York: Pantheon Books, 1982). Two rabbits—one drawn by a pencil and one cut from colored paper by scissors—are content with life in their two-dimensional world until they discover a *real* three-dimensional carrot casting a shadow.

The Little Rabbit, Judy Dunn, photographs by Phoebe Dunn (New York: Random House, 1980). Readers learn about rabbits along with Sarah, who cares for and enjoys her new pet as it matures and gives birth to seven babies.

Little Rabbit's Loose Tooth, Lucy Bate, pictures by Diane De Groat (New York: Crown Publishers, Inc., 1975). In this humorous story about a common experience for young children, Little Rabbit has to adjust to the idea of her first loose tooth, ponders what to do with it once it falls out, and has to decide if she believes in the tooth fairy.

The Little Rabbit Who Wanted Red Wings, Carolyn Sherewin Bailey, illustrated by Jacqueline Rogers (New York: The Putnam & Grosset Book Group, 1931, 1961, 1978). Little Rabbit always wishes he could look like other animals in the forest until, with the help of wise Old Mr. Groundhog and magic from the wishing pond, he discovers that he is not happy wearing the red wings he'd so coveted and that himself is just who he wants to be.

Mama, If You Had a Wish, Jeanne Modesitt, illustrated by Robin Spowart (New York: Simon & Schuster Books for Young Readers, 1993). Little Bunny learns about unconditional love as his mother assures him that, even if she could wish it, she wouldn't change anything about him (even the things he perceives as weaknesses) because she loves him just as he is.

Mr. Rabbit and the Lovely Present, Charlotte Zolotow, illustrated by Maurice Sendak (New York: Harper & Row, 1962). In full-page color illustrations and predictable, repetitive text, Mr. Rabbit helps a little girl discover a wonderful present for her mother's birthday: a basket of fruit—green pears, yellow bananas, red apples, and blue grapes.

Rabbit Makes a Monkey of Lion: A Swahili Tale, retold by Verna Aardema, illustrated by Jerry Pinkney (New York: Puffin Pied Piper/Dial Books for Young Readers, 1989). Try as he may, Lion can never catch the clever and fast trickster, Rabbit, who, Lion realizes, is behind the tricks the animals play on him to steal the honey from his calabash tree and to make a monkey (or fool) of him.

The Rabbit's Escape, Suzanne Crowder Han, illustrated by Yumi Heo (New York: Henry Holt and Company, 1995). In this pourquoi tale, because the only cure for the illness of the Dragon King of the East Sea is a rabbit liver, a faithful turtle tricks rabbit into a visit to the ocean bottom, but rabbit outwits the king and returns safely to land. The text is written in Korean and English on each page. An author's note provides information about the Korean alphabet.

Rabbit's Good News, Ruth Lercher Bornstein (New York: Clarion Books, 1995). Illustrations in pastels capture a young rabbit's adventure when spring beckons her from her burrow; she enjoys the coming of the season with her senses, and then announces its arrival to others.

Rockabye Rabbit, Kersten Hamilton, illustrated by Saundra C. Winokur (Boca Raton, Florida: Cool Kids Press, 1995). When Rockabye Rabbit—Jonathan's stuffed animal that shares in everything he does, including living under the Twelfth Street Bridge—is stolen by a dog, Jonathan thinks he and his mother will have to move into the Family Home without it—until a friend finds it for him.

The Runaway Bunny, Margaret Wise Brown, illustrated by Clement Hurd (New York: Harper & Row, 1942, 1970, 1972). A young rabbit considers running away but decides to stay at home with his loving mother after he proposes destinations and she describes her plans to be with him wherever he goes.

Seven Little Rabbits, John Becker, illustrated by Barbara Cooney (New York: Walker & Company, 1973). In this counting book with irresistible rhythm and rhyme and repeating pattern, seven rabbits set out to walk to visit their friend toad, but, one by one, the rabbits tire and are left safely behind to nap in mole's hole. In the end, all seven rabbits sleep and toad receives a visit only in the last rabbit's dream.

The Tale of Benjamin Bunny, Beatrix Potter (New York: Frederick Warne & Co., Inc., 1902, 1904). When Benjamin Bunny and his cousin Peter Rabbit return to the garden of Mr. McGregor to retrieve the jacket and shoes Peter left there during his recent adventure, they are held captive under a basket by a cat and rescued by Benjamin's father.

The Tale of Peter Rabbit, Beatrix Potter (New York; Frederick Warne & Co., Inc., 1902). In this classic home-adventures-home story, Peter Rabbit defies his mother's warning and goes to Mr. McGregor's garden, where he feasts and, after a series of adventures, escapes the angry Mr. McGregor and returns home.

The Tale of Rabbit and Coyote, Tony Johnston, Tomie dePaola (New York: G. P. Putnam's Sons, 1994). In this combination trickster and pourquoi tale from the Zapotec Indians of Mexico that explains why coyotes howl at the moon and why, in Mexican tradition, there is a rabbit (not a man) in the moon, cunning Rabbit outwits Coyote again and again. Contains a glossary of Spanish expressions that appear in the text of the story.

Too Many Rabbits, Peggy Parish, illustrated by Leonard Kessler (New York: Macmillan Publishing Co., Inc., 1974). Not long after she takes in a fat stray rabbit, kindhearted Miss Molly needs to find a home for a houseful of rapidly reproducing rabbits, but then she discovers a pregnant stray cat!

Tops and Bottoms, Janet Stevens (San Diego: Harcourt Brace & Company, 1995). In a trickster tale in the tradition of both Europe and the South of the United States, Hare tricks lazy Bear out of his inherited wealth in a business partnership, in which Hare plants just the right crops each time to win—no matter whether Bear chooses tops, bottoms, or tops *and* bottoms of the produce Hare's family grows on Bear's land.

What Have You Done, Davy?, Brigitte Weninger, illustrated by Eve Tharlet, translated by Rosemary Lanning (New York: North-South Books, 1996). Through a series of mishaps, little Davy the rabbit angers his sister, brothers, and mother, but his relationships with family members improve greatly when he repairs the damage he has caused.

Who's in Rabbit's House?: A Masai Tale, Verna Aardema, illustrated by Leo and Diane Dillon (New York: The Dial Press, 1969, 1977). This retelling of a Masai folk tale is a play performed by villagers in masks and costumes. In the play, Rabbit refuses the aid of a series of her friends, who offer to help her get a frightening intruder out of her house, until frog—posing as a poisonous spitting snake—scares the creature, who turns out to be just a caterpillar.

ZOMO The Rabbit: A Trickster Tale from West Africa, Gerald McDermott (San Diego: Harcourt Brace Jovanovich, Publishers, 1992). In this combination trickster, pourquoi, and quest tale that explains why rabbits run fast, small but clever Zomo the rabbit earns wisdom by accomplishing three trials considered impossible: He brings to Sky God the scales of Big Fish, the milk of Wild Cow, and the tooth of Leopard.

Literature Extension Activities

1. According to an author's note that accompanies ***Brother Rabbit: A Cambodian Tale***, folktales in Cambodia were traditionally told to village children in the evening by grandparents. As well, small traveling

troupes of actors presented folk plays (*yikay*) by pantomiming the action as the narrator sang while being accompanied by drums or a two-stringed Khmer violin. Students pantomime the action (and, optionally, accompany on drums or violin) as you read the story of trickster Brother Rabbit.

2. After they hear a read-aloud of ***Let's Make Rabbits: A Fable***, students each draw one rabbit with a pencil and cut a second rabbit out of scraps of colored paper with scissors, as they observed in the book. They tape or glue popsicle or wooden craft sticks to the back of each rabbit and act out the story, drawing a pencil carrot for the first rabbit and a carrot cut from orange and green paper for the second rabbit. They help their rabbits eat a *real* three-dimensional carrot (that you supply) to add realistic sound effects but, unlike the rabbits in the book, they do *not* eat the greens! *Note:* Position a bright light appropriately to provide shadows for the dramatization.

3. If you have a live rabbit in the classroom during this unit, compile photographs with students and compose a book about the care and habits of a pet rabbit after you share ***The Little Rabbit***.

4. As a group project, students make an illustrated map of the adventures of characters in each of three books in this unit that follow a home-adventures-home pattern: ***Ella and the Rabbit***, ***The Tale of Peter Rabbit***, and ***The Tale of Benjamin Bunny***. They compare and contrast the maps and relate their observations to the characteristics and habits of rabbits.

5. After you share ***Rabbit's Good News*** in read-aloud, have students experiment with pastels to make pictures of the four seasons (or of spring, or of a favorite or the current season) that show things they could enjoy in each season using their senses of sight, touch, hearing, smell, and taste.

6. Students, in masks and costumes, perform the play of ***Who's in Rabbit's House?: A Masai Tale*** as you, as narrator, read it aloud.

Items for the Mystery Box

Whenever possible, select items for this unit that are **red** in color.

Inedible Items: **rabbit**, race car, raccoon, racket, radio, raft, rag, rainbow, raincoat, rake, ram, rat, rattle (baby's), raven, razor, recipe (in a book or on a card), rectangle, refrigerator, reindeer, rhinoceros, ribbon, rickrack, riddles (in a book or on cards for students to solve after they have guessed the item), ring, robe, robin, robot, rock, rocket, rocking chair, roller skates, roof (from a building set or on a house or building), rooster, roots (on bulbs, potatoes), rope, rose, ruby, rug, ruler, rust (on a metal item)

Edible Items: radicchio, radishes, raisins, raita, ramen, raspberries, ratatouille, relish, Reuben sandwich, rhubarb, rice (brown, white), rice cakes (variety), rice pudding, ricotta cheese, roast, rolls, romaine lettuce, rosemary, rutabaga, rye bread

Rhymes, Songs, Fingerplays, and Tongue Twisters

Rabbit Theme

Bye, baby bunting: 5, 20, 28, 32, 33, 34, 38, 39, 40, 50, 73, 76

Creeping/Creeping, creeping, creeping: 19

Eeny, meeny, miney, mo,/Catch a rabbit by the toe: 79

Little Bunny/There was a little bunny who lived in the wood: 19

*Little cabin in the wood: 55, 78

Little white rabbit: 4

A rabbit skipped: 51

Tongue Twisters: 1, 13

Too Many Rabbits/Gail and Sue had two little rabbits: 75

Who ever saw a rabbit: 28

Letter-Sound r (r)

*Rock-a-bye, Baby: 5, 6, 20, 28, 29, 33, 34, 38, 39, 40, 41, 46, 50, 52, 53, 58, 62, 67, 73, 76

Round and round the rugged rock: 34

*R with R is carry: 18

Tongue Twisters: 7, 13, 60, 74, 80

Cloze Sentences

1. A <u>r</u>ing is jewel**r**y that I wea**r** on my finge**r**.

   (On my finge**r**, I wear jewel**r**y called a <u>r</u>ing.)

2. <u>R</u>ock is anothe**r** name fo**r** a stone.

   (Stone is another name fo**r** a <u>r</u>ock.)

3. A <u>r</u>uler can be used to measu**r**e a piece of pape**r**.

   (To measu**r**e a piece of pape**r**, you can use a <u>r</u>ule**r**.)

4. <u>R</u>abbits a**r**e small, fu**rr**y animals that have long ea**r**s and that hop and eat ca**rr**ots.

   (Small, fu**rr**y animals that have long ea**r**s and that hop and eat ca**rr**ots are <u>r</u>abbits.)

1. **R**ibbon can be used to tie a birthday present.
   (To tie a birthday present, you can use **r**ibbon.)
2. After it **r**ains, we sometimes see a **r**ainbow in the sky.
   (Sometimes we see a **r**ainbow in the sky after it **r**ains.)
3. A **r**azor is something a person can use to shave.
   (A person can shave with a **r**azor.)
4. A **r**ug is another name for a carpet.
   (A carpet is another name for a **r**ug.)

R r

Little cabin in the wood,

Little man by the window stood,

Little rabbit hopping by,

Knocking at the door.

"Help me! Help me, sir!" he said,

" 'fore the farmer bops my head."

"Come on in," the little man cried,

"Warm up by the fire."

Name _____   Date _____

R r

R with R is carry,

R with R is barrow

Rapid run the railroad cars

Carrying sugar

for tomorrow.

Erre con erre cigarro,

Erre con erre barril,

Rápido corren los carros

Cargados de azúcar

al ferrocarril.

Name _____

Date _____

Rhymes . . . 2

R r

Rock-a-bye, Baby, on the treetop,

When the wind blows, the cradle will rock;

When the bough breaks, the cradle will fall,

And down will come Baby, cradle and all.

Name _____   Date _____

R r

COMPLETE IT

ring	Rock
1	2
ruler	Rabbits
3	4

A <u>ring</u> is jewelry that I wear on my finger.
    1

<u>Rock</u> is another name for a stone.
    2

A <u>ruler</u> can be used to measure a piece of
    3
paper.

<u>Rabbits</u> are small, furry animals that have long
    4
ears and that hop and eat carrots.

Name _____ Date _____

Cloze Sentences . . . 1

R r

COMPLETE IT

Ribbon
1

rains
2

razor
3

rug
4

<u>Ribbon</u> can be used to tie a birthday present.
   1

After it <u>rains</u>, we sometimes see a rainbow in the
      2
sky.

A <u>razor</u> is something a person can use to shave.
  3

A <u>rug</u> is another name for a carpet.
  4

Name _____ Date _____

R

r

S s   snake

TEACHER REFERENCE

Annotated Book List

A Look Around Snakes, Janet Lambert, illustrated by Ray Keane (Worthington, Ohio: Willowisp Press, Inc., 1988). Colored photographs and drawings illustrate this book of facts about snakes: physical characteristics, habits, food, defense and protection, medicines made from venom, beliefs about snakes, and snakes as pets—with special sections about pit vipers, African boomslangs, rattlesnakes, horned and sand vipers, boas, pythons, anacondas, and cobras. Contains information about visiting wilderness areas and actions to take when bitten by a snake.

Amazing Snakes: Eyewitness Juniors, Alexandra Parsons, photographed by Jerry Young (New York: Alfred A. Knopf, 1990). Remarkable close-up colored photographs, drawings, diagrams, text, and captions reveal information about snakes, including physical characteristics, habits, food and drink, habitat, young, medicines made from venom, protection and defense, and beliefs about snakes—with separate sections about sunbeam, egg eater, cobra, rattler, milk, flying, tree boa, and vine snakes. Includes an index.

Baby Rattlesnake, Te Ata, illustrated by Mira Reisberg (San Francisco: Children's Book Press, 1989). Baby Rattlesnake begs and cries for a rattle long before he is old enough, but the elders decide to honor his wish in order to teach him a lesson. An author's note describes how this story, originally told by an internationally known Chickasaw storyteller, ninety-two year old Te Ata, came to be written as a book.

Crictor, Tomi Ungerer (New York: HarperCollins Publishers, 1958). In this classic, Crictor is sent from Africa to Madame Bodot by her son, and the rapidly growing nonpoisonous boa constrictor becomes quite a help to her during daily activities, at the school where she teaches, playing with children, and, most dramatically, when he saves her from a burglar's attack—for which he is honored by the entire French town.

The Day Jimmy's Boa Ate the Wash, Trinka Hakes Noble, pictures by Steven Kellogg (New York: Penguin Books USA Inc., 1980). In this first book in a series about Jimmy's boa, a pet constrictor, brought on a field trip to a farm, starts a chain of humorous events that makes the outing memorable—especially to the farmer and his wife, who keep it in the end.

The Great Snake Escape, Molly Coxe (New York: HarperCollins Publishers, 1994). Rather than being a threat to Mirabel the goose and Mazie the frog, a king cobra, who has escaped from the zoo to return to his home in India, becomes their hero.

Great Snakes!, Fay Robinson, illustrated by Jean Day Zallinger (New York: Scholastic Inc., 1996). This easy-to-read informational book with rhyming text—labeled drawings and a few lines of large print—on each page, provides information about physical characteristics, habitat, habits, young, food, and defense and protection of snakes. A section at the end of the book identifies each snake pictured.

The Greedy Python, Richard Buckley, illustrated by Eric Carle (Saxonville, Massachusetts: Picture Book Studio, USA, 1985). Rhyming lines and collage illustrations present the story of a python with a tremendous appetite, who becomes sick after he swallows whole and coughs out ten animals but learns nothing from the experience. He eats the next thing he spies and disappears, for it is his own tail!

Green Snake Ceremony, Sherrin Watkins, illustrated by Kim Doner (Tulsa, Oklahoma: Council Oak Publishing Co., Inc., 1995). Hilarious illustrations (filled with puns) on each page show the parallel drama of Mary Greyfeather and her grandparents' search for a snake for a Shawnee good luck and health tradition, and of the snake that lives under their porch as it attempts to avoid being put inside the girl's mouth for the ceremony. An author's note provides information about Native American and Shawnee traditions and about two kinds of green snakes, invites readers to create snake jokes, and provides directions for making a "windsnake" (windsock).

Hide and Snake, Keith Baker (San Diego: Harcourt Brace Jovanovich, Inc., 1991). In this interactive book, readers locate the partially hidden snake in each double-page illustration as it engages in activities, ending in *-ing* and identified in rhyming text, in a variety of settings.

How Snake Got His Hiss, Marguerite W. Davol, illustrated by Mercedes McDonald (New York: Orchard Books, 1996). This brilliantly illustrated pourquoi story tells how Snake, a vain and selfish creature who once was round, got his hiss and his current shape, and how Hyena, Lion, Ostrich, Monkey, and Crocodile got some of their characteristics.

Julian, Dream Doctor, Ann Cameron, illustrated by Ann Strugnell (New York: Random House, Inc., 1990). In this short chapter book, Julian, his brother Huey, and friend Gloria (introduced in ***The Stories Julian Tells*** by the same author) misunderstand what Julian's father mumbles in his sleep and go to great lengths to get him for his birthday what they *think* is his dad's greatest dream. The snakes they give him turn out to be his worst nightmare, which, when confronted, provide a gift his father will never forget.

Mufaro's Beautiful Daughters: An African Tale, John Steptoe (New York: William Morrow & Company, Inc., 1987). In this Cinderella story variant, two sisters, kind Nyasha and jealous, greedy, and bad-tempered Manyara, journey to be judged by the King as he chooses a wife. Nyasha acts kindly to those she meets on her way and discovers that they (and the garden snake she'd befriended at home) had been the King in disguise, who rewards her by marrying her and making her sister their servant.

Singing Snake, Stefan Czernecki and Timothy Rhodes, illustrated by Stefan Czernecki (New York: Hyperion Books for Children, 1993). This pourquoi tale, with illustrations influenced by Australian aboriginal paintings and legends, explains the origin of the didgeridoo (one of the oldest known musical instruments), the phrase "snake in the grass," and the snake's hiss. In the story, snake swallows lark to use her voice to win Old Man's singing contest and have a musical instrument fashioned in his likeness. An author's note provides information about the making and playing of the didgeridoo.

Small Green Snake, Libba Moore Gray, illustrated by Holly Meade (New York: Orchard Books, 1994). Colorful full-page illustrations and lively rhythmic text filled with alliteration, repetition, and onomatopeoia capture the adventures of a young garter snake who ignores his mother's warning not to wander away.

Snake: Animals in the Wild, Mary Hoffman (Milwaukee: Raintree Publishers, 1986). Text and colored photographs provide information about a variety of snakes: young, defense and protection, physical characteristics, habits, and food, plus facts about specific snakes, including vine, tree, rattler, boa, viper, king, ladder, and cobra.

Snake: Life Story, Michael Chinery, photography by Barrie Watts (Mahwah, New Jersey: Troll Associates, 1991). Text, photographs, and drawings present the life cycle of the corn snake, including its body, habits, method of catching prey, young, and habitat. Contains an engaging introductory summary, a section of fascinating facts, and an index.

Snakes: A New True Book, Ray Broekel (Chicago: Childrens Press, 1982). Photographs and diagrams accompany short sentences and paragraphs that describe the snake's body, diet, young, habits, habitat and range, and predators. Contains a table of contents, index, and glossary with pronunciation guide for important terms.

Snakes Are Hunters: Let's-Read-and-Find-Out Science, Patricia Lauber, illustrated by Holly Keller (New York: Harper & Row, Publishers, 1988). Colored drawings and text present facts about a variety of snakes: physical characteristics; habits; habitat; young; life expectancy; locating, catching, and eating prey; and defense and protection.

A Snake's Body, Joanna Cole, photographs by Jerome Wexler (New York: William Morrow and Company, Inc., 1981). Black-and-white photographs, drawings, and diagrams complement text that presents information about a number of different snakes: physical characteristics, internal organs, and skeletal system; senses; habits; detecting, catching, and eating prey; and young.

Take a Look at Snakes, Betsy Maestro, illustrated by Giulio Maestro (New York: Scholastic Inc., 1992). Text, illustrated with colored drawings and maps, presents common beliefs about snakes; physical characteristics, internal organs, and skeletal system; habitat and range; shelters; habits; senses; finding, killing, and eating prey; defense and protection; and young in a variety of snakes. A "Did You Know That . . . ?" section provides additional facts.

Literature Extension Activities

1. With students, experiment with different ways snakes move without legs or arms, described in *A Look Around Snakes*, *Amazing Snakes, Snake, Snakes Are Hunters, A Snake's Body, Take a Look at Snakes,* and additional fiction and nonfiction books. Movements may include slithering, climbing, sidewinding, wriggling, creeping, sliding, gliding, swimming, waving (undulating), bunching, looping, and the concertina and caterpillar (described in the books listed above).

2. Students make an illustrated interactive book with with *-ing* word labels (dictated or written), as an individual or group project, patterned after *Hide and Snake*.

3. Information about the author of *How Snake Got His Hiss* explains that the book began as a story for preschoolers, who participated in the telling by acting out Snake's movements and repeating his sounds. As you read the book aloud, students participate in the reading as the original listeners did when the story was created, acting out Snake's actions and imitating the sounds he makes—written in bold print and with appropriate shapes in the book.

4. After students enjoy *Singing Snake* in read-aloud and learn about the didgeridoo, have them make and play wind instruments, like the didgeridoo made by Old Man, fashioned in the likeness of a snake. They use paper towel and other tubes and decorate them with designs inspired by the book's illustrations.

5. *Small Green Snake* must be read aloud! Read it aloud several times so that students can savor the rich language. They move their bodies, clap their hands, and tap their feet to the rhythm in repeated readings.

   Students in a group interpret the story by matching movements and actions to the highly descriptive text as you, another adult, or a student reads it aloud.

   With students, discuss the similarities and differences between *Small Green Snake* and another book in which an animal character ignores his mother's warning and puts himself in danger: *The Tale of Peter Rabbit* (Chapter 18).

Items for the Mystery Box

Whenever possible, select items for this unit that are silver in color.

Inedible Items: saddle, sailboat, sandpaper, scale, scissors, screwdriver, seagull, seal, seeds, seven, sink, six, skate (ice), ski(s), skunk, sled, slide (playground), slipper, snail, **snake**, snow animal or person, snowflake, soap, soccer ball, sock, sombrero, spider, sponge, spoon, square, squid, squirrel, stamp (postal), star, starfish, stick, stocking, stone, stop sign, stove, straw (drinking), string, submarine, suitcase, sun, sunglasses

Edible Items: sage, salad, salami, salmon, salsa, salt, sandwich, sauce (for ice cream, variety), sauerkraut, sausage, scallions, scallops, scones, seaweed, seeds (pumpkin, sesame, sunflower), slaw (coleslaw), s'mores, soda (variety), soda bread, soufflé, soup (variety), soybeans, soy milk, soy sauce, spaghetti, spinach, sprouts (variety), squash, squid, star fruit, stew, strawberries, streusel, stroganoff, strudel, stuffed peppers, stuffing, submarine (sandwich), succotash, sundaes, sushi, sweet potatoes, swiss cheese, swordfish, syrup

Rhymes, Songs, Fingerplays, and Tongue Twisters

Snake Theme

As I was walking near the lake: 4
Fishes swim in the water clear: 5
Oh, a-hunting we will go: 44, 47, 79
*Slippery snakes slipping and sliding: (Tongue Twister: Cynthia Conway Waring)
*Snake, snake, run in the grass: 51
Tongue Twisters: 7, 13, 60, 63, 80

Letter-Sound s (s)

A sailor went to sea, sea, sea: 5, 36

The eentsy weentsy spider: 5, 12, 14, 29, 32, 33, 34, 49, 51, 53, 76, 78
Little Tom Tucker sang for his supper: 5, 26, 28, 33, 34, 38, 39, 40, 42, 46, 50, 52, 58, 62, 73, 76
Sally go round the sun: 5
Sing a song of sixpence: 3, 5, 26, 28, 29, 32, 33, 34, 37, 38, 39, 41, 46, 50, 52, 53, 58, 59, 62, 67, 73, 76
*Swan swam over the sea: 5, 25, 28, 33, 34, 50
Three little ghostesses: 73, 76
Tongue Twisters: 1, 7, 13, 60, 74, 80

Cloze Sentences

1. A <u>sandwich</u> that I like to eat for lunch is peanut butter and jelly.
(For lunch, I like to eat a peanut butter and jelly <u>sandwich</u>.)
2. I put on my <u>socks</u> before I put on my **sneakers**.
(Before I put on my **sneakers**, I put on my <u>socks</u>.)

3. <u>Six</u> is the number that comes after five.
   (The number that comes after five is <u>six</u>.)

4. A <u>snake</u> is an animal that slides through the grass and has no legs.
   (An animal that slides through the grass and has no legs is a <u>snake</u>.)

1. <u>Seven</u> is the number that comes after six.
   (The number that comes after six is <u>seven</u>.)

2. I use a <u>spoon</u> to eat my soup.
   (When I eat my soup, I use a <u>spoon</u>.)

3. A <u>spider</u> is an animal that spins a web.
   (An animal that spins a web is a <u>spider</u>.)

4. I use <u>soap</u> and water when I clean my hands.
   (When I clean my hands, I use water and <u>soap</u>.)

S s

SNAKE, SNAKE, RUN IN THE GRASS

Snake, snake, run in the grass
And I'll not hurt you as you pass.

Name _____   Date _____

S s

Slippery snakes slipping and sliding

Slippery snakes slipping and sliding

Slippery snakes slipping and sliding

Name _____   Date _____

Rhymes . . . 2

S s

Swan swam over the sea,

Swim, swan, swim!

Swan swam back again,

Well swum, swan!

Name _____   Date _____

S s

COMPLETE IT

sandwich	socks
1	2
Six	snake
3	4

A <u>sandwich</u> that I like to eat for lunch is peanut
   1
butter and jelly.

I put on my <u>socks</u> before I put on my sneakers.
     2

<u>Six</u> is the number that comes after five.
 3

A <u>snake</u> is an animal that slides through the
    4
grass and has no legs.

Name _____ Date _____

S s

COMPLETE IT

Seven	spoon
1	2
spider	soap
3	4

<u>Seven</u> is the number that comes after six.
 1

I use a <u>spoon</u> to eat my soup.
 2

A <u>spider</u> is an animal that spins a web.
 3

I use <u>soap</u> and water when I clean my hands.
 4

Name _____ Date _____

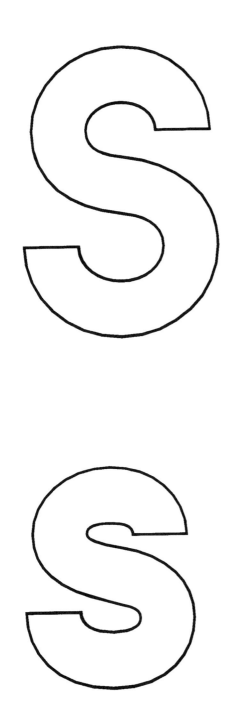

T t turtle

TEACHER REFERENCE

Annotated Book List

A Boy, a Dog, a Frog and a Friend, Mercer and Marianna Mayer (New York: Dial Books for Young Readers, 1971). In this wordless book, a boy, a dog, and a frog catch a turtle while fishing, and his mischief annoys them until he plays dead and they realize that they would miss him.

The Aesop for Children, Milo Winter (Chicago: Rand McNally & Co., 1919, 1947, 1984). In Winter's terse retelling of the fable "The Hare and the Tortoise," the Hare takes a nap to show the Tortoise just how laughable his attempt is to challenge him in the race.

Aesop's Fables Retold in Verse, Tom Paxton, illustrated by Robert Rayevsky (New York: Morrow Junior Books, 1988). In Paxton's retelling of the fable "The Hare and the Tortoise," in rhyming verse illustrated in rich natural tones, the Hare is his most prideful, boasting self and the Tortoise is his most determined.

Albert's Toothache, Barbara Williams, illustrated by Kay Chorao (New York: NAL Penguin Inc., 1974). No one in his immediate family believes Albert the turtle when he insists that he has a toothache because, after all, everyone knows that turtles don't have teeth. Then wise grandmother really *listens* to Albert who shows her where his toothache is—on his toe, where a gopher bit him.

Anansi Goes Fishing, Eric A. Kimmel, illustrated by Janet Stevens (New York: Holiday House, 1992). Anansi, the lazy and mischievous spider (from ***Anansi and the Moss-Covered Rock*** by the same author), returns in a combination trickster and pourquoi tale, in which he tries to trick Turtle into going fishing for him, but wise Turtle outsmarts him. The story tells how spider webs began.

And Still the Turtle Watched, Sheila MacGill-Callahan, illustrated by Barry Mosher (New York: Dial Books for Young Readers, 1991). Carved out of rock by an old man to watch over the Delaware people, the turtle observes other people as they destroy the forest, cultivate the land, build cities, and blind and deface the turtle with spray paint. Finally, the turtle is restored and placed in a botanical garden (like the one in New York City, which inspired this story).

Box Turtle at Long Pond, William T. George, pictures by Lindsay Barrett George (New York: William Morrow & Company, Inc., 1989). As they follow his activities in his pond environment from dawn to nightfall, readers discover information about a box turtle: habitat, shelter, habits, food and drink, senses, predators, and physical characteristics in text richly illustrated with colored paintings.

Evan's Corner, Elizabeth Starr Hill, pictures by Sandra Speidel (New York: Penguin Books USA Inc., 1967, 1991). In this new picture book edition of the beloved story, when Evan has what he wanted most—a place of his own in the corner of the two-room apartment he shares with seven members of his family— he finds that, even with a pet turtle, he's not happy until he helps his younger brother, who admires him, to fix a corner of his own.

The Foolish Tortoise, Richard Buckley, illustrated by Eric Carle (Saxonville, Massachusetts: Picture Book Studio, 1985). Tired of being encumbered and slow, Tortoise takes off his shell, in this rhyming story and fable, and finds that he's far too vulnerable without its protection.

Franklin in the Dark, Paulette Bourgeois, illustrated by Brenda Clark (Toronto: Kids Can Press Ltd., 1986). In this book, which introduces a series, Franklin, the turtle, is afraid of the dark and of being in small, cramped places. When he learns from other animals and his mother that they have their own fears, he is more comfortable sleeping in his shell—with his night light on! A plush hand puppet of Franklin is available from Kids Can Press Ltd.

The Hare and the Tortoise, Brian Wildsmith (Oxford, England: Oxford University Press, 1966). Characteristic full-page Wildsmith illustrations embellish this version of the famous race between the boastful Hare and the persevering Tortoise.

How Turtle's Back Was Cracked: A Traditional Cherokee Tale, retold by Gayle Ross, illustrated by Murv Jacob (New York: Dial Books for Young Readers, 1995). In this pourquoi story, when his bragging leads him into trouble with the wolves, Turtle is able to save himself with his guile—but not without cost. His once smooth shell cracks in the process, leaving the lines we see today. An author's note traces the evolution of the tale from oral storytelling tradition, and another provides information about the Cherokee nation.

I Can't Get My Turtle to Move, Elizabeth Lee O'Donnell, illustrated by Maxie Chambliss (New York: Morrow Junior Books, 1989). In this counting book, farm animals in groups from two to ten respond to a young girl's invitations to move in different ways, but it is not until the end of the book that animal number one, the turtle, decides to move when offered a lettuce leaf for lunch.

Into the Sea, Brenda Z. Guiberson, illustrated by Alix Berenzy (New York: Henry Holt and Company, 1996). Detailed and accurate illustrations and text in this picture book show the life cycle of a sea turtle that returns to the beach where she hatched, to lay her own eggs after braving life at sea.

Kanahena: A Cherokee Story, Susan L. Roth (New York: St. Martin's Press, 1988). As she stirs the Kanahena (hominy or cornmeal mush) in her pot, an old woman tells a girl an old pourquoi and trickster tale about Kanahena and how the trickster Terrapin got the scars on his shell when he tricked some angry wolves. Includes a recipe for Kanahena.

Little Turtle's Big Adventure, David Harrison, illustrated by J. P. Miller (New York: Random House, 1969, 1978). A little turtle is forced out of his pond home when people with bulldozers and steam shovels build a road. He survives the four seasons and tries out several locations before he finds a suitable new home.

Look Out for Turtles!: Let's-Read-and-Find-Out Science, Melvin Berger, illustrated by Megan Lloyd (New York: HarperCollins Publishers, 1992). The book describes both the characteristics of the turtle that have enabled it to survive on land and in the ocean for nearly 200 million years (including body parts, eating habits, hibernation, reproduction, and life expectancy) and its vulnerabilities, with suggested behaviors that protect turtles from becoming endangered or extinct.

The Rabbit's Escape, Suzanne Crowder Han, illustrated by Yumi Heo (New York: Henry Holt and Company, 1995). In this pourquoi tale, because the only cure for the illness of the Dragon King of the East Sea is a rabbit liver, a faithful turtle tricks rabbit into a visit to the ocean bottom, but rabbit outwits the king and returns safely to land. The text is written in Korean and English on each page. An author's note provides information about the Korean alphabet.

Stick-in-the-Mud Turtle, Lillian Hoban (New York: Bantam Doubleday Dell Publishing Group, Inc., 1977). Everyone except Mr. Turtle (whom Mrs. Turtle calls "Stick-in-the-Mud Turtle") has to experience the negative side of the fancy life and material possessions of the new turtle family that moves into the pond neighborhood, before they are again content with their own simple life.

The Stinky Cheese Man and Other Fairly Stupid Tales, Jon Scieszka, illustrated by Lane Smith (New York: Viking, 1992). In "The Tortoise and the Hair," one of eleven humorous modern retellings of well-known traditional tales, the Hare challenges the Tortoise to run faster than the Hare can grow his hair.

Thirteen Moons on Turtle's Back: A Native American Year of Moons, Joseph Bruchac and Jonathan London, illustrated by Thomas Locker (New York: The Putnam & Grosset Group, 1992). An Abenaki boy's question about the number of scales on a turtle's back prompts his grandfather to tell him one traditional story from North American Native peoples (Northern Cheyenne, Potawatomi, Anishinabe, Cree, Huron, Seneca, Pomo, Menominee, Micmac, Cherokee, Winnebago, Lakota Sioux, and Abenaki) for each of the thirteen moons of the year, the same as the number of turtle's scales. A note from the authors provides background for the book.

The Tortoise and the Hare: An Aesop Fable, Janet Stevens (New York: Holiday House, Inc., 1984). In Stevens's humorous retelling of the familiar Aesop fable with a contemporary setting, Tortoise's friends help him train for the race, and Hare wears jogging shorts and Tortoise wears running shoes.

Tricky Tortoise, Mwenye Hadithi, illustrated by Adrienne Kenaway (Boston: Little, Brown and Company, 1988). In this combination trickster and pourquoi story, to put an end to being stepped on, Tortoise triumphs over a boastful Elephant and shows him and the other animals that he can jump over the elephant's head through trickery and help from his identical brother—and thus, that power does not necessarily depend on size.

The Turtle and the Monkey: A Philippine Tale, Paul Galdone (New York: Clarion Books, 1983). Turtle tricks Monkey—not once, but three times—when she asks Monkey's help to plant a banana tree she found, and Monkey greedily takes his portion—or more.

The Turtle and the Moon, Charles Turner, illustrated by Melissa Bay Mathis (New York: Penguin Books USA Inc., 1991). Brief text, illustrated with pastel drawings, presents the tale of a lonely turtle, who discovers a perfect nighttime companion that plays tag and hide-and-seek, dives, and shimmers in the water with him—the moon's reflection.

Turtle and Tortoise: Animals in the Wild, Vincent Serventy (Milwaukee: Raintree Publishers, 1985). Two or three lines of text and a colored photograph on each page present similarities and differences between the closely related reptiles, and information about their physical characteristics, habitats, habits, food, young, and protection.

Turtle Bay, Saviour Pirotta, illustrated by Nilesh Mistry (New York: Farrar, Straus & Giroux, 1997). Jiro-San, the old man Taro and his sister Yuko have watched sweep the beach with a broom, introduces them to the secret of the old friends he patiently awaits—the Japanese loggerhead turtles who return each year to lay their eggs on the beach Jiro-San readies for them. An author's note provides information about sea turtles.

Turtle Spring, Lillian Hoban (New York: Bantam Doubleday Dell Publishing Group, Inc., 1978). One spring day, the whole turtle family thinks the bump in the garden is a bomb, and no one does anything but think about it until ten baby turtles hatch from it.

Yertle the Turtle and Other Stories, Dr. Seuss (New York: Random House, 1950, 1951, 1977, 1979, 1986). In "**Yertle the Turtle,**" a tale told in rhyme, King Yertle the Turtle experiences a literal fall from power when he is accidentally shaken off the pile of his subjects that he's ordered assembled so that he can climb up to increase his view and thus, his kingdom.

Literature Extension Activities

1. Students, individually or in a group, provide words for the story depicted in the illustrations of the wordless book ***A Boy, a Dog, a Frog and a Friend***. They record their story on an audiotape, dictate it to a teacher, another adult, or a child, or write it. They compare and contrast this book and its rewrite with another wordless book by Mayer and its rewrite, ***A Boy, a Dog and a Frog*** (Chapter 10).

2. After they enjoy ***Evan's Corner***, have students draw the items, including a pet, that they would include in a special corner of their own.

3. After you read ***Franklin in the Dark***, share with students more of the many books in the series about the young turtle, Franklin. Individual students complete a companion book to the series, ***Franklin and Me: A Book About Me, Written and Drawn by Me (With a Little Help from Franklin)***, Paulette Bourgeois, illustrated by Brenda Clark (Toronto: Kids Can Press Ltd., 1994). The illustrated book, in album format, provides information about aspects of Franklin's life and spaces for children to record information about their own, including family, home, friends, neighborhood, doctor, dentist, school, daily schedule, favorites, feelings, birthday celebration, and more.

4. With students, make a class counting book about a turtle with animals of the students' choice patterned after ***I Can't Get My Turtle to Move***.

5. With students, bake and eat rolls in the shape of turtles. Follow the "Twist and Roll" recipe in ***My First Cook Book: A Life-Size Guide to***

Making Fun Things to Eat, Angela Wilkes, photography by David Johnson (New York: Alfred A. Knopf, 1989). The cookbook is designed to introduce children to the tools and procedures for cooking and baking, and, in the Dorling Kindersley tradition, combines colored photographs, brief text, and labeled captions.

6. In some retellings of the "Tortoise and the Hare" fable, the moral is written and, in others, it is implied. Help students to provide morals for the versions they read that do not contain one. As well, have them offer suggestions for a lesson or moral for **"Yertle the Turtle,"** which is a modern fable with an implicit moral.

Items for the Mystery Box

Inedible Items: table, tack, tadpole, tambourine, tank, tape (audio), tape (mending), taxi, teabag, teapot, Teddy bear, teeth, telephone, telescope, television, ten, tennis ball, tent, tie (neck), tiger, tile, timer, tipi (teepee), tire, tissue, toad, toadstool, toboggan, toes, tomahawk, toothbrush, toothpaste, toothpick, top, totem pole, towel, tower, tractor, train, tray, tree, triangle (musical instrument), triangle (shape), tricycle, truck, trumpet, trunk (elephant's), trunk (storage), tulip, tunnel, turban, turkey, **turtle**, tusks (on elephant), tutu, two, typewriter

Edible Items: tabouli, tacos, tahini, tamales, tamari, tangerine, tarragon, tartar sauce (with vegetables), tarts, tea (herbal), tempeh, thyme, toast, toffee, tofu, tomato, torte, tortilla, tostadas, truffles, tuna, turkey, turnip

Rhymes, Songs, Fingerplays, and Tongue Twisters

Turtle Theme

My Turtle/This is my turtle: 12
There was a little turtle: 14
Tongue Twisters: 13
*Tricky turtles tickling toad's toes: (Tongue Twister: Cynthia Conway Waring)

Letter-Sound t (t)

I'm a little teapot: 3, 12, 29, 31, 48, 53, 78
Little Tommy Tittlemouse: 5, 25, 28, 33, 34, 40, 46, 50, 73, 76

*Little Tom Tucker sings for his supper: 5, 26, 28, 33, 34, 38, 39, 40, 42, 46, 50, 52, 58, 62, 73, 76
Star light, star bright: 3, 34, 37, 51, 73, 76
There once were two cats of Kilkenny: 20, 25, 28, 33, 50, 51, 73, 76
Tom, Tom, the piper's son: 5, 20, 26, 28, 32, 33, 38, 39, 41, 46, 50, 62, 67, 73, 76
Tongue Twisters: 1, 7, 13, 60, 74, 80
*Twinkle, twinkle, little star: 6, 26, 28, 32, 34, 40, 42, 43, 49, 51, 53, 58, 62, 73, 76, 78

Cloze Sentences

1. A <u>turtle</u> is a slow-moving animal that can pull its head and legs into its hard shell.

   (A slow-moving animal that can pull its head and legs into its hard shell is a <u>turtle</u>.)
2. On a <u>telephone</u>, you can talk to a friend who is not near you.

   (You can talk to a friend who is not near you on a <u>telephone</u>.)
3. You may use a <u>towel</u> to dry your wet hands.

   (To dry your wet hands, you may use a <u>towel</u>.)
4. We use <u>tape</u>, glue, or paste to fix ripped paper.

   (To fix ripped paper, we use glue, paste, or <u>tape</u>.)

1. In a <u>tent</u>, campers may sleep outdoors.

   (Campers may sleep outdoors in a <u>tent</u>.)
2. We sit at a <u>table</u> to eat most of our meals.

   (To eat most of our meals, we sit at a <u>table</u>.)
3. A <u>top</u> shelf is not a bottom shelf.

   (A bottom shelf is not a <u>top</u> shelf.)
4. <u>Tomatoes</u> are what we use to make pizza and spaghetti sauce.

   (Pizza and spaghetti sauce are made with <u>tomatoes</u>.)

T t

Tricky turtles tickling toad's toes

Trickly turtles tickling toad's toes

Tricky turtles tickling toad's toes

Name _____   Date _____

Rhymes . . . 1

T t

Little Tom Tucker

Sings for his supper.

What shall he eat?

White bread and butter.

Name _____ Date _____

T t

Twinkle, twinkle, little star,

How I wonder what you are!

Up above the world so high,

Like a diamond in the sky.

Name _____   Date _____

T t

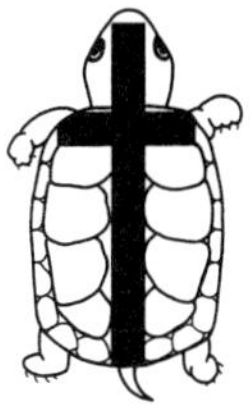

COMPLETE IT

turtle
1

telephone
2

towel
3

tape
4

A <u>turtle</u> is a slow-moving animal that can pull its
   1
head and legs into its hard shell.

On a <u>telephone,</u> you can talk to a friend who is
      2
not near you.

You may use a <u>towel</u> to dry your wet hands.
        3

We use <u>tape</u>, glue, or paste to fix ripped paper.
    4

Name _____   Date _____

T t

COMPLETE IT

tent   table
1   2
top   Tomatoes
3   4

In a <u>tent</u>, campers may sleep outdoors.
     1

We sit at a <u>table</u> to eat most of our meals.
     2

A <u>top</u> shelf is not a bottom shelf.
    3

<u>Tomatoes</u> are what we use to make pizza
    4
and spaghetti sauce.

Name _____   Date _____

Cloze Sentences . . . 2

U u umbrella

u

TEACHER REFERENCE

Annotated Book List

A Letter to Amy, Ezra Jack Keats (New York: Harper & Row, 1968). A misunderstanding about his friend Amy's invitation to his party, nearly lost in the rain, almost ruins Peter's birthday, but all ends well when Amy and her parrot arrive in time for the cake and Peter's secret wish.

Amy Loves the Rain, Julia Hoban, pictures by Lillian Hoban (New York: HarperCollins Publishers, 1989). As a young girl and her mother drive to pick up her father, she notices the sights, sounds, and feelings of the rainy day, and that her dad has forgotten his umbrella. In exchange for a hug, she lends him her umbrella.

Bringing the Rain to Kapiti Plain: A Nandi Tale, Verna Aardema, illustrated by Beatriz Vidal (New York: Dial Books for Young Readers, 1981). In this cumulative tale, Ki-pat shoots an arrow through a rain cloud and ends the terrible drought that had killed the vegetation and forced the animals to leave Kapiti Plain.

The Enchanted Umbrella: with a Short History of the Umbrella, Odette Meyers, pictures by Margot Zemach (San Diego: Harcourt Brace Jovanovich, 1988). In a story based on a French folktale, homeless after being cheated out of his inheritance from a kind umbrella maker, young Patou finds that his old, torn umbrella protects him from thieves, carries him through the air by its handle, saves him from drowning, and makes him a king. Includes a brief history of umbrellas.

The Legend of the Bluebonnet: An Old Tale of Texas, Tomie dePaola (New York: G. P. Putnam's Sons, 1983). A little girl sacrifices her most valued possessions to bring rain to save her people from drought and famine, and blue flowers grow from the scattered ashes of her treasured doll. This pourquoi story tells the origin of bluebonnet wildflowers.

Mushroom in the Rain, Mirra Ginsburg, adapted from the Russian of V. Suteyev, illustrated by José Aruego and Ariane Dewey (New York: Aladdin Books, 1974). In this cumulative story, animal after animal—ant, butterfly, mouse, sparrow, and rabbit—squeezes under a mushroom for shelter until it stops raining. A wise frog tells the amazed animals the secret of how they could all fit: Mushrooms grow in the rain!

Noah's Ark, Peter Spier (New York: Doubleday & Company, Inc., 1977). Realistic details in the ink and watercolor illustrations distinguish this version of the traditional story of the Ark, Noah, his family, and the animals before, during, and after the Flood.

Peter Spier's Rain, Peter Spier (New York: Bantam Doubleday Dell Publishing Group, Inc., 1982). Spier captures the outdoor and indoor adventures and discoveries of a brother and sister during a day and night of rain in this wordless picture book with watercolor and ink illustrations.

Rain, Donald Kalan, illustrated by Donald Crews (New York: Mulberry Books, 1978). Simple, bold illustrations and a few words (often in the colors they name) describe familiar parts of the environment during a rain shower. Repeated lines of the word *rain* appear in diagonal streams across the page during the storm.

The Rain, Michael Laser, illustrated by Jeffrey Greene (New York: Simon & Schuster Books for Young Readers, 1997). The picture book shows a tall man in a city, a teacher in a town, and a young brother and sister in a forest as they enjoy their separate and unrelated activities on a rainy day. It then reveals that the four are members of one family who return home in a surprise ending.

Rain Player, David Wisniewski (New York: Clarion Books, 1991). With the help of Jaquar, Quetzal, and the sacred water, Pik brings rain to his parched land and earns the name Rain Player when he challenges and defeats the rain god in *pok-a-tok*, a game of ball. An author's note includes information about the Maya culture.

Rain Song, Lezlie Evans, illustrated by Cynthia Jabar (Boston: Houghton Mifflin Company, 1995). Brightly illustrated rhyming verse captures the sounds, feelings, sights, and activities before, during, and after a summer thunderstorm enjoyed by two young girls.

Rainy Day Dream, Michael Chesworth (New York: Farrar, Straus & Giroux, 1992). In this wordless picture book, watercolor illustrations invite the reader to travel along with a boy who is swept on a fantasy rainy-day adventure as he holds onto the handle of his umbrella.

Time of Wonder, Robert McCloskey (New York: The Viking Press, 1957). Foggy mornings, sunny days, starlit nights, and a dramatic hurricane—McCloskey's text and watercolor illustrations create the summer world of an island in Penobscot Bay in Maine.

Umbrella, Taro Yashima (New York: Puffin Books, 1958, 1986). Three-year-old Momo impatiently awaits the first rainy day after she receives her first umbrella as a birthday gift. When that day finally arrives, she takes her umbrella as she walks to and from school and delights in the experiences of the sounds of the rain on her umbrella and in feeling grown-up.

The Umbrella Day, Nancy Evans Cooney, illustrations by Melissa Bay Mathis (New York: The Putnam & Grosset Group, 1989). At her mother's insistence that it is an umbrella day, Missy reluctantly takes a large, old umbrella with her as she goes out to play. During Missy's real and fantasy adventures that day, the umbrella proves its value.

We Hate Rain!, James Stevenson (New York: Greenwillow Books, 1988). When his grandchildren complain about a rainy day, Grandpa tells a tall tale about the time it poured for a month when he and his brother were children and water filled the four stories of their house.

We Play on a Rainy Day, Angela Shelf Medearis, illustrated by Sylvia Walker (New York: Scholastic Inc., 1995). One or two words or lines of rhyming text in large print on each page, and illustrations that give clues to meaning, show young children as they enjoy outdoor activities on a sunny day, run inside when it begins to rain, and don rainwear and grab umbrellas to enjoy activities outside in the rain.

Wet World, Norma Simon, illustrated by Alexi Natchev (Cambridge, Massachusetts: Candlewick Press, 1954, 1995). Watercolor illustrations capture the wet world, described with alliterative language featuring the letter *w*, experienced by a young child on a rainy day.

What Makes It Rain?: Usborne Starting Point Science, Susan Mayes, designed by Mike Pringle, illustrated by Richard Deverell and Mike Pringle (Tulsa, Oklahoma: EDC PUBLISHING, 1989). An introduction poses questions about the water cycle and related weather conditions, and short passages of text, illustrated with colored drawings and frequently presented in several outlined boxes on a page, provide answers and describe simple experiments for exploration. Includes a glossary and index.

Winnie-the-Pooh, A. A. Milne, illustrated by Ernest H. Shepard (New York: Dell Publishing Co., Inc., 1926, 1954). This book introduces the adventures of a boy, Christopher Robin, and his toy bear, who's come to life as Winnie-the-Pooh, and their friends Piglet, Eeyore, Kanga and Roo, and Rabbit. In "**Surrounded by Water**," Pooh proves himself a hero when he (and Christopher Robin aboard Christopher Robin's umbrella) rescues Piglet, who is stranded when rain floods the Forest.

Yagua Days, Cruz Martel, illustrated by Jerry Pinkney (New York: Penguin Books USA Inc., 1976). Friends and family tell Anan about "yagua days" as he is growing up in New York City, but he does not understand their enthusiasm until he visits family in Puerto Rico. There, on a rainy day, he slides down the hill into the river on his stomach on a yagua (the outer covering of a palm frond). Contains a glossary of Spanish words that appear in the story.

Literature Extension Activities

1. The section of the book that presents a brief history of umbrellas in ***The Enchanted Umbrella: With a Short History of the Umbrella*** shows a number of simple umbrellas for the daily needs of common people and fancy umbrellas for royalty and ceremonies. With students, design and draw umbrellas for people with different needs and occupations and for different occasions. Optionally, compile the drawings into a group book entitled *An Umbrella for Everyone*. Text that accompanies each illustration follows a repetitive pattern: An umbrella for _____ .

2. As an individual or group project, students make props, puppets, and scenery out of paper, cloth, or other materials for a puppet show of ***Mushroom in the Rain***. They make animal puppets out of paper attached to wooden craft or popsicle sticks or pencils, hand puppets out of socks, or finger puppets from the fingers cut off old gloves. A child-size umbrella makes a fine mushroom.

   Students act out the story of ***Mushroom in the Rain***. They dramatize the events in costume with a large, adult-size umbrella. A beach or golf umbrella works well.

3. After they have heard ***Rain Song*** read aloud, students in a group, in pairs, or individually act out each line with body movements.

   Students use homemade or commercially made drums or found drums (pots, pans, boxes) to punctuate the beats of the verses in ***Rain Song*** as you, another adult, or a student reads it aloud. They drum slowly as the storm approaches, more rapidly through the crescendo as the thunder reaches its peak, and slowly again as the storm fades off into the distance and the sun comes out again.

4. Illustrations for the pages of ***Umbrella***—on which Momo listens, on her way to and from school, to the raindrops as they fall on her umbrella— show a xylophone and mallets. Have students use a xylophone, a similar

percussion musical instrument, or a box or wooden block and mallets to accompany your reading of the rhythmic, onomatopoetic lines that capture the music of the sounds Momo hears.

5. After you share *The Umbrella Day* in read-aloud, generate and illustrate with your students a list of uses, real and fantasy, for an umbrella.

Items for the Mystery Box

Inedible Items: 7-UP® soda bottle or can, udder (on a cow), **umbrella**, umpire, uncle (photograph of your uncle, or a man who looks like an uncle), Uncle Sam (photograph of famous poster), under (in a picture), underpants (baby's or doll's), undershirt (baby's or doll's), underwear (long, baby's or doll's), up (arrow pointing up), upside-down (photograph or picture)

Edible Items: Ugli fruit™, 7-UP® soda, upside-down cake

Rhymes, Songs, Fingerplays, and Tongue Twisters

Umbrella Theme

*Doctor Foster went to Glo'ster: 5, 28, 32, 33, 34, 37, 38, 39, 46, 50, 73, 76
*A dog and a cat went out together: 9, 28, 33
Here's my umbrella: 19
It's raining, it's pouring: 5, 34, 36, 42, 51, 73, 76, 78
Pitter-pat, pitter-pat/The rain goes on for hours: 12

Raindrops/I listen to the raindrops fall: 75
The rain is raining all around: 51
Rain on the green grass: 34, 51, 73
Rain, rain, go away: 5, 20, 25, 28, 32, 33, 34, 38, 40, 43, 50, 51, 58, 73, 76, 78
Tongue Twisters: 13, 74

Letter-Sound u (u)

*Lazy Mary will you get up: 26, 53
Tongue Twisters: 1, 13, 60, 74, 80

Cloze Sentences

1. An **u**ndershirt is a shirt that I may wear **u**nder my shirt.
   (**Under** my shirt, I may wear an **u**ndershirt.)
2. An **u**mpire is the person who calls balls and strikes in a baseball game.
   (The person who calls balls and strikes in a baseball game is an **u**mpire.)

3. **U**p is the direction an arrow points if it points to the sky.

   (If an arrow points to the sky, it points **u**p.)

4. My **u**ncle may be my mother or father's brother, or he may be married to my a**u**nt.

   (The man who is my mother or father's brother, or who is married to my a**u**nt, is my **u**ncle.)

1. **U**nderwear is clothing I wear **u**nder my clothes.

   (The clothing I wear **u**nder my clothes is my **u**nderwear.)

2. When something is **u**nder something else, it is below it and not above it.

   (When something is below and not above something else, it is **u**nder it.)

3. An **u**mbrella is something with a handle that I place over my head to keep myself dry when it rains.

   (Something with a handle that I place over my head to keep myself dry when it rains is an **u**mbrella.)

4. I am **u**pside-down when I stand on my hands with my feet in the air.

   (When I stand on my hands with my feet in the air, I am **u**pside-down.)

U u

u

A dog and a cat went out together,

To see some friends just out of town;

Said the cat to the dog,

"What d'ye think of the weather?"

"I think, ma'am, the rain will come down;

But don't be alarmed, for I've an umbrella

That will shelter us both," said this amiable fellow.

Name _____ Date _____

U u

u

Doctor Foster went to Glo'ster,

In a shower of rain;

He stepped in a puddle, up to his middle,

And never went there again.

Name _____   Date _____

U u

u

Lazy Mary, will you get up,

Will you get up,

Will you get up?

Lazy Mary, will you get up

So early in the morning?

No, no, mother, I won't get up,

I won't get up, I won't get up,

No, no, mother, I won't get up

So early in the morning.

Name _____   Date _____

U u

COMPLETE IT

undershirt   umpire
1   2

Up   uncle
3   4

An <u>undershirt</u> is a shirt that I may wear under my
1

shirt.

An <u>umpire</u> is the person who calls balls and
2

strikes in a baseball game.

<u>Up</u> is the direction an arrow points if it points to
3

the sky.

My <u>uncle</u> may be my mother or father's brother,
4

or he may be married to my aunt.

Name _____   Date _____

U u

COMPLETE IT

Underwear
1

under
2

umbrella
3

upside-down
4

<u>Underwear</u> is clothing I wear under my clothes.
1

When something is <u>under</u> something else, it is
2
below it and not above it.

An <u>umbrella</u> is something with a handle that I
3
place over my head to keep myself dry when it
rains.

I am <u>upside-down</u> when I stand on my hands
4
with my feet in the air.

Name _____   Date _____

Cloze Sentences . . . 2

V v valentine

TEACHER REFERENCE

Annotated Book List

Arthur's Great Big Valentine, Lillian Hoban (New York: Harper & Row, Publishers, 1989). In this easy-to-read book, Arthur the monkey discovers that Valentine's Day can be a very lonely time without friends until he and his former best friend give each other valentines that help them reconnect.

Arthur's Valentine, Marc Brown (Boston: Little, Brown and Company, 1980). In this book in the series about Arthur the anteater, as Valentine's Day approaches, Arthur's curiosity grows as he receives a number of valentines from his secret admirer, but he has to wait until February 14th, when a letter in the mail and a movie ticket help him solve the mystery.

Cranberry Valentine, Wende and Harry Devlin (New York: Simon & Schuster Children's Publishing Division, 1986). In this book in the series of "Cranberry" holiday books, Mr. Whiskers is not sure he likes receiving unsigned valentines and fears that he is being pursued by a secret admirer, until he discovers that they were sent by members of Grandmother's sewing circle. Includes a recipe for cranberry upside-down cake.

Four Valentines in a Rainstorm, Felicia Bond (New York: Harper & Row, Publishers, 1983). A young girl catches hearts that magically fall from the sky during a rainstorm and makes a special valentine for each of four friends.

Heart to Heart, George Shannon, illustrated by Steve Bjorkman (Boston: Houghton Mifflin Company, 1995). Having forgotten Valentine's Day, Squirrel rushes to make his friend Mole a fancy card, but in the process he thinks of a unique gift only a best friend could make—a memory box decorated with souvenirs of their shared adventures.

How Spider Saved Valentine's Day, Robert Kraus (New York: Scholastic Inc., 1985). When Spider notices that the two caterpillars who constantly sleep in the back of the classroom were overlooked and have not received any valentines, he turns his friends Fly and Ladybug and himself into living cards for what have become two butterflies.

It's Valentine's Day, Jack Prelutsky, pictures by Yossi Abolafia (New York: William Morrow & Company, 1983). This collection of humorous, yet poignant, poems expresses a variety of feelings frequently experienced by young children around Valentine's Day.

Lots of Hearts, Maryann Cocca-Leffler (New York: Grosset & Dunlap, 1996). A little girl refuses the help of her dog when she makes valentines for her father, mother, goldfish, and dog, and then hides the cards for them to find. Then, she discovers that all have disappeared—into the doghouse, along with a surprise litter of puppies.

The Mysterious Valentine, Nancy Carlson (Minneapolis: Carolrhoda Books, Inc., 1985). When Louanne pig receives an unsigned valentine, she looks for her secret admirer everywhere but at home, where one of her greatest fans, her father, reveals clues to the reader (but not to Louanne) that he is the sender of the card.

Nate the Great and the Mushy Valentine, Marjorie Weinman Sharmat, illustrations by Marc Simont (New York: Bantam Doubleday Dell Publishing Group, Inc., 1994). In this detective story from the series, Nate the Great helps his dog Sludge and his friend Annie solve two Valentine's Day mysteries that involve the same valentine.

One Very Best Valentine's Day, Joan W. Blos, illustrated by Emily Arnold McCully (New York: Simon & Schuster Children's Publishing Division, 1990). Unable to put back together her broken heart bracelet, a young girl secretly makes gifts from it for each member of her family for Valentine's Day.

One Zillion Valentines, Frank Modell (New York: Greenwillow Books, 1981). Marvin shows his friend Milton how to make valentines, and after they deliver the cards to all of their neighbors, they sell the leftover cards and buy each other a very special valentine —the edible kind!

Things to Make and Do for Valentine's Day, Tomie de Paola (New York: Franklin Watts, Inc., 1976). This Valentine's Day activities book, liberally illustrated with de Paola drawings, provides directions for making sponge print cards with envelopes, a valentine mailbag, and baker's clay gifts; jokes, riddles, and tongue twisters; an I Spy hearts activity; recipes for sandwiches and dessert; and instructions for playing a relay race and the heartbeat game and for doing a card trick.

Valentine, Carol Carrick, illustrated by Paddy Bouma (New York: Clarion Books, 1995). Heather is disappointed when her mother has to work on Valentine's Day, but when she bakes Valentine cookies and helps her grandmother save the life of a newborn lamb, it becomes a day she will never forget.

Valentine Bears, Eve Bunting, illustrated by Jan Brett (New York: Clarion Books, 1983). Mr. and Mrs. Bear have never shared a Valentine's Day because they hibernate, but one Valentine's Day Mrs. Bear sets her alarm for February 14th so that she can make preparations to surprise her husband, and she finds that he has prepared surprises for her as well.

Valentine Cats, Jean Marzollo, illustrated by Hans Wilhelm (New York: Scholastic Inc., 1996). In this book with a repeated pattern, a rhyming line on each illustrated page describes an activity of writer cats, artist cats, and postal cats as they prepare and deliver valentines.

Valentine Mice!, Bethany Roberts, illustrated by Doug Cushman (Boston: Houghton Mifflin Company, 1997). One or two lines of rhyming text for each colorfully illustrated page describe the actions and adventures of four lively mice as they deliver valentines to their animal friends in the forest.

Literature Extension Activities

1. After students enjoy *Cranberry Valentine* in read-aloud, follow the recipe in the book and bake and eat cranberry upside-down cake.

2. As one alternative to making Valentine's Day cards, you and your students can make Valentine memory boxes for friends, family, or community members (whether it's Valentine's Day or not, for this is a thoughtful gift at any time of the year). Students use small objects that remind them of special times shared with the recipient of the gift— similar to the box Squirrel gives his friend Mole in *Heart to Heart*.

3. As time permits, engage in activities for Valentine's Day that can be enjoyed at any time of the year, from *Things to Make and Do for Valentine's Day*.

4. In *Valentine*, preschooler Heather and her grandmother make cut-out cookies using cookie cutters shaped like Grandma's farm animals— chickens, cats, and sheep— and in the shape of Valentine hearts. Using a favorite recipe for cut-out cookies, with students, roll out, cut, decorate with colored decorating sugars, and eat cookies made in their favorite shapes. As you enjoy the cookies together, have students talk about a Valentine's Day they will never forget or Valentine's Day traditions and activities that are special to them.

5. In *Valentine Bears*, Mr. and Mrs. Bear prepare special food treats that a bear would enjoy—honey, dried beetles and bugs, and chocolate-

covered ants. After they hear the book read aloud, students (individually, in pairs, or in groups) choose a favorite animal and draw and label pictures of Valentine food treats their animal would enjoy. Then, students enjoy a special snack that you have prepared in advance.

Items for the Mystery Box

Inedible Items: vacuum cleaner, **valentine**, valley, vampire, van, vane (weather), vase, Vaseline® petroleum jelly, vegetables (mixed—in photograph), V-8® juice can, veil, Velcro®, velvet, vest, village, vine, violet, violin, vise, visor, vitamin bottle, volcano (made with baking soda and vinegar), volleyball, vulture

Edible Items: vanilla, vanilla ice cream, vanilla pudding, vanilla wafers, veal, vegetable marrow (British squash), vegetable soup, vegetables (variety, with dips), V-8® juice, venison, vermicelli, vichyssoise, vinaigrette dressing (with vegetables), vinegar

Rhymes, Songs, Fingerplays, and Tongue Twisters

Valentine Theme

*Good morrow to you, Valentine: 73
The rose is red, the violet's blue: 73
*Roses are red, violets are blue: 5, 20, 51, 73, 76

Letter-Sound v (v)

*The Queen of Hearts: 3, 5, 28, 32, 33, 34, 35, 38, 39, 46, 50, 52, 73, 76
Tongue Twisters: 1, 13, 80

Cloze Sentences

1. A <u>v</u>alentine is a heart-shaped card that people give and receive on **V**alentine's Day.

   (A heart-shaped card that people give and receive on **V**alentine's Day is a <u>v</u>alentine.)

2. A <u>v</u>olcano is a mountain that can erupt and have steam, ashes, and lava come out of an opening at the top.

   (A mountain that can erupt and have steam, ashes, and lava come out of an opening at the top is a <u>v</u>olcano.)

3. <u>V</u>egetables are plants grown as food that can be carrots, peas, corn, or beans.

   (Plants grown as food such as carrots, peas, corn, and beans are <u>v</u>egetables.)

4. <u>V</u>anilla is a flavor of ice cream that is a white or cream color.

   (A flavor of ice cream that is a white or cream color is <u>v</u>anilla.)

1. A <u>v</u>ase is a container with water in it that holds flowers.

   (A container with water in it that holds flowers is a <u>v</u>ase.)

2. A <u>v</u>est is a piece of clothing that is like a shirt or a jacket, but it has no sleeves.

   (A piece of clothing that is like a shirt or a jacket, but has no sleeves, is a <u>v</u>est.)

3. A <u>v</u>acuum cleaner is a tool that people use to suck up dirt from a rug.

   (A tool that people use to suck up dirt from a rug is a <u>v</u>acuum cleaner.)

4. A <u>v</u>an is a **v**ehicle that is larger than a car and smaller than a bus.

   (A **v**ehicle that is larger than a car and smaller than a bus is a <u>v</u>an.)

V v

Roses are red,

Violets are blue,

Sugar is sweet,

And so are you.

I LOVE YOU.

BE MY VALENTINE!

Name _____   Date _____

V v

Good morrow to you, Valentine.

Curl your locks as I do mine,

Two before and three behind.

Good morrow to you, Valentine.

Name _____   Date _____

V v

The Queen of Hearts,
She made some tarts
All on a summer's day;

The Knave of Hearts,
He stole those tarts
And took them clean away.

Name _____   Date _____

V v

COMPLETE IT

valentine
1

volcano
2

Vegetables
3

Vanilla
4

A <u>valentine</u> is a heart-shaped card that
　　1
people give and receive on Valentine's Day.

A <u>volcano</u> is a mountain that can erupt
　　2
and have steam, ashes, and lava come out of an
opening at the top.

<u>Vegetables</u> are plants grown as food that
　　　3
can be carrots, peas, corn, or beans.

<u>Vanilla</u> is a flavor of ice cream that is a
　　4
white or cream color.

Name _____　Date _____

V v

COMPLETE IT

vase   vest
1   2
vacuum   van
3   4

A <u>vase</u> is a container with water in it that
   1
holds flowers.

A <u>vest</u> is a piece of clothing that is like a
   2
shirt or a jacket, but it has no sleeves.

A <u>vacuum</u> cleaner is a tool that people
    3
use to suck up dirt from a rug.

A <u>van</u> is a vehicle that is larger than a car
   4
and smaller than a bus.

Name _____   Date _____

W w   water

TEACHER REFERENCE

Annotated Book List

Alejandro's Gift, Richard E. Albert, illustrated by Sylvia Long (San Francisco: Chronicle Books, 1994). To fill the hours of his lonely life in his desert home with only his burro for company, Alejandro plants a garden that attracts animals who come for water and inspire him to dig a water hole for all of the animals to enjoy.

The Boy Who Held Back the Sea, Thomas Locker (New York: Dial Books for Young Readers, 1987). Rich oil paintings combine with detailed text to tell the story of the Dutch boy who saves his town from flooding by holding his finger over a hole in the dike until help comes.

Children of the Wind and Water: Five Stories About Native American Children, Stephen Krensky, illustrated by James Watling (New York: Scholastic Inc., 1994). The short stories in this collection show Native American children from five different tribes as they interact, in work and play, with their environments and learn, from family and community members, important traditions and skills needed for survival. An introduction highlights common experiences of Native American children, and a glossary and map provide information about each of the people represented in the stories: Muskogee, Dakota, Huron, Tlingit, and Nootka.

Come Away from the Water, Shirley, John Burningham (New York: Thomas Y. Crowell, 1977). While her overprotective parents absentmindedly toss warnings at her from their beach chairs, Shirley has an exciting action-packed adventure on a ship filled with pirates!

A Drop of Water: A Book of Science and Wonder, Walter Wick (New York: Scholastic Inc., 1997). Extraordinary full-color photographs (many with magnification) and easy-to-understand text explore the varied states of water (droplets, bubbles, ice, vapor, clouds, snowflakes/ice crystals, frost, dew, and rainbows) and related concepts (elasticity, surface tension, adhesion, capillary attraction, molecular motion, evaporation, condensation, refraction, and the water cycle). An author's note suggests extension observations and experiments.

Follow the Water from Brook to Ocean: Let's-Read-and-Find-Out Science, Arthur Dorros (New York: HarperCollins Publishers, 1991). Illustrations show two young children who follow water after a rain storm as it flows downhill to a puddle, brook, stream, spring, river, waterfall, pond, lake, reservoir, and ocean. Text provides information about water: sources; effects on surrounding land; animals and vegetation; erosion; floods, dams, and electricity; and pollution.

The Golden Flower: A Taino Myth from Puerto Rico, Nina Jaffe, illustrated by Enrique O. Sánchez (New York: Simon & Schuster Books for Young Readers, 1996). In this pourquoi story, a child plants seeds he finds in his barren world, from which a vine with a golden flower and then a yellow shining globe grow. From this shining pumpkin (calabaza) pour waters that cover the earth, leaving the island of Boriquén, or Puerto Rico. An afterword provides information about the traditional tale and the Taino people.

The Hole in the Dike, Norma Green, illustrated by Eric Carle (New York: Scholastic Inc., 1974). A young boy puts his finger in a hole in a dike until it can be repaired and saves his town in Holland from being flooded.

I Am Water, Jean Marzollo, illustrated by Judith Moffatt (New York: Scholastic Inc., 1996). In this book with layered collage illustrations and one or a few lines of large-print text that follow a repeated " I am . . ." pattern, the water provides information about its many forms and roles.

Letting Swift River Go, Jane Yolen, illustrated by Barbara Cooney (Boston: Little, Brown and Company, 1992). Under the stars one night, a woman is able to find peace with the loss and her memories of the Swift River Valley towns in western Massachusetts, where she had lived as a child until they were evacuated and flooded to create the Quabbin Reservoir between 1927 and 1946.

The Magic School Bus at the Waterworks, Joanna Cole, illustrated by Bruce Degen (New York: Scholastic Inc., 1986). In this informational book in the series (in which running text is complemented by text in illustrations, drawings, cartoon bubble dialogue, and student reports), Mrs. Frizzle and her class don scuba diving outfits and shrink to fit inside raindrops to learn about water during their visit to the waterworks.

Mouse Tales, Arnold Lobel (New York: HarperCollins Publishers, 1972). In this collection of short tales, Papa mouse sits by their bed and tells one bedtime story for each of the mouse boys until all seven of them are asleep. In **"The Bath,"** when a mouse takes a bath, he does not turn off the water in the tub until after it has flooded the entire town.

My Life with the Wave, based on the story by Octavio Paz, translated from Spanish and adapted for children by Catherine Cowan, illustrated by Mark Buehner (New York: Lothrop, Lee & Shepard Books, 1997). The ocean wave a boy brings home is a wonderful companion until she shows the dark sides of her moods and the family decides to return her to the sea.

Noah's Ark, Peter Spier (New York: Doubleday & Company, Inc., 1977). Realistic details in the ink and watercolor illustrations distinguish this version of the traditional story of the Ark, Noah, his family, and the animals before, during, and after the Flood.

No More Water in the Tub!, Tedd Arnold (New York: Dial Books for Young Readers, 1995). When the bathtub faucet breaks, a flood of water carries William and the bathtub, floor by floor, down from the top of his apartment building, gathering his neighbors with him and putting out a fire on the way.

On the River ABC, Caroline Stutson, illustrated by Anna-Maria L. Crum (Niwot, Colorado: Roberts Rinehart Publishers, 1993). As an ant floats downstream in a river on an aspen leaf, she sees wild animals whose names begin with each letter of the alphabet (except *x*) that are part of the world in and around the waterway. An afterword contains information about each of the animals featured that are native to western and southwestern United States.

The Perfect Spot, Robert J. Blake (New York: Philomel Books, 1992). As his father searches along a stream for a setting for his painting, a boy slips and falls in as he tries to catch a cricket frog. Amid shared laughter and water play, they realize that they have already discovered the perfect spot for his dad's work.

Rain Drop Splash, Alvin Tresselt, pictures by Leonard Weisgard (New York: William Morrow & Company, Inc., 1946, 1990). Text and illustrations of this Caldecott Honor Book follow rain drops as they become a puddle, pond, brook, lake, river, and sea, and show the vegetation, animals, and people they impact on their way. An afterword describes the process of writing the book.

Raven Returns the Water, Anne Cameron (Madeira Park, B.C., Canada: Marbour Publishing Co. Ltd., 1987). In this combination pourquoi and trickster tale from oral tradition that tells why frogs croak and ravens call, raven saves the world from drought when she teaches a giant frog, who hoards the missing water in her belly, to respect and share the element and return it to all living things.

A River Ran Wild, Lynne Cherry (San Diego: Harcourt Brace & Company, 1992). Full-page watercolor illustrations and borders, and informative text, trace the history of the Nashua River in Massachusetts from its natural state—preserved by the native people before the 1600s when the English arrived—to a time of pollution from nearby mills and factories, during which it was declared ecologically dead, and through cleanup efforts in the 1960s to restore it. An author's note, map, and time line provide background information.

Science with Water: Usborne Science Activities, Helen Edom, designed by Jane Felstead, illustrated by Simone Abel (Tulsa, Oklahoma: EDC PUB-LISHING, 1990). Short passages of text, with colorful illustrations, describe simple experiments using common objects that explore the properties of water.

Shaker Lane, Alice and Martin Provensen (New York: Penguin Books USA Inc., 1987). Only Old Man Van Sloop and his dog and chickens remain after the rest of the residents of Shaker Lane move away when a dam and reservoir are built and their community is flooded. He lives with his animals on a houseboat!

Three Monks, No Water, Ting-Xing Ye, illustrated by Harvey Chan (New York: Annick Press, 1997). Each of the three monks who live in a mountain temple offers excuses why he should not be the one to carry the water for their use, until a fire threatens their home and they learn to cooperate. The story proposes the origin of the expression "It's typical. Three monks, no water." An afterword explains the background of the book, the Chinese calligraphy translation of the expression that appears in the illustrations, and the seal on the cover that depicts the saying.

To Climb a Waterfall, Jean Craighead George, illustrated by Thomas Locker (New York: Philomel Books, 1995). George's text, which speaks directly to the reader, and Locker's richly detailed paintings complement each other effectively in this stunning picture book invitation to climb alongside a mountain water-fall.

Water, Frank Asch (San Diego: Harcourt Brace & Company, 1995). This rich watercolor tribute explores the forms, uses, and locations in the environment of this important element.

Water: A First Discovery Book, Gallimard Jeunesse and Pierre-Marie Valat, illustrated by Pierre-Marie Valat (New York: Scholastic Inc., 1991). A plastic protective covering for all pages, plastic see-through pages with illustrations on both sides, and a spiral binding distinguish this book that provides information about water: forms; cycle; journey to the sea; uses; reservoirs, dams, and electricity; irrigation; fire-fighting; recreation; and animals.

Water Dance, Thomas Locker (San Diego: Harcourt Brace & Company, 1997). In poetic prose from the point of view of the water itself, and with rich paintings, the book presents a variety of forms in which water appears. A section about the water cycle at the book's end provides factual information about each form.

Water Music: Poems for Children, Jane Yolen, photographs by Jason Stemple (Honesdale, Pennsylvania: Wordsong/Boyds Mills Press, 1995). A collection of poems, written by the author in response to the photographs of water taken by her son that illustrate the book, celebrate water in a variety of forms. An author's note describes the mother-son collaboration that culminated in this book.

Water, the Source of Life: Scholastic Voyages of Discovery, Gallimard Jeunesse (New York: Scholastic Inc., 1996). This interactive book with plastic protected pages, transparent plastic pages, flaps, cut-away pages, liquid bubble, and reusable vinyl stickers in a spiral-bound format invites readers to explore water's nature and history throughout the earth and space. Includes annotated lists (books; addresses; people; myths, legends, and monsters; words; and notable waterways), a time line, and an index.

Waters, Edith Newlin Chase, illustrated by Ron Broda (Buffalo, New York: Firefly Books [U.S.] Inc., 1995). One or a few poetic lines and watercolored paper-sculpture illustrations on each page trace the journey of a small brook to the sea and show the animals and plants that live near the waterways. An author's note describes ways in which creatures depend on water and identifies the creatures pictured in the text.

The Water's Journey, Eleonore Schmid, translated by Rada Matija AG (New York: North-South Books, 1989). Detailed paintings with accompanying text trace water's journey from precipitation on a mountaintop to brook, stream, waterfall, lake, small river, reservoir, and larger river until it joins the ocean and evaporates into mist to begin the cycle again.

Wet World, Norma Simon, illustrated by Alexi Natchev (Cambridge, Massachusetts: Candlewick Press, 1954, 1995). Watercolor illustrations capture the wet world, described with alliterative language featuring the letter *w,* experienced by a young child on a rainy day.

What Makes It Rain?: Usborne Starting Point Science, Susan Mayes, designed by Mike Pringle, illustrated by Richard Deverell and Mike Pringle (Tulsa, Oklahoma: EDC PUBLISHING, 1989). An introduction poses questions about the water cycle and related weather conditions. Short passages of text, illustrated with colored drawings and frequently presented in several outlined boxes on a page, provide answers and describe simple experiments for exploration. Includes a glossary and index.

Why Are There Waves?: Questions Children Ask About WATER, (New York: Dorling Kindersley Ltd., 1997). A table of contents introduces eight commonly asked questions about water answered in easy-to-understand text, with colored photographs of children and adults interacting with the element in a variety of contexts around the world.

Why the Sun and the Moon Live in the Sky: An African Folktale by Elphinstone Dayrell, illustrated by Blair Lent (Boston: Houghton Mifflin Company, 1968). Characters in this pourquoi tale wear costumes in the story of a visit from the water and his people that crowds the sun and his wife, the moon, out of their house on earth and forces them to live in the sky.

The Woman Who Outshone the Sun: The Legend of Lucia Zenteno/La mujer que brillaba aún más que el sol: La leyenda de Lucía Zenteno, from a poem by Alejandro Cruz Martinez, story by Harriet Rohmer and David Schecter, pictures by Fernando Olivera, translated by Rosalma Zubizarreta (Emeryville, California: Children's Book Press, 1991). In this legend, from the oral history of the Zapotec people of Oaxaca, Mexico and written in parallel text in English and Spanish, the cruelty of people from the village where the wondrous Lucia Zenteno appears drives away Lucia and the river who loves her. Compassionate when people beg forgiveness, Lucia asks the river to return. She remains, as a spirit, to help them live with kindness and understanding of those who, like her, are different.

Literature Extension Activities

1. Have students showcase what they know and learn about water in individual or group books they make, written from the point of view of the water, patterned after ***I Am Water***, with layered collage illustrations.

2. With students, compare and contrast ***No More Water in the Tub!*** with its companion book by the same author ***No Jumping on the Bed*** (Chapter 2). Then, record and illustrate the rhyming descriptions of William's neighbors, who are swept along on his watery adventure, including Uncle Nash in the trash, Patty Fuzzle's puzzle, and Mr. Bellow with his cello.

3. After you share ***Water*** in read-aloud with students, add to the list of forms, uses, and locations of water in the environment presented in the book (and in other books in this unit). Help students compile a group list and illustrate their entries, using watercolors as Asch did in his illustrations.

4. After you share ***Waters***, trace on a map the journey of a local brook, stream, or river to the sea. Students can find photographs or drawings, draw or paint pictures, of the animals and plants that live near local waterways, and make up a list of them. Compare ***Waters*** with other books with paper-sculpture illustrations.

5. Students make and wear costumes influenced by African cultures, like those worn by the characters in ***Why the Sun and the Moon Live in***

the Sky: An African Folktale by Elphinstone Dayrell, and present a play of the tale.

Items for the Mystery Box

Whenever possible, select items for this unit that are **w**hite in color.

Inedible Items: wagon (covered), wagon (toy), wall, wallet, walnut shell, walrus, wand (magic), wardrobe, washing machine, wasp, watch, **water** (*Note:* Begin the activity by silently pouring water into a clear glass and then drinking it.), watering can, wave, wax (candle), wax paper, weasel, weaving, web (spider's), wedding, week (on a calendar), weights, well, whale, wheat, wheel (steering, from play vehicle), wheel (from play vehicle), wheelchair, whisk (cooking), whiskers, whistle, wick (of a candle), wig, wigwam, willow, windmill, window (from building set), window box, wing (airplane), wing (bird), wire, wishbone, witch, wizard, wolf, wood, woodpecker, wool, worm

Edible Items: Cream of Wheat® cereal, wafers, waffles, Waldorf salad, walnuts, wax beans, **water** (bottled, tap), water chestnuts, watercress, watermelon, wheat crackers, wheat germ, Wheaties® cereal, whipped cream, wild rice, winter squash, wonton, wonton soup

Rhymes, Songs, Fingerplays, and Tongue Twisters

Water Theme

*The eentsy weentsy spider: 5, 12, 14, 29, 32, 33, 34, 49, 51, 53, 76, 78
Jack, Jack, pump the water: 79
Jack and Jill went up the hill: 5, 20, 26, 28, 31, 32, 33, 34, 38, 39, 40, 46, 49, 50, 52, 53, 58, 62, 67, 73, 76, 78
Mother, may I go out to swim?: 5, 46
There's a hole in the bucket, dear Liza, dear Liza: 17, 55, 65
Tongue Twisters: 13

Letter-Sound w (w)

Bow-wow-wow: 3, 20, 27, 28, 33, 46, 50, 73
*Cocks crow in the morn: 5

In and Out the Window: 47
Little Tom Tucker sang for his supper: 26, 28, 33, 34, 38, 39, 40, 42, 46, 50, 52, 58, 62, 73, 76
Lazy Mary will you get up: 26, 53
This little piggy went to market: 3, 5, 14, 20, 25, 26, 28, 29, 31, 32, 33, 34, 37, 38, 39, 42, 43, 46, 50, 52, 73, 76
Tongue Twisters: 1, 7, 13, 60, 74, 80
*Wee Willie Winkie: 3, 5, 20, 28, 32, 33, 34, 39, 40, 49, 50, 53, 73, 76
Where is Thumbkin?: 12, 14, 31, 78
Where, oh where, has my little dog gone?: 5, 27, 34, 39, 62, 73, 76
Whistle, daughter, whistle: 5

Cloze Sentences

1. **W**hen is is **w**indy, it is fun to fly a kite.
   (It is fun to fly a kite **w**hen it is **w**indy.)
2. **W**ings are things that help both birds and airplanes to fly.
   (Birds and airplanes both have things that help them fly called **w**ings.)
3. I **w**ash my hands with **w**ater and soap before I eat.
   (Before I eat, I **w**ash my hands with soap and **w**ater.)
4. A **w**itch rides a broom through the sky on Hallo**w**een.
   (On Hallo**w**een, through the sky on a broom rides a **w**itch.)

1. To see ho**w** many pounds **w**e **w**eigh, **w**e stand on a scale.
   (**W**e stand on a scale to see ho**w** many pounds **w**e **w**eigh.)
2. **W**heels are round and are on cars, bicycles, **w**agons, trucks, buses, and vans.
   (On cars, bicycles, **w**agons, trucks, buses, and vans are round **w**heels.)
3. A **w**atch or a clock can tell me **w**hat time is it.
   (To find out **w**hat time it is, I can look at a clock or a **w**atch.)
4. I look out a **w**indow **w**hen I **w**ant to see **w**hat is happening outside.
   (**W**hen I **w**ant to see **w**hat is happening outside, I look out a **w**indow.)

W w

The eentsy, weentsy spider
Climbed up the waterspout.

Down came the rain
And washed the spider out.

Out came the sun
And dried up all the rain.

And the eentsy, weentsy spider
Climbed up the spout again.

Name _____   Date _____

W w

Wee Willie Winkie runs through the town,

Upstairs and downstairs, in his nightgown,

Rapping at the window, crying at the lock,

"Are the children in their beds,

for now it's ten o'clock?"

Name _____   Date _____

W w

Cocks crow in the morn

To tell us to rise,

And he who lies late

Will never be wise;

For early to bed

And early to rise

Is the way to be healthy,

And wealthy and wise.

Name _____   Date _____

W w

COMPLETE IT

windy
1

Wings
2

water
3

witch
4

When it is <u>windy</u>, it is fun to fly a kite.
       1

<u>Wings</u> are things that help both birds and
  2
airplanes to fly.

I wash my hands with <u>water</u> and soap
               3
before I eat.

A <u>witch</u> rides a broom through the sky on
    4
Halloween.

Name _____   Date _____

W w

COMPLETE IT

weigh	Wheels
1	2
watch	window
3	4

To see how many pounds we <u>weigh</u>, we
                          1
stand on a scale.

<u>Wheels</u> are round and are on cars,
 2
bicycles, wagons, trucks, buses, and vans.

A <u>watch</u> or a clock can tell me what time
    3
is it.

I look out a <u>window</u> when I want to see
          4
what is happening outside.

Name _____ Date _____

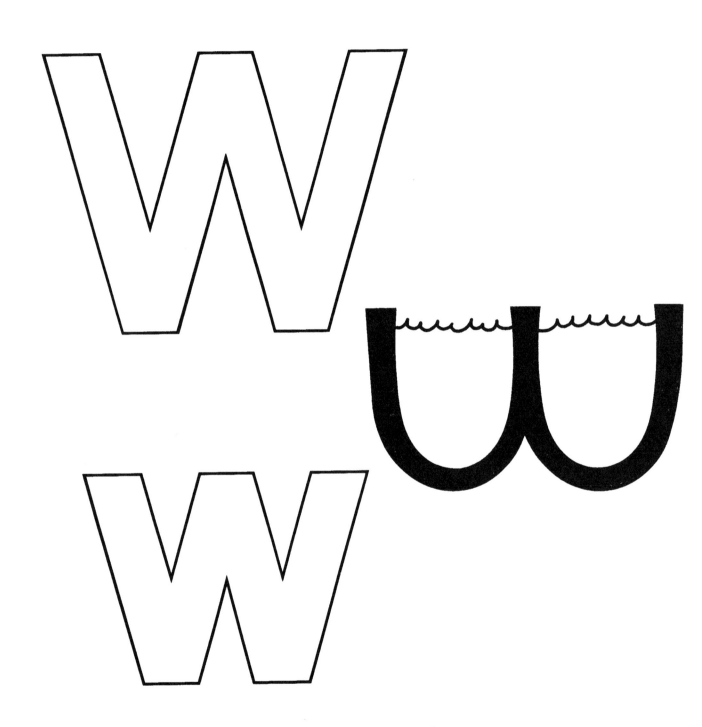

X x  fox

TEACHER REFERENCE

Annotated Book List

Chanticleer and the Fox, Geoffrey Chaucer, adapted and illustrated by Barbara Cooney (New York: Thomas Y. Crowell Company, 1958). In this traditional fable, the fox's flattery tricks proud Chanticleer, the rooster, into crowing with his eyes closed so he can capture Chanticleer, but Chanticleer outsmarts the fox and escapes his mouth when he tricks the fox into speaking.

Chicken Little, Steven Kellogg (New York: William Morrow and Company, Inc., 1985). Kellogg's story is a modern, humorous retelling of the traditional tale with a contemporary setting and police rather than a king. In the end, the plotting and poultry-loving fox villain is sentenced to prison and a vegetarian diet, and the hen tells her grandchildren the story under an oak tree she plants (from the acorn, of course).

Doctor De Soto, William Steig (New York: Farrar, Straus & Giroux, 1982). Tiny Doctor De Soto, the mouse and dentist, and his wife outsmart the large and hungry fox, who comes to their office to have a tooth pulled, with good thinking and a secret formula that glues the gullible and easily flattered fox's teeth together.

Father Fox's Pennyrhymes, Clyde Watson, illustrated by Wendy Watson (New York: Thomas Y. Crowell Company, 1971). In Watson's detailed illustrations, a variety of foxes dressed in rural Vermont farm clothes dramatize the action and add comments that provide the context for a collection of short rhymes.

Flossie & the Fox, Patricia C. McKissack, illustrations by Rachel Isadora (New York: Penguin Books USA Inc., 1986). On her way to take a basket of eggs to a neighbor for her grandmother, Flossie meets and outsmarts a fox by taking advantage of his vanity. Conversational dialect and glowing illustrations create the rural southern United States setting for the drama featuring one of literature's most independent heroines.

The Fox, Margaret Lane, pictures by Kenneth Lilly (New York: Penguin Books USA Inc., 1982). Lovely colored illustrations and informative text provide facts about foxes: habits, enemies and protection, young, shelter, physical characteristics, food, senses, and fox hunting as a sport.

Fox in Socks, Dr. Seuss (New York: Random House, 1965). Mr. Knox resists a fox's attempts to engage him in a series of complex tongue twisters until the end of the book, when he has the last word*s* and the last laugh as *he* ends the game.

The Fox on the Box, Barbara Gregovich, illustrated by Robert Masheris (Grand Haven, Michigan: School Zone Publishing Company, 1992). Simple patterned sentences composed of a few words describe the adventures and misadventure of a gentle fox and his companions, who are pictured in soft watercolor illustrations.

Fox on the Job, James Marshall (New York: Penguin Books USA Inc., 1988). In this book in a series, when fox shows off to impress the girls, he wrecks his bike and is forced to find a job (or, in his case, a *series* of ill-fitting jobs) to earn the money to replace it. He finally discovers the job for which he is perfectly suited—being a sleeping model for a bed in the front window of a furniture store!

Fox Song, Joseph Bruchac, illustrated by Paul Morin (New York: Philomel Books, 1993). After her great-grandmother dies, Jamie remembers their shared times, Grama's stories about the wisdom and traditions of their Abenaki people, and a song her Grama taught her. This rich legacy, along with a special visit from a fox, reassures Jamie that her beloved Grama is always near.

Fox's Dream, Tejima (New York: Philomel Books, 1985, 1987). The poetic prose and award-winning illustrations capture a lonely fox's winter dream-wish for a family and its fulfillment when he meets a vixen.

The Fox Went Out on a Chilly Night: An Old Song, Peter Spier (New York: Bantam Doubleday Dell Publishing Group, Inc., 1961). Spier's illustrations for the well-known traditional song show in detail a fox's successful hunting exploits one night in a farmer's poultry yard and the feast he happily shares afterward with his family. Includes the music for the song.

Gray Fox, Jonathan London, illustrations by Rober Sauber (New York: Penguin Books USA Inc., 1993). A fox's life in the wild with his vixen wife and cubs is brought to an abrupt end when he chases a rabbit across a road into the path of a truck, but his spirit goes on in the memory of a young boy who respectfully lays his body to rest and in the lives of his cubs.

Hattie and the Fox, Mem Fox, illustrated by Patricia Mullins (New York: Macmillan, Inc., 1986). The suspense builds in this story with a repetitive refrain when Hattie, the hen, is the only animal in the barnyard who notices in the bushes, first a nose, then two eyes, then two ears . . . and, finally, *all* of a—fox!

Henny Penny, H. Werner Zimmermann (New York: Scholastic Inc., 1989). Amusing watercolor illustrations and easy-to-read large print combine to tell the familiar cumulative story of a hen who, after she is hit on the head by an acorn, passes on her panic about the sky falling to an increasing collection of friends. She leads them, on the way to tell the king, to an untimely end in the fox's cave.

The Hungry Fox and the Foxy Duck, Kathleen Leverich, illustrated by Paul Galdone (New York: Parents Magazine Press, 1978). A wise duck outsmarts a hungry fox by insisting that the shared meal he proposes be eaten properly. The meal is postponed as the fox gets a table, plates and cups, and a tablecloth—a large, *red* tablecloth that excites a bull, who shares the field with the duck and conveniently chases the fox away.

Little Fox Goes to the End of the World, Ann Tompert, illustrated by John Wallner (New York: Crown Publishers, Inc., 1976). While she sews her a new jacket, Little Fox's sensitive mother actively engages with her daughter as the young fox tells about her adventures during an imaginary trip to the end of the world.

Mole's Hill: A Woodland Tale, Lois Ehlert (San Diego: Harcourt Brace & Co., Inc., 1994). Illustrations inspired by ribbon appliqué and sewn beadwork embellish this story based on a Seneca tale, in which Fox, with Skunk and Raccoon, demands that Mole remove her hill so they can build a path to the pond. Mole executes a clever plan that leads Fox to suggest a compromise—a tunnel, dug by Mole, for the path to go *through* her hill.

Moon Rope/Un lazo a la luna: A Peruvian Folktale, Lois Ehlert, translated into Spanish by Amy Prince (San Diego: Harcourt Brace Jovanovich, 1992). Written in English and Spanish, this adaptation of a Peruvian pourquoi legend tells the adventures of mole and fox as they climb to the moon on a grass rope ladder and why moles live underground and a fox's face is in the moon.

Mother Goose and the Sly Fox, Chris Conover (New York: Farrar, Straus & Giroux, 1989). Rich, two-page illustrations alternate with illustrated text in Conover's story set in Holland, in which Mother Goose tricks Fox, who tricked her seven goslings.

One Fine Day, Nonny Hogrogian (New York: Macmillan Publishing Company, 1971). In this cumulative tale, a fox drinks a woman's milk, and she cuts off his tail. To get the milk she requests in trade for sewing on his tail, the fox satisfies the requests of a series of characters.

Percy and the Five Houses, Else Homelund Minarik, illustrated by James Marshall (New York: Viking, 1989). Percy, the beaver, had heard of a Book of the Month Club but not a House of the Month Club, until a fox sells him a membership. Percy finds that the houses he receives are not as good for him or his family as their lodge.

Rosie's Walk, Pat Hutchins (New York: The Macmillan Company, 1968). In this book with few words, the action is in the illustrations. While Rosie, the hen, walks nonchalantly through the barnyard completely unaffected by the fox that wants to eat her for dinner, the fox is thwarted at every turn by one mishap after another.

Seasons of a Red Fox: Smithsonian Wild Heritage Collection, Susan Saunders, illustrated by Jo-Ellen Bosson (Norwalk, Connecticut: Trudy Management Corporation, 1991). Facts about red foxes (including young; hunting, playing, and mating habits; food; and physical characteristics) are presented by following a male red fox from his birth through the seasons of his first year, in this book with beautiful close-up colored drawings. Includes a glossary and a section with facts and points of interest in the book.

Tales for a Winter's Eve, Wendy Watson (New York: Farrar, Straus & Giroux, 1988). The evening after little Freddie, the fox, hurts his paw while skiing, his grandmother, Bert Blue Jay, and Nellie Mouse each tell the fox family a humorous story about other animals that live on Vinegar Lane.

Three Aesop Fox Fables, Paul Galdone (New York: Clarion Books, 1971). The fox is tricked in the first two fables but wins in the third, in this collection of three fox fables from Aesop: "The Fox and the Grapes," "The Fox and the Stork," and "The Fox and the Crow."

Wild Fox: A True Story, Cherie Mason, illustrated by JoEllen McAllister Stammen (Camden, Maine: Down East Books, 1993). The author shares the details of the six-month period during which a male fox, injured by a steel-jawed trap, frequents her home in Maine before he returns instinctively to the wild.

Winter Fox, Jennifer Brutschy, illustrated by Allen Garvis (New York: Alfred A. Knopf, 1993). Though she knows that the fox has eaten her beloved pet rabbit, a young girl stops her father from shooting it when she sees how hungry and thin the fox looks as it struggles to survive the winter.

Literature Extension Activities

1. After they hear you twist your tongue while reading ***Fox in Socks***, students try their tongues at other tongue twisters by Dr. Seuss in ***Oh Say Can You Say?*** (New York: Random House, Inc., 1979) and in other collections. A list of books that includes collections of tongue twisters is located in Appendix B.

2. An author's note at the end of ***Fox Song*** explains that the book was based on a story from the author's family. If they choose to do so, students can share with you about special times with grandparents (or other family members or close friends), stories they may have heard about the traditions of their people, or family songs they have learned.

3. ***The Fox Went Out on a Chilly Night: An Old Song*** contains the music for the song on a left-hand page and all of the verses, written out fully, on the facing right-hand page. Sing the song with students after you have read and discussed the book (if they were able to resist singing during the first reading!) They clap their hands, stamp their feet, or use rhythm instruments to mark the beat and accompany their singing.

4. Students, in costumes or headbands that identify their characters, dramatize the cumulative tale, ***One Fine Day***, as you, the narrator, read it aloud.

5. After they enjoy ***Rosie's Walk*** in read-aloud, students provide text for the story told from the fox's point of view. Individually or in a group, students dictate (or write) words to accompany the illustrations of the misadventures of the foiled fox. They include the fox's thoughts, feelings, motivations, and reactions as the drama unfolds behind Rosie.

6. Put out blue and black construction paper and pastels for classroom members to try their hand at day and night scenes with foxes, after they look carefully at the pastel illustrations in ***Winter Fox***.

Items for the Mystery Box

Inedible Items: ax, box, Chex® cereal box, Crispix® cereal box, exit sign, **fox**, jack-in-the-box, Kix® cereal box, Mueslix® cereal box, mix box (brownie, cake), mixer, ox, Red Sox (baseball card), six, tax form, toy box, Trix® cereal box, Twix® candy wrapper, wax (vehicle), wax (candle), wax paper

Edible Items: Chex® cereal, Crispix® cereal, Kix® cereal, lox (with bagels), Müeslix® cereal, Trix® cereal, Twix® candy, wax beans

Rhymes, Songs, Fingerplays, and Tongue Twisters

Fox Theme

*Foxes mixing socks in boxes: (Tongue Twister: Cynthia Conway Waring)

*Oh, a-hunting we will go: 44, 47, 79

*The fox jumped up on a moonlight night; or The fox went out on a chilly night: 16, 17, 28, 33, 51, 67

Tongue Twisters: 13, 54

Letter-Sound x (ks)

Tongue Twisters: 1, 13, 80

Cloze Sentences

1. A <u>box</u> is a container that is often made of cardboard, and it can have crackers or cookies inside it.

    (A container that is often made of cardboard and that can have crackers or cookies inside it is a <u>box</u>.)

2. When you <u>mix</u> something as you cook or bake, you stir it up.

    (When you stir up something as you cook or bake, you <u>mix</u> it.)

3. <u>Six</u> is the number that comes after five and before seven when we count.

    (When we count, the number that comes after five and before seven is <u>six</u>.)

4. An <u>ax</u> is a tool that can be used to chop down trees or to cut up wood.

    (A tool that can be used to chop down trees or to cut up wood is an <u>ax</u>.)

1. A <u>fox</u> is an animal that looks like a dog and has reddish-brown or gray fur, a bushy tail, and a pointed nose.

    (An animal that looks like a dog and has reddish-brown or gray fur, a bushy tail, and a pointed nose is a <u>fox</u>.)

2. <u>Wax</u> is the material that makes up the part of a candle around the wick.

    (The material that makes up the part of a candle around the wick is <u>wax</u>.)

3. <u>Tax</u> money is money that people pay to a town, state, or country where they live, and that is used to pay for roads, police and fire protection, schools, and other services that people need.

    (Money that people pay to a town, state, or country where they live, and that is used to pay for roads, police and fire protection, schools, and other services that people need is called <u>tax</u> money.)

4. The Red <u>Sox</u> professional baseball team is from Boston, Massachusetts.

    (A professional baseball team from Boston, Massachusetts, is the Red <u>Sox</u>.)

X x

Oh, a-hunting we will go,

A-hunting we will go;

We'll catch a fox

And put him in a box,

And then we'll let him go!

Name _____   Date _____

X x

THE FOX JUMPED UP ON A MOONLIGHT NIGHT

The fox jumped up on a moonlight night;

The stars were shining, and all things bright;

"Oho!" said the fox, "it's a very fine night

For me to go through the town, e-ho!"

Name _____   Date _____

X x

Foxes mixing socks in boxes

Foxes mixing socks in boxes

Foxes mixing socks in boxes

Name _____   Date _____

X x

COMPLETE IT

box	mix
1	2
Six	ax
3	4

A <u>box</u> is a container that is often made of
 1
cardboard, and it can have crackers or cookies
inside it.

When you <u>mix</u> something as you cook or bake,
 2
you stir it up.

<u>Six</u> is the number that comes after five and
 3
before seven when we count.

An <u>ax</u> is a tool that can be used to chop down
 4
trees or to cut up wood.

© 1999 by Cynthia Conway Waring

Name _____ Date _____

Cloze Sentences . . . 1

X x

COMPLETE IT

fox	Wax
1	2
Tax	Sox
3	4

A <u>fox</u> is an animal that looks like a dog and has
  1
reddish-brown or gray fur, a bushy tail, and a
pointed nose.

<u>Wax</u> is the material that makes up the part of a
 2
candle around the wick.

<u>Tax</u> money is money that people pay to a town,
 3
state, or country where they live, and that is used to
pay for roads, police and fire protection, schools,
and other services that people need.

The Red <u>Sox</u> professional baseball team is from
       4
Boston, Massachusetts.

Name _____ Date _____

X

x

Y y   yarn

TEACHER REFERENCE

Annotated Book List

Abuela's Weave, Omar S. Castañeda, illustrated by Enrique O. Sanchez (New York: Lee & Low Books Inc., 1993). Sanchez's paintings of the Guatemalan countryside where Esperanza and her grandmother, Abuela, weave together, and of the city of Guate where they sell their work at market, richly complement the story of tradition, art, and wisdom passed on in a close family.

Amos's Sweater, Janet Lunn, illustrated by Kim LaFave (Toronto, Ontario: Groundwood/Douglas & McIntyre Ltd., 1988). Old, cold, and tired of giving up all of his wool, Amos the sheep puts up a fight when Aunt Hattie shears his wool. Finally, after several dramatic attempts, he claims the sweater she knitted from it for Uncle Henry and wears it himself.

Angelita's Magic Yarn, Doris Lecher (New York: Farrar, Straus & Giroux, 1992). In this book, inspired by the author's travels in the South American Andes, after Angelita, the finest knitter in her mountain village, suffers a series of misfortunes and loses her donkey, her yarn, and her home, she follows the mountain's advice to gather the sun's rays. From the rays, she knits everything that she needs so that she can return to her work.

Annie and the Old One, Miska Miles, illustrated by Peter Parnall (Boston: Little, Brown and Company, 1971). Though she tries at first to stop time and her mother's weaving to prevent her beloved grandmother's approaching death, Annie is able to understand the legacy she shares with past and future generations as she takes her grandmother's stick and begins to weave.

Boys Don't Knit, Janice Schoop, illustrated by Laura Beingessner (Toronto: Women's Press, 1986). Marvin discovers that boys *do* knit when his friend's grandfather, who learned how to knit in the Navy, mends the sweater his grandmother gave him and teaches him how to knit. Then, as a first project, Marvin knits a scarf for his grandmother. A section with diagrams provides directions for knitting a scarf.

Charlie Needs a Cloak, Tomie dePaola (New York: Simon & Schuster Books for Young Readers, 1973). One of Charlie the shepherd's sheep—a mischievous rascal—tries to thwart him at each step of the process as Charlie makes a new cloak from its wool. In a wordless subplot, an industrious mouse secretly stores some of Charlie's possessions in its stump for the winter. Contains a glossary of key vocabulary.

A Gift for Tía Rosa, Karen T. Taha, illustrated by Dee deRosa (New York: Bantam Doubleday Dell Publishing Group, Inc., 1986). Carmela's beloved neighbor, Tía Rosa, has given her many gifts during their friendship, including teaching her how to knit, and, in gratitude after Tía Rosa's death, Carmela makes her a gift. She finishes knitting the baby blanket Tía Rosa began for her granddaughter.

The Goat in the Rug, as told to Charles L. Blood and Martin Link by Geraldine, illustrated by Nancy Winslow Parker (New York: Macmillan Publishing Company, 1976). Geraldine the goat describes each step in the process of making her mohair into a Navaho rug—clipping, washing and drying, carding, spinning, dyeing, and weaving. Contains a glossary of vocabulary with diagrams.

Kente Colors, Debbi Chocolate, illustrated by John Ward (New York: Walker and Company, 1996). Rhyming lines of text accompany each stunning double-page painting, with Kente cloth borders, that show the significance of the colors and patterns of the traditional cloth in the lives and customs of the people who weave and wear it. An author's note explains the history of the Kente cloth woven by the Ashanti and Ewe people of Ghana and the Ewe people of Togo and describes the process involved in weaving the colorful cloth—including the symbolism of the patterns, designs, and colors used.

The Little Weaver of Thái-Yên Village/Cô Bé Thò-Dêt Làng Thái-Yên, written in Vietnamese by Trân-Khánh-Tuyêt, translated into English by Christopher N.H. Jenkins and Trân-Khánh-Tuyêt, illustrated by Nancy Hom (San Francisco: Children's Book Press, 1987). In this book, with parallel text in English and Vietnamese, while she is in the United States for surgery following a serious injury she receives when her village is bombed, a young girl sends home to Viet-Nam blankets she weaves with an image of Viet-Nam's spirit bird to inspire her people. Footnotes on each page provide pronunciation and meaning of Vietnamese words. An author's note provides background to the story.

The Magic Cap: Inspired by an Old Swedish Tale, Flavia Weedn & Lisa Weedn Gilbert, illustrated by Flavia Weedn (New York: Hyperion Books for

Children, 1995). The cap a mother makes for her son from scraps of yarn and thread is filled with magic that others who covet it cannot steal—the magic of a mother's love that only her son can feel.

The Mitten: A Ukranian Folktale, Jan Brett (New York: The Putnam Publishing Group, 1989). In this retelling, when a boy drops into the snow one of the new mittens his grandmother has knitted for him, a parade of animals squeezes into and then explodes out of the packed mitten when a bear sneezes. The boy brings home to his incredulous grandmother two mittens—one greatly stretched.

The Mitten: An Old Ukrainian Folktale, Alvin Tresselt, adapted from the version by E. Rachev, illustrated by Yaroslava (New York: William Morrow & Co., Inc., 1964). A little boy drops an old mitten in the snow and larger and larger animals climb in to keep warm. When a tiny cricket tries to squeeze in, the mitten splits open and tosses everyone back into the snow.

Mr. Nick's Knitting, Margaret Wild, Dee Huxley (San Diego: Harcourt Brace & Company, 1988). Mr. Nick and Mrs. Jolley knit side by side every day during their train ride to the city until Mrs. Jolley is hospitalized for a long time. Mr. Nick knits her a blanket with squares showing the scenes from the windows of the train so that they can continue to share the same sights as they knit together in their different locations.

Navaho ABC: A Diné Alphabet Book, Luci Tapahonso and Eleanor Schick, illustrated by Eleanor Schick (New York: Simon & Schuster Books for Young Readers, 1995). Colored pencil drawings and accompanying one or two words—some in English and some in the Diné language—show objects and elements of the daily life (including weaving) of the T' á á Diné, which means "The People," also called the Navajo. A glossary and pronunciation guide present words in Diné and English languages.

A New Coat for Anna, Harriet Ziefert, illustrated by Anita Lobel (New York: Alfred A. Knopf, 1986). After World War II, Anna's mother has no money to buy her a new coat, but she trades family treasures with the farmer for wool, with a woman to spin it, and with a tailor to make it. With Anna, she dyes the coat red with berries.

No Roses for HARRY!, Gene Zion, pictures by Margaret Bloy Graham (New York: Harper & Row, Publishers, 1958). Harry, introduced in ***Harry the Dirty Dog*** by the same author, hates the wool sweater with the roses that the children's grandmother knit for him. Finally, after a number of unsuccessful tries, he is able to get rid of the sweater when a bird unravels it and uses the yarn to make a nest.

Pelle's New Suit, Elsa Beskow, translated by Marion Letcher Woodburn (New York: Harper & Row). When he outgrows his old suit, Pelle shears his lamb and barters his labor with family and townspeople, who complete parts of the process to make him a new wool suit.

Socks for Supper, Jack Kent (New York: Parents' Magazine Press, 1978). A poor farmer's wife unravels her husband's sweater to make socks to trade with their neighbors for food. The neighbor's wife uses the yarn from the socks to knit a sweater too big for her husband but a perfect fit for the farmer.

Songs from the Loom: A Navajo Girl Learns to Weave, Monty Roessel (Minneapolis: Lerner Publications, 1995). Colored photographs show the author's family as they pass on to the next generation traditional stories, songs, and steps in the process of weaving. Text, map, photographs, and diagrams present information about contemporary life on the Navajo reservation in Arizona. In a preface, the author writes about the role of weaving, songs, and storytelling to his people, the Diné. Includes a glossary and list of further readings.

The Spinner's Gift, Gail Radley, illustrated by Paige Miglio (New York: North-South Books, 1994). The cloth for the queen's gown, woven from thread spun by a poor spinner, is passed on and reused in a variety of forms until it returns, by chance, to the spinner, who makes it into a quilt for the queen's grandchild.

Tonight Is Carnaval, Arthur Dorros, illustrated by the Club de Madres Virgen del Carmen of Lima, Peru (New York: Penguin Books USA, 1991). In this book, illustrated with hand-quilted *arpilleras* (wall hangings used in storytelling), a boy who plays in the band, along with friends and members of his extended family, at the pre-Lenten Carnaval celebration in the high Andes Mountains, describes his everyday and Carnaval experiences. Contains a section, with colored photographs, that describes the process involved in making *arpilleras,* and a glossary. Available also in a Spanish edition, ***Por fin es Carnaval***.

The Whispering Cloth: A Refugee's Story, Pegi Deitz Shea, illustrated by Anita Riggio, stitched by You Yang (Honesdale, Pennsylvania: Boyds Mills Press, 1995). A young girl in a refugee camp in Thailand learns to embroider as she helps her grandmother make a pa'ndau (story cloth) to sell, but the pa'ndau she makes by herself contains the story of her difficult past and her hopes for the future, and it is not for sale. Contains a glossary.

Literature Extension Activities

1. Throughout the unit, provide balls, skeins, and scraps of yarn for students' experimentation. Also, furnish simple looms for weaving, large

knitting needles with blunt ends, large crochet hooks, and large embroidery needles for students' use in projects inspired by the books in which they are featured.

2. As you read the books in this unit about the process involved in preparing wool for use in yarn, garments, or a rug—including "*Charlie Needs a Cloak*," *The Goat in the Rug, A New Coat for Anna, Pelle's New Suit*, and *Songs from the Loom: A Navajo Girl Learns to Weave*—compile and illustrate with your students a list (or, optionally, a class book) of the steps, in sequence, that the characters in the books follow. As time permits, students experiment in class with each step of the process.

3. After they listen to *A Gift for Tía Rosa*, students, with support, experiment with basic knitting (with needles or finger knitting). Individually, or as a group project (with students taking turns adding stitches or rows of knitting), they make a scarf with fringe like the one Carmela makes for her father, with Tía Rosa's help, in the book. They follow directions you provide for knitting a scarf, or those included in *Boys Don't Knit*. Optionally, they donate their finished scarf or scarves to a survival center, homeless shelter, or other appropriate agency in their community.

4. Students, individually or in groups, present puppet shows or plays of one or both versions of "The Mitten" story suggested for this unit: *The Mitten: An Old Ukrainian Folktale* and *The Mitten: A Ukrainian Folktale*. They make paper animal puppets attached to wooden popsicle or craft sticks or pencils, sock puppets, or finger puppets using fingers cut from gloves; for the mitten they use a small pillowcase or a potholder mitt. Students act out the story in costume, with a sleeping bag or sheet as the mitten.

Items for the Mystery Box

Whenever possible, select items for this unit that are **y**ellow in color.

Inedible Items: yacht, yak, yard (area in front or back of a building), yard (measurement, on tape measure), **yarn**, yawn, year (on a calendar), yellow (on crayon), yellow jacket, yes, yodel (on an audiotape played inside the Mystery Box), yoga, yogurt container, yoke, young (photograph of you when you were young), yo-yo

Edible Items: yams, yeast (in bread/rolls dough), yeast (brewer's, on popcorn), yellow pea soup, yellow split peas, yogurt (variety of flavors), yogurt bread, yolk (hard-boiled egg), Yorkshire pudding

Rhymes, Songs, Fingerplays, and Tongue Twisters

Yarn Theme

*Baa, baa, black sheep: 3, 5, 9, 19, 20, 26, 28, 29, 32, 33, 34, 38, 39, 40, 41, 42, 43, 46, 50, 52, 53, 58, 62, 67, 73, 76

Cross patch, draw the latch: 5, 28, 33, 34, 38, 39, 50, 73

*Some little mice sat in a barn to spin: 5, 9, 28, 33, 34, 46, 51, 62, 73, 76

Letter-Sound y (y)

Dance to your daddy: 29, 32, 33, 34, 62, 73

The Hokey-Pokey/You put your right hand in: 29, 79

If you're happy and you know it: 12, 55, 78

Lazy Mary, will you get up: 26, 53

*Three young rats with black felt hats: 5, 25, 33, 34, 37, 73, 76

Yellow-belly, yellow-belly, come and take a swim: 4

Tongue Twisters: 1, 13, 60, 80

Cloze Sentences

1. **Y**ellow is the color of lemons and of the sun.
   (The color of lemons and of the sun is **y**ellow.)

2. **Y**ears are what **y**ou count to tell **y**our age.
   (What **y**ou count to tell **y**our age is **y**ears.)

3. **Y**arn is thread made from spinning wool that **y**ou can use for knitting and weaving.
   (Thread made from spinning wool that **y**ou can use for knitting and weaving is **y**arn.)

4. A **y**o-**y**o is a round to**y** on a string that **y**ou pull up and down.
   (A round toy on a string that **y**ou pull up and down is a **y**o-**y**o.)

1. **Y**ou are **y**oung, and **y**our grandmother is old.
   (**Y**our grandmother is old, and **y**ou are **y**oung.)

2. The **y**olk is the **y**ellow part of an egg.
   (The **y**ellow part of an egg is the **y**olk.)

3. **Y**es is the opposite of no.
   (No is the opposite of **y**es.)

4. In our **y**ard behind our house, we have a swing set and a sandbox.
   (Behind our house, we have a swing set and a sandbox in our **y**ard.)

Y y

Baa, baa, black sheep

Have you any wool?

Yes, sir, yes, sir,

Three bags full,

One for the master,

One for the dame,

And one for the little boy

Who lives down the lane.

Name _____   Date _____

Y y

Some little mice sat in a barn to spin.

Pussy came by and popped his head in.

"Shall I come in and cut your threads off?"

"Oh, no, kind sir. You would snap our heads off."

Name _____   Date _____

Y y

Three young rats with black felt hats,

Three young ducks with white straw flats,

Three young dogs with curling tails,

Three young cats with demi-veils,

Went out to walk with two young pigs

In satin vests and sorrel wigs.

But suddenly it chanced to rain

And so they all went home again.

Name _____ Date _____

Y y

COMPLETE IT

Yellow   Years
   1   2
Yarn   yo-yo
   3   4

Yellow is the color of lemons and of the
  1
sun.

Years are what you count to tell your age.
  2

Yarn is thread made from spinning wool
  3
that you can use for knitting and weaving.

A yo-yo is a round toy on a string that you
     4
pull up and down.

Name _____   Date _____

Y y

COMPLETE IT

young	yolk
1	2
Yes	yard
3	4

You are <u>young</u>, and your grandmother is
     1
old.

The <u>yolk</u> is the yellow part of an egg.
   2

<u>Yes</u> is the opposite of no.
 3

In our <u>yard</u> behind our house, we have a
     4
swing set and a sandbox.

Name _____ Date _____

Y y

Z z zebra

TEACHER REFERENCE

Annotated Book List

Cincuenta En La Cebra: Contando Con Los Animales/ Fifty on the Zebra: Counting with the Animals, Nancy María Grande Tabor (Watertown, Massachusetts: Charlesbridge Publishing, 1994). Cut-paper illustrations show an ascending number of animals in this counting book, with parallel text in Spanish and English that poses questions that challenge readers to find answers by counting, naming, and problem solving.

Do Pigs Have Stripes?, Melanie Walsh (Boston: Houghton Mifflin Company, 1996). In this interactive book, the first set of double pages poses a facetious question "Does a bird have a big black wet nose?" and contains an illustration of that animal attribute; the second set presents the answer in text, "No, a dog does," and an illustration. This pattern continues for a series of animals (crocodile, elephant, cow, anteater, deer, and giraffe), but, for the final animal, the answer is "Yes!"

Greedy Zebra, Mwenye Hadithi, illustrated by Adrienne Kennaway (Boston: Little, Brown and Company, 1984). In this pourquoi story, Zebra is so greedy for food that he arrives too late at the cave where all of the other plain, dull animals in Africa are sewing on horns and tails and brightly colored fur and skin coats. He finds nothing but a small amount of black material, from which he makes himself a coat that bursts open around his fat stomach, leaving him stripes!

On Beyond Zebra!, Dr. Seuss (New York: Random House, 1955). In characteristic rhyme and illustration, Seuss, in the person of a little boy, explores an imaginative alphabet that begins where the traditional English alphabet ends—complete with invented letters and corresponding fantastic creatures.

The Stories Huey Tells, Ann Cameron, illustrated by Roberta Smith (New York: Alfred A. Knopf, 1995). In this large-print book, it is Huey's turn to tell stories about their family and friend Gloria (introduced in ***The Stories Julian Tells*** by

369

the same author) and to show himself to be more than Julian's little brother, for, in *his* stories, Huey is a problem solver, adventurer, chef, tracker, and dog owner! In "**Tracks,**" when Julian won't share his library book with him, Huey tricks him. He sneaks the book and copies animal tracks in the dirt near their house that are so realistic that Julian and Gloria make a zebra cage and sleep out on the porch to look for it.

Underwear!, Mary Elise Monsell, iluustrated by Lyn Munsinger (Morton Grove, Illionois: Albert Whitman & Company, 1988). Zachary Zebra and Orfo Orangutan are extremely happy to wear different kinds of fancy underwear, but they are even happier when sharing their love of underwear cheers up ill-tempered Bismark Buffalo, who discovers that buffaloes *do* need to have fun, too.

Zebra: Animals in the Wild, Mary Hoffman (Milwaukee: Raintree Publishers, 1985). Full-color one- and two-page photographs and accompanying text, in one or two lines of bold print, provide information about zebras: physical characteristics, young, habits, predators, and food and water.

The Zebra-Riding Cowboy: A Folk Song from the Old West, collected by Angela Shelf Medearis, illustrated by María Brusca (New York: Henry Holt and Company, 1992). In this picture book based on a frontier cowboy song, a well-educated man, thought to be a greenhorn, proves himself a highly capable cowboy when he meets the challenge and rides the highly spirited Zebra Dun, a horse with zebralike stripes. An afterword provides background and describes the goal of the book: to correct the oversight of books and media that fail to include Mexican and African American cowboys in portrayals of the Old West.

Zella Zack and Zodiac, Bill Peet (Boston: Houghton Mifflin Company, 1986). In this story written in rhyme, Zella the zebra rescues and raises an abandoned ostrich chick, whom she names Zack. Later, full-grown Zack, in return, saves Zella's young colt, Zodiac, from the attack of a hungry lion and becomes his vigilant protector.

Literature Extension Activities

1. Create a counting book starring zebras only, patterned after ***Cincuenta En La Cebra: Contando Con Los Animales/ Fifty on the Zebra: Counting with the Animals***. With students—and perhaps with the help of school staff, family, and community members—provide parallel text in English, Spanish, or other languages spoken by members of the community.

2. Students discover that there is no illustration for the question in the title of ***Do Pigs Have Stripes?*** To fill this void, individual students create the

two double pages for this question, patterned after the entries in the book. On the first page, you (or students who are writing) write the question; on the second, students draw the attributes, stripes. On the third and fourth pages, you (or students who are writing) write the answer, "No, a zebra does." and students draw a zebra. Optionally, students create individual or group books featuring the attributes of additional animals, following the same pattern.

3. Students use bits of brightly colored cloth and fake fur, plus colored construction paper, to make coats, horns, and tails for themselves like those worn by the animals in **Greedy Zebra**. They wear their costumes and play rhythm instruments as they parade to other classrooms where you read the book aloud.

4. Students compare and contrast the story of a kindness repaid in **Zella Zack and Zodiac** with a tale with a similar theme, the "Androcles and the Lion" story. In preparation for their discussion, they reread one or both versions suggested for Chapter 12: **Androcles and the Lion** and **Andy and the Lion: A Tale of Kindness Remembered or the Power of Gratitude**.

Items for the Mystery Box

Inedible Items: zebra, zero, zigzag, zinnia, ZIP code, zipper, zoo animals

Edible Items: zest (of citrus fruits—lemons, limes, oranges), ziti, zucchini, zucchini bread

Rhymes, Songs, Fingerplays, and Tongue Twisters

Zebra Theme

Tongue Twisters: 1, 13
*Zippy zebras zipping zippers: (Tongue Twister: Cynthia Conway Waring)

Letter-Sound z (z)

*Bee, bee, with buzzing wing
Boom! Bang! THUNDER!: 75
Bumblebee/Bumblebee was in the barn: 78

Daddy's taking us to the zoo tomorrow: 17
*Fuzzy Wuzzy was a bear: 51
Here is the beehive: 12, 19, 78
Here we go to the zoo in the park: 3
Lazy Mary, will you get up: 26, 53
There's a hole in the bucket, dear Liza, dear Liza: 17, 55, 65
Tongue Twisters: 74, 80

Cloze Sentences

1. <u>Z</u>ero means nothing, and it is the number that comes before one when we count.

   (The number that comes before one when we count and that means nothing is <u>z</u>ero.)

2. You can use a <u>z</u>ipper to zip or to unzip your coat.

   (When you want to zip or to unzip your coat, you can use a <u>z</u>ipper.)

3. A <u>z</u>ebra is an animal that you might see in a zoo, that looks like a horse and has black and white stripes.

   (An animal that you might see in a zoo, that looks like a horse and has black and white stripes, is a <u>z</u>ebra.)

4. At a <u>z</u>oo, you might see lions, zebras, elephants, and monkeys in cages or in fenced-in areas.

   (You might see lions, zebras, elephants, and monkeys in cages or in fenced-in areas at a <u>z</u>oo.)

1. Your <u>Z</u>IP Code is the number for the town you live in, that you write after the address on the envelope of a letter you mail.

   (The number for the town you live in, that you write after the address on the envelope of a letter you mail, is your <u>Z</u>IP Code.)

2. A skier may <u>zigz</u>ag as he or she skis around trees in the way.

   (When a skier skis around trees in the way, he or she may <u>zigz</u>ag.)

3. <u>Z</u>ucchini is a green summer squash that looks like a cucumber.

   (A green summer squash that looks like a cucumber is a <u>z</u>ucchini.)

4. A <u>z</u>innia is a flower that people grow in their gardens, and it can be many different colors.

   (A flower that people grow in their gardens, and that can be many different colors, is a <u>z</u>innia.)

Z z

Zippy zebras zipping zippers

Zippy zebras zipping zippers

Zippy zebras zipping zipper

Name _____   Date _____

Z z

FUZZY WUZZY

Fuzzy Wuzzy was a bear.

Fuzzy Wuzzy had no hair.

So Fuzzy Wuzzy wasn't fuzzy,

Was he?

Name _____   Date _____

Z z

BEE, BEE, WITH BUZZING WING

Bee, bee, with buzzing wing,

I'll steal your honey, if you sting.

Name _____   Date _____

Z z

COMPLETE IT

Zero	zipper
1	2
zebra	zoo
3	4

<u>Zero</u> means nothing, and it is the number
  1
that comes before one when we count.

You can use a <u>zipper</u> to zip or to unzip
        2
your coat.

A <u>zebra</u> is an animal that you might see
    3
in a zoo, that looks like a horse and has black and
white stripes.

At a <u>zoo</u>, you might see lions, zebras,
     4
elephants, and monkeys in cages or in fenced-in
areas.

Name _____ Date _____

Z z

COMPLETE IT

ZIP	zigzag
1	2
Zucchini	zinnia
3	4

Your <u>ZIP</u> Code is the number for the town
     1
you live in, that you write after the address on the
envelope of a letter you mail.

A skier may <u>zigzag</u> as he or she skis
         2
around trees in the way.

<u>Zucchini</u> is a green summer squash that
   3
looks like a cucumber.

A <u>zinnia</u> is a flower that people grow in
    4
their gardens, and it can be many different colors.

Name _____ Date _____

CH ch chair

TEACHER REFERENCE

Annotated Book List

Abuelita's Paradise, Carmen Santiago Nodar, illustrated by Diane Paterson (Morton Grove, Illinois: Albert Whitman & Company, 1992). After her grandmother dies, Marita sits in the special rocking chair her abuelita left her, remembers her grandmother and the stories she told of her life as a little girl in Puerto Rico, and dreams of visiting her abuelita's beloved country, her paradise.

A Chair for My Mother, Vera B. Williams (New York: William Morrow & Company, Inc., 1982). In this first book in a series about Rosa's family, Rosa, Mama, Grandma (and even Aunt Ida and Uncle Sandy) save their coins in a big jar to buy Mama a chair to rest in after work as a waitress in a diner.

Deep in the Forest, Brinton Turkle (New York: E. P. Dutton & Co., Inc., 1976). A bear cub, in this wordless picture-book version of the "Goldilocks and the Three Bears" story, visits the cabin of a family of three people—mother, father, and little girl—samples their porridge, tries out their chairs and breaks the smallest, and romps on their beds.

Goldilocks and the Three Bears, Jan Brett (New York: G. P. Putnam's Sons, 1987). Borders that frame the illustrations provide additional details in Brett's retelling of the traditional tale of Goldilocks's visit and misadventures at the bear family's home, while they take a walk as their porridge cools.

Goldilocks and the Three Bears, James Marshall (New York: Penguin Books USA, Inc., 1988). Mischievous Goldilocks, in Marshall's humorous retelling of the story, defies her parents' warning and wanders through the forest and into the home of the three bears.

Home: A Collaboration of Thirty Distinguished Authors and Illustrators of Children's Books to Aid the Homeless, edited by Michael J. Rosen (New

York: HarperCollins Publishers, 1992). Through prose and poem, thirteen writers and seventeen illustrators describe the places that evoke a feeling of home—from in and under the bed to the front stoop, from an old chair to an apartment lightwell, from a closet to an elevator, from the refrigerator and grandmother's table in the kitchen to the attic, and from the window to the back porch to the garden—to benefit efforts by Share Our Strength (SOS) for the homeless. The poem **"Comfortable Old Chair,"** written by Karla Kuskin and illustrated by Karen Barbour, celebrates an old chair as the best place to read, rest, think, plan, and imagine.

The Lady's Chair and the Ottoman, Noel Tennyson (New York: Lothrop, Lee & Shepard Books, 1987). In a story with a delightful ending, the high-backed wing chair known as a lady's chair and the ottoman that matches it and that longs to be with it are separated until, by a quirk of fate after the death of their owner, they are reunited in a used furniture store.

Mr. Bear's Chair, Thomas Graham (New York: Penguin Books USA Inc., 1987). After Mrs. Bear's chair breaks as she sits down to breakfast, step by step, Mr. Bear makes her a new one just in time for supper. Then, as he sits down to eat, *his* chair breaks, and he sets off again to make a new one.

Music, Music for Everyone, Vera B. Williams (New York: Mulberry Books, 1984). In the final of three books about Rosa's multigenerational family, when Grandma is sick, Rosa thinks of a way to cheer her up and fill the empty coin jar, and the idea is born for Rosa and her friends to create the Oak Street Band.

The Old Red Rocking Chair, Phyllis Root, illustrated by John Sandford (New York: Arcade Publishing, Inc., 1992). Pieces of the old red rocking chair slowly break off as it is repeatedly discarded with the trash and claimed by new owners until, without arms, it becomes a footstool for its first owner.

The Patchwork Quilt, Valerie Flournoy, illustrated by Jerry Pinkney (New York: Dial Books for Young Readers, 1985). Every day Tanya's beloved Grandma sits in her favorite chair sewing pieces of fabric and the stories of the lives of her family into a patchwork quilt, until she becomes ill. Then, Tanya works on it until Grandma recovers and can finish it.

Peter's Chair, Ezra Jack Keats (New York: Harper & Row, 1967). At first, Peter resists giving up his place as only child when the cradle and crib he has outgrown are painted pink for his baby sister, but his desire to paint his small chair for her marks his transition to his new role in the family.

Poppy's Chair, Karen Hesse, illustrated by Kay Life (New York: Macmillan Publishing Company, 1993). During her first summer visit after her grandfather Poppy's death, Leah finds her grandmother napping in Poppy's chair, and they are able, for the first time, to talk together about living after the death of someone they have loved.

Somebody and the Three Blairs, Marilyn Tolhurst, illustrations by Simone Abel (New York: Orchard Books, 1990). While Mr. and Mrs. Blair and Baby Blair take a walk in the park at breakfast time, a bear samples their packaged breakfast cereal, tries out their chairs, plays with toys, gets a drink, and, finally, falls asleep in the crib by the time the Blairs return home and discover the mess he's made, in this modern version of the "Goldilocks and the Three Bears" story.

Something Special for Me, Vera B. Williams (New York: Mulberry Books, 1983). In this second of three books about Rosa's family who live in a city in the United States, when Rosa finds it difficult to select a birthday present worthy of the coins in the savings jar, she chooses an accordion like the one her grandmother played.

The Three Bears, Paul Galdone (New York: Clarion Books, 1972). Print size in the text of Galdone's version of "Goldilocks and the Three Bears" shows the ascending order of the three bears and their possessions in the well-known tale of a girl's adventures as an intruder in the house of a bear family.

Uncle Jed's Barbershop, Margaree King Mitchell, illustrated by James Ransome (New York: Simon & Schuster Books for Young Readers, 1993). It isn't until Sarah Jean is an adult that her Uncle Jed, at age seventy-nine, is able to twirl her around in one of the barber chairs in his own shop—a dream he had pursued despite many challenges, since she was a little girl in the 1920s in the segregated South.

When Goldilocks Went to the House of the Bears, illustrated by Jenny Rendall (New York: Scholastic Inc., 1986). The traditional story of "Goldilocks and the Three Bears" is made highly supportive with a refrain combined with repeated words and a rhyming pattern.

When We Were Very Young, A. A. Milne, decorations by Ernest H. Shepard (New York: Dell Publishing Co., Inc., 1924, 1952). This collection of poems immortalizes the experiences and perspective of Christopher Robin and his friends (introduced in **Winnie-the-Pooh** by the same author). In "**Nursery Chairs,**" the four chairs in the nursery of an imaginative young boy are South America for him as adventurer, a cage when he is a lion, a ship at sea for him as sailor, and a high chair when he pretends he is a baby.

The Wishing Chair, Rick Dupré (Minneapolis, Minnesota: Carolrhoda Books, Inc., 1993). It is not until he is an adult that Eldon realizes that his childhood wishes, made while sitting in his grandmother's wishing chair and listening to her stories, were made possible by the people from his grandmother's stories whose photographs lined her walls: Fannie Lou Hamer, Medgar Evers, Martin Luther King, Jr., Septima Clark, Langston Hughes, and others.

Literature Extension Activities

1. After sharing "**Comfortable Old Chair**" in *Home: A Collaboration of Thirty Distinguished Authors and Illustrators of Children's Books to Aid the Homeless,* have students draw their favorite chair. They illustrate or describe (orally or in dictation/writing) the activities they enjoy in their special chair and the things and places they imagine the chair to be, as the young boy imagines in "**Nursery Chairs**" in *When We Were Very Young*.

2. After they have listened to them in read-aloud and have compared and contrasted them, students dramatize one or more of the six versions of the "Goldilocks and the Three Bears" story suggested for this unit: *Deep in the Forest*, *Goldilocks and the Three Bears* (Brett), *Goldilocks and the Three Bears* (Marshall), *Somebody and the Three Blairs*, *The Three Bears*, and *When Goldilocks Went to the House of the Bears*. They memorize or read lines and present them with voices that differentiate individual characters as you read the story as narrator, act them out in a play with props and masks or costumes, or present them as puppet plays.

3. With students, compare the theme of recycling items in *The Old Red Rocking Chair* and *Peter's Chair* from this unit, and in *The Spinner's Gift* (Chapter 25). Have students share (dictate or write and illustrate) what they do when they outgrow clothes or other items. If several family members, friends, or community agencies or organizations are part of their recycling chain, they provide illustrations and dictate or write labels for a diagram showing the journey of one piece of clothing or hand-me-down item. They compare and contrast their experiences with the experiences of the characters in the books.

4. After they hear *Wishing Chair* read aloud, students take turns sitting in a chair designated as the classroom wishing chair (preferably a large, old, and comfortable chair similar to Eldon's grandmother's). They draw and dictate or write labels or captions for a wish that has come true for them and the person(s) who helped make it possible. Students display their pictures on the wall above the chair, just as Eldon's grandmother hung photographs of the people in her inspiring stories.

5. Students play games of noncompetitive Musical Chairs. In this variation, the number of chairs is the same as the number of players. The goal of the game is for each player to sit in a chair as quickly as possible when

the music stops. No player is ever eliminated. The fun is in the scurrying to a chair!

Items for the Mystery Box

Inedible Items: chain, **chair** (doll-size), chalk, chalkboard, Chap Stick®, charge card, charm (bracelet), check (bank, voided), checkers, chest (treasure), chick, chicken, child, chimney, chimpanzee, chimes (a small set, played inside Mystery Box as a clue), chin, chips bag (corn or potato), chipmunk, chopsticks, church

Edible Items: Cheerios® cereal, chapati, chard, cheddar cheese, cheese (variety), cheesecake, cherries, chestnuts, chestnuts (water), chicken, chicken soup (variety), chickpeas (garbanzo beans), chicory, chiles (mild), chili, chips (variety, including blue corn, corn, potato, tortilla), chives, chocolate (candy, chips, pudding, sauce), chopped liver, chop suey, chowder (corn or fish), bok choy, chutney, cottage cheese

Rhymes, Songs, Fingerplays, and Tongue Twisters

Chair Theme

Anna Elise, she jumped with surprise: 5

Chairs to mend, old chairs to mend: 77

If I'd as much money as I could spend: 5, 28, 33, 50

Kittens/Five little kittens sleeping on a chair: 19

*Pussy cat, pussy cat, where have you been?: 5, 9, 25, 26, 28, 33, 34, 37, 38, 39, 40, 42, 46, 50, 52, 58, 62, 73, 76

Letter-Sound ch (ch)

The ants go marching: 55

Changing bedrooms number 1, 4

*Chook, chook, chook, chook, chook: 5, 12, 34, 73

*How much wood would a woodchuck chuck: 5, 34, 74

Sweep, sweep chimney sweep: 5

Ten Little Witches/One little, two little, three little witches: 78

Tongue Twisters: 1, 7, 13, 60, 74, 80

Cloze Sentences

1. Coming out of a **ch**imney on top of a house may be smoke from a stove, fireplace, or furnace inside.

   (You may see smoke from a stove, fireplace, or furnace inside a house coming out of a **ch**imney on top of the house.)

2. **Ch**ests are large boxes with lids, where pirates sometimes kept their treasures.

   (The large boxes with lids, where pirates sometimes kept their treasures, are **ch**ests.)

3. **Ch**ocolate is usually brown, and it is the flavor of some fudge, candy bars, hot cocoa, and **ch**ips in cookies.

   (The flavor of some fudge, candy bars, hot cocoa, and **ch**ips in cookies, that is brown in color, is **ch**ocolate.)

4. A **ch**erry is a small, round fruit that grows with a stone in the middle, and that is sometimes put on the top of an ice cream sundae.

   (A small, round fruit that grows with a stone in the middle, and that is sometimes put on the top of an ice cream sundae, is a **ch**erry.)

1. A **ch**air is a piece of furniture that makes a good seat when you sit at a desk or a table.

   (A piece of furniture that makes a good seat when you sit at a desk or a table is a **ch**air.)

2. **Ch**ips that I buy in a bag at the store and eat as a snack are usually made out of potatoes or corn.

   (A snack that I buy in a bag at the store, that is usually made out of potatoes or corn, is **ch**ips.)

3. A **ch**ild is a young person, and he or she is not an adult.

   (A person who is young and is not an adult is a **ch**ild.)

4. **Ch**opsticks are small sticks that can be used to eat **Ch**inese food at home or at a restaurant.

   (Small sticks that can be used to eat **Ch**inese food at home or at a restaurant are **ch**opsticks.)

CH ch

"Pussy cat, pussy cat, where have you been?"

"I've been to London to look at the queen."

"Pussy cat, pussy cat, what did you see there?"

"I frightened a little mouse under the chair."

Name _____   Date _____

CH ch

How much wood would a woodchuck chuck,

If a woodchuck could chuck wood?

It would chuck as much wood

As a woodchuck could chuck

If a woodchuck could chuck wood.

Name _____   Date _____

CH ch

Chook, chook, chook, chook, chook,

Good morning, Mrs. Hen.

How many chickens have you got?

Madam, I've got ten.

Four of them are yellow,

And four of them are brown,

And two of them are speckled red,

The nicest in the town.

Name _____   Date _____

CH ch

COMPLETE IT

chimney
1

Chests
2

Chocolate
3

cherry
4

Coming out of a <u>chimney</u> on top of a
                        1
house may be smoke from a stove, fireplace, or furnace inside.

<u>Chests</u> are large boxes with lids, where
   2
pirates sometimes kept their treasures.

<u>Chocolate</u> is usually brown, and it is the
      3
flavor of some fudge, candy bars, hot cocoa, and chips in cookies.

A <u>cherry</u> is a small, round fruit that grows
    4
with a stone in the middle, and that is sometimes put on the top of an ice cream sundae.

Name _____   Date _____

CH ch

COMPLETE IT

chair	Chips
1	2
child	Chopsticks
3	4

A <u>chair</u> is a piece of furniture that makes
   1
a good seat when you sit at a desk or a table.

<u>Chips</u> that I buy in a bag at the store and
  2
eat as a snack are usually made out of potatoes
or corn.

A <u>child</u> is a young person, and he or she
    3
is not an adult.

<u>Chopsticks</u> are small sticks that can be
    4
used to eat Chinese food at home or at a
restaurant.

Name _____   Date _____

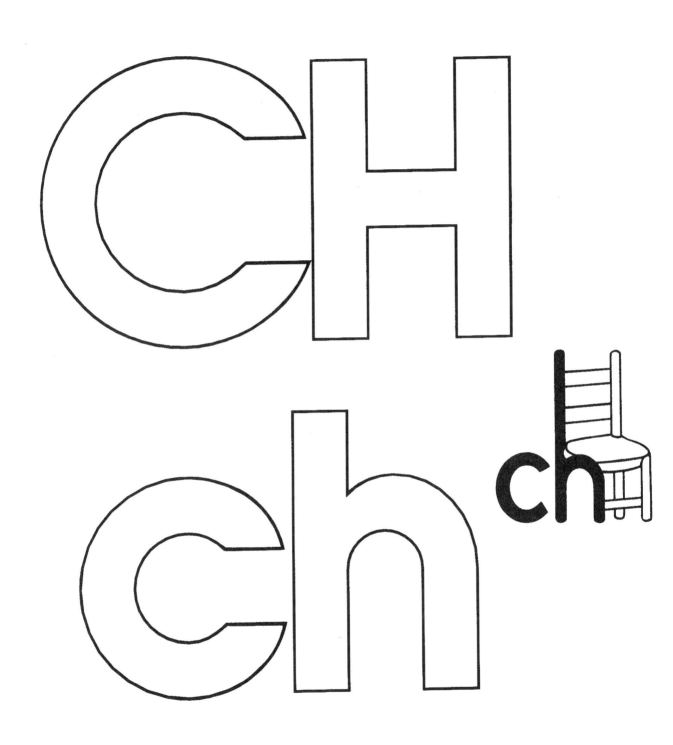

SH sh shark

TEACHER REFERENCE

Annotated Book List

Amazing Fish: Eyewitness Juniors, Mary Ling, photographed by Jerry Young (New York: Alfred A. Knopf, 1991). Collections of colored photographs and drawings amplify text that provides information about the physical characteristics of fish (including color, shape, and body parts) and their habits (in particular feeding and hunting), with special focus sections on sharks, rays, eels, sea horses, and salmon.

The Best Way to See a Shark: Rookie Read-About Science, Allan Fowler (Chicago: Childrens Press, 1995). This informational book with photographs makes the distinction between sharks that are dangerous and those that do not present threats to humans, presents information about the body of the shark, and shows the best way for nonscientists to observe sharks—in an aquarium or marine park. Contains an index and illustrated list of important words.

Dolphins at Daybreak, Mary Pope Osborne, illustrated by Sal Murdocca (New York: Random House, 1997). In order to become Master Librarians to help Morgan LeFay, Annie and Jack pilot a disabled minisubmarine, encounter an octopus and a hammerhead shark, are rescued by a pair of dolphins, and solve the first of four riddles in the ninth book in the "Magic Tree House" series.

Fascinating Facts About Sharks, Jane Walker, illustrated by Ian Thompson, cartoons by Tony Kenyon (Brookfield, Connecticut: The Millbrook Press, 1993). Colored drawings, cartoons, and maps amplify text that provides information about a variety of sharks. Includes a shark quiz, "More Fascinating Facts" section, glossary, and index.

The Great White Man-Eating Shark—A Cautionary Tale, Margaret Mahy, illustrated by Jonathan Allen (New York: Dial Books for Young Readers, 1990). Wearing a dorsal fin, Norvin pretends to be a shark to scare away the other swimmers so that he can have the cove to himself, but he is soon frightened out of the water himself—by a female shark with marriage intentions!

The Greedy Gray Octopus, based on a story by Christel Buckley and her class, illustrations by David Pearson (Crystal Lake, Illinois: Rigby, 1988). In this book with a repetitive, predictable pattern, a hungry octopus invites a series of sea creatures to play with him, but each anticipates his intentions and is wise enough to refuse and flee. Finally, a shark accepts the octopus's invitation and eats *him*.

Hungry, Hungry Sharks, Joanna Cole, illustrated by Patricia Wynne (New York: Random House, 1986). Brief passages of large-print, easy-to-read text, illustrated with colored drawings, provide information about sharks: kinds, sizes, physical characteristics, habitat, habits, food, young, and defense.

A Look Inside Sharks and Rays: A Remarkable First Visual Reference, Keith Banister, Ph.D., illustrated by Steve Johnson and Alex Pang (Westport, Connecticut: Joshua Morris Publishing, Inc./A Reader's Digest Young Families Book, 1995). Acetate windows sandwiched between cut-out sections in heavy board pages show both sides of cross-sections of sharks, plus ray and skate relatives, in color. Captioned illustrations, diagrams, and maps complement the informative text. Contains a table of contents.

Ottie and the Star, Laura Jean Allen (New York: Harper & Row, Publishers, 1979). In this easy-to-read book of fiction, Ottie, a young otter, attempts to catch a star by diving into the sea after its reflection and, with the help of a friendly dolphin, escapes a shark before he finds a starfish. Back home, his mother explains the difference between a star and a starfish, and Ottie returns it to its ocean home.

Punia and the King of Sharks: A Hawaiian Folktale, adapted by Lee Wardlaw, illustrated by Felipe Davalos (New York: Dial Books for Young Readers, 1997). Young Punia devises a series of clever plans to trick the sharks and their king so that he can take home to his poor mother the delicious lobsters they guard in their cave. Includes a glossary and pronunciation guide to Hawaiian terms.

Questions and Answers About Sharks, Ann McGovern, illustrated by Pam Johnson (New York: Scholastic Inc., 1976, 1995). The table of contents lists the twenty-six often-asked questions about sharks that are answered in the clearly written, easy-to-read text, illustrated with drawings.

Rainbow Fish to the Rescue!, Marcus Pfister, translated by J. Alison James (New York: North-South Books Inc., 1995). In this sequel to ***The Rainbow Fish,*** by the same author and with similar illustrations, Rainbow Fish and his friends save the life of a little striped fish from the attack of a shark and welcome him into their play, after initially excluding him.

A Sea Full of Sharks, Betsy Maestro, illustrated by Giulio Maestro (New York: Scholastic Inc., 1990). This informative book—with brief text and colored drawings, diagrams, and maps—emphasizes the importance of the frequently misunderstood shark in the chain of living things, shows the great diversity among sharks, and presents facts about different kinds of sharks: physical characteristics, habits, habitat, food, senses, and young. Includes a section with additional facts.

Shark: Eyewitness Books, Miranda MacQuitty, special photography by Frank Greenaway and Dave King (New York: Alfred A. Knopf, 1992). Collections of captioned, colored photographs of sharks (and ray and skate relatives), related objects, and maps provide information about their traits and characteristics, life cycle, and habitat. Contains an index.

Sharks, Ann McGovern, pictures by Murray Tinkleman (New York: Scholastic Inc., 1976). This question-and-answer book, with black-and-white illustrations, provides information about physical characteristics, young, habits, habitat, food, and enemies of a variety of sharks. Includes a table of contents and index.

Sharks, Niki Walker and Bobbie Kalman (New York: Crabtree Publishing, 1997). Photographs and diagrams accompany text in one- to two-page sections about a shark's body, habitat, diet and feeding habits, young, relatives, and predators, and about a number of specific sharks. Includes a table of contents, glossary, index, and guide to photographs.

Sharks!, Lynn Wilson, illustrated by Courtney (New York: Grosset & Dunlap, Inc., 1992). Physical characteristics, habits, young, and food of a variety of sharks are presented in informative text and colored drawings.

Sharks: Explorer Books, Della Rowland (New York: The Trumpet Club, 1990). A single diagram and a collection of photographs in the book's center, all in black and white, are the only illustrations for this fifty-six page informative book, organized in chapters, that covers in detail a range of aspects of the life of the shark. Contains a list of aquariums in the United States.

Sharks: A Portrait of the Animal World, Andrew Cleave (New York: Smithmark Publishers Inc., 1994). Ninety-four spectacular photographs with captions and informative text present a large number of the more than 350 known species of sharks, with a discussion of close shark relatives, the skates and rays. The 9 1/2" x 12" book presents a balanced view of the shark as predator, with information about its life cycle, characteristics, and hunting behavior. Contains an index.

The Truth About Sharks: Young Readers' Series, Carol A. Amato, illustrated by David Wenzel (Hauppauge, New York: Barron's Educational Series, Inc., 1995). Readers accompany a teacher and his students as they visit an aquarium to learn about sharks' characteristics and habits, young, and predators through the students' and teacher's experiences and dialogue. Includes a table of contents, glossary and pronunciation guide for key vocabulary terms, a note to parents and educators, and guidelines for the series.

The Ultimate Shark & Whale Sticker Book, Helena Spiteri, illustrations by Martin Camm and Kenneth Lilly, photographs by Frank Greenaway and Dave King (New York: Dorling Kindersley Publishing, Inc., 1994). To complete the book, readers use more than sixty reusable labeled stickers made from colored photographs to match outlines of sharks and other sea creatures—captioned with additional informative text and organized by topic.

What If the Shark Wears Tennis Shoes?, Winifred Morris, illustrated by Betsy Lewin (New York: Simon & Schuster Children's Publishing Division, 1990). Young Stephen is in bed, but he can't sleep because he's worried that a shark might come and eat him. He counters every one of his mother's assurances with a creative scenario about the shark, but when he imagines himself outwitting the shark, he finally vanquishes his fears.

Literature Extension Activities

1. Inspired by the illustrations in ***Ottie and the Star***, students experiment with ink and watercolor paints to create underwater scenes featuring sharks that illustrate information they know or learn about these fascinating sea animals.

2. At the beginning of their study of sharks, list with students questions they have about sharks in one column. As they discover the answers to their questions, record them in a second column, opposite the corresponding question. At the end of the unit, you, another adult, or students record the questions and answers in book form, with one question and answer on each page. Students then make drawings to illustrate a "Questions and Answers About Sharks" book of their own, similar to ***Questions and Answers About Sharks,*** as an individual, partner, or group project.

3. For classroom display, after reading ***Shark*** (Eyewitness Books), create with students collections of captioned colored photographs, related objects, and maps to provide information about their *own* traits and characteristics, life cycle, and habitat—similar to those in the book.

4. After you share ***What If the Shark Wears Tennis Shoes?*** in read-aloud, talk about students' own imaginative scenerios starring the shark, to counter each one of Stephen's mother's assurances that a shark will not eat him in bed. Then, they illustrate their scenes for a class wall display or book.

Items for the Mystery Box

Inedible Items: shaker (salt), shampoo, shamrock, **shark**, shaver, shawl, sheep, sheet (baby or doll size), shell (egg), shell (sea), shield, ship, shirt, shoe, shoelace, shop (store), shot (from a play doctor's kit), shoulder, shovel, Shredded Wheat™ cereal box

Edible Items: shake (milk), shells (pasta, stuffed), shepherd's pie, sherbet, shrimp, shortbread, shortcake (strawberry), shoyu (soy sauce), Shredded Wheat™ cereal

Rhymes, Songs, Fingerplays, and Tongue Twisters

Shark Theme

*Six sharp shiny sharks seeing ships sinking: (Tongue Twister: Cynthia Conway Waring)
Tongue Twisters: 7, 60, 63, 80

Letter-Sound sh (sh)

I know an old lady who swallowed a fly: 23, 24, 51, 66
I'm a little teapot: 3, 12, 29, 31, 48, 53, 78
Little Betty Blue lost her holiday shoe: 5, 28, 33, 46, 50, 73

She'll be comin' 'round the mountain: 17, 47, 55, 56, 57, 77, 78
*She sells sea shells on the seashore: 5, 25, 46, 74
Star light, star bright: 3, 34, 37, 51, 73, 76
*There was an old woman who lived in a shoe: 5, 20, 28, 32, 33, 34, 37, 38, 39, 40, 46, 49, 50, 53, 58, 73, 76
Tongue Twisters: 7, 13, 60, 74, 80
Wynken, Blyken, and Nod: 3

Cloze Sentences

1. A **sh**ark is a fish that often has a large fin that sticks out above the water when it swims.

   (A fish that often has a large fin that sticks out above the water when it swims is a **sh**ark.)

2. I put my **sh**oes on my feet after I put on my socks.

   (After I put my socks on my feet, I put on my **sh**oes.)

3. **Sh**eep are animals that have thick, white wool, and they make a "baa-ing" sound.

   (Animals that have thick, white wool and that make a "baa-ing" sound are **sh**eep.)

4. **Sh**ampoo is a liquid soap that is used to wash people's hair and animals' fur.

   (A liquid soap that is used to wash people's hair and animals' fur is **sh**ampoo.)

1. A **sh**eet is a piece of cloth used to sleep on or under, and it is usually placed under a blanket or other covering on a bed.

   (A piece of cloth used to sleep on or under, and usually placed under a blanket or other covering on a bed, is a **sh**eet.)

2. A **sh**ip is a large boat with masts and sails for sailing on the sea.

   (A large boat with masts and sails for sailing on the sea is a **sh**ip.)

3. A **sh**irt is a piece of clothing made of cloth that I wear on the upper part of my body.

   (A piece of clothing made of cloth, that I wear on the upper part of my body, is a **sh**irt.)

4. The **sh**ells that I find on the beach are the hard outer coverings of sea animals that lived in them at one time.

   (The hard outer coverings of sea animals that once lived in them, and that I find on the beach, are **sh**ells.)

SH sh

Six sharp shiny sharks seeing ships sinking

Six sharp shiny sharks seeing ships sinking

Six sharp shiny sharks seeing ships sinking

Name _____   Date _____

SH sh

She sells sea shells on the seashore.

The shells she sells are sea shells, I'm sure.

So if she sells sea shells on the seashore,

It's seashore shells she sells for sure.

Name _____   Date _____

SH sh

There was an old woman who lived in a shoe.

She had so many children

she didn't know what to do.

Name _____   Date _____

SH sh

COMPLETE IT

shark	shoes
1	2
Sheep	Shampoo
3	4

A <u>shark</u> is a fish that often has a large fin
    1
that sticks out above the water when it swims.

I put my <u>shoes</u> on my feet after I put on
      2
my socks.

<u>Sheep</u> are animals that have thick, white
  3
wool, and they make a "baa-ing" sound.

<u>Shampoo</u> is a liquid soap that is used to
   4
wash people's hair and animals' fur.

Name _____ Date _____

SH sh

COMPLETE IT

sheet	ship
1	2
shirt	shells
3	4

A <u>sheet</u> is a piece of cloth used to sleep
    1
on or under, and it is usually placed under a
blanket or other covering on a bed.

A <u>ship</u> is a large boat with masts and sails
    2
for sailing on the sea.

A <u>shirt</u> is a piece of clothing made of
    3
cloth that I wear on the upper part of my body.

The <u>shells</u> that I find on the beach are the
     4
hard outer coverings of sea animals that lived in
them at one time.

Name _____ Date _____

SH

Sh

TH th thumb

TEACHER REFERENCE

Annotated Book List

The Adventures of Thumbelina Starring* You: *Make Believe It's You #3, Margaret and Carson Davidson, illustrated by Yuri Salzman (New York: Scholastic Inc., 1987). This "readers choose their own adventures" book, based on the original Thumbelina story by Hans Christian Andersen, contains characters and plot choices of the traditional tale, plus new, original ones. Readers are given an opportunity to read the basic plot of the story as it appears in Andersen's original version if they follow the choices to read the corresponding pages listed in an end note.

Dick Bruna's Tom Thumb, Dick Bruna (Chicago: Follett Publishing Company, 1966). The youngest of a poor woodcutter's seven children is called Tom Thumb because he is so small, but he shows that it is his cleverness, not his size, that matters when he saves himself and his siblings from a giant, when they are abandoned in the woods, and his family from starvation.

Ed Emberley's Great Thumbprint Drawing Book, Ed Emberley (Boston: Little, Brown and Company, 1977). In this book in a series by the author, readers follow drawings that show progressive steps for adding shapes, scribbles, and filler lines to thumbprints to make a variety of people, animals, and seasonal and holiday objects. Includes directions for making thumbprints or carrot and potato prints using a variety of media.

Hand, Hand, Fingers, Thumb, Al Perkins, illustrated by Eric Gurney (New York: Random House, Inc., 1969). In this highly rhythmic rhyming book, more and more monkeys join a monkey as he drums on his drum until there are millions of monkeys, fingers, and thumbs drumming.

Right Thumb, Left Thumb, Osmond Molarsky, illustrated by John E. Johnson (Reading, Massachusetts: Addison-Wesley, 1969). Victor's clever mother ties a string to his right thumb to remind him to make several right turns on the way to the store, and the alert storekeeper reties it onto Victor's left thumb for the return trip home.

Thumbelina, Hans Christian Andersen, retold by Amy Ehrlich, pictures by Susan Jeffers (New York: Penguin Books USA Inc., 1979). Jeffer's pastel one- and two-page drawings create the fantasy world in this highly effective retelling of the traditional tale of Thumbelina, who grows from a magic seed into a young woman the size of a thumb and, with the help of animal friends, survives a number of adventures before she meets a thumb-sized king and becomes his queen.

Thumbelina, Hans Christian Andersen, translated by Erik Haugaard, illustrated by Arlene Graston (New York: Bantam Doubleday Dell Publishing Group, 1974, 1996). Muted tones in new illustrations for Haugaard's unabridged translation of Andersen's tale show Thumbelina as she grows from a magic seed to experience a number of adventures, before she finds her place in the world with a tiny king and his people who are just her size—the size of a thumb.

Thumbelina: Ladybird Favorite Tales, Hans Christian Andersen, retold by Sarah Ketchersid, illustrated by Petula Stone (New York: Penguin Books USA Inc., 1996). This brief retelling, designed for developing readers, of the traditional tale of thumb-sized Thumbelina, who becomes princess in the land of the Flower People, contains several lines of illustrated text, with short sentences on each page.

Tom Thumb, retold and illustrated by Richard Jesse Watson (San Diego: Harcourt Brace & Company, 1989). Rewarded for their kindness to Merlin the wizard, a poor farmer and his wife are given a clever and brave son no bigger than a thumb. After a series of misadventures due to his small size, he brings honor and riches to his parents when he is made Sir Thomas Thumb, the smallest knight of the Round Table, in this retelling with one- and two-page illustrations in egg tempera and watercolor.

Literature Extension Activities

1. Inspired by the tales of characters no bigger than a thumb suggested for this unit—*The Adventures of Thumbelina Starring* **You,** *Dick Bruna's Tom Thumb, Thumbelina* (Ehrlich), *Thumbelina* (Haugaard), *Thumbelina: Ladybird Favorite Tales*, and *Tom Thumb*—use art materials with students to make thumb-sized folk of

their own invention or in the likeness of the characters in the books you have shared.

2. With students, refer to the drawings and follow the steps provided in ***Ed Emberley's Great Thumbprint Drawing Book*** to make people, animals, and seasonal and holiday objects by adding shapes, scribbles, and filler lines to thumbprints, and students can also invent their own thumbprint creations. They follow the directions to make thumbprints with ink stamp pads, water color or poster paint on a brush, or frosting color on a sponge or cloth—or they substitute carrot or potato prints or round painted shapes.

3. Students clap their hands, stamp their feet, or use rhythm instruments to accompany you as you reread the highly engaging ***Hand, Hand, Fingers, Thumb,*** with its irresistible beat.

4. Plan several routes around the classroom or the school that require a series of right turns to arrive at the desired destination, and a series of left turns to retrace the route during the return trip, similar to the route Victor followed to and from the store in ***Right Thumb, Left Thumb***. Students, with a string tied to the appropriate thumb, take turns following your oral directions to retrieve an object, note, or other item located at the indicated destination.

5. Frequently during the unit, enjoy with students the fingerplay "Where is Thumbkin?" with corresponding finger motions featured in four books listed in Appendix B of this book: ***The Eentsy, Weentsy Spider: Fingerplays and Action Rhymes*** (no.12), ***Finger Rhymes*** (no.14), ***The Lap-Time Song and Play Book*** (no. 31), and ***Wee Sing: Children's Songs and Fingerplays*** (no. 78).

6. With students, bake and eat cookies with thumbprints pressed into the dough and filled with jam, following "Thumbprint Clues" in an illustrated cookbook featuring reduced-sugar recipes and designed with easy-to-follow directions for children, ***My First Baking Book*** by Rena Coyle, illustrated by Tedd Arnold (New York: Workman Publishing Company, Inc., 1988.

Items for the Mystery Box

Inedible Items: Thanksgiving (photograph, e.g., on a calendar), thank-you note, thermometer, thimble, third (arrow points to third in line in photograph or picture), thistle, thorn, thread, three, throat, throne, **thumb**

Edible Items: Thousand Island™ dressing (with vegetables), three-bean salad

Rhymes, Songs, Fingerplays, and Tongue Twisters

Thumb Theme

Dance, Thumbkin, dance: 28, 29, 33, 50

*I had a little husband, No bigger than my thumb: 5, 28, 33, 34, 50

*Little Jack Horner: 3, 5, 26, 28, 33, 34, 37, 38, 39, 40, 41, 43, 46, 50, 58, 62, 73, 76

Sleepy Fingers/My fingers are so sleepy: 14

This old man: 12, 26, 30, 51, 55, 68, 69

Tongue Twisters: 60, 80

Where is Thumbkin?: 12, 14, 31, 78

Letter-Sound th (th)

The farmer in the dell: 26, 47, 79

Here we go round the mulberry bush: 5, 25, 26, 29, 33, 34, 38, 41, 47, 50, 62, 67, 73, 76, 78

*Little Bo Peep: 5, 20, 26, 28, 33, 34, 38, 39, 41, 43, 46, 50, 53, 58, 62, 67, 73, 76

Thatcher of Thatchwood: 28, 33

Theophilus Thistle, the successful thistle sifter: 33

This little piggy went to market: 3, 5, 14, 20, 25, 26, 28, 29, 31, 32, 33, 34, 37, 38, 39, 42, 43, 46, 50, 52, 73, 76

This is the house that Jack built: 5, 28, 32, 33, 34, 46, 50, 76

Three blind mice: 5, 26, 29, 32, 34, 37, 38, 39, 40, 41, 46, 49, 50, 52, 62, 67, 73, 76, 77

Three jovial huntsmen: 70, 73

Three little kittens: 5, 9, 26, 27, 28, 33, 34, 37, 51, 62, 71, 72, 73, 76

Tongue Twisters: 7, 60, 74, 80

Cloze Sentences

1. I look at a **th**ermometer to find out **the** temperature.

   (To find out **the** temperature, I look at a **th**ermometer.)

2. A **th**rone is **the** special seat where kings and queens sit.

   (**Th**e special seat where kings and queens sit is a **th**rone.)

3. **Th**read and a needle are what I need when I sew.

   (When I sew, I need a needle and **th**read.)

4. **Th**ree is **the** number **th**at comes after two and before four when we count.

   (When we count, **the** number **th**at comes after two and before four is **th**ree.)

1. I have a **th**umb and four fingers on each of my hands.

   (On each of my hands, I have four fingers and a **th**umb.)

2. A **th**ank-you note is something I write to **th**ank someone for a gift.

   (Something I write to **th**ank someone for a gift is a **th**ank-you note.)

3. If I am <u>th</u>ird in line, **th**en I am after **th**e person who is second in line.
   (If I am after **th**e person who is second in line, **th**en I am <u>th</u>ird in line.)
4. When I have a sore <u>thr</u>oat, it hurts when I swallow.
   (It hurts when I swallow when I have a sore <u>thr</u>oat.

TH th

I had a little husband,

No bigger than my thumb;

I put him in a pint pot,

And there I bid him drum.

Name _____   Date _____

TH th

Little Jack Horner

Sat in a corner

Eating a Christmas pie;

He put in his thumb,

And pulled out a plum,

And said: "Oh, what a good boy am I!"

Name _____   Date _____

TH th

Little Bo-peep has lost her sheep,

And can't tell where to find them.

Leave them alone, and they'll come home

And bring their tails behind them.

Name _____   Date _____

TH th

th

thermometer	throne
1	2
Thread	Three
3	4

I look at a <u>thermometer</u> to find out the
        1
temperature.

A <u>throne</u> is the special seat where kings
    2
and queens sit.

<u>Thread</u> and a needle are what I need
     3
when I sew.

<u>Three</u> is the number that comes after two
    4
and before four when we count.

Name _____   Date _____

TH th

COMPLETE IT

thumb   thank
1   2
third   throat
3   4

I have a <u>thumb</u> and four fingers on each
           1
of my hands.

A <u>thank</u>-you note is something I write to
     2
thank someone for a gift.

If I am <u>third</u> in line, then I am after the
         3
person who is second in line.

When I have a sore <u>throat</u>, it hurts when I
                4
swallow.

© 1999 by Cynthia Conway Waring

Name _____   Date _____

Cloze Sentences . . . 2

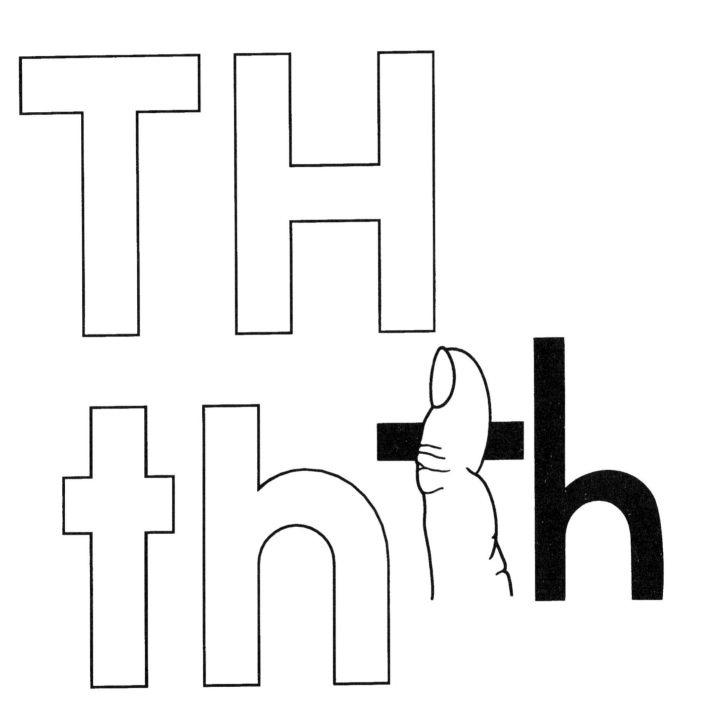

Appendix A

REPRODUCIBLE MASTERS FOR LETTER-SOUND-KEY WORD/PICTURE CARDS AND CARD MASK

Letter-Sound-Key Word/Picture Cards are approximately 3" x 5" in size. They are made by phototcopying the reproducible masters in this Appendix onto white card stock. Make a set of cards for each group of students or for individual students in tutorial. You may choose to color some of the key word/pictures, including *p* (pumpkin), *v* (valentine), *w* (water), and *y* (yarn).

Each card is divided vertically by lines into three segments or frames, with the following information represented:

1. On the left is the letter or letters that represent a phoneme/sound.

2. In the middle is the sound represented by the letter(s), which is enclosed in parentheses.

3. On the right is a key word and picture. For most sounds, the letters are embedded in the picture.

Use a card as a mask to cover the last two frames (middle and right) of each card during the one-frame-exposed activity described in the directions for the Review Letter-Sound-Key Word/Picture Cards activity on page 6. A template for making a mask from colored card stock or oak tag is included with the reproducible masters in this Appendix.

Reproducible Masters

for
Letter-Sound-Key
Word/Picture Cards
and
Card Mask

Template
for
Mask

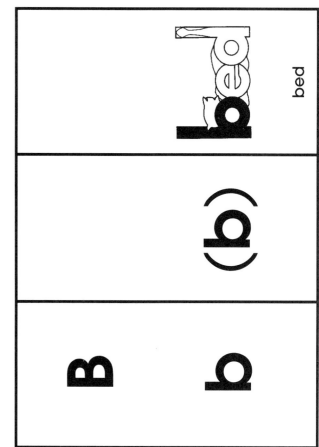

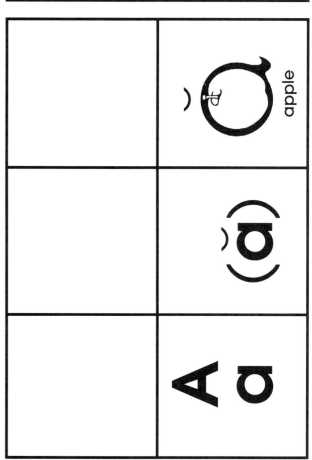

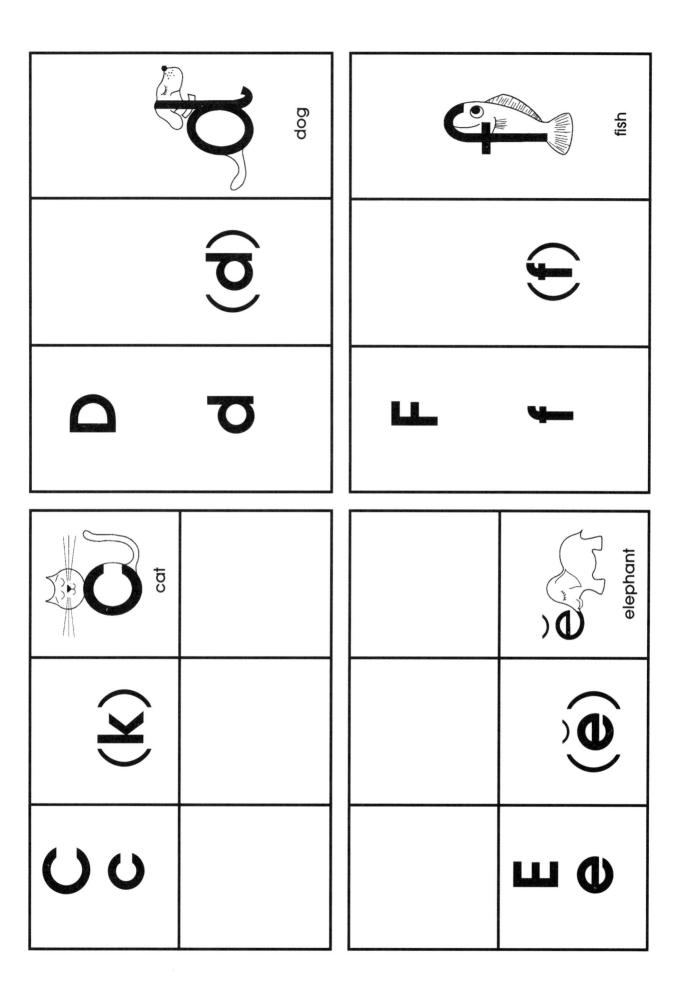

D d (d) dog

F f (f) fish

C c (k) cat

E e (e) elephant

hat

(h)

H h

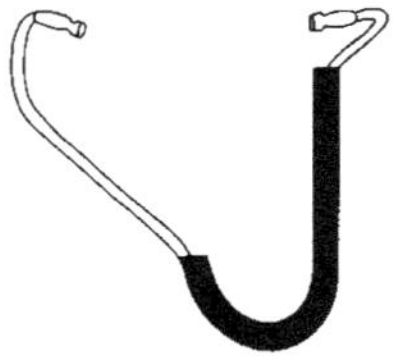

jump rope

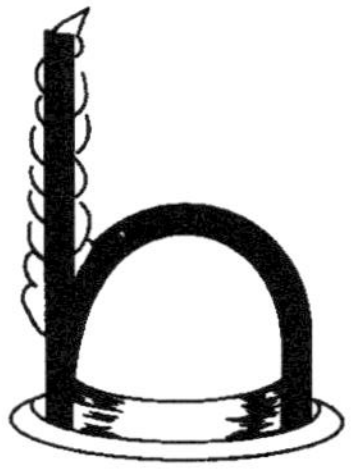

(j)

J j

goat

(g)

G g

igloo

(i)

I i

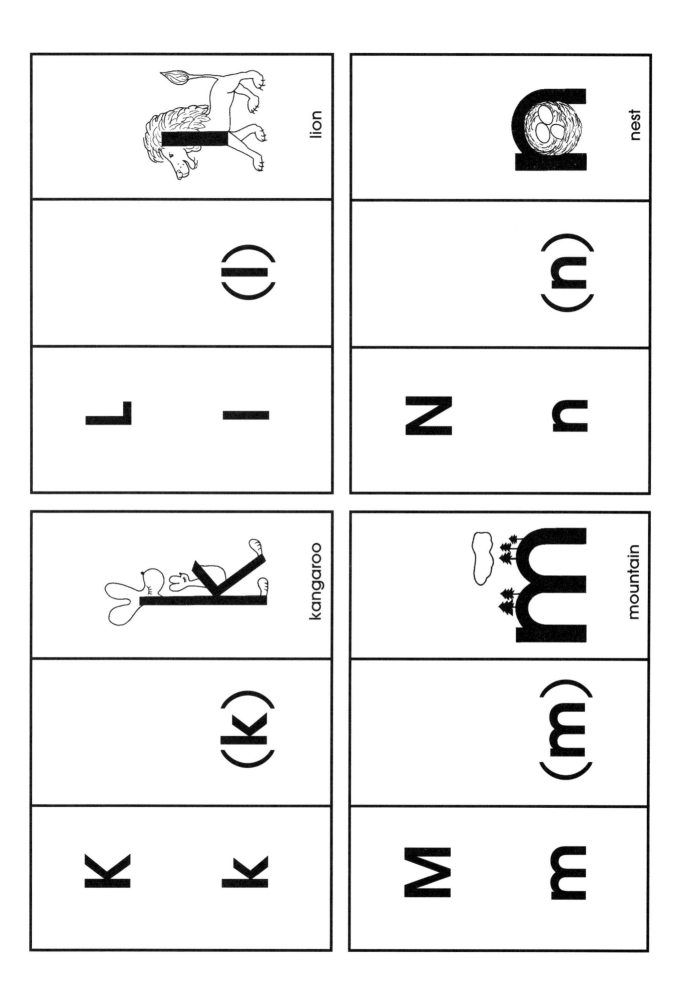

L l lion

N n nest

K k kangaroo

M m mountain

P   (p)   pumpkin

R   (r)   rabbit

O o   (o)   octopus

Qu   (kw)   quilt
qu

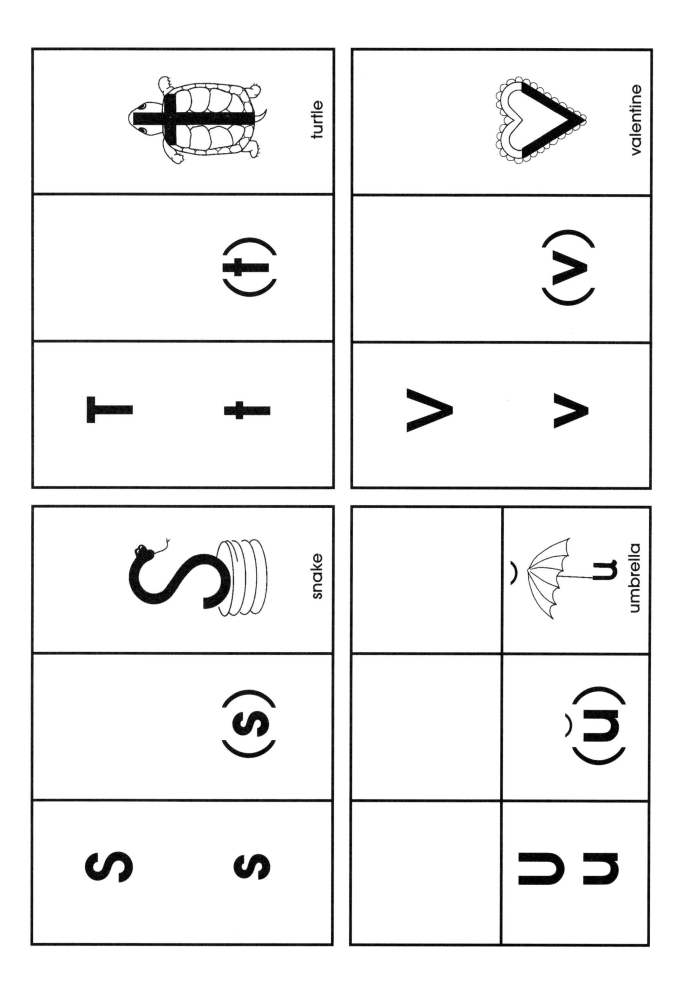

T   t

turtle

(t)

V   v

valentine

(v)

S   s

snake

(s)

U   u

umbrella

(u)

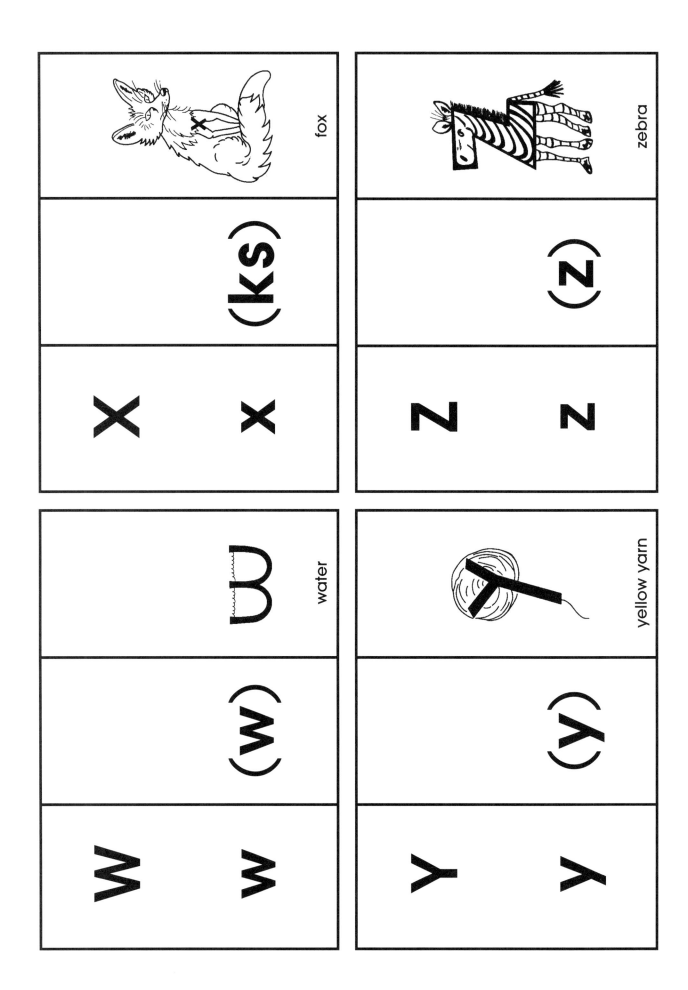

X x (ks) fox

W w (w) water

Z z (z) zebra

Y y (y) yellow yarn

Consonant Digraphs

CH ch (ch)

chair

TH th (th)

the thumb

SH sh (sh)

sh! shark

Appendix B

BOOKS THAT CONTAIN RHYMES, SONGS, FINGERPLAYS, AND TONGUE TWISTERS

1. *A Beastly Circus,* Peggy Parish, pictures by Peter Parnall (New York: Simon & Schuster Children's Book Division, 1969).
2. *The Alaska Mother Goose,* Shelley Gill, illustrations by Shannon Cartwright (Homer, Alaska: Paws IV Publishing Company, 1987).
3. *Animal Crackers: A Delectable Collection of Pictures, Poems, and Lullabies for the Very Young,* Jane Dyer (Boston: Little, Brown and Company, 1996).
4. *Anna Banana: 101 Jump-Rope Rhymes,* Joanna Cole, illustrated by Alan Tiegreen (New York: William Morrow and Company, Inc., 1989).
5. *The Arnold Lobel Book of Mother Goose: A Treasury of 306 Timeless Nursery Rhymes,* selected and illustrated by Arnold Lobel (New York: Random House, Inc., 1986).
6. *The Baby's Bedtime Book,* Kay Chorao (New York: E. P. Dutton, Inc., 1984).
7. *Busy Buzzing Bumblebees and Other Tongue Twisters,* Alvin Schwartz, illustrated by Paul Meisel (New York: HarperCollins Publishers, 1982, 1992).
8. *Cat Goes Fiddle-i-fee,* adapted and illustrated by Paul Galdone (New York: Clarion Books, 1985).
9. *Cats by Mother Goose,* selected by Barbara Lucas, pictures by Carol Newsom (New York: William Morrow & Company, 1986).
10. *Down by the Bay: Raffi Songs to Read,* illustrated by Nadine Bernard Westcott (New York: Random House, Inc., 1987).
11. *Each Peach Pear Plum,* Janet and Allan Ahlberg (New York: Viking Penguin Inc., 1978).
12. *Eentsy, Weentsy Spider: Fingerplays and Action Rhymes,* Joanna Cole and Stephanie Calmenson, illustrated by Alan Tiegreen (New York: William Morrow and Company, Inc., 1991).
13. *Faint Frogs Feeling Feverish & Other Terrifically Tantalizing Tongue Twisters,* Lilian Obligado (New York: Viking Penguin Inc., 1983).
14. *Finger Rhymes,* collected and illustrated by Marc Brown (New York: Penguin Books USA Inc., 1980).
15. *Five Little Pumpkins,* Iris Van Rynbach (Honesdale, Pennsylvania: Boyds Mills Press, Inc., 1995).

16. *The Fox Went Out on a Chilly Night: An Old Song,* illustrated by Peter Spier (New York: Bantam Doubleday Dell Publishing Group, Inc., 1961).

17. *Gonna Sing My Head Off!: American Folk Songs for Children,* collected and arranged for piano and guitar by Kathleen Krull, introductory note by Arlo Guthrie, illustrated by Allen Garns (New York: Alfred A. Knopf, 1992).

18. *Grandmother's Nursery Rhymes/ Las Nanas de Abuelita: Lullabies, Tongue Twisters, and Riddles From South America,* compiled by Nelly Palacio Jaramillo, translated by Raquel Jaramillo, illustrated by Elivia (New York: Henry Holt and Company, Inc., 1994).

19. *Hand Rhymes,* collected and illustrated by Marc Brown (New York: Penguin Books USA Inc., 1985).

20. *Hey Diddle Diddle & Other Mother Goose Rhymes,* Tomie dePaola (New York: The Putnam & Grosset Book Group, 1985, 1988).

21. *Hush, Little Baby,* Margot Zemach (New York: E. P. Dutton, 1976).

22. *Hush Little Baby: A Folk Lullaby,* illustrated by Aliki (New York: Simon & Schuster Books for Young Readers, 1968).

23. *I Know an Old Lady,* Rose Bonne, music by Alan Mills, pictures by Abner Graboff (Skokie, Illinois: Rand McNally & Company, 1961).

24. *I Know an Old Lady Who Swallowed a Fly,* retold and illustrated by Nadine Bernard Westcott (Boston: Little, Brown and Company, 1980)

.25. *James Marshall's Mother Goose,* James Marshall (New York: Farrar, Straus & Giroux, 1979).

26. *Jane Yolen's Mother Goose Songbook,* selected, edited, and introduced by Jane Yolen, musical arrangements by Adam Stemple, illustrations by Rosekrans Hoffman (Honesdale, Pennsylvania: Boyds Mills Press, 1992).

27. *Jane Yolen's Old MacDonald Songbook,* selected, edited, and introduced by Jane Yolen, musical arrangements by Adam Stemple, illustrations by Rosekrans Hoffman (Honesdale, Pennsylvania: Boyds Mills Press, 1994).

28. *The Jessie Willcox Smith Mother Goose: A Careful and Full Selection of the Rhymes With Numerous Illustrations in Full Color and Black and White,* Jessie Willcox Smith, foreword by Edward D. Nudelman (Gretna, Louisiana: Pelican Publishing Company, Inc., 1914, 1991).

29. *The Kingfisher Nursery Rhyme Songbook: With Easy Music to Play for Piano and Guitar,* compiled by Sally Emerson, illustrated by Colin and Moira Maclean (New York: Larousse Kingfisher Chambers Inc., 1991).

30. *Knick Knack Paddywack,* written and illustrated by Marissa Moss (Boston: Houghton Mifflin Company, 1992).

31. *The Lap-Time Song and Play Book,* edited by Jane Yolen, musical arrangements by Adam Stemple, pictures by Margot Tomes (San Diego: Harcourt Brace & Company, 1989).

32. *The Little Dog Laughed and Other Nursery Rhymes,* Lucy Cousins (New York: Penguin Books USA Inc., 1989).

33. *Marguerite de Angeli's Book of Nursery and Mother Goose Rhymes,* Marguerite de Angeli (New York: Doubleday & Company, Inc., 1953, 1954).

34. *Michael Foreman's Mother Goose,* Michael Foreman, foreword by Ionia Opie (San Diego: Harcourt Brace & Company, 1991).

35. *The Missing Tarts,* story by B. G. Hennessy, pictures by Tracey Campbell Pearson (New York: Viking Penguin Inc., 1989).

36. *Miss Mary Mack and Other Children's Street Rhymes,* Joanna Cole and Stephanie Calmenson, illustrated by Alan Tiegreen (New York: William Morrow and Company, Inc., 1990).

37. *Mother Goose,* illustrated by Aurelius Battaglia (New York: Random House, Inc., 1973).

38. *Mother Goose,* illustrated by Tasha Tudor (New York: Random House Inc., 1944, 1971).

39. *Mother Goose: A Collection of Nursery Rhymes,* Brian Wildsmith (Oxford, England: Oxford University Press, 1964).

40. *Mother Goose: A Collection of Classic Nursery Rhymes,* selected and illustrated by Michael Hague (New York: Holt, Rinehart and Winston, 1984).

41. *The Mother Goose Songbook,* arranged for the piano by Carol Barratt, illustrated by Jacqueline Sinclair (New York: Crown Publishers, 1984).

42. *My Little Mother Goose,* Amye Rosenberg (Racine, Washington: Western Publishing Company, Inc., 1981).

43. *Nursery Rhymes From Mother Goose Told in Signed English,* Harry Bornstein and Karen L. Saulnier, illustrated by Patricia Peters, line drawings by Linda C. Tom (Washington, DC: Gallaudet University Press, 1992).

44. *Oh, A-Hunting We Will Go,* John Langstaff, pictures by Nancy Winslow Parker (New York: Macmillan Publishing Company, 1974).

45. *Old Mother Hubbard,* Alice and Martin Provensen (New York: Random House, Inc., 1977).

46. *The Opie Book of Nursery Rhymes,* Iona and Peter Opie, illustrated by Pauline Baynes (New York: Penguin Books USA Inc., 1963, 1997).

47. *Party Rhymes,* collected and illustrated by Marc Brown (New York: Penguin Books USA Inc., 1988).

48. *Play Rhymes,* collected and illustrated by Marc Brown (New York: Penguin Books USA Inc., 1987).

49. *The Puffin Book of Nursery Rhymes,* Nick Butterworth (New York: Penguin Books USA Inc., 1981, 1990, 1995).

50. *The Real Mother Goose,* illustrated by Blanche Fisher Wright (Chicago: Rand McNally & Co., 1916, 1944).

51. *The Real Mother Goose Book of American Rhymes,* selected by Debby Slier, illustrated by Patty McCloskey-Padgett, Bernice Loewenstein, and Nan Pollard, cover art by Lynn Adams (New York: Scholastic Inc., 1993).

52. *The Real Mother Goose Picture Word Rhymes,* illustrated by Blanche Fisher Wright (New York: Macmillan, Inc., 1916, 1944, 1987).

53. *The Rebus Treasury,* compiled by Jean Marzollo, art by Carol Devine Carson (New York: Dial Books for Young Readers, 1986).

54. *See You Later Alligator: A First Book of Rhyming Word-Play,* Barbara Strauss and Helen Friedland, illustrated by Tershia d'Elgin (Los Angeles: Price Stern Sloan, Inc., 1986, 1987).
55. *Shari Lewis Presents 101 Games and Songs for Kids to Play and Sing,* Shari Lewis, illustrated by Lisa Goldrick (New York: Random House, Inc., 1993).
56. *She'll Be Coming Around the Mountain,* Emily Coplon, Doris Orgel, and Ellen Schecter, illustrated by Rowan Barnes-Murphy (New York: Bantam Doubleday Dell Publishing Group, Inc., 1994).
57. *She'll Be Comin' 'Round the Mountain,* illustrations by Alan and Lea Daniel (Bothell, Washington: The Wright Group, 1990).
58. *Sing a Song of Mother Goose,* Barbara Reid (New York: Scholastic Inc., 1987).
59. *Sing a Song of Sixpence,* pictures by Tracey Campbell Pearson (New York: Dial Books for Young Readers, 1985).
60. *Six Sick Sheep: 101 Tongue Twisters,* Joanna Cole and Stephanie Calmenson, illustrated by Alan Tiegreen (New York: William Morrow and Company, Inc., 1993).
61. *Sleep Rhymes Around the World,* edited by Jane Yolen, illustrated by 17 international artists (Honesdale, Pennsylvania: Boyds Mills Press, 1994).
62. *Songs From Mother Goose With the Traditional Melody for Each,* compiled by Nancy Larrick, illustrated by Robin Spowart (New York: Harper & Row, Publishers, 1989).
63. *Squeeze a Sneeze,* Bill Morrison (Boston: Houghton Mifflin Company, 1977).
64. *Street Rhymes Around the World,* edited by Jane Yolen, illustrated by 17 international artists (Honesdale, Pennsylvania: Boyds Mills Press, 1992).
65. *There's a Hole in the Bucket,* pictures by Nadine Bernard Westcott (New York: Harper & Row, Publishers, 1990).
66. *There Was an Old Lady Who Swallowed a Fly,* illustrated by Pam Adams (Child's Play International Ltd, 1973, 1989).
67. *Thirty Old-Time Nursery Songs,* arranged by Joseph Moorat and pictured by Paul Woodroffe (New York: The Metropolitan Museum of Art and Thames and Hudson, 1980).
68. *This Old Man,* illustrated by Carol Jones (Boston: Houghton Mifflin Company, 1990).
69. *This Old Man: A Musical Counting Book,* illustrated by Tony Ross, designed by Jon Z. Haber, paper engineering by Rodger Smith (New York: Macmillan Publishing Company, 1990).
70. *Three Jovial Huntsmen: A Mother Goose Rhyme,* adapted and illustrated by Susan Jeffers (Mahwah, New Jersey: Troll Associates, 1973).
71. *Three Little Kittens,* Paul Galdone (Boston: Houghton Mifflin Company, 1986).
72. *Three Little Kittens,* illustrated by Lilian Obligado (New York: Random House, Inc., 1974).

73. ***Tomie de Paola's Mother Goose,*** Tomie dePaola (New York: G. P. Putnam's Sons, 1985).

74. ***Tongue Twisters,*** Charles Keller, illustrated by Ron Fritz (New York: Simon & Schuster Books for Young Readers, 1989).

75. ***Too Many Rabbits and Other Fingerplays About Animals, Nature, Weather, and the Universe,*** Kay Cooper, illustrated by Judith Moffatt (New York: Scholastic Inc., 1995).

76. ***A Treasury of Mother Goose,*** illustrated by Hilda Offen (New York: Simon & Schuster Books for Young Readers, 1984).

77. ***Wee Sing™ Around the Campfire,*** Pamela Conn Beall and Susan Hagen Nipp (Los Angeles: Price/Stern/Sloan Publishers, Inc., 1982).

78. ***Wee Sing™ Children's Songs and Fingerplays,*** Pamela Conn Beall and Susan Hagen Nipp (Los Angeles: Price/Stern/Sloan Publishers, Inc., 1977, 1979).

79. ***Wee Sing and Play™ Musical Games and Rhymes for Children,*** Pamela Conn Beall and Susan Hagen Nipp (Los Angeles: Price/Stern/Sloan Publishers, Inc., 1981).

80. ***World's Toughest Tongue Twisters,*** Joseph Rosenbloom, drawings by Dennis Kendrick (New York: Sterling Publishing Co., Inc., 1986).

Teacher Notes

Teacher Notes

Teacher Notes

Teacher Notes

Teacher Notes

Teacher Notes

Teacher Notes

Teacher Notes